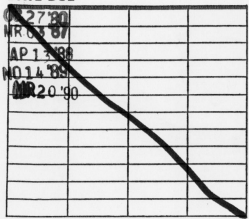

THE
ADMINISTRATIVE
PROCESS
AND
DEMOCRATIC
THEORY

Under the editorship of

RICHARD P. LONGAKER

*University of California
at Los Angeles*

THE ADMINISTRATIVE PROCESS AND DEMOCRATIC THEORY

LOUIS C. GAWTHROP

State University of New York at Binghamton

HOUGHTON MIFFLIN COMPANY Boston

New York
Atlanta
Geneva, Illinois
Dallas
Palo Alto

Library of Congress Catalog Card Number: 70–122910

TO
TRACY

PREFACE

The purpose of this volume is to trace the development of certain basic concepts and premises of the public administration process in the United States and to relate these concepts and premises to various principles of democratic theory. Following the format set forth in Chapter One, thirty-two selections from the writings of Presidents, economists, politicians, political scientists, philosophers, and administrators form the core of the book. In addition each chapter includes an extended interpretive commentary by the author. These commentaries are designed (1) to synthesize the selections presented within each chapter, (2) to integrate the several themes developed among the different chapters, and (3) to supplement the selections in each chapter with additional relevant information.

I am, of course, indebted to the many authors who have graciously consented to have selections of their scholarship reprinted in this volume. In addition, invaluable technical assistance in the preparation of the manuscript has been provided by Joan Kaufman and Dawn Daniels. My colleagues at the State University of New York, Binghamton, provided a constant source of encouragement and advice which I have freely exploited. Finally, the vital intangibles that go into any effort of this type are derived from a wide variety of sources. In this instance, as in all other of my endeavors, my wife represents the most important contributor.

TABLE
OF
CONTENTS

THE
ADMINISTRATIVE
PROCESS
AND
DEMOCRATIC
THEORY

THE NORMATIVE PENDULUM OF PUBLIC ADMINISTRATION

1

INTRODUCTION

The function of government, it could be argued, is to simplify the complex in a manner which provides relevant responses to the needs of individuals. To solve the complex social, economic, and political problems of a nation is a challenge which every democratic government must face; to solve the relatively simple social, economic, and political problems of the individual is a challenge which no democratic government can avoid.

But simple needs, such as routine garbage collection, adequate street lighting, a neighborhood playground, are all too frequently lost in the growing complexities of the day, and as more of the talents, techniques, and resources of our administrative systems are directed toward the search for grand macro-solutions affecting total systems at the subnational, national, and transnational levels, the direct relevance, or payoff, for the lone individual entombed in a black ghetto, for instance, is minimal. If one puts together—as Dwight Waldo did in a recent speech—the revolution taking place *in* science and technology and the growing reaction *against* science and technology; the reaction against gradualism, the increase in the use of violence, and the increasing force *against* the use of violence; the crisis in race relations; the revolution between generations; the urban revolution; the mounting wave of disorganized crime; and the revolution in morals and values,* it should be apparent that to many of the dissatisfied and alienated groups in our contemporary society, the

* "Public Administration in a Time of Revolutions," Address delivered to Capital District Chapter of the American Society for Public Administration, Albany, New York, April 2, 1968, pp. 3–6 (mimeo.).

3

public administrator and the administrative process represent major forces standing in opposition to change.

But how are public policy decisions to be made in a nation of two hundred million people? How are the finite resources of our governmental system to be allocated among a body politic which is capable of expressing a virtually unlimited set of demands? Our judicial and certainly our legislative branches of government are required to provide answers to these questions daily, but to a very real extent the ultimate burden of responsibility in this regard falls on the executive branch and its administrative officials. Shall resources be allocated incrementally on the basis of bargained agreements, or shall they be allocated systematically on the basis of a comprehensive plan devised by highly specialized analysts? With a choice between the threat of a loss of identity in the latter instance and the denial of the right to participation in the former, neither approach appears capable of satisfying the demands of an equitable *and* efficient allocative process.

For example, the destruction of the computer center on the campus of Sir George Williams University in Montreal by rioting students could be viewed in the extreme as a dramatically symbolic act committed in the name of all the impersonalized, alienated, and frustrated little people in the world today. As the symbol of a highly centralized and rational bureaucracy, the computer becomes a way-of-life to avoid as well as a machine to destroy. But what of the alternative to the highly centralized and rational bureaucracy—the pluralist-bargaining-incremental framework* which integrates the administrative process into our politically hypersensitive governmental system? This process fares no better and is increasingly being threatened by rejection. "America is pluralistic," says the Reverend Jesse Jackson. "There is talk about it being a melting pot. But it really is more like vegetable soup. There are separate pieces of corn, meat, and so on, each with its own identity. The blacks have been pushed down to the bottom of the pot. We are going to come up and be recognized, or turn the pot over."†

For some, undoubtedly, the problem is insoluble, given the enormous complexity of our contemporary society. As we face the prospect of discovering the secrets of the universe, the challenge to government of satisfying the basic physiological, psychological, and biological needs of man in the most equitable and efficient manner seems somehow related to a simpler, distant period, a less complex age. And yet, a moment's reflection should convince us that the goal

---

* The subject of Chapter Six.

† *The New York Times,* June 2, 1969, p. 31. The Reverend Jackson is the Southern Christian Leadership Conference coordinator for Operation Breadbasket in Chicago.

of combining administrative efficiency with social equity is one of the most elusive ever to have faced mankind. Plato did not even try; Machiavelli asked, "Why bother?"; Pontius Pilate was driven almost to despair in attempting their reconciliation. But despite the failure on the part of rational man to achieve a meaningful unity between efficiency and equity, the search for a solution has continued through the centuries. Not surprisingly, therefore, do we find that both elements were introduced into our governmental system in the very earliest beginnings of our republic. As usual, one must turn to Leonard White to place our administrative process in historical perspective.

The administrative system, as well as the political system of the United States was founded on the divergent theories and objectives of two of America's greatest statesmen—Hamilton and Jefferson. Each developed a coherent, well-considered plan of administration supported by deep-seated but conflicting preferences concerning the type of society toward which they hoped America would grow and buttressed by equally deep-seated differences of personality and aptitude. Hamilton triumphed for a brief period of magnificent construction; but Jefferson's spirit ruled over the subsequent century. The American system of administration in the troubled years of this generation has moved back toward the ideals of Hamilton but against popular preferences set in motion by Jefferson which still carry extraordinary weight. Neither ideal has been able to secure certain dominance over the other; neither can be driven from the field; and their reconciliation remains in considerable measure an unsolved problem.[*]

Two observations should be made concerning White's historical interpretation of our administrative system. In the first place, considering his comment, written in 1946, that "the American system of administration *in the troubled years of this generation* has moved back toward the ideals of Hamilton but against the popular preferences set in motion by Jefferson which still carry extraordinary weight," one cannot fail to be impressed by the pertinence of this observation as applied to our current social situation. In fact, the ideals of Hamilton for greater administrative efficiency have been embraced with even greater enthusiasm in the troubled years of this current generation. At the same time and with surprising resiliency, the ideals of Jefferson for greater social equity have recently reappeared.

In the second place, although the pendulum of public administration in the United States has swung between these two divergent approaches to administration, it is important to emphasize at the

[*] Leonard D. White's introduction to Lynton K. Caldwell's *The Administrative Theories of Hamilton and Jefferson,* p. vii. Copyright 1944 by the University of Chicago. All rights reserved. Published September 1944. Composed and printed by The University of Chicago Press, Chicago, Illinois, U.S.A.

outset that, as White implies, they also represent two equally divergent sets of democratic values. Thus, both Hamilton and Jefferson developed, ". . . deep-seated but conflicting preferences concerning the type of society toward which they hoped America would grow. . . ." In short, the administrative techniques advocated by each were simply means to a higher end—the "good life"—and in each instance, the techniques, the structure, the process all became meaningless if not applied toward their appropriate end.

In this introductory chapter a set of selected readings are presented to illustrate the current manifestation of this "unsolved problem." Briefly stated, an administrative device called the planning-programming-budgeting system (PPBS) was formally introduced into the executive branch of the federal government in 1965 by an executive order from the President. This decision was made when former President Lyndon B. Johnson was obviously satisfied that the techniques of systems analysis brought into the Defense Department by Secretary Robert McNamara in 1961 could profitably be applied throughout the entire federal structure. The selections which follow present President Johnson's executive order, one congressional committee's response to the executive order, a description of the application of PPB in the Defense Department by a former Assistant Secretary of Defense, some casual reflections and "hard" questions concerning the future of PPB from an eminent academician, an articulate defense of the use of systems analysis in government by the president of the RAND Corporation, and a political philosopher's attempt to present a logical justification for the primacy of politics and political rationality as essential elements in the public policy decision-making process. By presenting these six selections in this introductory chapter, it is hoped that the reader will at least have a base point that can be applied in the chapters which immediately follow.

A STATEMENT BY THE PRESIDENT

LYNDON B. JOHNSON

I have asked you to meet with me this morning to discuss the introduction of a new planning and budgeting system throughout the Government.

The objective of this program is simple: to use the most modern management tools so that the full promise of a finer life can be brought to every American at the least possible cost.

This program is aimed at finding new ways to do new jobs faster, better, less expensively; to insure sounder judgment through more accurate information; to pinpoint those things we ought to do more, and to spotlight those things we ought to do less; to make our decision-making process as up-to-date as our space-exploring equipment. In short, we want to trade in our surreys for automobiles, our old cannon for new missiles.

Everything I have done in both legislation and the construction of a budget has been guided by my deep concern for the American people—consistent with wise management of the taxpayer's dollar.

In translating this principle in action, and with the help of an outstanding Congress, we have passed more progressive legislation than in any comparable period in history.

We have been compassionate. We have also been prudent.

But we can and must do better if we are to bring the Great Society closer to all the people.

Good government demands excellence.

From *Public Papers of the Presidents of the United States: Lyndon B. Johnson,* August 25, 1965, Book II.

It demands the fullest value for each dollar spent. It demands that we take advantage of the most modern management techniques.

This is what I want to introduce today—a new planning-programming-budgeting system developed by our top management experts led by Budget Director Charles Schultze. Once in operation, it will enable us to:

1. Identify our national goals with precision and on a continuing basis;

2. Choose among those goals the ones that are most urgent;

3. Search for alternative means of reaching those goals most effectively at the least cost;

4. Inform ourselves not merely on next year's costs, but on the second, and third, and subsequent years' costs of our programs;

5. Measure the performance of our programs to insure a dollar's worth of service for each dollar spent.

This system will improve our ability to control our programs and our budgets rather than having them control us. It will operate year round. Studies, goals, program proposals, and reviews will be scheduled throughout the year instead of being crowded into "budget time."

To establish this system and carry out the necessary studies, each of you will need a central staff for program and policy planning accountable directly to you. To make this work will take good people, the best you now have and the best you can find.

I intend to have the 1968 budget and later-year programs presented in this new form by next spring.

With these programs will go the first studies produced by your planning and policy staffs.

It is important to remember one thing: no system, no matter how refined, can make decisions for you. You and I have that responsibility in the executive branch. But our judgment is no better than our information. This system will present us with the alternatives and the information on the basis of which we can, together, make better decisions. The people will be the beneficiary. . . .

PLANNING-PROGRAMMING-BUDGETING

THE JACKSON SUBCOMMITTEE

PPBS: WHAT IS IT?

Sitting at the apex of the Federal Government, a President is keenly aware of the shortage of resources for pursuing desirable goals of public policy, and of the difficult choices this hard fact of life imposes. Some goals must be eliminated, some postponed, others reduced in order to tailor the desirable to the feasible. A President needs the best help he can get in establishing an intelligent scale of priorities, choosing policies that would achieve desired results at the least cost, and marshaling, through Congress, the required resources.

In matters of defense and foreign policy, a President seeks aid from many quarters—State and Defense, his own staff, the National Security Council, task forces, other departments and agencies involved with national security matters, members of Congress, and private citizens. In addition, the budgetary process helps to bring things into focus—to weigh domestic versus foreign needs and to set priorities, to compare costs and benefits of competing programs, and once the budget has been fixed, to exercise Presidential direction and control of the operations of the Executive Branch.

The Planning-Programming-Budgeting System is one more step in a continuing endeavor to make the budgetary process a more versatile and helpful instrument of the President and his principal advisers. As its name suggests, it is an effort to tie forward planning to budgeting via programming. Key elements in the approach are program budgeting and systems analysis.

From *Planning-Programming-Budgeting: Initial Memorandum,* Government Operations Subcommittee on National Security and International Operations, U.S. Senate, 90th Congress, 1st Session, 1967, committee print, pp. 1–8.

The traditional budget has been prepared and presented in terms of objects of expenditure, or "inputs," in the new jargon. In this form the budget has not shown the link between agency spending and agency purposes—between the resources an agency uses and its missions or tasks, now, of course, called "outputs." By linking resources to purposes, inputs to outputs, in a program, and by planning ahead for several years, the program budget is expected to contribute to better appraisal by decision-makers of what a budget cut or increase would mean in terms of an agency's program—the goals to be pursued and the goals to be sacrificed or deferred.

Systems analysis is intended to present decision-makers with a systematic and comprehensive comparison of the costs and benefits of alternative approaches to a policy goal, taking advantage of techniques variously described as operations research or cost-effectiveness studies. There is an emphasis on quantitative analysis. Computers have made it possible to handle large quantities of data and applied mathematics has provided ingenious statistical techniques for dealing with some kinds of uncertainty.

Some of the less historically-minded proponents of PPBS strongly imply that it is something brand new, providing decision-makers for the first time with a rational basis for choosing between alternative policies. Actually, cost-benefit analysis seems to have begun in the Garden of Eden (see *Genesis*, 3), and the problem from the outset has been to avoid an underestimation of costs and an overestimation of benefits. Costs and gains have been compared throughout our government's history whenever a decision to spend or not to spend had to be made, and Congress explicitly called for cost-benefit studies as far back as the Rivers and Harbors Act of 1902. Operations research demonstrated its usefulness in World War II. Statistical control, pushed by Robert Lovett as Assistant Secretary of War for Air in World War II, was the forerunner of many functions of the Comptroller of the Defense Department and a predecessor of systems analysis. The idea of performance or program budgeting can be traced back at least to President Taft's Commission on Economy and Efficiency, which published its path-breaking report, "The Need for a National Budget," in 1912. And program budgets for periods extending well into the future have long been the rule in progressive banks and business firms.

PPB may for the first time identify these techniques as a "system," give them a special name, and advertise them, but the approach itself is as old as the problem of the buyer who would like to make two purchases and has money only for one.

Some of the more enthusiastic advocates of PPBS seem to suggest that it can work miracles in all corners of government. But it is no magic wand. It is a set of sharp tools which in experienced hands and guided by sound judgment can be a helpful aid in some of the business of government. . . .

THE EXPERIENCE IN DEFENSE

The major experiment to date with PPB began in the Department of Defense in 1961, and the system has been applied to six defense budgets—Fiscal Years 1963 through 1968. . . .

This Defense PPB system has, of course, been applied only during a period of rising national defense budgets (from $54.3 billion in FY 1963 to about $75 billion in FY 1967). It is not clear that the system would ease the problems of managing a contraction of the military services and of deciding, in a period of declining appropriations, what combination of forces would best promote the national interest.

Even in Defense the benefits of the PPB system have been overplayed by its proponents. It is not a statistical litmus paper, scientifically sorting good projects from bad. It may be used as easily to rationalize a decision as to make a rational choice. It is no substitute for experience and judgment, though men of experience and judgment may find it helpful.

The PPB approach was used to justify the purchase of a $277 million oil-fueled aircraft carrier that was obsolete before it was launched. Also, a perversion of cost-effectiveness was used, after the fact, in the largest single military aircraft contract in history, to rationalize the choice of an airplane whose costs are soaring, if not its performance. The latter case demonstrates that cost-effectiveness study, like any other management tool, can be misused—to becloud rather than illuminate judgment in the Executive Branch and Congress.

A major goal of PPB, according to Charles Hitch, was to enable the Secretary of Defense to run his Department on a unified basis, and PPB has meant a greater centralization of decision-making and control. A consequence, whether intended or not, is that it may be more difficult for voices of doubt and dissent at lower levels to make themselves heard at high levels. It means, among other things, less bargaining between OSD and the service departments and the services. This in turn makes it easier for OSD to ignore or simply not to hear things it would rather not hear—other beliefs about technological change, different estimates of costs and gains, conflicting views of the contingencies and the uncertainties. Defense programs may therefore be more nearly tailored to one estimate of the future and to one cost-benefit calculus than in a period when decision-making was less centralized.

All this underlines the fact that "unifying" is not without its dangers, particularly for the innovation of new weapons systems. Professor Roland McKean points out: ". . . rivalry under a rather decentralized system more than good analysis was probably responsible for the early development of Polaris and the subsequent Air Force interest in reducing vulnerability." The evidence is not all in on how increased centralization has affected major force-level decisions, aircraft production rates, and initiatives on new major weapons systems, including the ABM. But there are obvious risks to which the President and Congress should be alert and which may suggest the need for reforms in Defense, at the Presidential level, and in Congress.

PPB aims at a systematic analysis of significant costs and benefits of alternative policies. But as a politician knows, sometimes the costs of an action, or failure to act, are heaviest not in dollars, but in a loss of confidence or a failure of will or a collapse of morale. Benefits also may show up in an improvement in these intangible factors of will and psychology rather than on the cash register. Priceless is not a synonym for worthless. An analysis which emphasizes cost-effectiveness and gives special attention to quantification runs the risk of short-changing or ignoring non-quantifiable costs and benefits. Skybolt presumably did not meet the Defense tests of cost-effectiveness, but one wonders whether, in estimating the costs of its cancellation, allowance was made for the impact on the British Government and perhaps on French policies in Atlantic and West European affairs. . . .

RELEVANCE TO THE STATE DEPARTMENT
AND RELATED AGENCIES

The State Department, like a number of other agencies, may find PPBS of little use. The differences between decision-making in defense and in foreign affairs, of course, make it impossible just to transfer budgetary procedures from Defense to State, AID, USIA and other national security programs.

In the nature of things, Defense must plan and program far ahead because of the time required to turn ideas into weapons. Foreign policy is more sensitive to day-to-day actions of other governments.

Furthermore, the difficulties of quantifying objectives, costs and benefits, in Defense are minor compared with the difficulties in foreign affairs. Defense deals in large part with end products that one can see, touch, measure, test-fire and ride in. State itself has virtually none of that; it deals mainly with the battle of ideas and interests called diplomacy. Also, the budgetary process as a whole does not serve effectively to bring foreign policy choices into focus.

Even apart from these factors, there has been no preparatory work in the foreign policy field remotely comparable to the decade of intensive work by RAND and others which preceded the large-scale application of programming and systems analysis in Defense, and the number of people trained and skilled in both the conduct of foreign affairs and the techniques of modern management is very limited. Charles Hitch himself has sounded a cautionary note:

... there are risks and dangers as well as opportunities in trying to move too far too fast in the application of new management techniques like these, including the risk of discrediting the techniques.

The foreign affairs agencies are still grappling with PPBS to learn what it means for them.

A special problem: the Office of the Secretary of State has not yet found means to take the proffered role of Presidential agent for the "overall direction" of interdepartmental activities overseas, and to play it vigorously. The difficulties are great, and it is unlikely that PPBS provides an answer to the problem. An effort has been made to assist State by establishing a Senior Interdepartmental Group (SIG) with the Under Secretary of State as its Executive Chairman, and Interdepartmental Regional Groups (IRG), chaired by the regional Assistant Secretaries of State. This experiment, however, seems to be languishing.

These questions follow:

1. What problems have been encountered in implementing the President's directive on PPBS with respect to State and related agencies?

2. To what extent are the difficult foreign policy decisions that must be faced by the President, the Secretary of State, and the heads of related agencies ones on which budgetary considerations are of great or determining influence?

3. At this stage of the development of systems analysis, can it play a constructive role in foreign policy decision-making?

4. Are some aspects of the operations of State, AID, and other foreign affairs agencies adapted to programming and cost-benefit analysis?

5. Would PPBS be helpful in any way in the work of the Senior Interdepartmental Group (SIG) and the Interdepartmental Regional Groups (IRG)?

6. An attempt is being made to develop an "inter-agency foreign affairs programming system." Does this contemplate a more prominent role in policy-making for the Bureau of the Budget in relation to State and other departments? What arguments are advanced by proponents and opponents of the system?

IMPLICATIONS FOR THE PRESIDENT AND CONGRESS

Does PPBS provide a wholly rational basis for decision-making? Have we arrived at that technocratic utopia where judgment is a machine-product?

Not even the zealots of PPBS would answer these questions affirm-atively, although some of them talk as though we should be moving in this direction. Professor Frederick Mosher, for example, has noted the frequency of authoritarian language:

> In all the literature I have read about PPBS . . . only a very few authors have even mentioned the executive and legislative processes of review and decision. The President and Congress seem to be regarded as enemies of rationality. . . . Much of the literature of PPBS resembles that of the tech-nocrats of the thirties; its aim seems to be to eliminate *politics* from de-cisionmaking.

It would be as easy of course to take H₂O out of water as to take politics out of decisions. Our political system is a system for making decisions on matters of public interest. We do not propose to dele-gate this task to a dictator, no matter how benevolent, or to an ex-pert, no matter how objective, or to a computer, no matter who pro-grams it. Indeed, we do not propose to leave it to any one person, but have built what we call "checks and balances" into our decision-making system. At the heart of our democratic form of government are the principles of executive accountability and Congressional re-view of Executive action.

The temperate proponents of PPBS claim only that their approach will help to sharpen the intuition and improve the judgment of de-cision-makers by providing them with more, better, and more timely information. They do not aspire to replace our decision-makers al-though they might want to arrange the contents of their in-boxes.

It is easy to agree that good analysis is preferable to poor analysis. If the President and his principal assistants believe that PPBS studies and analyses are helpful and an improvement over what they had before they will surely want to see the techniques developed and extended.

It is not clear however that PPBS will win or should win a Presi-dent's unqualified support. A President needs and wants, for example, freedom to shift his plans and respond flexibly to new situations. Professor Aaron Wildavsky points out:

> It is well and good to talk about long-range planning; it is another thing to tie a President's hands by committing him in advance for five years of expenditures. Looking ahead is fine but not if it means that a President cannot negate the most extensive planning efforts on grounds that seem sufficient to him. He may wish to trade some program budgeting for some political support.

To some extent, the planner and the politician are and ought to be at odds. The planner tries to foresee, in order to plan intelligently.

A plan rests on today's best estimates of future needs. A politician knows how dimly we can foresee at best, how inadequate the information on the basis of which he must decide and act, how full of surprises history is, how desirable, therefore, to postpone decisions that can be postponed, and how much one depends, in the final analysis, on intuition and judgment based on experience.

A President will look at a program budget skeptically—or should —for he will sense that some costs may have been overlooked and some benefits overestimated—and he may also sense the temptation of assistants to write plans and programs that rationalize their hunches. He will take seriously the lesson of the struggle to get nuclear propulsion for the Navy—a lesson described in these words by Admiral Rickover:

> Nuclear power has served to demonstrate the fallibility of expert cost accountants. In so doing, this issue has served a useful purpose. This has resulted in delay in achieving a stronger Navy, but in the long run it may have been worthwhile.
>
> Out of this issue has again been demonstrated the fact that politics is more difficult than physics or cost accounting, and that it is politicians who saw the truth before the cost accountants. The primacy of politics should not again be subordinated to the doctrinaire and unproved claims of specialists—particularly when these specialists are in a position of overall authority and do not encourage or permit contrary views to be voiced or to be asserted.

Congress, too, may not welcome all the implications of PPBS. The experience to date does not suggest that the Department of Defense is likely to place before Congressional committees the analyses of costs and benefits of competing policies and programs on which the Department based its own choices. Without such comparisons, however, Congress will be in the dark about the reasons for selecting this policy over that. It may be that Congress will wish to improve its own capability for systematic analysis of public problems in order to compete on more even terms with the Executive Branch. Furthermore, the more centralized decision-making becomes in the Executive Branch, the more important some competition of this sort from Congress might be.

Congress may also be concerned with the impact of PPBS on the distribution of power within the Executive Branch. The centralizing bias of PPBS may be more important than the anticipated technical improvements of the budgetary process, because of a lessening of competitive forces within the Executive Branch. Congress will also be interested, of course, in how the changes in the Executive Branch will affect the role of Congress in the formulation of national security policy and the establishment of national security budgets.

If PPBS develops into a contest between experts and politicians, it will not be hard to pick the winners. They will be the politicians in the Congress and the White House. It has been said, and correctly, that as interesting as observing what happens to government when confronted with PPB will be watching what happens to PPB when confronted with government.

DECISION-MAKING IN LARGE ORGANIZATIONS

CHARLES J. HITCH

I have referred to the management techniques which comprise PPBS. What are they? There are two, related and mutually supporting but distinct, in fact so distinct that it is possible to use either without the other. One is called "program budgeting," or more simply "programming." Since "program budgeting" is sometimes used more broadly to mean the whole PPB system, I will use the simpler term "programming" to describe this part of the system. Programming as an activity produces a program or program budget which has the following characteristics. First, it is organized or classified by programs rather than, as traditional budgets are, by objects of expenditure. Or, if you prefer, it is classified by "outputs" which are objective-oriented rather than "inputs." Secondly, the resource requirements and the financial or budget implications are linked to these programmed outputs. And thirdly, the program extends far enough into the future to show to the extent practical and necessary the full resource requirement and financial implications of the programmed outputs. In the Department of Defense programmed outputs are usually shown for eight years and the financial implications for five years.

The second of the two management techniques in PPB is variously named "systems analysis," "cost effectiveness analysis," or "cost benefit analysis," as well as by various other names, including operations or operational research. The whole system seems to be singularly

Royal Society Nuffield Lecture, London, England, October 25, 1966. Charles J. Hitch, former Assistant Secretary of Defense, is currently President of the University of California. Reprinted with permission of the author.

plagued by terminological confusion. I hope that, like someone said of the music of Wagner, it is better than it sounds. Let me call the second technique "systems analysis" . . . since that is its official name in the Department of Defense. Systems analysis in this sense is analysis, explicit quantitative analysis to the extent practical, which is designed to maximize, or at least increase, the value of the objectives achieved by an organization minus the value of the resources it uses.

These two techniques, programming and systems analysis, were introduced into the Department of Defense by Secretary McNamara for one purpose—to improve high level planning in the Department, i.e., planning at the level of Department of Defense headquarters, Service headquarters, and the headquarters of the unified commands. Other management functions in the Department of Defense, such as control and operations, were not affected except indirectly by these particular McNamara innovations. Even the format of the annual operating budget as appropriated by Congress and accounted for by the Department's accounting staffs was unaffected, at least initially. Instead, and this I believe proved to be satisfactory enough, we developed a torque converter for translating the five-year program into the budget format and vice versa.

I emphasize the exclusive relation of these techniques to the planning function for clarity in explaining their rationale, certainly not to disparage them, for I consider planning in its various aspects to be *the* important function of top management in any large organization, whether government, business, or education. Before saying more about the technique let me make some general remarks about the nature of planning. The planning function can be analyzed in a number of different ways. First, of course, by how distant the future time period with which it is concerned. We have short-range planning—planning for the use of existing facilities and resources. We have intermediate-range planning—the planning of procurement and construction of new facilities. And we have long-range planning— the planning of new developments with very long lead times, like new major weapons systems in Defense or new campuses for the University of California. In Defense we generally found a ten-year planning cycle long enough for most of our developments. In the University of California the lead times are longer. New campuses require that we look 35 years ahead, to the year 2000, and we attempt to do so.

Another distinction which is critical to much of my discussion is that between substantive planning and fiscal planning. Fiscal planning is the planning of future budgets—how much money and how to spend it. Substantive planning is the planning of objectives—ultimate objectives and intermediate objectives. In the Department of Defense substantive planning is called military planning; in the University it is called academic planning. Both fiscal and substantive planning can be short, intermediate, or long-range.

I repeat, the reason we introduced the two techniques of programming and systems analysis in the Department of Defense in 1961 was to improve the exercise of the planning function, which we found in disarray. We introduced programming to make the military planning of the Department realistic, to make it face up to the hard choices by linking it to fiscal planning, from which it had been divorced. And we introduced systems analysis to provide a criterion or standard for making the hard choices, to achieve some rationality and optimality in the planning.

When I say that planning was in disarray at the beginning of 1961 I mean just that. There was plenty of planning activity of all sorts: short-range, intermediate-range, long-range, substantive and fiscal. The key to the disarray was the almost complete separation between substantive or military planning and fiscal planning. These two types of planning were performed by two different groups—the military planning by the Joint Chiefs of Staff and the military planners in the Services, and fiscal planning by the civilian secretary and the comptroller organization throughout the Department. Secondly, these two types of planning were couched in different terms, not readily translatable and in general not translated. Military planning was in terms of army divisions, navy ships, fighter aircraft squadrons, and so forth —military units or weapons systems, the "outputs" of the department. Fiscal planning was in terms of budget categories, which were military personnel, operations and maintenance, procurement, research and development, military construction—"input" categories. In practice, the long-range and intermediate-range military plans of the Joint Chiefs of Staff and the Services were either not costed out in terms of their budget requirements or this was done so roughly and unreliably as to be unuseable. Thirdly, the two types of planning were for different time periods. There were intermediate-range and long-range military plans but no fiscal plans extending beyond the next budget year.

In consequence, the intermediate-range and long-range military planning was largely ineffective. The Department of Defense, one of the world's largest organizations, had no approved plans extending more than one year into the future. Each year the Joint Chiefs of Staff would produce its massive intermediate-range plan called the Joint Strategic Objective Plan (JSOP) with Force Tabs extending five to ten years into the future, and would send it to the Secretary of Defense, who would note it and file it. Before McNamara no JSOP was ever approved. Then in the budget season, in October and November, the real life decisions were made by civilian secretaries advised in the main by the comptroller organization. Why was the

JSOP ignored? Primarily because it was financially infeasible. It was more or less a pasting together of the wish lists of the four military Services. If costed out, the budgets it required would be far in excess of what any Secretary of Defense or President or Congress would approve. The system in short did not require the military planners to face up to the hard choices that are part of responsible management. Let me emphasize that this was not the fault of the military planners but of the system. In organizations with similar systems, academic planners and business planners act just like the military planners.

But since the military planners didn't make the hard choices, the civilian secretary had to as best he could in his budget review, and without much help from intermediate-range or long-range military plans. The method which he used in his budget review, lacking any other, might be described generally as the "budget ceiling" approach. The President would indicate the general level of defense budget he felt was appropriate to the international situation and to his over-all economic and fiscal policies. The Secretary of Defense, by one means or another, would allocate this figure among the three military departments. Each military department would in turn prepare its basic budget submission, allocating its ceiling among its own functions, units, and activities. It was recognized long ago that this was a rather inefficient way to go about preparing the defense budget. For one thing, the budget submissions didn't provide the right kind of information for program decisions. It wasn't organized by programs and it extended only one year into the future. Secondly, the decisions were too decentralized to achieve a balanced over-all program. Each Service naturally tended to exercise its own priorities, favoring its own unique missions to the detriment of joint missions, striving to lay the groundwork for an increased share of the budget in future years by concentrating on alluring new weapon systems, and protecting the over-all size of its force structure. The Air Force, for example, gave overriding priority to the strategic retaliatory bombers and missiles, starving as necessary the tactical air units needed to support Army ground operations and the airlift units needed to move limited war forces quickly to far off trouble spots. The Navy gave overriding priority to its own nuclear attack forces, notably the aircraft carriers, while its anti-submarine warfare capability was relatively neglected and its escort capability atrophied. The Army used its limited resources to preserve the number of its divisions, although this meant that they lacked equipment and supplies to fight effectively for more than a few weeks. Moreover, because attention was focused only on the next fiscal year, the Services had every incentive to propose large numbers of new starts, the full cost dimensions of which would only become apparent in subsequent years. This is the "foot in the door" or "thin edge of the wedge" technique which one-year-at-a-time approaches to budgeting greatly encourage.

So every year the plans and programs of each of the Services had to be cut back to fit the budget ceiling by program cancellations, stretchouts, or postponements—but only for that year. Beyond the budget year unrealistic plans continued to burgeon. Perhaps next year the budget would be higher.

We introduced the program, the official name of which is the "Five Year Force Structure and Financial Program," to correct the basic flaw in the system, namely the separation of planning and budgeting. You will recall that the program is organized by outputs like the military plans, which can be related to national, military, and foreign policy objectives far more readily than the traditional budget categories. The basic elements of the program are force units, like Army Infantry Divisions, or weapons systems, like Minuteman Missiles, or development projects, like the Nike-X Antimissile Missile. The sum total of the program elements, of which there are about a thousand when one includes the overhead elements, is the total program of the Department. You will also recall that each program element has with it its full resource and financial costs year by year, five years into the future, for all the men, equipment, supplies and installations required to make it effective, irrespective of the budget category in which the funds are appropriated. The total dollars required for the program each year are within limits which the Secretary of Defense considers appropriate and feasible. The program shifts the emphasis from cost in next year's budget to cost to complete and operate a weapons system or program.

The program, once established in 1961, is continuously in being. There is always a program, an approved program, but a program change procedure results in several billion dollars worth of changes in the program each year. Any office of the Department of Defense may propose a change in the program at any time. All major changes have to be approved by the Secretary of Defense after review and recommendations by the Joint Chiefs of Staff. So we end up with a planning, programming, budgeting system with the program linking the military plans on the one side and the budget on the other.

The function of the planning in the planning-programming-budgeting system is to develop alternatives—better alternatives—to those in the current approved program. The planning is carried out at all levels of the Department and it takes three forms. One of these is the more or less traditional military planning like that which was embodied in the JSOP, which continues. The second is systems analysis, about which I will say more later, and the third consists of blends of the two. The budget has become in effect the first annual slice of the five-year program. The annual budget review continues but it has become an intensive final analysis of the financial requirements of the program for the next fiscal year, rather than a review of the program itself.

The second of the management techniques which comprise the PPB system is called "systems analysis" or "cost effectiveness" or "cost benefit analysis" or "operations research." It is nothing more or less than economic analysis applied to the public sector. Economic analysis is concerned with the allocation of resources. Its basic maxim is: maximize the value of objectives achieved minus the value of the resources used. In business this reduces itself to maximizing profits, both income and outgo being measured in dollars. In Defense and generally in the public sector we lack a common valuation for objectives and resources and therefore have to use one of two weaker maxims—maximize objectives for given resources, or minimize resources for given objectives. This is what a systems analysis attempts to do—assist the decision-maker to choose weapon systems and modes of operating them which maximize some military objective or objectives (for example, the number of attacking bombers or missiles shot down) for given resources (for example, budget dollars) available. The function of the program is to cost out the plans to keep them feasible and realistic, to make the planners face up to the hard choices. The function of systems analysis is to get dollars into the calculations at an earlier stage—into the planning process, into the evaluation of alternative ways of achieving a military objective. You can't choose the optimal way or even a good way without knowing about the alternatives—what the alternatives achieve and what they cost. . . .

Let me digress to emphasize the very partial role which systems analysis necessarily plays in optimizing decisions. I have said that it assists the decision-maker. It attempts to inform and sharpen his intuition and judgment; it does not itself make the decision. In operations research it is customary to distinguish between optimizing models and predictive models. In this application the two blend into each other. Our aim is to help the decision-maker. What help does he need in making a decision—in choosing among alternatives? He needs to know the consequences of his choices—positive consequences, in achieving his objectives, and negative consequences or "costs" in a broad sense. If he has a single measurable objective and is interested in only one kind of cost—say budget cost—it might well be possible to design an optimizing model—a systems analysis—which would, in effect, make the decision for him. I have never encountered such a pure case in the real world, although I know of some which approximate it. In the typical case there are several objectives—some intangible—and several relevant costs. The systems analyst must predict the important consequences, i.e., those which are important in assisting the decision-maker to make his own intuitive optimizing choice.

So, in summary, the program provides the link between planning and budgeting, relating forces and their costs to national security objectives, while systems analysis provides the quantitative analytical foundation in many areas, by no means all, for making sound choices among the alternative means of achieving the objectives. Between them they give the Secretary of Defense the tools which are necessary for planning a program with balance and some rationality, and therefore for the unified management of his $60-billion-a-year department. For the first time the Secretary of Defense is capable of exercising the authority given him in the National Security Act of 1947, which attempted to unify the military services.

I have spent so much time explaining what happened in the Department of Defense that I have little left to answer the question "Whither?" This is perhaps as well for I know more about the past than about the future. Let me speculate with some shorthand points. First, all large organizations, whether government, business, or mixed, have many problems in common. I am very impressed with their similarities, having recently moved from one large organization to another which sounds very different, but which has many of the same problems. Among these is the problem of achieving realistic, balanced, rational plans. I found academic planning in U.C. in the same kind of disarray as military planning in the Department of Defense, and for the same reason. So I am sure that similar techniques have widespread application in other organizations.

Secondly, in fact they already have widespread application. The Department of Defense is not the first organization to develop a financial plan or program which extends more than a year into the future, and which has evolved budget categories more suitable for planning—for intermediate and long-range fiscal planning—than objects of expenditure. Other organizations have confronted and more or less satisfactorily solved the problems of unrealistic and too decentralized planning. Similarly, many well managed businesses make explicit, quantitative economic analyses of, for example, alternative equipment and facility plans, which are indistinguishable from what is called systems analysis in the Department of Defense. . . . Operations researchers have assisted military [and] other governmental and business planners with varying degrees of success for the past 25 years. What is different in the Department of Defense is that systems analysis has there become a generally accepted way of life, perhaps for the first time in any large public organization.

Thirdly, there are risks and dangers as well as opportunities in trying to move too far too fast in the application of new management techniques like these, including the risk of discrediting the techniques. Although it did not appear easy at the time, there is no doubt in my mind that the Department of Defense (or much of it) is easier to program and to analyze quantitatively than many areas of civilian government. For example, it is easier than the foreign affairs area, where I have perhaps foolhardily been attempting to advise the State Department on how to install a planning-programming-budgeting system. And quite apart from ease or difficulty the substantive problems in other areas are different and new. In Defense we had several hundred analysts at the RAND Corporation and elsewhere developing programming and systems analysis techniques for a decade before the Department attempted any large scale general application. No remotely similar preparatory effort has gone into any other governmental area and the number of trained and skilled people is so limited that they are inevitably spread far thinner in other departments of government than they were and are in Defense.

But fourth and finally, to end on an encouraging note, although these techniques are mutually supporting, we are not dealing here with a matter of either/or. There is an infinity of degrees. Not only may one introduce a program budget without systems analysis or vice versa, but each may be used in limited areas or ways, and sometimes quite productively. For example, in foreign affairs, where quantification of objectives and therefore full systems analysis is so difficult, one can, I think, organize the budget more meaningfully for planning purposes. In many areas a systems *cost* analysis is possible and useful although a full systems analysis, involving measurement of objectives, is not as yet. I am convinced that there are some American institutions . . . which are quite ripe for the application of some efficiency-inducing management techniques, and for basically the same reason that the military was ripe. American hospitals, for example, have, like armies and navies, traditionally and proudly operated on a not-for-profit basis. Just as the Generals and Admirals asked: "What do dollars matter when national security is at stake?", the doctors and hospital administrators ask "What do dollars matter when life is at stake?". (I have heard educators ask "What do dollars matter when the quality of the next generation is at stake?".) Well, the dollars do matter. Granted that these are all high priority claimants on the national purse and that there is a kernel of truth in each protesting cry, the importance of objectives does not justify ignoring the canons of economy and efficiency—which are to achieve the most from whatever limited resources the nation, in its wisdom or unwisdom, places at our disposal.

PPBS: TWO QUESTIONS

FREDERICK C. MOSHER

LETTER TO EDITOR-IN-CHIEF

Over the last few years and particularly the last few months, I have been searching for "satisficing" answers to two questions about PPBS. First, what is really new and distinctive about it? Second, in what directions is it really influencing governmental decision-making and the conduct of governmental operations?

I was therefore particularly gratified to learn that *PAR* would devote a complete issue to PPBS, and I read all of it with unusual (for me) care and thoroughness. It was a very good and rewarding issue. Yet I cannot honestly say that these articles resolved my questions; indeed, I am somewhat more confused now than before. Most of your authors, like others before them, differ among each other as to what PPBS really is; few of them say or predict what its real effects are or will be—beyond the confident assurance that decisions will be more rational, governmental operations more efficient (excepting, of course, Mr. Wildavsky's alarums from the wilderness of political science). I am in sympathy with most of PPBS and its constituent elements insofar as I understand what they are. In fact, I have been a supporter for about thirty years—ever since I took a course in budgeting taught by Bob Steadman in 1936. But apparently I have been missing some things. These are what I am searching to identify.

From *Public Administration Review*, Vol. 27 (March 1967), pp. 67–71. Frederick C. Mosher is Professor of Government and Foreign Affairs, University of Virginia. Reprinted with permission of the author and the American Society of Public Administration.

Mr. Greenhouse's article on "Planning-Programming-Budgeting System: Rationale, Language, and Idea-Relationships" is described as particularly aimed at "distinguishing it (PPBS) from earlier management systems", so his piece seems an appropriate point of departure. Greenhouse advises us that PPBS has two basic ingredients which distinguish it from what has gone before. The first is a new and different concept of accountability. The second consists of a set of eight terms and expressions, none of which is new according to Mr. Greenhouse, but their rearrangement provides them "subtle differences of flavor and shade" which renders the totality distinctly different and new.

The more intriguing of these two ingredients of PPBS is the first one, accountability, since most of the literature on the subject has been singularly devoid of concern about accountability. Greenhouse advises us that, under the PPBS concept, each agency is primarily accountable to the President (and Congress) "for the distribution of these goods and services to the American people." Before PPBS, he says, agencies were accountable to provide "administrative support" to the President (and Congress). This seems to me a singular interpretation of agency accountability prior to PPBS, whether it is construed as a description of legal and formal accountability or of attitudinal and behavioral accountability. It is the more extraordinary coming from an official of the Veterans' Administration where many of us have thought, and some have deplored, that for many decades the primary accountability was to the veterans (and their organizations) for the "distribution of goods and services to (a sector of) the American people." If, as Mr. Greenhouse says, PPBS hinges on this "new" concept of accountability, it is strange that the source and fountainhead of PPBS practice and experience—indeed to this date almost the only example—is the Department of Defense where it was applied primarily to the fashioning of weapon systems for possible delivery to potential enemies of the American people. While the protection of the American people is perhaps the principal objective of Defense, the distribution of protection does not seem to have been a determining and underlying concept in the development of PPBS with regard to weapons.

The eight distinguishing terms of PPBS, according to Greenhouse, are: "objectives, programs, program alternatives, outputs, progress measurements, inputs, alternative ways to do a given job, and systems analysis". I find few "differences of flavor and shade" in Mr. Greenhouse's discussion of these terms. The objective-plans-programs-operations-measurements sequence is very "old-hat" among budgeteers and among scholars. His extension of the meaning of objectives to "market objectives" seems a rather curious perversion of the word "market," but the idea is an old one to students of government and administration. I find little to debate in Mr. Greenhouse's definition of PPBS "programs," bearing in mind, as he asks us, that "*this* idea of program is very different from the traditional governmental usage." I would bear in mind too that the "traditional usage" has been repeatedly challenged over the past sixty years with a great deal of success in some areas, well before "PPBS" was coined. Unless I am mistaken, the PPBS definition of, and concentration upon, programs has been standard doctrine in the literature about, and the teaching of, budgeting since the thirties. And, so far as I can recall, there is no essential change in the meaning of "program" and its identification with objectives from what I was taught then.

Dr. Hirsch, in his "Toward Federal Program Budgeting," is less explicit in distinguishing the elements of PPBS. He argues that it "should help overcome some of the major shortcomings of the existing administrative budget, where budgetary requests are presented in line-item form—personnel, supplies, maintenance, etc." The drive against the line-item and toward more programmatic appropriations, presentations, justifications, and thinking has been pushed for a good many decades both by budgeteers and by budgetary reformers. As a matter of fact, great progress toward this objective was made during the decade following World War II and partly in consequence of the first Hoover report (which made a very similar statement). If, as Dr. Hirsch suggests, the major shortcomings of Federal budgeting reside in the fact that "budgetary requests are presented in line-item form," it is at least interesting that the presentation of the Defense Department in the President's Budget has changed in no material way since 1961 and still accords with the cost-category structure instituted a decade and a half ago under the direction of then Defense Comptroller Wilfred McNeil. Program budgeting has apparently gone on *behind* the formal presentation in Defense, and one wonders whether its essence may not have been going on behind the formal presentations of a good many other agencies. How significant a test is the formal presentation? . . .

My own guess is that PPBS has made significant contributions to budgetary concepts and potentially to budgetary practice in providing not new ideas but new emphasis. These include its emphases upon alternatives, upon cost-benefit analysis, and upon the reexamination of objectives and what should be done about them—i.e., programs. It has provided Presidential support, and in a few cases, departmental support for the intensive analysis, utilizing whatever analytical tools are available, of public—and therefore budgetary—problems. PPBS has made more respectable—indeed more mandatory —the application of the newer techniques of computerization of quantitative data to public decision-making. It has laid new stress on the assessment of outputs against inputs and therefore on the evaluation of effects of governmental programs, as far as possible quantifiable. It has encouraged a longer-range view—three or five or ten years—beyond the one-year budget projection, though this is by no means a new idea or practice. And it has fostered and given respectability to intensive analysis of programmatic and budgetary problems in depth, taking into account both costs and benefits. In these various ways I would hope that PPBS will contribute significant accretions to rationality in the budget process. The goal is not new any more than are the means. But PPBS has brought a sudden and unexpected Presidential push about which none of us should quibble.

These are guesses and hopes. Opposite them I would pose some other guesses and fears. First among these seems to me, generously, the ignoring of, or less generously, contempt for, democratic values and processes. In all the literature I have read about PPBS, including your recent *PAR* issues, only a few authors have even mentioned the executive and legislative processes of review and decision. The President and Congress seem to be regarded as enemies of rationality. Dr. Hirsch raises a variety of value-loaded questions such as: "Have we the right mix between the budget for U.S. military forces and the other national security activities?" and: "Should the Federal Government spend only $1.4 billion on primary and secondary education?" Who is to answer such questions? An analyst? Or are they to be answered through normal budgetary procedures, enlightened as far as possible by studies of analysts? At no point does one gain the impression that the budget process is a "due process" of administration wherein the facts, the analyses, the interests, the politics and the prejudices of people enter. Much of the literature of PPBS resembles that of the technocrats of the thirties; its aim seems to be to eliminate *politics* from decisionmaking. I hope that some apostle of PPBS may soon draft a rationalization of the system with political democracy. I think this can be done but not in the technocratic and authoritarian language we have seen to date.

My second reservation about the literature on PPBS—and some of its practice—is the apparent lack of sophistication about organization and administration. Perhaps I am underrating the proponents; maybe they know (and intend) that their efforts will shift decision-making power from one group to another, from one level to another, however much some of them prefer to describe their system as "politically neutral." I am grateful to Dr. Wildavsky for his penetrating discussion of program budgeting as "system politics," though I am less concerned than he regarding the possible dire consequences of "unlimited efficiency," perhaps because of my faith, which may be naive, in checks and balances, in competition among bureaucracies, in political executives, and in the Congress. While PPBS is avowedly intended to improve decision-making, there has been surprisingly little treatment of *who* would or should make the decision. In fact, the potential effects of PPBS on power distribution within the government are surely as important as the technical improvements which are hoped for it. Most of the government lacks the "unitaryness" of the Defense Department where the decisive power of the Secretary was enhanced by PPBS and at the same time contributed assurance of authoritative treatment of PPBS findings. But this is hardly possible in fields like education, foreign affairs, natural resources, and many others. Will PPBS move all program decision-making in these fields up to the Budget Bureau or the White House? Is this its intent? Secondly, what will be the relationship between the budget analysts and the decision-makers? Will this new style of experts be on top or on tap? Thirdly, what will be the relationship between the program budgeteers and the old-style budgeteers, who deal with such mundane problems as line-items and presentations to higher levels and Congress? And what will be their relationship with the existing, usually professionalized, offices of programming and planning which one finds in most of the Federal bureaus?

Dr. Hirsch states that more than 40 Federal agencies are engaged in educational activities. I understand that over 50 are engaged in foreign affairs. Comparable numbers are involved in other major governmental efforts (or programs): natural resources, transportation, urban development, etc. One reads vague expectations in the PPBS literature that agencies will be reorganized to accord with programs. While some reorganizations in this direction would undoubtedly be helpful, the objectives of different organizations will inevitably cross over into others, however they are defined; all have multiple purposes. All have, and inevitably will have, their own committees and subcommittees in Congress, including the appropriations subcommittees. How then to develop rational program budgets? I pose these questions not as unanswerable or insoluble but as questions that many apostles of PPBS have conspicuously neglected. Who is to seek answers to the many questions that Hirsch and others have raised? And, more important, who is to make decisions about them?

My third fear about PPBS arises from its lack of "historicism." I can find no better word than this slightly obsolescent one to depict an ignorance or deliberate rejection of historical precedents and an absence of recognition of developments over a considerable period. The article by Allen Schick on "The Road to PPB" provided a particularly valuable historical perspective, conspicuous by its absence in most of the writings on the subject. The majority would have us believe that PPBS has come to us as Aphrodite from the sea, full-blown, fresh, beautiful, and topless. Dr. Hirsch advises us that the early beginnings came in World War II in the War Production Board and that David Novick developed the concept in the mid-fifties. The expression "program budgeting" goes back a good many decades. As you know, I wrote a book in 1954 with this title and I believe with the same theme—the rational relating of objectives, plans, programs, and budgets. Since World War II, there have been innumerable articles and monographs on the subject—local, state, national, and international. As indicated above, I am still searching for the differences in concept between the Novick-Rand-Defense PPBS and the traditional idea of program budgeting which goes back several decades. My own questions about the meaning and the significance of PPBS perhaps arise from the lack of historicism of most of the writers on the subject. It is hard to point up what is new if one does not know or does not acknowledge what has gone before.

I hope that PPBS may not grow and blossom and fade as some other management "fads" have because of a failure to synchronize it with the development of our society, orientations, and experiences. I hope that the 90, more or less, Federal employees now training for PPBS in various universities (and the 150, more or less, next year) may learn enough about public administration and politics that they are not completely frustrated when they return to their jobs. I hope that we not oversell this thing; that we keep our feet on the ground; that our political-administrative system may be educated as far as possible with rationality but that economic rationality may not overtake political and administrative responsibility. If my understanding of the meaning of PPBS is near the mark, let us have it but only in terms that are consonant with the ideals of American politics, administration, and democracy.

BARGAINING AND ANALYSIS IN GOVERNMENT

HENRY S. ROWEN

No observant person intimately involved in affairs of Government can fail to be impressed by the contrast between current theories of Government and what actually seems to be going on about him. Part of the discrepancy comes from the complexity of the operations of Government. But much comes from the fact that there have been few systematic attempts to record and analyze actual bureaucratic behavior. Until a great many more behavioral studies have been done, and done with a higher standard of rigor than has been typical so far, we are not likely to make a great deal of progress. (My observations below on Government should not be regarded as inconsistent with this assertion.)

In the absence of such rigorous analysis, the best we have to go on are the more superficial observations and reasoning based on them by participants and spectators of the bureaucratic process.

TWO APPROACHES

The two principal approaches to the operations of Government are what have been called the Hierarchical one and the Bargaining one. The former derives from traditional administrative and economic theories, the latter from pluralist concepts of democratic government.

Paper delivered before the American Political Science Association Annual Meeting, New York City, September 1966. Henry S. Rowen is President of the Rand Corporation. Reprinted with permission of the author and the American Political Science Association.

The former has emphasized hierarchies of objectives, lines of authority, division of labor among organizational units, coordination of policies and programs, and systems efficiency. It is in this tradition that the economics of public expenditures has developed, including in recent years the technique of systems analysis. The bargaining approach is concerned mainly with the fact that individuals and groups with differing values exist, with the power they possess, and with the processes of adjustment among these groups in the workings of government. This approach is rooted in the concept of equity in a democratic society.

In recent years the bargaining view has been very much in the ascendency. For several reasons. It has deep roots in the pluralist tradition, a tradition which is widely and deeply shared in American culture. It seems to be more consistent with the actual workings of government than does the traditional hierarchically oriented administrative theory. The bargaining theorists have, of course, gone further and have not only pointed out that things don't work the way the traditional view would have it, they have adduced strong arguments as to why they shouldn't and can't. Third, important aspects of the theory of public expenditures have come under severe criticism. For example, the conditions to be met for Pareto optimality* generally aren't met and the divergences often seem large and difficult or impossible to overcome.

So perhaps the bargaining approach is the only contender of consequence left on the field. I think it is not.

HOW WELL DOES THE PRESENT SYSTEM WORK?

The theory has been developed in its most interesting and recent form by C. E. Lindblom. In his latest book on this subject he asserts that independent, partisan decision makers can be coordinated in several ways in the absence of a central coordinator; that such partisan mutual adjustment is characteristic of the real world; that complex decision making is necessarily fragmented, disjointed and incremental; that having a multiplicity of interacting quasi-independent decision makers promotes rationality; that central decision making doesn't work very well; that partisan mutual adjustment facilitates agreements on values and actions; and that the process promotes consent to democratic government.

One comment on this view is that Lindblom has described the way the Government mainly works. The pulling and hauling, adversary dealings, promotion of programs, compromising, marginal adjusting,

* Editorial note: As defined by Allen Schick, Pareto optimality denotes the "best that could be achieved without disadvantaging at least one group."

and related activities are highly visible aspects of governmental behavior from the precinct level on up. It is an important contribution to our understanding of bureaucracy to have the importance of this kind of behavior properly emphasized and to have begun to analyze it systematically.

But if this is not an inaccurate description of the workings of much of the government much of the time, how good are the results of this process, and to the extent they seem not good what can be done to improve things?

If one holds the view that means the ends of government action are indistinguishable and that all of our issues are issues of equity in a pluralistic society, it is difficult to say anything meaningful about the goodness or badness of the functioning of government. Presumably the search for objective measures of governmental performance is fruitless. Any program the system produces will do as well as any other and the goodies might as well be distributed one way as another.

This is an extreme view and, I think, not tenable. (The symmetrically opposite, strict hierarchical view is even less tenable.) Not tenable for the following reasons:

Some ends are widely deemed to be better than others. Individuals and groups have preferences, not only on "Who's Right?", but also on "What's Right?". "What's Right?" often commands a high degree of agreement. There are consequences of government action that come pretty near to being objectively "good" or "bad". For example, avoidance of nuclear war, reduction of poverty at home and abroad, providing at least a minimal level of protection from crime and violence, improvement in the status of Negroes. These are widely shared objectives. Although objectives like these are abstractions, and they sometimes conflict with each other and with other objectives, and there are wider differences about ways to accomplish these ends than there is about the ends themselves, these ends do matter. And some actions do better than others at achieving these ends.

That is, efficiency matters also. This assertion might seem trivial. But if means are regarded as ends and if the purpose of the game of government is only income distribution, then why be efficient? One reason is that it has a prominent place in American culture. Another is that if one holds that there are some important objectives, it takes some minimal level of efficiency to get there. Moreover, it may take not only a strong bargaining position but even a degree of efficiency in getting income transferred to the groups deemed worthy of receiving it.

Consider technical efficiency. It seems to make a difference. Some designs of supersonic transports or space vehicles, or sewage treatment plants are better than others in the sense that payload—range or payload—thrust or plant output-input ratios—differ and some designs work better than others. In space, in defense, in transportation, in health, in crime, in flood control, in postal delivery there are many decisions made about which the question of technical efficiency is relevant.

But this is too limited a concept of efficiency. More general is an economic efficiency concept—the least cost combination of factor inputs to accomplish a given objective. Still more general is the measure of both benefits and costs in money terms.

One must be careful, however, to be sure that the same objective is being met by the various means. In the early stages of the manual lunar landing program, the two principal alternatives considered called for an earth-orbiting and a moon-orbiting stage respectively. The object in both cases was to get at least one American to the moon and back alive by 1970. There was little question about the objective being the same. (Even in examples of this kind, some members of our society might prefer one approach based not on technical or social economic criteria but on a preference among manufacturers.)

Clearly there are many cases of a type Lindblom cites where members of society have important differences both among ends and among the means of achieving given ends. The least cost solution on a highway *won't* do for many. But, the least cost solution (or at least a relatively low cost solution) is relevant and the partisan mutual adjustment process isn't all that likely to throw it up.

That is, we should not just assume that good (i.e., efficient in one of the senses described above) technical and economic decisions will be made, or even taken into account, by a system operating primarily in a partisan mutual adjustment mode. We should not assume so for several reasons:

(a) Large bureaucracies have remarkable inertia. I use the word "inertia" in the sense used in physics, as the tendency for matter (organizations) to remain at rest, if at rest, or if moving, to keep moving in the same direction. The inner life of organizations and their imperviousness to changes in the external environment is often extraordinary. The celebrated case of the survival of the cavalry for decades past its useful life is a case in point, as is the continued survival of some other governmental anachronisms. The ability of a well-established organization to develop a doctrine, a theory which justifies any defense behavior against outside influences is impressive. The absence of market prices for most of the goods and services produced by government helps to maintain the inertia. So does the restricted nature of the competition that government "firms" also face.

One result is to suppress options, to conceal possibilities that don't conform. Anomalies can exist for very long periods of time with no corrective action being taken.

For example, in our Defense Department we had for many years a situation in which two services were preparing for quite different kinds of wars. Their force structure, their readiness, their logistics, and their ordnance were incompatible. These gaps persisted despite the fact than many people were aware of the problem. But doctrine was too strong. A similar gap existed between our alliance policies abroad and the forces to back up these policies.

One difficulty with leaving important issues to be thrashed out by the parties that happen to express an interest is that they can argue over the wrong issues. Some years ago there was some debate over the size of the Soviet bomber force versus our own; several years later there was a similar debate over strategic missiles. In both cases, the main issue debated was the number of vehicles on either side; the main real issue was largely undebated: the implications for the vulnerability of the forces.

(b) There are not only wide differences in the bargaining power of the "firms," this bargaining power is not necessarily very highly correlated with the information or the power to take relevant action to accomplish objectives with a high degree of efficiency.

No one can deny the power of the Bureau of Public Roads; one might question the extent to which it has the information to enable it to shape the structure of cities differently than it now does through its urban highway programs or the extent to which it would regard this as its mission of life. This power may reflect widely shared values or the intensity with which values are felt. But the price in technical and economic diseconomies are often high. If all one uses as a criterion is the pragmatic test of the firm's "sales" (the disputes it wins, the new programs introduced, the old ones sustained, the share of the budget obtained), one hasn't much. And resources wasted often count as much as resources well used on these criteria.

(c) Even where counteravailing power is present, one cannot assert a high probability that the common interest will benefit. If private firms and organized labor are capable of striking bargains which act against the common interest one shouldn't assume that government agencies are not.

Other examples can be cited: We invest quite a lot to move air passengers from airport to airport but have paid little attention to the increasingly significant links in the journey from portal to and from airports. Our maritime policies which have traditionally been worked out via the bargaining mode include an operating subsidy which is structured so as to create a positive incentive to overmanning of ships. Our water resources policies favor expensive means of reducing water pollution over less expensive means. These policies have also produced flood control projects which have generated incentives for people to overbuild in still vulnerable flood plains. In agriculture we pay both to take land out of agricultural production while bringing reclaimed land in. We have a sugar subsidy program which seems to cost three times the net incomes of the sugar producers. We spend ten times on urban roads as on urban mass transit without the balance between these two types of transportation being examined.

It might be held that some of these examples simply illustrate the principle that our political system has decided to transfer income to specific groups, that a politically feasible way has been found to do this, and the fact that apparently contradictory actions are taken by different parts of the government is either evidence of income being transferred to *other* groups or is compensatory action to correct undesirable overall effects of particular subsidies.

This is undoubtedly true—in some cases. But it is my belief, that, on the average, instances of this type are at least as much due to the reasons cited above: bureaucratic inertia, random differences in bargaining power, absence of market forces, unregulated intra-governmental monopolistic practices.

WHAT CAN BE DONE?

Neither model will do. Lindblom is right about the undesirability and infeasibility of a rigidly hierarchical system. But he is, I think, too hopeful about the virtues of the largely bargaining system we have. We need analysis as well.

What do I mean by analysis? For present purposes suffice it to mean an attempt to define objectives, to describe alternative means to these ends, to invent new objectvies and new alternative means, to assess benefits and costs, to take account of uncertainties, to quantify what looks useful to quantify, to isolate decisions that can be deferred from those that can't, to create options. All this may appear ordinary. It is, but it is often difficult to do and it hasn't been attempted much in a systematic way on major public decisions. But it has begun to be done in a significant way with results in the Defense Department that are impressive; I predict that results throughout other parts of government will, in time, be at least as impressive.

There are several necessary conditions for doing better: one is that there exist a structure of adversary relationships, that over a wide range of governmental behavior there exist mechanisms for one group to challenge and debate issues of common interest with other centers. This doesn't work well if left to chance. It requires action from a higher level. This is a familiar problem in the operation of big corporations. It is more an important problem in areas where market mechanisms are weak or absent. Therefore, one subject for systematic analysis is to improve the bargaining phenomena.

Another necessary condition is that there be a system of analysis involving many groups working from many points of view. For no one group can assemble all of the relevant data on a complex issue; values and facts *do* get inter-mixed; ends and means often *do* interact; problems must be decomposed for analysis; analysis must be partial; all optimizations are, in some sense, suboptimizations. One can expect, however, through more systematic analysis to narrow the vast areas in which governmental action is uninformed, arbitrary, and based on unenlightened opinion rather than data and analysis. One can create larger conceptual "islands" in which relatively good predictions can be made about the consequences of taking alternative decisions. One can even expect to connect some islands to each other through the development of broader theories. Just as economic theory was extended over time from separate theories on production and consumption and money into a unified macro-theory with major consequences for the conduct of public affairs, so we should expect to develop broader theories of health, of education, of law enforcement. And some of these might even connect. How far can this process continue? Indefinitely. (But I confess my mind boggles at the notion of the unified theory, for example, of postal service, foreign aid, and outer space.) We needn't be concerned about running out of new phenomena. New ones will be identified or become ripe at at last the rate at which old ones are mastered.

Finally, in carrying out analyses what should be done about the absence of conditions for Pareto optimality? Two things. Firstly, try in making analyses, to make corrections that move the results in what seems to be the right direction. Secondly, take some solace from the bargaining viewpoint: our system doesn't mind making interpersonal comparisons, and the interactions, over time, of partisan mutual adjusters will see that rough justice gets done.

SCOPE
OF
POLITICAL
DECISIONS

PAUL
DIESING

Political decisions are necessary whenever an organization, or society, or person is faced with a political problem; that is, whenever there is a deficiency in its decision structure. The deficiency may be some form of narrowness, in that the structure is not receptive to an adequate range of facts, or that it is not able to break away from well-known formulas in its estimates of problems and suggestions for action, or that it is insufficiently self-critical and slow to admit error, or that its procedures are excessively rigid and thus shut out novelty. The deficiency may be some form of indecisiveness or internal conflict, in that decisions are excessively difficult to achieve, or that they are nullified or changed by concealed internal opposition, or that the system "changes its mind" too readily after reaching a decision.

The symptom of political deficiency is the existence of numerous and increasing nonpolitical problems for the organization. Since the function of a decision structure is to deal with problems, any deficiency in functioning leads to an accumulation of unsolved problems. Also the way in which the problems accumulate points to the specific kind of deficiency. If the accumulating problems are apparent to an outsider but not to the decision structure, the deficiency exists in the information receptors; if the problems are recognized but solutions are late and erratic in appearing, the difficulty is one of indecisiveness; if solutions consistently fail, the deficiency is one of inventiveness; if erroneous courses of action are not readily changed the

From *Reason in Society* (Urbana: The University of Illinois Press, 1962), pp. 227–232. Paul Diesing is Professor of Political Science at the State University of New York, at Buffalo. Reprinted with permission of the publisher.

deficiency is one of self-criticism; and so on. Sometimes political deficiencies can be discovered directly, by studying the internal workings of the structure and comparing it with similar structures, but the easiest way to locate deficiencies is to work back from the results.

Though a political problem is always accompanied by numerous nonpolitical problems, the political problem is always basic and prior to all the others. Sometimes one of the other problems has a temporal priority in the sense that if something is not done about it within two weeks the organization will go out of existence. This may be the case with threatened bankruptcy, or with a violent internal dispute which is about to force crucial members out of the organization. These are emergencies, to be settled by whatever temporary expedient will succeed. But nothing is basically solved until the political problems of an organization are solved. The reason is that without a well-functioning control system the organization, or society or person, is unable to deal with its other problems in a continuing fashion. They may be temporarily solved by outside help or some emergency action, but they are sure to reappear and get worse unless the organization is politically sound. Conversely, once the decision structure has been put into working order, the organization can be expected to take care of its other problems as they come up.

This means that any suggested course of action must be evaluated first by its effects on the political structure. A course of action which corrects economic or social deficiencies but increases political difficulties must be rejected, while an action which contributes to political improvement is desirable even if it is not entirely sound from an economic or social standpoint. It sometimes happens that political and nonpolitical problems can be solved together, but if this is not possible, the political problem must receive primary attention.

Further, a person who is dealing with a nonpolitical problem must always be ready to ask whether his problem is a symptom of some political deficiency. This is especially necessary if his problem is a persistent one, if it keeps reappearing in various forms. Isolated, unusual problems are likely to be the result of environmental circumstances, but a persistent problem is likely to be the result of some political inability to deal with that kind of problem. If it does appear that a political deficiency exists, attention should be turned away from the original problem to the political problem. Unless this is done, attempts to solve the original problem are likely to be futile, as the political deficiency will cause the same problem to reappear in another form. . . .

So far I have argued that whenever political and nonpolitical problems occur together, the political problem must be solved before one can hope to achieve a lasting solution of the nonpolitical problems. But the primacy of politics extends beyond this. Even when no marked political deficiency exists, a person dealing with nonpolitical problems should make sure that his solutions do not produce a political deficiency, as this is likely eventually to undo any nonpolitical improvements he can make. This point is not so important in dealing with small, isolated problems, as changes here are not likely to affect the political structure markedly. But it is important when one is initiating large-scale long-term changes which are likely to alter the whole organization or society considerably.

For instance, strategies planning a national technological development program should consider the long-term political effects of the changes they are initiating. What will be the optimum-size producing unit with the new technology? If it is small, will this decentralize economic power to a new small-holding class, and can the political system absorb the resulting increased participation? If it is large, will this unduly centralize power and promote a narrow oligarchical political system? Can the economic power of large-scale units be diffused through co-operative ownership or other forms of mixed control? What effects will expected population shifts have on kinship, status systems, life patterns, and what effects will these changes have on levels of personal security and political toleration? What effects will new patterns of experience have on belief systems and on political ideologies? These are difficult questions and in many cases it is not yet possible to answer them, but if any answers which are possible disclose a likelihood of producing political deficiencies, the development program should be modified. Usually there is enough indeterminacy in the requirements of technological development to make modifications possible, and the planner sensitive to political effects will find these modifications as he proceeds.

Political decisions, then, are relevant whenever a political problem exists, and political considerations can be raised whenever a political problem is likely to be produced by planned secular changes. But this means that politics is almost always relevant, because there rarely, if ever, has been a decision structure which was both perfectly adequate for all its tasks and immune to long-term change. And wherever political considerations are raised, they have priority over other considerations. Political rationality is the fundamental kind of reason, because it deals with the preservation and improvement of decision structures, and decision structures are the source of all decisions. Unless a decision structure exists, no reasoning and no decisions are possible; and the more rational a decision structure is, the more rational are the decisions it produces. There can be no conflict between political rationality and any other kind of rationality, because the solution of political problems makes possible an attack on any other problem, while a serious political deficiency can prevent or undo all other problem solving.

COMMENTARY

Without getting into the technical details of PPB, which are dealt with more thoroughly in Chapter Seven, it is possible to detect in these six selections numerous themes which relate directly to our general inquiry into the means and ends of administration. For instance, insofar as the administrative process itself is concerned, both Rowen and Hitch are unequivocal proponents of increased operating efficiency through systems analysis. Rowen's main thrust stresses the value of efficient systems analysis as a necessary aid in making more rational allocative decisions, while Hitch warns that, "dollars do matter" and "the importance of objectives does not justify ignoring the canons of economy and efficiency." But, although this may be the kind of statement that one might normally expect from a cost-analysis oriented executive official, it obviously does not reflect an operating principle that either the Jackson subcommittee or Diesing are prepared to accept. The latter speaks as a philosopher; the former, as a politician. The one tends to reinforce the other.

Thus, for Diesing the primacy of politics is the highest of all values. As long as political considerations are granted priority over all nonpolitical considerations, the system will operate effectively— the canons of economy and efficiency notwithstanding. The primacy of politics concept advanced by Diesing is reflected even more intensely in the Jackson subcommittee memorandum. Here, when the political intuition and judgment of experienced legislators confront the analytical facts, estimated projections, and logical deductions of the executive planner, the primacy of politics must, and will, prevail. Viewed in this context, broad public policy decisions simply cannot

41

be controlled by quantitative data reduced to economic factors. The administrative means favored by Diesing and the Jackson subcommittee for the allocation of available resources is the bargaining model described by Rowen. The Jackson subcommittee memorandum strongly implies a preference for the bargaining-incremental approach. Diesing, as can be noted from the following passage found elsewhere in his excellent book, *Reason in Society,* is much more explicit.

Nonpolitical decisions are reached by considering a problem in its own terms and by evaluating proposals according to how well they solve the problem. The best available proposal should be accepted regardless of who makes it and who opposes it, and a faulty proposal should be rejected or improved no matter who makes it. Compromise is always irrational; the rational procedure is to determine which proposal is the best, and to accept it. In a political decision, on the other hand, action is never based on the merits of the proposal but always on who makes it and who opposes it. . . . The best available proposal should never be accepted just because it is the best; it should be deferred, objected to, discussed, until major opposition disappears. Compromise is always a rational procedure, even when the compromise is between a good and bad proposal.*

The interesting theme which emerges from this statement, and one which is implicitly emphasized throughout the Jackson subcommittee memorandum, is the personification of the decision-making process in terms of the individual who makes the decisions or the proposals for public policy action. Thus, according to Diesing, in nonpolitical decisions the best proposal must always be accepted and the faulty proposal must always be rejected no matter who makes it; whereas, the selection of a political proposal is never to be based on the merits of the proposal, but rather, on *who* favors it and *who* opposes it. Similarly, the Jackson subcommittee appears to be less concerned with how our governmental system is to be administered —i.e., toward what end?—than with the question of who is to administer the system—i.e., who is to propose and decide, or, ultimately, who governs? This concern surfaces very emphatically and almost defiantly in the concluding paragraph of the memorandum: "If PPBS develops into a contest between experts and politicians, it will not be hard to pick the winners. They will be the politicians in the Congress and White House. It has been said, and correctly, that as interesting as observing what happens to government ˙when confronted with PPB will be watching what happens to PPB when confronted with government."

This shift in emphasis is significant. If one's primary concern

* Diesing, *Reason in Society,* pp. 203–204.

rests with *how* a system is to be administered, then the answer to this query must be joined with some ultimate goal to be achieved. Thus if operating efficiency is to be maximized, or, if the available resources are to be allocated in the most equitable manner possible, the way in which the administrative system is organized to achieve either of these goals is of absolute significance. On the other hand, if one's primary concern is with *who* is to administer the system, it is possible that such ultimate goals as economy, efficiency, or equity may still be established as legitimate ends to be achieved, but it is equally possible, as is shown in Chapter Six, that this concern may develop into an end in itself.

The notion of Who Governs, of course, carries strong normative, or subjectively defined, value connotations, but what about the nation of *how* a system is to be governed? Is it also structured around a well-defined set of value preferences and normative judgments? Hamilton and Jefferson, as well as James Madison, had very strong preferences as to how their respective administrative systems should be organized, and yet, one of the major sources of concern for Mosher as he discusses some of the current literature on PPB, is its apparent ignorance of, or contempt for, democratic values and processes. His second reservation is directly related to the former: the disturbing claim of many of the proponents of PPB that their system is politically neutral. In other words, if Mosher's concerns prove valid, then a value-free administrative process would apparently represent a major departure from the value-oriented administrative plans advanced in the beginning days of our nation by Hamilton, Jefferson, and Madison.

These are just some of the questions that will be examined in more detail in the chapters that follow. From the six selections included in this chapter, the reader may be able to sense the broad dimensions of conflict which currently exist between divergent administrative approaches and certain fundamental concepts of democratic theory. The basic assumption on which this volume rests is that the essential elements of the current conflict have recurred periodically in varying forms since the beginning of our nation. Indeed, the remaining chapters will attempt to show that the various administrative philosophies that have been applied to our governmental system are all directly related to the basic premise various people have assumed concerning the manner in which governmental resources are to be allocated in a political system. As has been indicated, most approaches to public administration (as applied in democratic settings) attempt to maximize either operating efficiency or social equity. Thus, the chapters which follow will attempt to trace the historical continuity of these two major themes. Simply stated, the divergent lines of thought have developed as follows:

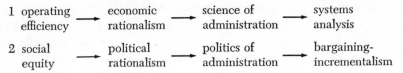

1 operating ⟶ economic ⟶ science of ⟶ systems
   efficiency   rationalism   administration   analysis

2 social ⟶ political ⟶ politics of ⟶ bargaining-
   equity   rationalism   administration   incrementalism

Presented in this manner there is the danger, of course, of thinking in terms of absolute extremes—either pure efficiency or pure equity. The subsequent readings and commentaries will, I think, guard against this tendency. Each of the above pairs can be (and have been) discussed as ideal models, but in actual practice public administrative processes have shifted along the continuum between the two extremes.

Just where the administrative process comes to rest between the polar points at any given time depends on the nature of the democratic and nondemocratic values prevalent in our society at that time. This proposition is to be read as a hypothesis, not as a categorical statement of fact. But if the basic premise one assumes concerning the manner in which resources are to be allocated in a political system tends to shape his preference for the administrative scheme best designed to accomplish this end, then it also seems reasonable to suggest that social, economic, and political values contributed to the intellectual development of that basic premise in the first place. Thus, an individual may assume—along with former President Johnson, for example—that only through maximizing operating efficiency may "the full promise of a finer life be brought to every American at the lowest possible cost." In this instance, the goal to be realized—the full promise of a finer life, etc.—is obviously based on certain normative judgments. On the other hand, one might conclude that "the full promise of a finer life" could only be realized in a pluralistic-bargaining-incremental context. In this case the ultimate goal is based on a set of diametrically opposite normative judgments. However, the position assumed in this volume is that the preference for any model to achieve some ultimate goal is itself based on a set of social, economic, and political values which may or *may not* correspond to the traditional values so frequently cited as integral aspects of our democratic creed. This proposition will consume the major attention of the inquiry which follows simply because the development of public administrative processes in the United States is inexplicable if analyzed apart from, first, the context of democratic theory in which each of these processes was developed, and second, the sets of value preferences from which these theoretical principles were formed.

HISTORICAL ANTECEDENTS 2

CONTRIBUTIONS OF HAMILTON AND JEFFERSON

LYNTON K. CALDWELL

Although in the opinion of the writer the political principles of Hamilton and Jefferson were not so far divided as most of their interpreters insist, it is their differences in administrative theory and practice which here require evaluation. Personal antipathies and political jealousies aside, the fundamental difference between the administrative ideas of Hamilton and Jefferson appears to be in their attitude toward the control of political power. . . . Thus Hamilton stood for responsible government and Jefferson for limited government. Hamilton admired the system of centralized ministerial responsibility which Walpole and Pitt had developed in Great Britain, but Jefferson preferred the accepted American notion of separation of powers and local home rule.

HAMILTON

The practical contributions of Alexander Hamilton to the administrative institutions and practices of the nation are very great and are largely obvious. One need only to cite his work in the establishment of the Treasury Department, the Mint, the first United States Bank, and the University of New York and to recall his proposals for the

From *The Administrative Theories of Hamilton and Jefferson*, pp. 230–241. Copyright 1944 by the University of Chicago. All rights reserved. Published September 1944. Composed and printed by The University of Chicago Press, Chicago, Illinois, U.S.A. Lynton Caldwell is Professor of Government at Indiana University.

creation of a national military academy, a national university, and a board of industry and agriculture to confirm Hamilton's position as a builder of administrative institution. His contributions to administrative practices in the funding of the national debt, in taxation, in the controlling of revenue, in purchasing, and in the organization of the Army of the United States were scarcely less valuable to the establishment of the national administrative system.

Had Hamilton's contributions to public administration been only to form and vitalize the greater part of our first truly national government, he would rank as one of the greatest constructive statesmen in the history of the nation. But his genius for creative thought exceeded the limitations of his practical accomplishments. In the realm of ideas Hamilton's constructive imagination had free rein, unobstructed by the hazards of personal defect or political opposition; and his great contribution to thought on public administration might have been made entirely apart from his distinguished administrative career. He formulated his administrative philosophy long in advance of the practical application of his ideas to the establishment of the national government; and his practical contributions afford exemplification of the scope and quality of his thinking.

Hamilton's contribution to thought on administration, reduced to its essence, may be stated in three propositions. First, public administration is a unifying process which must operate unimpeded throughout the area of its constitution. Second, the function of public administration is leadership in the systematic and comprehensive development of the area which it is designed to serve. Third, constitutional government requires the fixing of responsibility upon those administrative leaders to whom the guidance of social development is intrusted.

The first proposition might be applicable to any administrative system, but to Hamilton the national Union was the object of its application. The area of national administration was the federal Union—states, counties, municipalities, the nation as an entirety. National administration must operate throughout the nation in the fullest sense, knowing neither sovereign states nor local preference where national issues were concerned. The systematic and comprehensive development of the nation being the responsibility of public administration, the necessity for national planning by administrative leadership was obvious. And the execution of systematic and comprehensive national plans required a unified administrative system of nation-wide scope, which, cutting through all layers of government, would bring into action throughout the Union the plans which responsible administrators deemed necessary to the national welfare.

Hamilton therefore favored the centralization of administrative initiative and responsibility, and this was the basis of Jefferson's charge that Hamilton wished to administer the Union from a federal into a "consolidated" government. In his definition of the administrative relationship between the national government and the states, Hamilton's purpose is evident and Jefferson's fear substantiated. Hamilton would push as far as possible federal administrative direction of the states. His proposals in the Constitutional Convention of 1787 to place the appointment of state governors in the hands of the national executive and to give the governors an absolute veto on all state legislation indicate his belief that, where national interests were concerned, the national administrative system must comprehend and control state administrative action. Thus the states would have certain legislative autonomy, but for all national purposes they would become administrative units of the national system. To insure state subordination, Hamilton wished to reduce the size of the larger units so that the strength of no state or of a likely combination of states would be adequate to challenge the authority of the Union. Hamilton not only intended the subordination of state to national administration in the interest of unity but proposed to allow national administration to operate wherever possible upon the people directly. In April, 1802, he wrote to Gouverneur Morris: "It has ever appeared to me as a sound principle to let the federal government rest, as much as possible, *on the shoulders of the people*, and as little as possible on those of the State Legislatures."

Hamilton's conception of public administration as a unifying process reflected his dissatisfaction with the system of local home rule which then characterized American government. The dissensions of local governing bodies he saw only as obstructive of comprehensive national purposes. He did not share Jefferson's admiration for the New England town meeting. He believed that unified public policy required unitary government and that large measures required comprehensive organization. He did not object to local assemblies dealing with local measures, but with the greater issues of national policy and general welfare he believed they had no proper concern. Hamilton feared the jealous mischief of the states more than the provinciality of the counties and townships. His centralizing tendencies may have placed a higher value on efficiency and a lower value on local freedom than most Americans considered wise, but it was order and efficiency that America most needed in realizing the benefits of independence; local liberty she enjoyed in superabundance.

Thus Alexander Hamilton's conception of the unity of public administration represents a contribution to the theory of national-state relationship in the federal Union. He was the first and most persuasive advocate of national supremacy and a unified public administrative system; and it is fair to say that, without his contributions of thought and practical achievement, the unification of America would

have been substantially more difficult to realize. In the realm of political thought his nationalist and centralizing tendencies were not
unique, but in the building of the United States of America they were
indispensable.

The second major proposition in Hamilton's administrative theory
—that the systematic and comprehensive development of the area
which it serves is the proper function of administration—implies a
dynamic, a creative, role for administrators. Thus Hamilton's third
proposition logically follows—that responsibility for guiding social
development should be required of administrative leadership. . . .

To interpret the Hamiltonian conception of administrative responsibility as a forecast of the regimented economies and authoritarian
philosophies of the twentieth century would be utterly to misunder-
stand Hamilton's point of view. If he rejected the laissez faire theories of late eighteenth-century liberalism, he likewise questioned the
omniscience of public administrators. He favored a greater degree of
governmental guidance and control than nineteenth-century America
was willing to accept, but he ever insisted that the area of individual
freedom and opportunity be enlarged. He would have government
regulate in order to liberate, to conserve, and to develop the material
resources of the nation, to increase the opportunities for individual
development and prosperity. He encouraged the organization of
private societies to co-operate with the government in this work.
Government was not the master of individual enterprise but rather a
senior partner. Thus in the cultivation of the national well-being,
administration encountered the inevitable problem of reconciling
freedom with order. To the solution of this problem Hamilton
brought a breadth of mind and a depth of practical understanding
adequate to the major contribution to administrative philosophy
which the problem required. . . .

JEFFERSON

During the greater part of the two centuries elapsed since the birth
of Thomas Jefferson, his thought has been an undeniable influence in
the shaping of American political institutions. This influence has been
of two sorts: the popular traditions of Jeffersonian government and
the actual beliefs and practices of Jefferson, which often vary from
generally accepted notions. Jefferson was a practical idealist, and it is
misleading to accept his speculations on what ought to be as invariably descriptive of his actual policy. Throughout his long political
and administrative career Jefferson deprecated the enjoyment of
authority and command. "I have no inclination to govern men," he
declared; "I should have no views of my own in doing it." He avowed
himself never so well pleased as when he could shift power from his

own shoulders to those of others. Actually, Jefferson did not lack political ambition, but his desire was to lead a host of willing followers. His wish was to reflect the will of the majority, but he sometimes read his preferences into his interpretation of public opinion. He preferred to exercise power through political leadership rather than through executive authority.

Jefferson's letters and public addresses expounded doctrine as often as they described practice, and much of the Jeffersonian tradition derives from the doctrine, whereas many of Jefferson's actual administrative contributions obtain from the practice. His theoretical desire for isolation from European political intrigue was tempered by his realistic judgment of what the national safety required, and the ideal of no treaties and few envoys gave way to proposals for an alliance with Great Britain and a diplomatic mission to Russia. His oft-voiced opposition to military expenditures and standing armies seemed to some the counsels of pacificism, but he favored selective military service from all male citizens and would include military science in collegiate training. He opposed executive expenditures of money without specific legislative approval, but in the purchase of Louisiana he contracted on behalf of the nation for an expenditure exceeding anything approaching the amounts his predecessors had spent out of general appropriations. He insisted that the power to put the nation into a state of war belonged to the Congress, and yet he directed an undeclared war against the Tripoli pirates upon the basis of his presidential responsibility for the defense of the national interests.

Jefferson was fond of speaking in generalities, and hence he was often misunderstood by persons with a literal turn of mind. Hamilton declared him a "contemptible hypocrite," and his more charitable colleagues often believed him inconsistent. That there was a large element of paradox in his thinking cannot be denied but where fundamental principles were concerned Jefferson's position was unmistakable. The key to his administrative theories was his concern over the control of power. He understood with Hamilton that power is indispensable to civil society, and he was prepared to exercise a degree of personal authority which he deemed dangerous in the hands of others less devoted to the freedom and welfare of men. But he believed also that power corrupts its possessor, and he therefore endeavored to find ways of controlling the power which any individual or group might possess. He observed the growth of federal powers under the administrations of Washington and Adams and feared that the centralization of political authority would destroy the equilibrium of the Union and lead to an ultimate monopoly of public policy for the exclusive benefit of "the one, the few, the well born or the many."

Jefferson's attempt to restrict the sphere of federal activity did not, however, imply a negative approach to administrative problems. He would have favored the use of federal revenue for the "great purposes of the public education, roads, rivers, canals, and such other objects of public improvement as it may be thought proper to add to the constitutional enumeration of federal powers," but the actual administration of these public works (a national research university excepted), he preferred to see in the hands of the states or at least to insure by law that the federal proportion of each state should be expended within that state.

Jefferson's desire to decentralize the administration of public affairs reflected his belief that government was republican in direct proportion to the participation of each citizen in its administration. The purest republics were those in which each citizen personally participated, and of these Jefferson described the New England township as "the wisest invention ever devised by the wit of man for the perfect exercise of self-government, and for its preservation." He believed decentralized democratic government to be the strongest in the world, for had he not seen the concentrated despotism of Louis XVI rendered impotent when the people would no longer obey; and had he not felt the foundations of the federal Union shaken under his feet by the New England townships resisting the enforcement of his embargo? He was convinced that the ultimate power of the New England town meeting exceeded whatever consolidated force generals and bureaucrats might muster, and he tried without success to promote the establishment of the township system in the southern states.

The principle of decentralization therefore emerges as one of Jefferson's major contributions to thought on public administration. Not only would he control the exercise of power in terms of space, but his theories of rotation in office reflect a desire to control the use of power in terms of time. He was concerned with the tenure of office in the policy-determining posts of government because he believed that it is in the nature of man to look upon that which he has long held as a personal possession. "The functionaires of every government have propensities to command at will the liberty and property of their constituents," he declared. He recognized the value of continuity of policy in public administration, but he believed that republican government required a change of hands at the helm at regular intervals. How long the tenure of office might safely be intrusted to the same person was a question to which Jefferson gave no precise answer, although he declared to a correspondent in 1813 that he preferred a presidential term of four years to that of seven, which he had first suggested with the proviso that perpetual ineligibility should follow the second quadrennial election of any one man.

The ultimate purpose of Jefferson's desire to decentralize government and limit the tenure of office was not the reduction of the public power but rather its control. Jefferson has often been described, and in a sense correctly, as an apostle of limited government, but his career and considered pronouncements show that he was prepared to carry the public authority to great lengths when necessary to effect the public welfare. He favored the limitation of power to the degree which he believed necessary to insure its control but never to an extent incommensurate with the public need.

From this practical view of the role of power the significance of Jefferson's theory of administrative responsibility becomes apparent. In the absence of constitutional or legislative guidance it was incumbent upon the executive to determine the nature and degree of power which the exigencies of society required. When constitutional and statutory measures directed executive conduct, the independent responsibility of the chief executive required that he interpret, in accordance with his understanding of the purpose of the measures, what they required of him. Thus the control of power required the accountability of an executive who must in large measure be the judge of his responsibility and authority. Jefferson was willing to use the checks and balances of eighteenth-century political theory to guard against executive usurpation, but he was too astute a student of history and politics to believe that power could be restrained by mere constitutional mechanics. At the bottom of Jefferson's philosophy of government lay his profound belief in the perfectibility of man and his conviction that in the end only an informed and responsible electorate could exact responsibility from government. "If a nation expects to be ignorant and free, in a state of civilization, it expects what never was and never will be." Thus, although beyond the scope of this inquiry, Jefferson's plans for universal public education must be considered as one of his positive contributions to thought on public administration.

Jefferson's insistence upon limited government can be properly understood only when read in the context of his equal insistence that government promote the public welfare and happiness. Although he believed that a large area of individual freedom was required for the public good, and therefore opposed paternalism as a philosophy of state, he recognized that the nature and degree of governmental authority required to serve the needs of societies varied with the dispositions of peoples. Because he feared the abuse of political power, he hoped that America would remain a nation of farmers and villagers and would avoid occasion for the elaborate administrative controls which he had observed in France. He encouraged the development of local government and opposed administrative centralization. Yet he was not doctrinaire in his attitude, for he recognized that

among the warring powers of Europe and in small nations a centralized constitution, an executive office more permanent, and a leader
more stable than the American system afforded would perhaps be
necessary.

Certainly it is true that Jefferson's administrative thought revolved
about a focus quite distinct from that which lay at the center of
Hamilton's thinking. Here political theory inevitably intrudes, for the
nation was the hub upon which Hamilton's thought turned, whereas
with Jefferson the *individual* was centermost. Both sought the general
welfare, each by his own means. Hamilton believed that, given
sufficient power, the government could guarantee the prosperity and
happiness of the nation. Jefferson dissented, holding that government
as such was incapable of creating conditions which obtained only
from the free labor and responsible conduct of the mass of people.
Thus Jefferson's wish that the government promote the public welfare was expressed not so much by the direct governmental aids
which Hamilton proposed in the *Report on Manufactures* as by encouraging conditions favorable to freedom of labor, thought, and
enterprise. Public education and a homestead law represented Jefferson's choice of methods to promote public happiness and prosperity.

Both leaders recognized the need for governmental leadership in
the formulation of public policy. They agreed that public policies
ought to be formed to promote the general interest in foreign affairs
and in matters of common concern as indisputable as defense, public
lands, Indians, and interstate commerce. But they differed in the
method by which public policy was to be determined and common
concerns defined. Hamilton advocated executive responsibility for the
formulation and execution of policy, with the legislature accepting or
rejecting the proposals of the administration. Public policy was therefore defined by the executive, subject to legislative ratification. Jefferson, although stoutly defending executive independence in the
execution of the law, and the necessity of discretion to responsible
administration, yet insisted that public policy was properly to be
determined by the legislative branch. The right of legislative veto
upon executive proposals he viewed as nugatory if the executive,
reinforced with patronage, the prestige of official opinion, and a relative security of tenure, should have the primary right of determining
the measures to receive legislative deliberation. Although he did not
question the power of the executive to propose and promote certain
measures in the legislature, he believed that these should be confined
to instances defined by constitutional law, and he rejected Hamilton's
notion of a general power of policy-making on the part of the administration.

The difference between Hamilton and Jefferson over the nature and extent of public policy was manifest in contrasting opinions in the details of administration. Hamilton, declaring that the general government must "not only have a strong soul, but *strong organs* by which that soul is to operate," favored lengthy tenure and substantial compensation for public officers. Jefferson declared conversely for rotation in office and considered it "a wise and necessary precaution against the degeneracy of the public servants" to offer them "drudgery and subsistence only." Hamilton favored a lofty and formal tone in the chief executive when dealing with administrative subordinates or with members of the House of Representatives, contrasting with Jefferson's informal methods of consultation and deference to the representatives.

Clearly, Hamilton and Jefferson favored contrasting theories of organization. The nationalistic centralizing objectives of Hamilton encouraged his view of organization from the top down, whereas the democratic decentralizing hopes of Jefferson led him customarily to view organization from the bottom up. It is probable that Hamilton's familiarity with military organization influence his thinking on the organization and administration of civil affairs and explains his emphasis on adequate executive power, clear lines of authority, the absolute responsibility of public officers, and the separation of auxiliary and staff from line functions. His papers on the organization of the civil administration of the War Department, particularly his interest in the organization of the auxiliary services of supply, illustrate the consolidating, integrating character of his thought. Jefferson's theory of organization was dominated by his desire to give to every citizen personally some part in the administration of public affairs, and his concern with the development of effective local government exceeded his interest in the organization of the central administration. . . .

And so one returns again to the basic disagreement of Hamilton and Jefferson over the control of political power. Hamilton is our great teacher of the organization and administration of public power; Jefferson, our chief expositor of its control. Jefferson's fear of unlimited centralized administrative authority inspired a corrective for Hamilton's overly sanguine expectation that the public interest would be served by responsible but unlimited public administration. The philosophy of government acting positively to promote the public welfare—a conception in which Hamilton and Jefferson concurred—is accepted by virtually all segments of public opinion, and it is as the great tasks of modern administration are undertaken that concern for effective execution and regard for individual liberties reveal the continuing relevance of the thought of Alexander Hamiltor ˑⁿᵈ Thomas Jefferson.

THE FEDERALIST NO. 70

ALEXANDER HAMILTON

There is an idea, which is not without its advocates, that a vigorous Executive is inconsistent with the genius of republican government. The enlightened well-wishers to this species of government must at least hope that the supposition is destitute of foundation; since they can never admit its truth, without at the same time admitting the condemnation of their own principles. Energy in the Executive is a leading character in the definition of good government. It is essential to the protection of the community against foreign attacks; it is not less essential to the steady administration of the laws; to the protection of property against those irregular and high-handed combinations which sometimes interrupt the ordinary course of justice; to the security of liberty against the enterprises and assaults of ambition, of faction, and of anarchy. Every man the least conversant in Roman story, knows how often that republic was obliged to take refuge in the absolute power of a single man, under the formidable title of Dictator, as well as against the intrigues of ambitious individuals who aspired to the tyranny, and the seditions of whole classes of the community whose conduct threatened the existence of all government, as against the invasions of external enemies who menaced the conquest and destruction of Rome.

There can be no need, however, to multiply arguments or examples on this head. A feeble Executive implies a feeble execution of the government. A feeble execution is but another phrase for a bad ex-

From *The Federalist* (Washington: Universal Classics Library, 1901), pp. 49–58.

ecution; and a government ill executed, whatever it may be in theory, must be, in practice, a bad government.

Taking it for granted, therefore, that all men of sense will agree in the necessity of an energetic Executive, it will only remain to inquire, what are the ingredients which constitute this energy? How far can they be combined with those other ingredients which constitute safety in the republican sense? And how far does this combination characterize the plan which has been reported by the convention?

The ingredients which constitute energy in the Executive are, first, unity; secondly, duration; thirdly, an adequate provision for its support; fourthly, competent powers.

The ingredients which constitute safety in the republican sense are, first, a due dependence on the people, secondly, a due responsibility.

Those politicians and statesmen who have been the most celebrated for the soundness of their principles and for the justice of their views, have declared in favor of a single Executive and a numerous legislature. They have with great propriety, considered energy as the most necessary qualification of the former, and have regarded this as most applicable to power in a single hand, while they have, with equal propriety, considered the latter as best adapted to deliberation and wisdom, and best calculated to conciliate the confidence of the people and to secure their privileges and interests.

That unity is conducive to energy will not be disputed. Decision, activity, secrecy, and dispatch will generally characterize the proceedings of one man in a much more eminent degree than the proceedings of any greater number; and in proportion as the number is increased, these qualities will be diminished.

This unity may be destroyed in two ways: either by vesting the power in two or more magistrates of equal dignity and authority; or by vesting it ostensibly in one man, subject, in whole or in part, to the control and co-operation of others, in the capacity of counsellors to him. Of the first, the two Consuls of Rome may serve as an example; of the last, we shall find examples in the constitutions of several of the States. New York and New Jersey, if I recollect right, are the only States which have intrusted the executive authority wholly to single men.[1] Both these methods of destroying the unity of the Executive have their partisans; but the votaries of an executive council are the most numerous. They are both liable, if not to equal, to

---

[1] New York has no council except for the single purpose of appointing to offices; New Jersey has a council whom the governor may consult. But I think, from the terms of the constitution, their resolutions do not bind him.

similar objections, and may in most lights be examined in conjunction. . . .

Wherever two or more persons are engaged in any common enterprise or pursuit, there is always danger of difference of opinion. If it be a public trust or office, in which they are clothed with equal dignity and authority, there is peculiar danger of personal emulation and even animosity. From either, and especially from all these causes, the most bitter dissensions are apt to spring. Whenever these happen, they lessen the respectability, weaken the authority, and distract the plans and operation of those whom they divide. If they should unfortunately assail the supreme executive magistracy of a country, consisting of a plurality of persons, they might impede or frustrate the most important measures of the government, in the most critical emergencies of the state. And what is still worse, they might split the community into the most violent and irreconcilable factions, adhering differently to the different individuals who composed the magistracy.

Men often oppose a thing, merely because they have had no agency in planning it, or because it may have been planned by those whom they dislike. But if they have been consulted, and have happened to disapprove, opposition then becomes, in their estimation, an indispensable duty of self-love. They seem to think themselves bound in honor, and by all the motives of personal infallibility, to defeat the success of what has been resolved upon contrary to their sentiments. Men of upright, benevolent tempers have too many opportunities of remarking, with horror, to what desperate lengths this disposition is sometimes carried, and how often the great interests of society are sacrificed to the vanity, to the conceit, and to the obstinacy of individuals, who have credit enough to make their passions and their caprices interesting to mankind. Perhaps the question now before the public may, in its consequences, afford melancholy proofs of the effects of this despicable frailty, or rather detestable vice, in the human character.

Upon the principles of a free government, inconveniences from the source just mentioned must necessarily be submitted to in the formation of the legislature; but it is unnecessary, and therefore unwise, to introduce them into the constitution of the Executive. It is here too that they may be most pernicious. In the legislature, promptitude of decision is oftener an evil than a benefit. The differences of opinion, and the jarrings of parties in that department of the government, though they may sometimes obstruct salutary plans, yet often promote deliberation and circumspection, and serve to check excesses in the majority. When a resolution too is once taken, the opposition must be at an end. That resolution is a law, and resistance to it punishable. But no favorable circumstances palliate or atone for the disadvantages of dissension in the executive department. Here, they are pure and unmixed. There is no point at which they cease to operate. They serve to embarrass and weaken the execution of the plan or measure to which they relate, from the first step to the final conclusion of it. They constantly counteract those qualities in the Executive which are the most necessary ingredients in its composition,—vigor and expedition, and this without any counterbalancing good. In the conduct of war, in which the energy of the Executive is the bulwark of the national security, every thing would seem to be apprehended from its plurality.

It must be confessed that these observations apply with principal weight to the first case supposed—that is, to a plurality of magistrates of equal dignity and authority a scheme, the advocates for which are not likely to form a numerous sect; but they apply, though not with equal, yet with considerable weight to the project of a council, whose concurrence is made constitutionally necessary to the operations of the ostensible Executive. An artful cabal in that council would be able to distract and to enervate the whole system of administration. If no such cabal should exist, the mere diversity of views and opinions would alone be sufficient to tincture the exercise of the executive authority with a spirit of habitual feebleness and dilatoriness.

But one of the weightiest objections to a plurality in the Executive, and which lies as much against the last as the first plan, is, that it tends to conceal faults and destroy responsibility. Responsibility is of two kinds—to censure and to punishment. The first is the more important of the two, especially in an elective office. Man, in public trust, will much oftener act in such a manner as to render him unworthy of being any longer trusted, than in such a manner as to make him obnoxious to legal punishment. But the multiplication of the Executive adds to the difficulty of detection in either case. It often becomes impossible, amidst mutual accusations, to determine on whom the blame or the punishment of a pernicious measure, or series of pernicious measures, ought really to fall. It is shifted from one to another with so much dexterity, and under such plausible appearances, that the public opinion is left in suspense about the real author. The circumstances which may have led to any national miscarriage or misfortune are sometimes so complicated that, where there are a number of actors who may have had different degrees and kinds of agency, though we may clearly see upon the whole that there has been mismanagement, yet it may be impracticable to pronounce to whose account the evil which may have been incurred is truly chargeable.

"I was overruled by my council. The council were so divided in their opinions that it was impossible to obtain any better resolution on the point." These and similar pretexts are constantly at hand, whether true or false. And who is there that will either take the trouble or incur the odium, of a strict scrutiny into the secret springs of the transaction? Should there be found a citizen zealous enough to undertake the unpromising task, if there happen to be collusion between the parties concerned, how easy it is to clothe the circumstances with so much ambiguity, as to render it uncertain what was the precise conduct of any of those parties?

In the single instance in which the governor of this State is coupled with a council—that is, in the appointment to offices, we have seen the mischiefs of it in the view now under consideration. Scandalous appointments to important offices have been made. Some cases, indeed, have been so flagrant that ALL PARTIES have agreed in the impropriety of the thing. When inquiry has been made, the blame has been laid by the governor on the members of the council, who, on their part, have charged it upon his nomination; while the people remain altogether at a loss to determine, by whose influence their interests have been committed to hands so unqualified and so manifestly improper. In tenderness to individuals, I forbear to descend to particulars.

It is evident from these considerations, that the plurality of the Executive tends to deprive the people of the two greatest securities they can have for the faithful exercise of any delegated power, *first,* the restraints of public opinion, which lose their efficacy, as well on account of the division of the censure attendant on bad measures among a number, as on account of the uncertainty on whom it ought to fall; and, *secondly,* the opportunity of discovering with facility and clearness the misconduct of the persons they trust, in order either to their removal from office or to their actual punishment in cases which admit of it. . . .

The idea of a council to the Executive, which has so generally obtained in the State constitutions, has been derived from that maxim of republican jealousy which considers power as safer in the hands of a number of men than of a single man. If the maxim should be admitted to be applicable to the case, I should contend that the advantage on that side would not counterbalance the numerous disadvantages on the opposite side. But I do not think the rule at all applicable to the executive power. I clearly concur in opinion, in this particular, with a writer whom the celebrated Junius pronounces to be "deep, solid, and ingenious," that "the executive power is more easily confined when it is ONE", that it is far more safe there should be a single object for the jealousy and watchfulness of the people; and, in a word, that all multiplication of the Executive is rather dangerous than friendly to liberty.

A little consideration will satisfy us, that the species of security sought for in the multiplication of the Executive, is unattainable.

Numbers must be so great as to render combination difficult, or they are rather a source of danger than of security. The united credit and influence of several individuals must be more formidable to liberty, than the credit and influence of either of them separately. When power, therefore, is placed in the hands of so small a number of men, as to admit of their interests and views being easily combined in a common enterprise, by an artful leader, it becomes more liable to abuse, and more dangerous when abused, than if it be lodged in the hands of one man; who, from the very circumstance of his being alone, will be more narrowly watched and more readily suspected, and who cannot unite so great a mass of influence as when he is associated with others. The Decemvirs of Rome, whose name denotes their number, were more to be dreaded in their usurpation than any ONE of them would have been. No person would think of proposing an Executive much more numerous than that body; from six to a dozen have been suggested for the number of the council. The extreme of these numbers, is not too great for an easy combination; and from such a combination America would have more to fear, than from the ambition of any single individual. A council to a magistrate, who is himself responsible for what he does, are generally nothing better than a clog upon his good intentions, are often the instruments and accomplices of his bad and are almost always a cloak to his faults.

I forbear to dwell upon the subject of expense; though it be evident that if the council should be numerous enough to answer the principal end aimed at by the institution, the salaries of the members, who must be drawn from their homes to reside at the seat of government, would form an item in the catalogue of public expenditures too serious to be incurred for an object of equivocal utility. I will only add that, prior to the appearance of the Constitution, I rarely met with an intelligent man from any of the States, who did not admit, as the result of experience, that the UNITY of the executive of this State was one of the best of the distinguishing features of our constitution.

THE FEDERALIST NO. 51

JAMES MADISON

To what expedient, then, shall we finally resort, for maintaining in practice the necessary partition of power among the several departments, as laid down in the Constitution? The only answer that can be given is, that as all these exterior provisions are found to be inadequate, the defect must be supplied, by so contriving the interior structure of the government as that its several constituent parts may, by their mutual relations, be the means of keeping each other in their proper places. Without presuming to undertake a full development of this important idea, I will hazard a few general observations, which may perhaps place it in a clearer light, and enable us to form a more correct judgment of the principles and structure of the government planned by the convention.

In order to lay a due foundation for that separate and distinct exercise of the different powers of government, which to a certain extent is admitted on all hands to be essential to the preservation of liberty, it is evident that each department should have a will of its own; and consequently should be so constituted that the members of each should have as little agency as possible in the appointment of the members of the others. Were this principle rigorously adhered to, it would require that all the appointments for the supreme executive, legislative, and judiciary magistracies should be drawn from the same fountain of authority, the people, through channels having no communication whatever with one another. Perhaps such a plan of con-

From *The Federalist* (Washington: Universal Classics Library, 1901), pp. 353–358.

structing the several departments would be less difficult in practice than it may in contemplation appear. Some difficulties, however, and some additional expense would attend the execution of it. Some deviations, therefore, from the principle must be admitted. In the constitution of the judiciary department in particular, it might be inexpedient to insist rigorously on the principle: first, because peculiar qualifications being essential in the members, the primary consideration ought to be to select that mode of choice which best secures these qualifications; secondly, because the permanent tenure by which the appointments are held in that department, must soon destroy all sense of dependence on the authority conferring them.

It is equally evident, that the members of each department should be as little dependent as possible on those of the others, for the emoluments annexed to their offices. Were the executive magistrate, or the judges, not independent of the legislature in this particular, their independence in every other would be merely nominal.

But the great security against a gradual concentration of the several powers in the same department, consists in giving to those who administer each department the necessary constitutional means and personal motives to resist encroachments of the others. The provision for defense must in this, as in all other cases, be made commensurate to the danger of attack. Ambition must be made to counteract ambition. The interest of the man must be connected with the constitutional rights of the place. It may be a reflection on human nature, that such devices should be necessary to control the abuses of government. But what is government itself, but the greatest of all reflections on human nature? If men were angels, no government would be necessary. If angels were to govern men, neither external nor internal controls on government would be necessary. In framing a government which is to be administered by men over men, the great difficulty lies in this: you must first enable the government to control the governed; and in the next place oblige it to control itself. A dependence on the people is, no doubt, the primary control on the government; but experience has taught mankind the necessity of auxiliary precautions.

This policy of supplying, by opposite and rival interests, the defect of better motives, might be traced through the whole system of human affairs, private as well as public. We see it particularly displayed in all the subordinate distributions of power, where the constant aim is to divide and arrange the several offices in such a manner as that each may be a check on the other—that the private interest of every individual may be a sentinel over the public rights. These inventions of prudence cannot be less requisite in the distribution of the supreme powers of the State.

But it is not possible to give to each department an equal power of self-defense. In republican government, the legislative authority necessarily predominates. The remedy for this inconveniency is to divide the legislature into different branches; and to render them, by different modes of election and different principles of action, as little connected with each other as the nature of their common functions and their common dependence on the society will admit. It may even be necessary to guard against dangerous encroachments by still further precautions. As the weight of the legislative authority requires that it should be thus divided, the weakness of the executive may require, on the other hand, that it should be fortified. An absolute negative on the legislature appears, at first view, to be the natural defense with which the executive magistrate should be armed. But perhaps it would be neither altogether safe nor alone sufficient. On ordinary occasions it might not be exerted with the requisite firmness, and on extraordinary occasions it might be perfidiously abused. May not this defect of an absolute negative be supplied by some qualified connection between this weaker department and the weaker branch of the stronger department, by which the latter may be led to support the constitutional rights of the former, without being too much detached from the rights of its own department?

If the principles on which these observations are founded be just, as I persuade myself they are, and they be applied as a criterion to the several State constitutions, and to the federal Constitution it will be found that if the latter does not perfectly correspond with them, the former are infinitely less able to bear such a test.

There are, moreover, two considerations particularly applicable to the federal system of America, which place that system in a very interesting point of view.

First. In a single republic, all the power surrendered by the people is submitted to the administration of a single government; and the usurpations are guarded against by a division of the government into distinct and separate departments. In the compound republic of America, the power surrendered by the people is first divided between two distinct governments, and then the portion allotted to each subdivided among distinct and separate departments. Hence a double security arises to the rights of the people. The different governments will control each other, at the same time that each will be controlled by itself.

Second. It is of great importance in a republic not only to guard the society against the oppression of its rulers, but to guard one part of the society against the injustice of the other part. Different interests necessarily exist in different classes of citizens. If a majority be united by a common interest, the rights of the minority will be insecure. There are but two methods of providing against this evil: the

one by creating a will in the community independent of the majority
—that is, of the society itself; the other, by comprehending in the
society so many separate descriptions of citizens as will render an
unjust combination of a majority of the whole very improbable, if
not impracticable. The first method prevails in all governments possessing an hereditary or self-appointed authority. This, at best, is but
a precarious security; because a power independent of the society
may as well espouse the unjust views of the major, as the rightful
interests of the minor party, and may possibly be turned against both
parties. The second method will be exemplified in the federal republic of the United States. Whilst all authority in it will be derived
from and dependent on the society, the society itself will be broken
into so many parts, interests, and classes of citizens, that the rights of
individuals, or of the minority, will be in little danger from interested
combinations of the majority. In a free government the security for
civil rights must be the same as that for religious rights. It consists in
the one case in the multiplicity of interests, and in the other in the
multiplicity of sects. The degree of security in both cases will depend
on the number of interests and sects; and this may be presumed to
depend on the extent of country and number of people comprehended under the same government. This view of the subject must
particularly recommend a proper federal system to all the sincere
and considerate friends of republican government, since it shows that
in exact proportion as the territory of the Union may be formed into
more circumscribed Confederacies, or States oppressive combinations
of a majority will be facilitated: the best security, under the republican forms, for the rights of every class of citizens, will be diminished; and consequently the stability and independence of some
member of the government, the only other security, must be proportionately increased. Justice is the end of government. It is the end
of civil society. It ever has been and ever will be pursued until it be
obtained, or until liberty be lost in the pursuit. In a society under the
forms of which the stronger faction can readily unite and oppress the
weaker, anarchy may as truly be said to reign as in a state of nature,
where the weaker individual is not secured against the violence of
the stronger; and as, in the latter state, even the stronger individuals
are prompted, by the uncertainty of their condition, to submit to a
government which may protect the weak as well as themselves; so, in
the former state, will the more powerful factions or parties be gradually induced, by a like motive, to wish for a government which will
protect all parties, the weaker as well as the more powerful. It can
be little doubted that if the State of Rhode Island was separated from
the Confederacy and left to itself, the insecurity of rights under the
popular form of government within such narrow limits would be
displayed by such reiterated oppressions of factious majorities that

some power altogether independent of the people would soon be called for by the voice of the very factions whose misrule had proved the necessity of it. In the extended republic of the United States, and among the great variety of interests, parties, and sects which it embraces, a coalition of a majority of the whole society could seldom take place on any other principles than those of justice and the general good; whilst there being thus less danger to a minor from the will of a major party, there must be less pretext, also, to provide for the security of the former, by introducing into the government a will not dependent on the latter, or, in other words, a will independent of the society itself. It is no less certain than it is important, notwithstanding the contrary opinions which have been entertained, that the larger the society, provided it lie within a practical sphere, the more duly capable it will be of self-government. And happily for the REPUBLICAN CAUSE, the practicable sphere may be carried to a very great extent, by a judicious modification and mixture of the FEDERAL PRINCIPLE.

COMMENTARY

These selections provide an excellent example of how three of America's early statesmen, each intensely concerned with the manner in which political power should be controlled in the new republic, attempted to make the administrative system of our federal government conform to their respective democratic theories. In their writings, if not in practice, Jefferson and Madison were, of course, the leading American exponents of the Lockean tradition of limited and representative government: for both, the primacy of the legislative branch was an *a priori* assumption. However, Jefferson and Madison perceived the main threat to the future of the new democratic nation quite differently, and, consequently, the theoretical manner in which each attempted to neutralize these perceived threats differed significantly.

For Jefferson cumulative executive-administrative power was the greatest danger to democracy. Conversely, the main strength of democracy was to be found in an enlightened, responsible, fully-participating citizenry. The nub of Jefferson's philosophy, therefore, was to play this strength against the potential danger in a manner designed to check the latter and enhance the former. Madison, on the other hand, while also fearful of the accumulation of power, visualized this threat emerging from the body politic in the form of a tyrannical majority and manifesting itself within the citadel of democracy—the legislative branch.

As seen by Jefferson, the most effective check against the threat of a tyrannical executive branch was a high degree of administrative decentralization, coupled with an equally high degree of citizen participation in the actual administration of government. Under this ideal set of circumstances, administrative responsibility could be insured and the ends of government—the active promotion of the public welfare and public happiness—could be obtained. It is important to note in this connection that despite Jefferson's substitution of the word "happiness" for Locke's term "property" in the Declaration of Independence, the latter term still retained significance in Jeffersonian principles to the extent that it implied a reciprocal respect among all citizens for the recognition of the human dignity of man. Certainly this ideal of social equity represented a paramount feature of Jeffersonian thought, and as an end to be achieved it represented a basic goal of government. Thus, the more administrative functions were decentralized, the more the body politic would become directly involved in the actual administrative implementation of public policy programs. Furthermore, the more executive power was separated, checked, and counterchecked, then the higher the probability that this basic goal of government—social equity—would be realized.

As pointed out in his Federalist No. 51, written in 1788, the basic goal of government for Madison was justice. Given the broad connotations associated with both equity and justice, one might assume that the Jeffersonian and Madisonian concepts were merely two sides of the same democratic coin. An equitable government would, by definition, be a just government, and certainly a just government would be equitable. However, if one considers the almost excessive preoccupation Madison displayed with the notion of "security," his concern for justice may be viewed in a different perspective. A government which made the individual secure from the capricious and arbitrary actions of a tyrannical majority was a government which had realized its ultimate goal—justice.

Madison's major contributions to the dialogue of politics in America were his institutionalization of prudence and his development of a unique style of prudential politics. Jefferson's belief in the perfectibility of man was never shared by Madison, who viewed political behavior in terms of conflicting self-interests and personal ambitions. His approach to democracy was much more qualitative than Jefferson's, and, as a consequence, his fear of an emerging tyrannical executive was much less acute. Given Madison's scheme of a pluralistic society, composed of a heterogeneous multiplicity of small, diverse groups, each seeking to maximize its own self-interests, the only way public policy conflict could be resolved without recourse to violence was by putting together what Dahl aptly described as a majority of minorities."* Under these circumstances, to Madison the

* Robert Dahl, A Preface to Democratic Theory (Chicago: The University of Chicago Press, 1956).

legislative branch emerged as the supreme coordinator of conflicting interests, and justice would be realized in direct proportion to the extent that conflicting interests could be accommodated through commonalty. In short, it was the responsibility of the legislature to insure that the private rights and interests of every citizen were adequately protected against the conflicting claims of any other individual, or groups of individuals, or even so-called majorities of individuals. This was the definition of security for Madison; it also was a definition of justice as he viewed it. Consequently, the executive branch and the administrative system became incidental considerations vis-à-vis the legislative branch, and, in terms of arbitrary executive power, Madison was satisfied that it would continue impotent as long as the power of the legislative assembly prevailed. The Madisonian theory, therefore, was not directly aimed at the control of the administrative system but rather at the structure of society itself. Fragmented, highly decentralized, isolated self-interest groups provided an adequate check and balance against a tyrannical executive, or even a legislative act. The real threat to democracy came from the body politic, and this threat could best be eliminated simply by insuring that no single group in society would ever presume to speak as a majority. The effects of Madison's philosophy on the executive branch, therefore, were indirect, yet the extent to which these indirect effects have manifested themselves is significant. We shall return to a more elaborate analysis of this point in later chapters*. For the present it is sufficient to note that the social equity sought by Jefferson, with its focus on the human dignity of man, was substantially different from the "political equity" sought by Madison in which the security of the private interests of each individual became almost sacrosanct.

Hamilton was something else again. In his view, a viable democracy was virtually synonymous with a strong, highly centralized administrative system. But Hamilton went even further: the preeminent branch of the *national* government (and with Hamilton it cannot be referred to as the federal government) was the executive and its administrative system. Only through the centralization of administrative regulation and operating efficiency could man become, in fact, truly liberated. Individual development, prosperity, and freedom were the legitimate ends of government for Hamilton, and the means to these ends were clearly set forth in his writings. Executive energy, efficiently applied in an unimpeded context, was the natural ingredient of a national unity in which man would be capable of developing a true sense of individualism.

In this regard, Hamilton and Jefferson were poles apart. Jefferson presented a model for social equity that was aimed at developing the

---

* See especially Commentaries, Chapters Four, Six, and Nine.

full measure of man. In this ideal state, a democratic government would emerge which, quite literally, was "of the people, by the people, and for the people." But the development of the individual as a responsible, respected, true human being was a necessary prerequisite for the emergence of the just state. Hamilton, on the other hand, viewed an efficient, unified, national government as the necessary prerequisite for the full realization of man's worth and provided a basic model of executive leadership which was directed primarily at the unification of the nation.

The unimpeded context in which Hamilton's "administrative man" was to operate raised ticklish questions of administrative responsibility and accountability. To whom were executive officials responsible? To whom were they ultimately accountable? Jefferson's answers to these questions were obvious; ultimate sovereignty of the state rested with the people, or their duly elected representatives, and functional responsibility for the administration of the state was to be completely decentralized among local political jurisdictions. For Hamilton, however, this was an unsatisfactory solution since legislative checks on administrative behavior would represent a serious impediment to the efficient and orderly process of national unification. But administrative responsibility and accountability were not ignored by Hamilton. Rather, the issue was viewed in terms of a personal code of ethics imposed on administrative behavior by the administrator himself. Thus, consistent with his overall approach to democratic theory which projected a prototypical image of David Riesman's inner-directed man, administrative responsibility and accountability were self-imposed sets of obligations.

The differences between Hamilton and Madison were equally substantial. Madison's theory of democratic pluralism was, in essence, summarily dismissed by Hamilton in his Federalist No. 70 of 1788. Writing specifically against the proposal for a plural executive (but applicable also to the theory of political pluralism in general), Hamilton stated that a plural decision-making process concealed faults, destroyed the concept of democratic responsibility, and weakened the power of an informed public opinion. The fragmentation of responsibility could only mean the fragmentation of accountability, and, for Hamilton, this inevitably meant the weakening of administrative efficiency and national unity. This reasoning alone turned Hamilton and Madison into intellectual strangers.

In any discussion of the development of administrative thought in America, the extent of our debt to Hamilton, Jefferson, and Madison can hardly be overstated. As one reviews the literature of nineteenth century administrative practice and theory as it developed in the wake of these three individuals, it becomes obvious that few men of comparable intellectual stature emerged. In evaluating the period from approximately 1800 to the end of the Civil War, White concluded, "These were not years . . . in which administrative doctrine was an object of attention. These were not years of innovation or experiment. . . . The great issues of organizational theory and administrative practice that had divided Hamilton and Jefferson remained the same. . . ."* And of the period extending from the end of the Civil War to the turn of the century he wrote, "Considering the state of administrative doctrine from 1870 to 1900, we must conclude that these were years of stagnation."†

By consolidating these two assessments it seems reasonable to conclude that the epoch-making events of the nineteenth century—the expanding frontier, the Civil War, the rise of the industrial city, the emergence of the corporate structure and a corporate way-of-life—brought forth no new theoretical concepts that could be applied to the administrative system of our federal government. Faced with an economic, political, and social environment of steadily increasing complexity, the administrative apparatus responded to the changing patterns in a practical, pragmatic, and political fashion. Dynamic, energetic growth of the administrative structure was certainly a characteristic of this period, but this growth was stimulated by an undisciplined energy which, seemingly, moved without purpose or direction. The innovative vacuum which prevailed in the administrative system for nearly three-quarters of the century was broken by only three major developments.

First, President Andrew Jackson effected a major change in our Hamilton-Jefferson-Madison legacy by democratizing the federal public service. This development was neither the cause of organizational changes in the administrative system, nor the consequence of such changes. Rather, the administrative system was simply overwhelmed by the rising spirit of democracy which swept across the nation at that time. This force was tied to the concomitant rise of political parties in America, and as a result, for better or worse, a crass political pragmatism was introduced into the administrative system, although the structure, the functions, and the processes of the executive branch remained essentially intact. Nevertheless, a tradition of a scant thirty-five years was broken with finality. The public service was "Americanized," and the ever-so-slight aristocratic bearing of the professional public administrator in the Federalist tradition was replaced by an ordinary man of much more modest credentials. The "new" public administrator was characterized as a politically attuned generalist who was to respond to social and political con-

* Leonard White, *The Jacksonians* (New York: The Macmillan Company, 1956), pp. 566, 563, 561.
† Leonard White, *The Republican Era* (New York: The Macmillan Company, 1963), p. 395.

siderations. This did not mean that considerations of economy and efficiency were stricken from the system.* It did mean, however, that a subtle—and, in some instances, a not-too-subtle—shift occurred in emphasis on which factors in the administrative decision-making process should be given preference. Jackson was the catalytic agent who unleashed a tremendous new force in American public administration. Unfortunately, the vitality inherent in the democratic spirit of public service incurred immediate costs which greatly exceeded any discernible benefits. The "free spirit" of the democratic, politically conditioned public administrator somehow had to be harnessed. One solution to this dilemma—civil service reform— represented the second major administrative development of the nineteenth century.

"Without doubt," wrote White, "the achievement of civil service reform in 1883 was a fundamental turning point in the history of the federal administration system."† An odd statement, indeed, if one simply considers the stormy history of the passage of the Pendleton Act and the ineffective implementation and enforcement of that act in the period immediately following its passage. However, its long-term consequences have been enormous, and from a mid-twentieth century vantage point one can agree with White that a fundamental turning point did, in fact, occur with the passage of the act. Interestingly, it introduced a Hamiltonian element of national unity and order into the career system of the federal service without destroying the egalitarian values of the Jefferson-Jackson tradition. Civil service reform substituted a vague sense of loyalty to a national public service for a sense of loyalty to a political party. The basic premise of the Pendleton Act was that operating efficiency would logically result from an absolutely equitable allocation of jobs and other occupational rewards. Thus, within the context of the civil service reform movement, efficiency and equity were mutually reinforcing terms; efficiency was inevitable if all personnel decisions were made in strict (and hence equitable) accordance with the established standards and regulations; and conversely, if allocative decisions were handled efficiently, equitable results would normally follow.

The basic philosophy of the Pendleton Act was built around its core concept of merit. No longer was there to be the practice of finding a job for a loyal supporter; the new system looked in the opposite direction and sought qualified personnel to fill established and authorized positions. The concept of merit, along with the egalitarian emphasis which preceded the reform period, did, indeed,

---

* See Albert Somit, "Andrew Jackson as Administrator," *Public Administration Review*, Vol. 8, (Summer 1948).
† *The Republican Era*, p. 393.

fundamentally alter the nature and character of federal career service programs. In this area, at least, the values and attitudes which prevailed at the end of the century were totally different from the situation which existed in the early years of the new republic. This difference was most dramatically measured in quantitative terms: more people became eligible for civil service positions by satisfactorily demonstrating their tangible abilities as impartially measured by objective examinations. No attempt was made to measure the extent to which the quality of the public service was improved as a result of the merit system, primarily because it was then—and even now in many quarters—generally assumed that intelligence was a reliable predictor of quality service. Nevertheless, it is true that in addition to the ethical and equitable implications that were associated with the concept of merit, the term was also utilized by its proponents to advance a notion of absolute scientific validity. This scientific orientation found its way into the governmental system primarily through the private business community, and it represented the third major administrative development of this period.

Throughout the twentieth century, one theme which has consistently prevailed in the literature of public administration is that government is business and should be operated on the basis of standard business principles. This was Charles Wilson's point when, as Secretary of Defense under former President Eisenhower, he stated that what was good for General Motors was good for the country. The attitude implicit in his statement was certainly no different than that expressed by Richard "Dick" Croker, boss of Tammany Hall during the 1890s, who patiently explained to the young and inexperienced reporter, Lincoln Steffens, why a political organization needed a "boss."

'It's because there's a mayor *and* a council *and* judges *and*—a hundred other men to deal with. A government is nothing but a business, and you can't do business with a lot of officials, who check and cross one another and who come and go, there this year, out the next. A business man wants to do business with one man, and one who is always there to remember and carry out the business.'

'Business? Business?' I repeated. 'I thought government was all politics.'
He smiled turning to look into my face.

'Ever heard that business is business?' he teased. 'Well, so is politics business, and reporting—journalism, doctoring—all professions, arts, sports —everything is business.'*

The "government is business" attitude is still very much with us, and its influence on our public policy decision-making process is

* *The Autobiography of Lincoln Steffens* (New York: Harcourt Brace and Co., 1931), pp. 236–237.

well documented. The point to be made here is that the introduction
of this attitude into our governmental system came toward the end
of the nineteenth century when the full implications of the corporation as a person came to be realized. From the 1870s through the
1890s traditional administrative theory may have become stagnated
as White concludes, but certainly during that period the influence of
the corporate philosophy on government, and especially on the administrative system, cannot be ignored. Fully developed theoretical
principles and models dealing with organization and management
concepts did not emerge until the 1900s, but the initial patterns of
business enterprise, particularly those dealing with operating efficiency, were introduced during this earlier period.

Civil service reform, as well as the infusion of basic Americana
into the veins of the federal career service, were both vitally significant developments in our administrative system. But the effects of
both were seen primarily in the manner in which the character of
the public administrator was altered. In this regard, the changes
came in *who* were the individuals to make the necessary administrative decisions. The main thrust of the "government is business"
syndrome was not at who would make decisions, or who would administer the government (although it was assumed that sound
business-oriented administrators would be selected), but rather, *how*
decisions would be made, and *how* government would be administered. And in this regard, it was further assumed that as in business
basic economic considerations would be recognized as primary.

Such an approach obviously deviated significantly from an administrative orientation which recognized the primacy of social and
political considerations. But the main argument advanced by the
business advocates of public administration was that political and
social values could not coexist with the scientifically valid tenets of
economics. By the end of the first quarter of the twentieth century,
the roots of this business orientation were firmly entrenched in our
governmental structure. A businesslike efficiency was emphasized
throughout the administrative system; a clear separation between
politics and administration was advocated; and public administration, viewed in terms of scientific principles of management, was
seen by many as the capstone victory of business over government,
of efficiency over equity, of economic principles over political prov-
erbs, of science over intuitive values.

ADMINISTRATION AS MANAGEMENT SCIENCE 3

THE STUDY OF ADMINISTRA- TION

WOODROW WILSON

ONE

The science of administration is the latest fruit of that study of the science of politics which was begun some twenty-two hundred years ago. It is a birth of our own century, almost of our own generation.

Why was it so late in coming? Why did it wait till this too busy century of ours to demand attention for itself? Administration is the most obvious part of government; it is government in action; it is the executive, the operative, the most visible side of government, and is of course as old as government itself. It is government in action, and one might very naturally expect to find that government in action had arrested the attention and provoked the scrutiny of writers of politics very early in the history of systematic thought.

But such was not the case. No one wrote systematically of administration as a branch of the science of government until the present century had passed its first youth and had begun to put forth its characteristic flower of systematic knowledge. Up to our own day all the political writers whom we now read had thought, argued, dogmatized only about the *constitution* of government; about the nature of the state, the essence and seat of sovereignty, popular power and kingly prerogative; about the greatest meanings lying at the heart of government, and the high ends set before the purpose of government by man's nature and man's aims. The central field of controversy was that great field of theory in which monarchy rode tilt

Reprinted with permission from the *Political Science Quarterly*, Vol. II (June 1887), pp. 198–201, 209–214, 217–222. Footnotes deleted.

against democracy, in which oligarchy would have built for itself
strongholds of privilege, and in which tyranny sought opportunity
to make good its claim to receive submission from all competitors.
Amidst this high warfare of principles, administration could command no pause for its own consideration. The question was always:
Who shall make law, and what shall that law be? The other question,
how law should be administered with enlightenment, with equity,
with speed, and without friction, was put aside as "practical detail"
which clerks could arrange after doctors had agreed upon principles.

That political philosophy took this direction was of course no
accident, no chance preference or perverse whim of political philosophers. The philosophy of any time is, as Hegel says, "nothing but
the spirit of that time expressed in abstract thought"; and political
philosophy, like philosophy of every other kind, has only held up
the mirror to contemporary affairs. The trouble in early times was
almost altogether about the constitution of government; and consequently that was what engrossed men's thoughts. There was little
or no trouble about administration—at least little that was heeded by
administrators. The functions of government were simple, because
life itself was simple. Government went about imperatively and
compelled men, without thought of consulting their wishes. There
was no complex system of public revenues and public debts to puzzle financiers; there were, consequently, no financiers to be puzzled.
No one who possessed power was long at a loss how to use it. The
great and only question was: Who shall possess it? Populations were
of manageable numbers; property was of simple sorts. There were
plenty of farms, but no stocks and bonds: more cattle than vested
interests. . . .

This is the reason why administrative tasks have nowadays to be
so studiously and systematically adjusted to carefully tested standards of policy, the reason why we are having now what we never
had before, a science of administration. The weightier debates of
constitutional principle are even yet by no means concluded; but
they are no longer of more immediate practical moment than questions of administration. It is getting to be harder to *run* a constitution than to frame one. . . .

There is scarcely a single duty of government which was once
simple which is not now complex; government once had but a few
masters; it now has scores of masters. Majorities formerly only underwent government; they now conduct government. Where government once might follow the whims of a court, it must now follow the
views of a nation.

And those views are steadily widening to new conceptions of state
duty; so that, at the same time that the functions of government are
every day becoming more complex and difficult, they are also vastly

multiplying in number. Administration is everywhere putting its hands to new undertakings. The utility, cheapness, and success of the government's postal service, for instance, point towards the early establishment of governmental control of the telegraph system. Or, even if our government is not to follow the lead of governments of Europe in buying or building both telegraph and railroad lines, no one can doubt that in some way it must make itself master of masterful corporations. The creation of national commissioners of railroads, in addition to the older state commissions, involves a very important and delicate extension of administrative functions. Whatever hold of authority state or federal governments are to take upon corporations, there must follow cares and responsibilities which will require not a little wisdom, knowledge, and experience. Such things must be studied in order to be well done. And these, as I have said, are only a few of the doors which are being opened to offices of government. The idea of the state and the consequent ideal of its duty are undergoing noteworthy change; and "the idea of the state is the conscience of administration." Seeing every day new things which the state ought to do, the next thing is to see clearly how it ought to do them.

This is why there should be a science of administration which shall seek to straighten the paths of government, to make its business less unbusinesslike, to strengthen and purify its organization, and to crown its duties with dutifulness. This is one reason why there is such a science.

TWO

The field of administration is a field of business. It is removed from the hurry and strife of politics; it at most points stands apart even from the debatable ground of constitutional study. It is a part of political life only as the methods of the counting-house are a part of the life of society; only as machinery is part of the manufactured product. But it is, at the same time, raised very far above the dull level of mere technical detail by the fact that through its greater principles it is directly connected with the lasting maxims of political wisdom, the permanent truths of political progress.

The object of administrative study is to rescue executive methods from the confusion and costliness of empirical experiment and set them upon foundations laid deep in stable principle.

It is for this reason that we must regard civil-service reform in its present stages as but a prelude to a fuller administrative reform. We are now rectifying methods of appointment; we must go on to adjust executive functions more fitly and to prescribe better methods of executive organization and action. Civil-service reform is thus but a moral preparation for what is to follow. It is clearing the moral atmosphere of official life by establishing the sanctity of public office as a public trust, and, by making the service unpartisan, it is opening the way for making it businesslike. By sweetening its motives it is rendering it capable of improving its methods of work.

Let me expand a little what I have said of the province of administration. Most important to be observed is the truth already so much and so fortunately insisted upon by our civil-service reformers; namely, that administration lies outside the proper sphere of *politics*. Administrative questions are not political questions. Although politics sets the tasks for administration, it should not be suffered to manipulate its offices.

This is distinction of high authority; eminent German writers insist upon it as a matter of course. Bluntschli, for instance, bids us separate administration alike from politics and from law: Politics, he says, is state activity "in things great and universal," while "administration, on the other hand," is "the activity of the state in individual and small things. Politics is thus the special province of the statesman, administration of the technical official." "Policy does nothing without the aid of administration"; but administration is not therefore politics. But we do not require German authority for this position; this discrimination between administration and politics is now, happily, too obvious to need further discussion.

There is another distinction which must be worked into all our conclusions, which, though but another side of that between administration and politics, is not quite so easy to keep sight of: I mean the distinction between *constitutional* and administrative questions, between those governmental adjustments which are essential to constitutional principle and those which are merely instrumental to the possibly changing purposes of a wisely adapting convenience.

One cannot easily make clear to everyone just where administration resides in the various departments of any practicable government without entering upon particulars so numerous as to confuse the distinctions so minute as to distract. No lines of demarcation, setting apart administrative from non-administrative functions, can be run between this and that department of government without being run up hill and down dale, over dizzy heights of distinction and through dense jungles of statutory enactment, hither and thither around "ifs" and "buts," "whens" and "howevers," until they become altogether lost to the common eye not accustomed to this sort of surveying, and consequently not acquainted with the use of the theodolite of logical discernment. A great deal of administration goes about *incognito* to most of the world, being confounded now with political "management," and again with constitutional principle.

Perhaps this ease of confusion may explain such utterances as that of Niebuhr's: "Liberty," he says, "depends incomparably more upon administration than upon constitution." At first sight this appears to be largely true. Apparently facility in the actual exercise of liberty does depend more upon administrative arrangements than upon constitutional guarantees; although constitutional guarantees alone secure the existence of liberty. But—upon second thought—is even so much as this true? Liberty no more consists in easy functional movement than intelligence consists in the ease and vigor with which the limbs of a strong man move. The principles that rule within the man, or the constitution, are the vital springs of liberty or servitude. Because dependence and subjection are without chains, are lightened by every easy-working device of considerate, paternal government, they are not thereby transformed into liberty. Liberty cannot live apart from constitutional principle; and no administration, however perfect and liberal its methods, can give men more than a poor counterfeit of liberty if it rest upon illiberal principles of government.

A clear view of the difference between the province of constitutional law and the province of administrative function ought to leave no room for misconception; and it is possible to name some roughly definite criteria upon which such a view can be built. Public administration is detailed and systematic execution of public law. Every particular application of general law is an act of administration. The assessment and raising of taxes, for instance, the hanging of a criminal, the transportation and delivery of the mails, the equipment and recruiting of the army and navy, *etc.*, are all obviously acts of administration; but the general laws which direct these things to be done are as obviously outside of and above administration. The broad plans of governmental action are not administrative; the detailed execution of such plans is administrative. Constitutions, therefore, properly concern themselves only with those instrumentalities of government which are to control general law. Our federal constitution observes this principle in saying nothing of even the greatest of the purely executive offices, and speaking only of that President of the Union who was to share the legislative and policy-making functions of government, only of those judges of highest jurisdiction who were to interpret and guard its principles, and not of those who were merely to give utterance to them. . . .

There is, indeed, one point at which administrative studies trench on constitutional ground—or at least upon what seems constitutional ground. The study of administration, philosophically viewed, is closely connected with the study of the proper distribution of constitutional authority. To be efficient it must discover the simplest arrangements by which responsibility can be unmistakably fixed upon officials; the best way of dividing authority without hampering it, and responsibility without obscuring it. And this question of the distribution of authority, when taken into the sphere of the higher, the originating functions of government, is obviously a central constitutional question. If administrative study can discover the best principles upon which to base such distribution, it will have done constitutional study an invaluable service. Montesquieu did not, I am convinced, say the last word on this head.

To discover the best principles for the distribution of authority is of greater importance, possibly, under a democratic system, where officials serve many masters, than under others where they serve but a few. All sovereigns are suspicious of their servants, and the sovereign people is no exception to the rule; but how is its suspicion to be allayed by *knowledge?* If that suspicion could be clarified into wise vigilance, it would be altogether salutary; if that vigilance could be aided by the unmistakable placing of responsibility, it would be altogether beneficial. Suspicion in itself is never healthful either in the private or in the public mind. *Trust is strength* in all relations of life; and, as it is the office of the constitutional reformer to create conditions of trustfulness, so it is the office of the administrative organizer to fit administration with conditions of clear-cut responsibility which shall insure trustworthiness.

And let me say that large powers and unhampered discretion seem to me the indispensable conditions of responsibility. Public attention must be easily directed, in each case of good or bad administration, to just the man deserving of praise or blame. There is no danger in power, if only it be not irresponsible. If it be divided, dealt out in shares to many, it is obscured; and if it be obscured, it is made irresponsible. But if it be centered in heads of the service and in heads of branches of the service, it is easily watched and brought to book. If to keep his office a man must achieve open and honest success, and if at the same time he feels himself intrusted with large freedom of discretion, the greater his power the less likely is he to abuse it, the more is he nerved and sobered and elevated by it. The less his power, the more safely obscure and unnoticed does he feel his position to be, and the more readily does he relapse into remissness. . . .

THREE

. . . Government is so near us, so much a thing of our daily familiar handling, that we can with difficulty see the need of any philosophical study of it, or the exact point of such study, should it be undertaken. We have been on our feet too long to study now the art of walking. We are a practical people, made so apt, so adept in self-government by centuries of experimental drill that we are scarcely any longer capable of perceiving the awkwardness of the particular system we may be using, just because it is so easy for us to use any system. We do not study the art of governing: we govern. But mere unschooled genius for affairs will not save us from sad blunders in administration. Though democrats by long inheritance and repeated choice, we are still rather crude democrats. Old as democracy is, its organization on a basis of modern ideas and conditions is still an unaccomplished work. The democratic state has yet to be equipped for carrying those enormous burdens of administration which the needs of this industrial and trading age are so fast accumulating. Without comparative studies in government we cannot rid ourselves of the misconception that administration stands upon an essentially different basis in a democratic state from that on which it stands in a nondemocratic state.

After such study we could grant democracy the sufficient honor of ultimately determining by debate all essential questions affecting the public weal, or basing all structures of policy upon the major will; but we would have found but one rule of good administration for all governments alike. So far as administrative functions are concerned, all governments have a strong structural likeness; more than that, if they are to be uniformly useful and efficient, they *must* have a strong structural likeness. A free man has the same bodily organs, the same executive parts, as the slave, however different may be his motives, his services, his energies. Monarchies and democracies, radically different as they are in other respects, have in reality much the same business to look to.

It is abundantly safe nowadays to insist upon this actual likeness of all governments, because these are days when abuses of power are easily exposed and arrested, in countries like our own, by a bold, alert, inquisitive, detective public thought and a sturdy popular self-dependence such as never existed before. We are slow to appreciate this; but it is easy to appreciate it. Try to imagine personal government in the United States. It is like trying to imagine a national worship of Zeus. Our imaginations are too modern for the feat.

But, besides being safe, it is necessary to see that for all governments alike the legitimate ends of administration are the same, in order not to be frightened at the idea of looking into foreign systems of administration for instruction and suggestion; in order to get rid of the apprehension that we might perchance blindly borrow something incompatible with our principles. . . .

We can borrow the science of administration with safety and profit if only we read all fundamental differences of condition into its essential tenets. We have only to filter it through our constitutions, only to put it over a slow fire of criticism and distil away its foreign gases. . . .

Let it be noted that it is the distinction, already drawn, between administration and politics which makes the comparative method so safe in the field of administration. When we study the administrative systems of France and Germany, knowing that we are not in search of *political* principles, we need not care a peppercorn for the constitutional or political reasons which Frenchmen or Germans give for their practices when explaining them to us. If I see a murderous fellow sharpening a knife cleverly, I can borrow his way of sharpening the knife without borrowing his probable intention to commit murder with it; and so, if I see a monarchist dyed in the wool managing a public bureau well, I can learn his business methods without changing one of my republican spots. He may serve his king; I will continue to serve the people; but I should like to serve my sovereign as well as he serves his. By keeping this distinction in view—that is, by studying administration as a means of putting our own politics into convenient practice, as a means of making what is democratically politic towards all administratively possible towards each—we are on perfectly safe ground, and can learn without error what foreign systems have to teach us. We thus devise an adjusting weight for our comparative method of study. We can thus scrutinize the anatomy of foreign governments without fear of getting any of their diseases into our veins; dissect alien systems without apprehension of blood-poisoning.

Our own politics must be the touchstone for all theories. The principles on which to base a science of administration for America must be principles which have democratic policy very much at heart. And, to suit American habit, all general theories must, as theories, keep modestly in the background, not in open argument only, but even in our own minds—lest opinions satisfactory only to the standards of the library should be dogmatically used, as if they must be quite as satisfactory to the standards of practical politics as well. Doctrinaire devices must be postponed to tested practices. Arrangements not only sanctioned by conclusive experience elsewhere but also congenial to American habit must be preferred without hesitation to theoretical perfection. In a word, steady, practical statesmanship must come first, closet doctrine second. The cosmopolitan what-to-do must always be commanded by the American how-to-do-it.

Our duty is, to supply the best possible life to a *federal* organization, to systems within systems; to make town, city, county, state, and federal governments live with a like strength and an equally assured healthfulness, keeping each unquestionably its own master and yet making all interdependent and co-operative, combining independence with mutual helpfulness. The task is great and important enough to attract the best minds.

This interlacing of local self-government with federal self-government is quite a modern conception. It is not like the arrangements of imperial federation in Germany. There local government is not yet, fully, local *self*-government. The bureaucrat is everywhere busy. His efficiency springs out of *esprit de corps*, out of care to make ingratiating obeisance to the authority of a superior, or, at best, out of the soil of a sensitive conscience. He serves, not the public, but an irresponsible minister. The question for us is, how shall our series of governments within governments be so administered that it shall always be to the interest of the public officer to serve, not his superior alone but the community also, with the best efforts of his talents and the soberest service of his conscience? How shall such service be made to his commonest interest by contributing abundantly to his sustenance, to his dearest interest by furthering his ambition, and to his highest interest by advancing his honor and establishing his character? And how shall this be done alike for the local part and for the national whole?

If we solve this problem we shall again pilot the world. There is a tendency—is there not?—a tendency as yet dim, but already steadily impulsive and clearly destined to prevail, towards, first the confederation of parts of empires like the British, and finally of great states themselves. Instead of centralization of power, there is to be wide union with tolerated divisions of prerogative. This is a tendency towards the American type—of governments joined with governments for the pursuit of common purposes, in honorary equality and honorable subordination. Like principles of civil liberty are everywhere fostering like methods of government; and if comparative studies of the ways and means of government should enable us to offer suggestions which will practicably combine openness and vigor in the administration of such governments with ready docility to all serious, well-sustained public criticism, they will have approved themselves worthy to be ranked among the highest and most fruitful of the great departments of political study. That they will issue in such suggestions I confidently hope.

THE FIRST YEAR OF THE BUDGET

CHARLES G. DAWES

ADDRESS OF PRESIDENT HARDING

GENERAL DAWES, VICE-PRESIDENT, MEMBERS OF THE CABINET, AND GENTLEMEN OF THE GOVERNMENT'S BUSINESS ORGANIZATION: This gathering is the second in which have been brought together the heads of the various departments of the government's organization. Something more than six months ago the first meeting of this kind was held to signalize the inauguration of the budgetary system of control over the detailed conduct of the government business. It is now possible to survey the accomplishments of this first half-year period, and I think we may well congratulate ourselves on the showing which has been made.

The report of the Director of the Budget is in your hands. It indicates that even in the formative period the Budget system has justified our most confident expectations. As a result of the higher systematization and better co-ordination of business methods the director notifies us that, at an almost insignificant cost, it has been possible to reduce the government's expenditures, from the scale based on $4,550,000,000, which was asked for the executive departments and independent establishments for the current fiscal year, to a scale of $3,974,000,000. It is true that this showing is based on the accomplishments of only one-half of the fiscal year, but it demonstrates the possibility of keeping the government's expenditures measurably within the scale forecasted in advance of the fiscal year's opening,

From *The First Year of the Budget of the United States* (New York: Harper & Row Publishers, 1923), pp. 166–178. Reprinted with permission of the publisher.

provided that no new legislation shall be enacted to increase the expenses.

This gathering has been summoned in pursuance of a policy of calling together the business heads of the government, precisely as would be done from time to time in any business organization. Here the President of the business establishment can meet those who are in direct charge of the business machinery. In order to insure continuing contacts with them throughout the business years, there have been created by Executive order the co-ordinating boards whose reports are in your hands. In accomplishing what has been achieved in the first six months of this organization's operation the director tells us that a staff has been engaged representing a scale of expenditure, not new but newly applied, of only $109,000, while the reports show direct savings of $32,000,000 that may be definitely measured and direct and indirect savings of $104,000,000 in a period somewhat more than four months.

The various co-ordinating boards were created, on recommendation of General Dawes, for the purpose of binding together in a common plan of unification the departments and independent establishments which formerly in large measure operated independently of one another.

Through these co-ordinating boards, agents representing the Executive, working under the supervision of the Director of the Budget, it is possible to impose and execute the general policy of the Executive, involving co-ordination, economy and efficiency. If there were any misunderstandings in the beginning as to the method and purpose in bringing about this co-operation, they have now happily been substantially all dissipated. It is now definitely understood that in detailing, by Executive order, any officer or employee of the government to serve as a co-ordinator or as aide to the Director of the Budget, it is the intention that there shall be created a primary responsibility to the President as the head of the business organization, and that responsibility is now recognized, not only by the detailed officer or employee but by all the departments and independent establishments.

In the beginning of this governmental reorganization there were those who feared that if we detailed from each department or establishment some person employed therein to serve with the Director of the Budget there would be created a sort of a double responsibility and a divided loyalty which might prove destructive of the highest efficiency. It was feared, in short, that these aides to the Director of the Budget might be moved more by their loyalty to and their interest in the department or establishment with which they were officially connected than by their obligations to the budgetary system. It is of the utmost importance that persons thus detailed shall understand most definitely that they are expected to extend their first loyalty and obligation to the general policy of the Budget bureau as an agency for the imposition of Executive plans. In practical operation it is manifestly impossible to find liaison officers for this service outside of the various departments, because these officers must be thoroughly familiar with the business of the departments. Otherwise they could not deal intelligently with them.

The liaison officer must, in short, be thoroughly familiar with the affairs of the department he represents, and at the same time devoted to the purpose of this co-ordination and economy program. Every person so detailed must understand and be assured that his service in this capacity will not be permitted to involve him in any embarrassment as to his present or future status in the department or establishment under which he formerly served. I want you all to be very certain that it will be my purpose to protect every one of you in his career and proper activities. In giving you this assurance I know I can be confident of the loyal co-operation of all the departments and establishments; and this is a good time to have it unanimously understood that we all serve one and the same government, and the common good, not departmental advantage, is the end at which every one of us must aim.

On the other hand, I expect that those who are detailed on this co-ordinating work will keep fully in mind, as a guide to their actions, the rights, the requirements, and the jurisdictions of the departments and establishments which they represent. In the inauguration of the Budget system it was the deliberate judgment of the director that best results would be obtained by employing as co-ordinating agents persons assigned from the departments or establishments equipped with thorough knowledge of their requirements. The wisdom of that determination has already been demonstrated. I believe it was and is the only method by which to produce such results as have been presented in the report which has been placed in your hands today.

Constant vigilance and intelligent activity on the part of the co-ordinating agencies make the one price at which we may secure and maintain the highest economy and efficiency in the conduct of the government's business. It is necessary that there shall be not only attention by the Executive to the work of the co-ordinating boards but also Executive attention to the departments and establishments in relation to the co-ordinating agencies. It is gratifying to be able to say that thus far the relations between the co-ordinating agencies and the departments or establishments have been highly satisfactory. The necessity for this arrangement has been everywhere recognized. A feeling of solidarity in the government business organization has grown up, and there is a conviction that the interests of economy and efficiency demand close co-operation under central leadership.

So effective has been this department during the four months of operation through these agencies of co-ordination that there has been practically no conflict between the co-ordinating boards and the government business organization requiring decision by me as between any department on the one side and the Director of the Budget on the other. I want you to know what great satisfaction there is in saying that. And I am going to add to it the statement that in any case which may arise in the future where an honest difference of opinion exists to the beneficial effect of a proposed order of co-ordination the matter will receive my promptest attention. Thus far we have had the most harmonious co-operation, resulting in the institution and functioning of a reorganized system of government practically without friction. It is hoped and believed that there will be a continuation of the same harmonious attitude in the future.

The report of the Director of the Budget indicates that the Executive can maintain, through agencies of co-ordination, an effective control over expenditures which will substantially eliminate the occasion for deficiency appropriations. It is true that emergencies, changes of legislative policy, and shifting business conditions, or excusable errors of judgment will make necessary at times deficiency appropriations; but it is expected that hereafter these will be, as compared with former years, very greatly reduced. From early in the administration the Executive set his face against deficiency appropriations, and an Executive order was issued discountenancing them. The fact that it has been possible to reduce the scale of expenditures so greatly as we have noted must convince us of the possibility, if estimates are made with proper intelligence and there is the necessary care in expenditures, of substantially avoiding deficiency appropriations.

It is true that the reports now before us cover only one-half of the current fiscal year. The exigencies of the coming months may modify somewhat the favorable showing which we now note with so much satisfaction. But, on the other hand, the Director of the Budget expects that new attention will be given by all of you to the continuing revision of expenditures with a view to still further economies wherever and whenever they are possible. To that end the director expects to give especial consideration to the accomplishments of each department for the entire fiscal year. It is particularly desirable that the careful and painstaking effort which has been made continuously during the first half year to effect reductions of expense shall be continued hereafter. In a business so great as that of the national government unexpected receipts will not infrequently swell the total of calculated revenues. It seems likely that this will be true during the current year. But despite this possibility it now seems probable that the restrictions upon expenditure which have been possible by reason of the administration's general policy and your splendid co-operation would have resulted in a surplus of receipts for the year. The prospect of such a surplus, when compared with the estimated deficiency of $24,500,000 that was outlined in the Budget figures submitted to Congress in December, is certainly an occasion of much satisfaction to all of us.

In conclusion, I want to tell you how much I have been pleased at the spirit of economy manifested all over the country, not only throughout the departments of the government activities, but among the people at large. I cannot but feel that the government has, in this Budget organization, set an example of care and thrift that has helped greatly to make saving fashionable. If to some extent the government has been a leader in so praiseworthy a cause we ought all to be gratified that we have had a part in such an affair. Much of the extravagance of government has been due to a lack of a sense of individual responsibility, and the same is true of the extravagance in the corporate businesses and the private affairs of the people. If our efforts here shall set a standard and inspire an ambition for greater economies and higher efficiency, we shall have served not only the government but the whole public particularly well. Perhaps our example will have been of service to the world.

In making my acknowledgments on this occasion I desire to commend those officials whose energy, judgment and ability have contributed to the remarkable results outlined by the Director of the Budget. Under his direction they have performed their work quietly, without seeking publicity or producing unnecessary internal conflict. I wish I could say a word that would bestow a proper meed of appreciation. I want to thank for his services Colonel Henry C. Smither, Chief Co-ordinator, General Supply. I want to thank his staff, Lieutenant Colonel McAdams, Lieutenant Colonel McAndrews, Lieutenant Colonel Morey, Lieutenant Colonel Wright, Lieutenant Commander Cairnes, Lieutenant Commander Stanley, Major Wainer, and Commander C. G. Mayo.

I wish I might personally express appreciation and gratitude to every individual member of the co-ordinating forces and all of those who have been contributing to the notable success of the Budget. Sometimes, aye ofttimes, the government compensates inadequately, and there is scant expression, if any, of that gratitude and appreciation which have been so well earned; but there must come to you that finer and dearer return which is the highest compensation men may know in the public service—the consciousness of a good work accomplished.

I suspect sometimes there are public servants in more conspicuous positions who find themselves momentarily discouraged by a lack of public understanding of the difficulties of their tasks and an ungenerous appraisal of things accomplished. Sometimes it is partisan, sometimes it is ignorance, not infrequently it borders on the malicious, which is designed to create unrest, and when I contemplate the unresisted flow of extravagance and the tendency to drift the ship of state on the rocks of bankruptcy, which is far too prevalent throughout the world, I must express to every one of you and to all in authority who have assisted you my appreciation for the splendid work done in bringing government business activities back to a state which intelligence may approve.

Perhaps other governments were brought to greater strains of expenditure and more difficult financial straits through their more intimate and heavier burdens of war; and notwithstanding that fact, and that we have suffered less comparatively, I doubt if any government in the world has made a more persistent and conscientious endeavor to cut down its expenditures and institute economies and restore sane and normal ways again.

You have inaugurated a very practical work of exceedingly great importance, and the results have been so gratifying and have proven of such advantage to both the government and the public that I am taking this opportunity of openly uttering to you the assurance of my appreciation and gratitude.

Now, if I may, I want to call to the presiding position the one genius whose devotion and personality and capacity have been the inspiration of the great success of the budgetary system, General Dawes.

ADDRESS OF CHARLES G. DAWES, DIRECTOR OF THE BUREAU OF THE BUDGET

MR. PRESIDENT, GENTLEMEN OF THE CO-ORDINATING BOARDS, AND MEMBERS OF THE BUSINESS ORGANIZATION OF GOVERNMENT: It is a great handicap to a business man, in a business meeting, called to discuss routine business, to have this kind of an introduction; to be surrounded by this intangible, imponderable atmosphere of dignity and restraint which pervades important government gatherings and which, unless dissipated, always interferes with the proper meeting of minds in business conference. The members of the business organization of government gathered here must not think of business in its relation to personal dignity or in its relation to personal prerogatives, just because it has been done in government business for over a hundred years. Despite these formal surroundings, despite the depressing psychology of a gathering of very high government officials, I must regard the President of the United States here today, not as one engaged in carrying out great policies of state, or the members of the Cabinet as his advisers upon these great policies, but as the head of a routine business organization, and the members of the Cabinet as nothing but the administrative vice-presidents of this organization, who heretofore, because of the absence of leadership and because of a system for which they were not to blame, have, with their predecessors, allowed a disgraceful and extravagant system of routine business to obtain in this government for one hundred and thirty years—a condition which President Harding started to rectify when, last June, six months ago, he called together the first meeting of the business organization of government in the one hundred and thirty years since its establishment.

There is no reason why, because the government of the United States does the largest business in the world, it should be the worst conducted. What I want you to do is to listen to a discussion of simple business principles in a simple way, just as if we were members of a smaller corporation, meeting not in the peace conference room, but in a business office, with only ordinary men around, discussing only ordinary things—to get attuned to that kind of an atmosphere —and not to have our thoughts diverted because the President of the United States is here, or the press is here, or all these uniforms are here, and all these other conditions that do not embarrass an ordinary business meeting.

Now, at the first meeting of the government business organization last June, the President assumed, for the first time, his position of responsibility as the head of the business organization of government. At that time there was no adequate machinery in the hands of the President for the transmission of Executive will and policy in the matter of routine business to the body of the business organization. The first meeting, therefore, was devoted to an effort on the part of the President to arouse the business organization to the overwhelming necessity for economy in governmental expenditures—to bring to each man the essential fact that he would be held personally responsible for participation in such a program. He let you know then that at the end of the year he would check you up, just as if he was in charge of a private business organization, to find out whether you had carried out his policy. That sort of pressure had its effect upon this great organization, and at the end of thirty days, during which you made a careful examination to determine the possibilities, you promised him that you would reduce your expenses in the sum of $112,000,000 per year. He continued this pressure, having in the meantime established agencies for such continuing imposition in the shape of these great co-ordinating boards, the representatives of which sit before you.

At the time the President commenced this effort the forecast of governmental expenditures for the present fiscal year, made by the heads of departments and establishments who had formulated their demands before Executive pressure had been instituted, amounted to the sum of $4,550,000,000. As a result of pressure, the President was able to announce in December that, instead of a reduction of only $112,000,000 first promised him, the reduction, including $170,-000,000 of public debt postponement, would be nearer $576,000,000, and that we would undertake to run the government for the fiscal year 1922 on the sum of $3,974,000,000, instead of $4,550,000,000.

The imposition of Executive pressure immediately removed the chief~cause for the riotous extravagance in government business which had theretofore run without a head, and where the chief object of every man connected with it seemed to be how much money he could get for the plans of his individual department, instead of how little he could get along with in carrying out a policy imposed by the President, who thought in terms not of departments, but of one government responsible to the public.

After this first meeting of the business organization, where just as in private business, the President imposed policy, there followed the creation, by Executive order, of these co-ordinating agencies, which not only transmit Executive policy and plan, but which become gatherers of information as to the business of government from the bird's-eye view, which, presented to him, assist him in his formulation of a unified policy. What the President did in creating these co-ordinating boards was a simple thing in the business world. He selected, not from strangers, but from the body of the existing business organization, men of experience in the business, with acquaintance in the business, with qualifications developed by continued contact with the business organization, and formed committees, imposing over them the authority of an agent representing Executive authority.

There is no finer body of business men in this country than these underpaid men of talent confronting me, who find in their public service a satisfaction which private employment cannot give. Let me say something here. These co-ordinating boards are not boards in the common acceptation of that word. They do not act as boards, either by majority vote or otherwise. They have no personnel. Authority lies only in the Chief Co-ordinator, who presides over them, acting under Executive authority. His power lies through orders of co-ordination alone, and from his orders there is always preserved the right of appeal of the head of a department or establishment to the Chief Executive himself. I mention this because these co-ordinating agencies have been established in accordance with law, and all the steps in the reorganization of the routine business of government have been taken with most careful regard to existing law. It may not seem so, but we in the Bureau of the Budget try to be the most cautious people in Washington. Every time we consider a new move we expect to have some old and forgotten law confront us which, if we walk over it, like a mine in the Argonne battle field left by the enemy, would explode under us. In every important step taken, before we act, we secure a departmental interpretation of law, and I say to you now, with deep regret, that in connection with official interpretation of law the mental *status quo* of legal advisers often seems one of enthusiastic support of the old *status quo* in government business and in the interest of the plans of departments as distinct from the new plan of a unified system for the whole government.

Until the President assumed his attitude of responsibility for a unified plan, the attitude of everybody from Cabinet, department heads, and bureau chiefs down to clerks, has always been one of hostility to anything which interfered with the plan of their separate jurisdictions, irrespective of the demoralizing effect of such an attitude upon the business interests of the government which they have sworn to serve. They have not been to blame for it; lack of system has been to blame for it; and for that lack of system the past Presidents of the United States have been to blame, for any one of them could have established a proper system.

The suggestion was made by some one the other day that in selecting these co-ordinators and agents from the body of the business organization to transmit his policies it would be impossible for the President to get men who would give him impartial judgments in connection with the imposition of a unified plan of business, because of their former allegiance to the particular department from which they were chosen—that he could not depend upon them for that absolute impartiality between the departments which is necessary in the work to which he called them. What folly! Has the President of the United States less power over his business organization than the president of a private organization? Need he be afraid, with his immense powers over personnel, including the heads of departments and establishments, to rely upon the loyalty of these agents? As the head of a bank, in selecting agents to transmit my policy, would I hesitate to call into my office service a man from the trust department, or the foreign exchange department, or the discount department, to use him in gathering information and transmitting policy, because I would fear that this man would be more loyal to the head of the discount department, or the trust department, or the foreign exchange department than he would be to me, and would I, therefore, go out into the street and hire Tom, Dick, and Harry, who knew nothing about the business, to do the work in his place?

The only reason we have gotten anywhere in this business reorganization of government is because we have not only completely absorbed, but I say completely demonstrated, the truth that the proper machinery with which to run governmental routine business must be similar to the machinery to run private routine business.

I say "demonstrated" because the President has told you that these co-ordinators, who are already in the government service, and who, in the aggregate, draw only $109,000 per year compensation, have, in about four months, effected measurable direct cash savings to the government of over $32,000,000, and directly and indirectly about $100,000,000.

In routine business there should always be but one head. In our republican form of government our Constitution provides a system of checks and balances which protect the liberty of the people in connection with the determination of governmental policy. In a free government like ours there is no central control in determination of general policy, but after policy is established under the methods prescribed by the Constitution, then in the routine business of government, concerned with the expenditure of money to carry out policy, the principle of one central control must obtain or you will go back to the riotous extravagance which has characterized governmental routine expenditure in the past.

We in the Bureau of the Budget are not concerned with matters of policy. The President, advised by the Cabinet, and Congress determine the great questions of policy. As for us, we are men down in the stokehole of the ship of state, and we are concerned simply with the economical handling of fuel. The President and Congress determine which way the ship sails, for that is a matter of policy, but we in the hold of the ship have something to do with how far she can sail through the way in which, in our humbler place, we apply common sense business principles.

These co-ordinators do not have their eyes upon the press gallery. And here I want to say something to the representatives of the press here present, as an expression of my deep appreciation of the fact that they have treated this new system of co-ordinating routine business in a constructive way—that they have not bothered it in quest for scandal. You members of the press, as faithful American citizens, are just as much interested in the success of this effort to save money for the government and to increase efficiency as is the President of the United States or the Director of the Bureau of the Budget, and you are showing it. It would be possible for you to do incalculable damage if you were so minded, but, Heaven be thanked, we have been spared the attention of the destructive newspaper critic—that kind of destructive critic who encourages public men to exploit their pitiful personalities at the expense of the public service by throwing monkey wrenches into usefully moving machinery. I would as soon invite one of that kind of newspaper men to a business meeting like this as to put rat poison in my breakfast food.

Now that we have this formal atmosphere dissipated and are down to matters of plain business common sense, just as if we were sitting in an ordinary business meeting, I am going to talk with perfect freedom to the members of the Cabinet as simply members of this business organization. I confess it is not easy to regard Secretary Hughes, for example, as anybody but the great Secretary of State, who, in the last few months has done so much for the world and for the future peace and happiness of humanity. That is the trouble down here in routine business. That is the trouble that our co-ordinators have. We have to rid ourselves of the idea that because Mr. Hughes is a man to whom the President of the United States and the world owes a debt, he is not a proper subject for that power of Executive control which, in his capacity as one of the administrators of routine business of government, must tie him into a routine business organization and enable him to save money. Mr. Hughes is so intelligent that we have no trouble in our relations with him. But that is not saying we do not have trouble with some officials of this government in less important positions.

I do not want to compare for a minute our work down in the stokehole of the ship with the work of those who are bringing better conditions of life and safeguarding the tranquillity of the world in connection with this peace conference, but I will say to you that in our work we will save to the taxpayers of the country every year double the amount that can be saved by the plan for the limitation of armament. And these business matters are, therefore, important enough to properly engross the attention of even the Secretary of State, the Secretary of the Navy, and every other member of the Cabinet.

I want to say here again that the Budget bureau keeps humble, and if it ever becomes obsessed with the idea that it has any work except to save money and improve efficiency in routine business it will cease to be useful in the hands of the President. Again I say, we have nothing to do with policy. Much as we love the President, if Congress, in its omnipotence over appropriations and in accordance with its authority over policy, passed a law that garbage should be put on the White House steps, it would be our regrettable duty, as a bureau, in an impartial, nonpolitical and nonpartisan way to advise the Executive and Congress as to how the largest amount of garbage could be spread in the most expeditious and economical manner.

That is not humorous. That is intended to serve notice on those who would seek to make political capital against this routine business reform of the President that the success of the Budget bureau depends upon our integrity and sincerity in a determination to be nonpartisan, nonpolitical and impartial. Whatever may be the political complexion of Congress, or the party affiliations of a President, this impersonal business agency of the Budget bureau, and these coordinating boards, concerned not at all with policy, must endeavor to see that the money of the government is spent in the most economical manner in routine administration along the lines of policy which are adopted by those charged by the Constitution with the duty of imposing them. . . .

SCIENCE, VALUES, AND PUBLIC ADMINISTRA- TION

LUTHER GULICK

Administration has to do with getting things done; with the accomplishment of defined objectives. The science of administration is thus the system of knowledge whereby men may understand relationships, predict results, and influence outcomes in any situation where men are organized at work together for a common purpose. Public administration is that part of the science of administration which has to do with government, and thus concerns itself primarily with the executive branch, where the work of government is done, though there are obviously administrative problems also in connection with the legislative and the judicial branches. Public administration is thus a division of political science, and one of the social sciences.

At the present time administration is more an art than a science; in fact there are those who assert dogmatically that it can never be anything else. They draw no hope from the fact that metallurgy, for example, was completely an art several centuries before it became primarily a science and commenced its great forward strides after generations of intermittent advance and decline.

It is fashionable for physicists, chemists and biologists who have achieved remarkable control and great predictive accuracy in narrow areas to ridicule all the social scientists, particularly those in government, because of the small body of verified knowledge thus far ac-

From *Papers on the Science of Administration* (New York: Institute of Public Administration, 1937), pp. 191–195. Professor Gulick is Chairman of the Board of the Institute of Public Administration. Reprinted with permission of the Institute of Public Administration.

cumulated and "laws" formulated outside of the field of the "exact sciences." It is even denied that there can be any "science" in social affairs. This naïve attitude is perhaps not to be wondered at in a group which has so recently arrived on the scene of man's intellectual theatre and has been permitted to play such a striking rôle for the past two centuries. Natural science, after all, has undertaken the comparatively simple and easy task of understanding the mechanistic and mathematical relationships of the physical world and has left to philosophy, ethics, religion, education, sociology, political science, and other social sciences the truly difficult and the truly important aspects of life and knowledge.

Social science rests at many points upon the physical sciences. Economics and politics, for example, are fundamentally conditioned by the discoveries of pure science and their technological application. The advance of certain of the exact sciences thus becomes of great concern and serves to condition and delay the advance of social science. The very fact that exact science has made a great forward surge in the past one hundred years, inevitably thrusts a whole new series of unsolved problems upon social science.

The social sciences are also mutually dependent. This is particularly true of political science because political science is not a unitary, but a co-ordinating science which deals on one side with man's political life, desires and behavior, and on the other with government and public administration in which must be utilized most if not all of the professions and sciences which man has developed.

The basic difference between the exact sciences and the social sciences, it has often been said, is that the social sciences must deal with values and ends. It is this which places them in a different category from the mechanistic sciences. It seems to the writer, however, that the importance of this element may be overemphasized, and that such overemphasis is certain to discourage the advance of social science as much as any other single factor. In many of the subsidiary but fundamental fields of social knowledge it is possible to put values and ends to one side, or to assume them as constants, just as is done in the pure sciences. For example, Gresham's law with regard to dear currency and cheap currency has validity entirely outside of any notion of what is "good" or "bad." Similarly Thorndike's studies in the age of learning, Boas' investigation of skulls and culture, Huntington's weather records, Buck's examination of public budget systems, Hurd's study of the movement of land values, King's analysis of income distribution, Mitchell's investigations of the price cycle do not depend for their validity upon the "good" or the "bad." Value finds its place in these studies not in the statement of variations and interrelationships, but in the social appraisal and application of the principles deduced. This does not mean that the social scientist will not be led on in his quest for truth by his individual value-interests, but it does mean that the results of his work, if scientifically done, may be used by others who have entirely different values in view. It would hardly be claimed that the structure of American democracy profited more from the thinking of the democrat Jackson than from that of the aristocrat Hamilton; nor that the concept of public and private law devised for the Roman Empire is of no value for a soviet republic.

It thus behooves the student of administration, along with other students of social science, to acquire the habit of separating (a) relationships and (b) value judgments as far as is possible in his work. In scientific literature, at least, he should endeavor to say: "Under conditions x, y and z conduct A will produce B; and conduct A^1 will produce C." He may have discovered this because he feels that B is desirable and C is undesirable, but if another student, or a statesman, confronts the same problem he may none the less be able to build upon and make use of the scientific work of the first student even though he has a reversed scale of values. Whenever a student of government says: "The mayor should now do A," this is to be interpreted:

1. Present conditions are xyz
2. Under conditions xyz, A gives B
3. B is good, therefore
4. Do A

If political scientists will make it a habit to split up every important "should" sentence in this way, they will not only make more useful to others the ideas which they develop, but may also introduce into their own work a new element of scientific validity. In other words, "should" is a word political scientists should not use in scientific discussion!

In the science of administration, whether public or private, the basic "good" is efficiency. The fundamental objective of the science of administration is the accomplishment of the work in hand with the least expenditure of man-power and materials. Efficiency is thus axiom number one in the value scale of administration. This brings administration into apparent conflict with certain elements of the value scale of politics, whether we use that term in its scientific or in its popular sense. But both public administration and politics are branches of political science, so that we are in the end compelled to mitigate the pure concept of efficiency in the light of the value scale of politics and the social order. There are, for example, highly inefficient arrangements like citizen boards and small local governments which *may* be necessary in a democracy as educational devices. It has been argued also that the spoils system, which destroys efficiency in administration, is needed to maintain the political party, that the political party is needed to maintain the structure of government, and that without the structure of government, administration itself will disappear. While this chain of causation has been disproved under certain conditions, it none the less illustrates the point that the principles of politics may seriously affect efficiency. Similarly in private business it is often true that the necessity for immediate profits growing from the system of private ownership may seriously interfere with the achievement of efficiency in practice. It does not seem to the writer, however, that these interferences with efficiency in any way eliminate efficiency as the fundamental value upon which the science of administration may be erected. They serve to condition and to complicate, but not to change the single ultimate test of value in administration.

In other words, the student of administration must take into account the conditions under which a given group of men are brought together to do a job. These conditions may include not only physical obstacles but also the democratic dogma, the fascist structure, a socialist economy, or the spoils system. But in any case the student of administration will not only explore relationships from the standpoint of efficiency within the framework afforded, but will consider also the effect of that framework upon efficiency itself wherever the opportunity is presented.

If it be true that the continual intrusion of varying scales of value has served to hinder the development of all of the social sciences, may it not be well to minimize this difficulty as is here suggested? This, it seems to the writer, is already possible in the study of public administration by regarding all value scales as environmental with the exception of one—efficiency. In this way it may be possible to approximate more nearly the impersonal valueless world in which exact science has advanced with such success.

But even so, great difficulties to scientific advance remain. If we may by various devices put fluctuating values to one side, and this is not as easy for other social sciences as it is for public administration, we are still confronted by two problems which the exact scientists have largely escaped. These are:

First, in dealing with human beings we encounter a rare dynamic element which is compounded in unknown proportions of predictable and of unpredictable, of rational and of emotional conduct.

Second, we are not able, except in the rarest circumstances, to set up controlled experiments or to test theories over and over at will.

The human psyche is significant, not entirely because it is dynamic and in part unpredictable and irrational, but also because human beings are so extraordinarily rare. There are in one cubic centimeter of air 15,000,000,000 times as many molecules as there are individual humans on this earth. It is this scarcity of phenomena which makes the individual variations so difficult and important. If we had as many humans to deal with as the exact scientist has electrons, we might more easily discover the pattern of conduct and the normal probability curves of social life. And in political science, when we turn to aggregates of human beings, organized in nations, we are confronted by a situation of still greater scarcity. There is only one Soviet Union, one Great Britain, one United States of America. With this paucity of phenomena to observe, it would be a miracle indeed if scholars were able to see through to the underlying laws and set them forth, certain that every significant variation was covered. This immensely important problem of variation, which is at the center of social science, was not even suspected to exist in the constitution of matter until a very few years ago, and even now presents a theoretical rather than a practical problem to the physicist because he, amid the plethora of phenomena, may rely on solid averages as a starting point.

Social experiments, moreover, must be made by men on men. This greatly restricts the process of verification of hypotheses not only because of the value and dignity of human life, but also because human beings continually interfere with experiments involving themselves.

There is no easy escape for social science from these two limitations. The number of human beings, though increasing, cannot remotely approach the gigantic statistical arrays which confront the physical scientist even within the confines of the smallest particle of matter. Nor may we follow the biologists and develop extensive controlled experiments to which human beings will readily submit over and over for the sake of pure science. Nor may we hope to develop laboratories in which outside social conditions may be reproduced for purposes of experimentation, for after all these laboratories must contain active elements which behave just like human beings in a normal human setting—and this is precisely that which human beings cannot provide outside of themselves.

Should we look, then, to the invention of instruments as the open sesame of social science? Do we need for social science microscopes, or telescopes, or cathode-ray tubes—that is, instruments to extend our sensory equipment? Do we need thermometers, balances, barometers—that is, instruments with which to make more accurate measurements? Or should our search be directed primarily in some other direction?

Though the writer has been greatly intrigued by the search for new instruments, useful particularly in public administration, and has contributed to the invention or development of some, it does not seem to him that the invention of instruments for the extension and refinement of the senses is the prime necessity at the present juncture. It is not mechanical instruments we need to enable us to see that which now escapes us. The great need is putting ourselves in a position to use the instruments which we already have.

What we require in the social sciences at the present time, it seems, is:

1. Analysis of phenomena from which we may derive standard nomenclature, measurable elements, and rational concepts;

2. The development of extensive scientific documentation based upon these analyses, and

3. The encouragement of imaginative approach to social phenomena, and the publication and circulation of hypotheses so that they may be scrutinized by others in the light of experience, now and in future years.

The analysis of phenomena, if it is to be of value in future years, or is to be added to the work of others and become part of a growing reservoir of knowledge, must be brought within a single system of definition and nomenclature. This is so obvious that it needs no further proof. It has been the device by which natural science has developed, and makes it possible for each scholar to stand on the shoulders of his predecessors, and not at ground level.

Definition requires careful analysis, analysis which must include the dynamic as well as the static facts. This will in itself show the way to the elements which can be measured, translated to mathematical terms, and thus brought into such form that they may be subjected to the most complete system of logic and inference which man has created. In the development of meaningful measurements, there may be room for new instruments. But, here again, instruments are not the first need. The first need is to discover and name the things that are to be measured. Surely we already have in the punch card, the instantaneous electrical transmission of information, automatic accounting, the electrical scoring of examinations and schedules, the perfected "straw vote," the photo-electric cell, the cinema, the decimal system of filing and classifying, and similar well-known devices, the basic instrumental equipment which is necessary for the advance of the social sciences. We have barely begun to use these devices. It will be observed that they are useful primarily in the summarization of experience for analysis. This is precisely the process which is needed because in the social sciences we start with the restless electron, and endeavor to build up the solid continuum.

The development of documentation is essential in the social sciences because it is the first step in accumulating sufficient data to submerge unimportant variables, and thus to furnish the basis of rational analysis. If we cannot have vast quantities of phenomena from which to work, we must at least accumulate those which we have from generation to generation so that scholars in considering the fate of mankind will not be confined to their own town and their own life span. The effort to "capture and record" administrative experience is surely fundamental. It is perhaps significant that modern science itself arose on the foundations of Greek analysis and documentation, and that science did not emerge even in civilizations further advanced than the Greek in some particulars, where such documentation was conspicuously absent.

And how may we encourage the imaginative approach, the formulation of generalizations, the statement of hypotheses, the building up and testing of theories? There is, of course, no simple answer. But three things are certain: first, we must subsidize social science research and philosophy through the universities and research institutes so that many men may be set free to study, think, and test out ideas; second, we must make it easy for those with ideas to secure their circulation among their fellows; and finally, we must contrive to give recognition to those who come forward with original and valid contributions. All of these factors played their part in the conquest of the natural world by exact science, and may be counted upon again to advance scientific knowledge and control in the world of human affairs.

COMMENTARY

"We do not study the art of governing," wrote Woodrow Wilson in 1887, "we govern. . . . Though democrats by long inheritance and repeated choice, we are still rather crude democrats." Thirty-five years later, the first director of the Bureau of the Budget, Charles G. Dawes, repeated essentially the same sentiment. "There is no reason why, because the government of the United States does the largest business in the world, it should be the worst conducted." The growth of corporate business enterprise from the end of the nineteenth century to 1928 represents one of the major developments in American history. Among other things, it introduced a business psychology into the American way-of-life in a manner which significantly altered a wide range of previously held attitudes and values. For example, the hero of American business enterprise, the small private entrepreneur, was suddenly faced with a formidable competitor in the more glamorous figure of the large corporation executive. The new "organization man" did not own a business enterprise; he managed a corporation, and, given the degree of pure competition which prevailed during most of this period, a corporation had to be managed effectively if it was to survive. Thus, for the corporation survival was directly related to a firm's comparable cost advantage over its competitors.

Efficiency became a function of costs, but, in addition, costs were directly related to the quality of management decisions. In other words, decreasing cost curves were *a priori* evidence of efficiency, and efficiency was seen as a function of sound management techniques and decisions. In this context, economic rationalism was the ideal model to emulate, and the main postulate of management science became the "minimax" strategy of minimum costs and maximum profits. This economic rationalism highlighted the mood of the nation during this period, and its spillover into the administrative system of government was inevitable. As revealed in the literature of this period, operating efficiency was viewed as a universal principle applicable to all administrative settings. Thus, management principles judged sound in the private sector were obviously just as sound for the public sphere.

Dawes, of course, epitomized the practical application of the business ethic in government. Gulick and Wilson were also concerned about improving the caliber of administrative performance in the executive branch, but neither approached the subject with the same hard-nosed, practical set of business values propounded by Dawes.

The Bureau of the Budget was created with the passage of the Budget and Accounting Act in 1921. This act was designed to correct the chaotic situation which had hitherto prevailed in the federal government's budgetary practices. Specifically, through the creation of the Bureau of the Budget and the House and Senate Appropriations Committees, the budgetary process was substantially modified in both the executive and legislative branches. The Budget Bureau was assigned the responsibility of collecting, inspecting, and collating all executive budget requests into a single document which would be submitted to Congress. The congressional appropriations committees were assigned exclusive jurisdiction over the legislative evaluation of these requests. Thus, the previous pattern of independent negotiations between every bureau and its legislative counterpart was abolished, and an element of centralized unity, especially on the executive side, was introduced into the budgetary process.

The full importance of the passage of the Budget and Accounting Act must remain implicit at this point. Neustadt has referred to it as one of the most significant developments in our entire constitutional history. "No other single innovation has so markedly enlarged the practical importance of the Presidency to the whole executive establishment."[*] An exposition demonstrating the validity of this proposition would divert the present discussion too far from its main focus. On the other hand, the selection by Dawes does contain three important themes which need to be developed in detail: first, a traditional bureaucratic theme; second, a theme of frugality; and third, a theme of political neutrality.

[*] Richard Neustadt, "Politicians and Bureaucrats," in *The Congress and America's Future*, David B. Truman (ed.) (Englewood Cliffs: Prentice-Hall, Inc., 1965), p. 110. See also by the same author, "Presidency and Legislation: The Growth of Central Clearance," *The American Political Science Review*, Vol. 48 (September 1954), and "Presidency and Legislation: Planning the President's Program," *Ibid.*, Vol. 49 (December 1955).

The concept of the bureaucratic model was an integral aspect of the management science literature of the period. Theoretically, all rational bureaucracies should be structured hierarchically according to graded ranks of authority. Furthermore, they should be characterized by a high degree of centralization of decision-making responsibilities, clearly defined disciplinary relationships between superiors and subordinates, and complete, willing subordination of one's personal values to those of the organization. For Dawes, the highest of all personal virtues were unity, discipline, and loyalty. As applied to the federal executive structure, the President symbolized the focal point of authority for the entire administrative system. Efficiency prevailed for Dawes to the extent that unity, discipline, and loyalty coalesced around the single figure of the President. Organizational efficiency, in terms of management values, would yield functional efficiency. Within this context, then, it seems reasonable to conclude that the basic concern of Dawes, as Director of the Bureau of the Budget, was *how* the internal managerial structure of the administrative system was to be organized, not *who* was to be in charge.

The second theme that runs through the Budget Director's statement is that of frugality. Of course, this is like saying the dominant theme of J. Edgar Hoover's statements is law enforcement. But the significance of this point should not be lost in its apparent obviousness. Efficiency, for Dawes, was indeed a function of cost. He absorbed this axiom from the private sector of pure competition. Costs were related to profits, and both were related to survival and growth. As Budget Director, however, Dawes established a precedent of focusing exclusively, and almost fanatically, on only one-half of this equation—cost reduction. "He who governs least, governs best," was changed to, "He who governs least expensively, governs best." The good administrator should not ask how much money he could get to operate his unit but, rather, he should ask, "how little he could get along with." Thus, Dawes inserted an actuarial zeal into the budgetary process of the federal government at a time when the management science orbit was approaching its apogee. Despite subsequent modifications of the original tenets of the management science approach, this attitude of frugality left a residual impression which, as will be seen, has been extremely difficult to modify.

The third theme stressed most emphatically by Dawes was that of administrative neutrality. "Ours is not to reason why," the humble stoker in the hold of the great Ship of State replies. If garbage must be dumped on the White House steps, so be it, but let it be done efficiently and impartially. As with Wilson, Dawes' "administrative man" was divorced from politics and political intrigue. The administrator became a specialist whose professional strength and integrity emerged from his dispassionate detachment from the political and social currents of the day. Administrative effectiveness in government was integrally related to administrative integrity. Involvement in political details by the public administrator could only dull the luster of this virtue, and administrative effectiveness would suffer accordingly. The administrator had to be frugal; he had to be a specialist; and he had to operate with the impersonal detachment worthy of a professional bureaucrat.

Gulick, writing in 1937, provided a theoretical base to the practical tenets of Dawes. In the science of administration the basic good was efficiency which was defined by Gulick as accomplishing a particular task at the least possible cost. In this regard there was no difference between Gulick and Dawes. Gulick did, however, get into a more sophisticated discussion on the question of values which must inevitably confront the administrator, and here his scientific orientation was most pronounced. Values—and particularly political values— may complicate the attainment of efficiency, but, as seen by Gulick, this fact alone was not enough to nullify efficiency as the ultimate goal to be attained. Efficiency was to be preferred over other values because it could be objectively measured, and for one who was concerned with developing a science of administration which was capable of predicting results and influencing outcomes, hard, tangible, and objective data had to be examined in a scientifically reputable framework—i.e., efficiency. It was Gulick who provided public administration with one of the first and one of the best statements on fact-value distinctions. In the governmental decision-making process politicians had the responsibility of considering the values included in any particular political conflict. The administrator, on the other hand, had the professional responsibility of contributing only the factual details to the decision-making process. The facts had to be collected, evaluated, and presented to the political decision-makers by the administrators in a purely scientific manner. The political neutrality of Dawes was translated into scientific purity by Gulick.

For Wilson, administrative neutrality was an equally relevant question. In fact, it was in his 1887 article that the first clear and precise delineation was presented between politics and administration. Although trained as a political scientist, Wilson considered that administration was more properly a field of business than a branch of politics. If a democracy was to be governed effectively, it had to be managed efficiently, and, given the rather seamy side of politics which was evidenced during the latter part of the nineteenth century, it was not surprising that Wilson, who was probably the last creditable political theorist we have had in the White House, became disillusioned with the fragmented, disorganized federal governmental structure. The proper distribution of authority was essential in our governmental system of separated powers but the assigned authority of each branch had to be inviolate. Specifically this meant that since the executive branch had the responsibility for administering the laws of the land, commensurate authority was needed to protect that responsibility. To this end it was Wilson who felt that extensive power and unhampered discretion were the indispensable conditions for executive leadership and responsibility. Divided responsibility meant obscured responsibility which, in turn, could only result in "irresponsible responsibility."

To paraphrase Walter Kaufman,* any discussion of the science of administration as applied to government without reference to Woodrow Wilson is like discussing Thomism without reference to Aristotle; but, to a very real extent, to call Wilson an administrative "scientist" is a little like calling Aristotle a Thomist. To be sure, Wilson, Gulick, and Dawes were of one mind insofar as the need for managerial efficiency was concerned, and with Hamilton, Wilson certainly appeared to argue forcefully for the primacy of the executive branch and especially its administrative system. However, a close reading of the Wilson selection also reveals a slight touch of the Madisonian influence. It was the pragmatic Wilson who observed, for instance, that administrative arrangements congenial to American habit must be preferred without hesitation to theoretical perfection, and that the "cosmopolitan what-to-do must always be commanded by the American how-to-do-it." In short, "Our own politics must be the touchstone for all theories." But for what purpose? In this connection the management science literature has significant implications.

For example, the administrative theories of Jefferson and Madison attempted to maximize individual happiness and justice. Even Hamilton's centralized administrative system was designed to achieve a fully developed and enlightened social man. In this regard, Wilson, perhaps, was more centrally concerned with a transcendental end or purpose of his administrative theory than either Gulick or Dawes, although even Wilson presented his concepts in a somewhat ambiguous framework. At one point he showed primary concern over the securing of individual liberty, and he concluded that a liberal constitution ingrained with liberal principles provided the only security for individual liberty. Administrative arrangements, therefore, were clearly secondary to constitutional guarantees. Political values formed the bedrock of Wilsonian thought, and liberal democracy was the mechanism best designed to attain these values. Unfortunately, Wilson never stated in concrete terms the role administration was to play in attaining the "good society." As a consequence, his administrative generalizations could be applied with no difficulty to the theories of Hamilton, Jefferson, or Madison, despite their significant differences.

* *Existentialism from Dostoevsky to Sartre* (New York: Meridian Books, 1956).

Who, indeed, could disagree with, "The principles on which to base a science of administration for America must be principles which have democratic policy very much at heart."? Certainly neither Hamilton, Jefferson, nor Madison. Administration may, in fact, be primarily concerned with "making what is democratically politic towards all, administratively possible towards each," but what does this provide in terms of a guide with which administrative behavior can be gauged as it carries out its functions? The primary responsibility of the "steady, practical statesman" (as opposed to the doctrinaire theorist) is "to supply the best possible life to a *federal* organization, to systems within systems. . . ." Wilson's focus in this instance was on the vast multitude of political jurisdictions throughout the United States from the federal government down to the town councils, and he envisioned a model of perfect integration and harmony among all of the many diverse political subsystems within the United States. In short, despite his urgings for a pragmatic, common-sense approach to administration, Wilson set up a political abstraction of the first order.

Dawes and Gulick were not as ambiguous as Wilson; their objectives were clear and precise, although certainly not transcendental as with Jefferson, Madison, and Hamilton. Both, in fact, would agree with Rowen and Hitch, as discussed in Chapter One that efficiency does matter, and that efficiency is, itself, a basic good. But efficiency for what purpose? For what end? Efficiency, after all, is simply a method of operation—a technique—which is designed to accomplish certain goals and to avoid others. Goals reflect values, and means are directly related to the ultimate values which are sought.

For Gulick the problem was resolved simply; the administrative process must develop as a science, and this meant that it must be capable of being evaluated objectively. Normative values could not be applied to evaluate administrative effectiveness. The only objective criterion that was available was efficiency. Therefore, the only "good" that administrators had to concern themselves with was efficiency. All other values such as justice, happiness, equity—while they may be legitimate concerns for politicians and policy makers—were of no concern to administrators if the administrative process was to attain scientific legitimacy. In other words, as seen by Gulick, within the context of a value-free administrative process, the ends to be attained through efficiency were irrelevant insofar as the administrator was concerned.

The political neutrality of Dawes has been discussed. He, like Wilson, saw a basic dichotomy between politics and administration, but, unlike Gulick, the "administrative man" of Dawes was by no means value-free. It might be said that, for Dawes, efficiency became an end in itself; not only a basic good but *the* basic value to be attained.

Efficiency carried with it its own normative justification, and any action which moved in the direction of efficiency was good while any action which moved in the opposite direction was, by definition, bad. But this explanation is really too simplistic, since Dawes was interested in not only efficiency but also unity, coordination, integration, and centralization of function within the executive branch. But, again, for what purpose?

One possible explanation is that he sought to increase the power of the President in the public policy process; his dutiful comments in this regard are numerous. If this is a valid conclusion then Dawes, like Machiavelli before him and Neustadt after him, was simply advising the Chief Executive as to how his power could best be utilized. But another explanation is suggested which is more significant in its implications. Both Machiavelli and Neustadt advised their respective Princes to be wary of their subordinate advisors—to become their own experts in the use of political power; in short, to trust no one. Dawes is much more pretentious. Despite his claims to the contrary, his philosophy would inevitably increase administrative influence over the executive policy-making process through the budgetary controls he applied. His pontifical tribute to the Secretary of the State, for example, indicated clearly that while foreign policy decisions were of no concern to the Bureau of the Budget, the manner in which the State Department implemented any decisions involving the expenditure of public funds was a matter of prime concern to the Budget Director. Thus, even for Dawes, efficiency was a means to an end which elevated economic considerations to a position of primacy in the public policy process. As a consequence, the executive branch inevitably emerged as the dominant branch of government since it alone—through the President and his efficiency oriented administrative advisors—was able to subordinate the political and social considerations involved in the public policy process to basic economic factors.

From this brief sample of management science themes and concepts which developed from approximately the 1890s to the 1920s, it seems reasonable to conclude that these were not years of stagnation, at least as far as administrative theory was concerned. The impact of this movement on the subsequent development of administrative practice and theory in America has been alluded to briefly, but, because of the significance of some of the characteristics implicit in the management science doctrines, a more detailed evaluation of four of these characteristics is essential.

First of all, there was a characteristic of suppression which tended to dominate the entire movement. The organization chart of the traditional hierarchical structure symbolized the scientific nature of the management movement in its most elaborate form. The pyramid of pyramids diagrammed quite precisely the internal superior-subordinate relationships, the line-staff patterns, and the inevitable chains of command. In short, a basic assumption of the movement was that operating efficiency could be achieved only if accountability and responsibility could be precisely pinpointed. In actual practice, this principle of accountability manifested itself most severely. Subordinates were directly accountable to their immediate superiors and, given the chain of command concept, no other route was available for subordinates to appeal the decisions or directives of their superiors. In terms of operating functions, each member of the organization was assigned a specific job in a specific administrative subunit. His duties and responsibilities in this regard were narrowly defined in order to avoid ambiguity. On the other hand, imaginative functional innovations which transcended the established functional jurisdictions could not be permitted since this, too, created ambiguity of accountability and responsibility. A more realistic assessment of the management science movement has been provided by psychologist Herbert Shepard, who describes the organization chart as a suppression chart— ". . . in the case of conflict the chart tells who can suppress whom."*

The second dominant characteristic of the administrative science approach was its punitive quality. This, of course, was directly related to suppression, although the two were not synonymous characteristics. Typically, the most elementary form of control is the simple superior-subordinate relationship in which the latter consistently responds correctly to the commands of the former. Failure to meet one's obligations and responsibilities in this regard normally results in the imposition of organizational sanctions and punishments, whereas correct responses are generally rewarded. However, both in the literature and the practice of the management science movement almost exclusive stress was placed on the sanctions and punishments that the organization would impose for substandard executive performance, while organizational rewards were generally alluded to in rather distant and vague terms. Dismissal, demotion, and disgrace were the prices one could expect to pay for the failure to recognize unity, discipline, and loyalty as the highest of all organizational values.

The third basic characteristic of the movement was frugality. Although this concept has been discussed in some detail above, it is important to stress that frugality does imply something different from mere efficiency. The total and absolute attention given to minimizing costs at the expense of all other considerations could only be

* "Responses to Competition and Conflict," in *Power and Conflict in Organizations,* Robert L. Kahn and Elise Boulding (eds.) (New York: Basic Books, 1964), p. 128.

described as frugality. In addition, of course, this attitude was directly related to the primacy of economic factors over all other non-economic considerations.

A final characteristic of the movement was the element of impersonality, which was seen as an essential feature of any rational bureaucratic structure. As related to the "value-free" notions of Gulick, for example, an impersonal attitude toward all normative considerations became an integral feature of the management science movement. For those who, like Gulick and others, saw administration as a value-free science, managerial efficiency was directly related to the impersonal detachment of the administrator. But, more significantly, for those who did not accept the value-free premise of the movement, the element of impersonality was still seen as a convenient rationalization which could be invoked to justify administrative noninvolvement in social and political conflict. As will be seen in later chapters, this was a most important contribution of the management science movement to subsequent administrative developments.

In terms of administrative theory, the management science doctrines were built around a narrow interpretation of the classical laissez-faire business ethic which prevailed at the time. Government was a business, and its main function was to operate efficiently. Therefore, such vague concepts as social happiness, equity, justice, and morality were redefined in terms compatible with the laissez-faire business ethic. Thus, efficiency yielded happiness; equity resulted from allowing every man to proceed at his own pace, in his own way, without governmental assistance; justice was guaranteed by the contract clause of the Constitution; and Calvinism provided a moral base befitting to all men in a democratic society.

By 1930, the management science movement was—along with everything else in government—in serious disorder. In the face of a deepening depression, its dogmas and its advocates were discredited. If government was business, then the nation was starkly confronted with the task of reassessing the efficacy of the American business ethic. What caused the Great Ship of State to flounder, to use Dawes' archaic metaphor, is much too complex a question to answer here. It is probably fair to say, however, that the laissez-faire tenets of management science were inapplicable to a rapidly changing and turbulent society.

In the middle of this violent social turbulence a new administration assumed office, and an entirely different set of managerial principles were immediately applied. As Franklin D. Roosevelt directed the executive apparatus, the shortest distance between two points no longer was necessarily a straight line and the least expensive government program was no longer necessarily the most efficient, if factors other than pure economic costs were taken into account.

Noneconomic factors were taken into account by the new administration to the extent that the primary goal of government was no longer considered to be economic efficiency, but, rather, political effectiveness.

Economic efficiency-inefficiency and political effectiveness-ineffectiveness are options which may be deliberately chosen by top level executive officials. The range of alternatives can be simply stated: The administrative system of any government may be—

1. economically efficient and politically effective
2. economically inefficient and politically ineffective
3. economically efficient and politically ineffective
4. economically inefficient and politically effective

At the outset of his administration, Roosevelt, in effect, chose the fourth option. As a consequence, the business of government was no longer business, but politics. Government was politics, politics was government. The two were inseparable, and both were inherent elements in the public policy process. Economic rationalism was replaced by political rationalism, the science of administration by the politics of administration. Even more importantly, the manner in which available governmental resources were to be allocated underwent a fundamental change in philosophy. The decentralization principles of Jefferson and the pluralism of Madison were revived and integrated with the element of the strong chief executive inherent in the Hamiltonian mode.

ADMINISTRATION AS POLITICS

4

PUBLIC ADMINISTRATION AS POLITICS

HAROLD STEIN

Many, perhaps most, of the insights gained from an understanding of public administration as process are insights that are also applicable to private administration as well. Yet there are differences between these two kinds of administration, the most important of which are derived, of course, from the political environment and purpose of the former.

In the United States, the study of public administration has been, and still is occasionally, confused by an attempt to define public administration in terms of the constitutional separation of powers. This has led to a series of meaningless and misleading generalizations, such as: "Congress creates policy, administrators carry it out," "the good public administrator pays no attention to politics," and so forth. Such artificial divisions (and other parallel ones) were, of course, not exclusively the result of treating public administration as a branch of public law; they were also in part the product of other intellectual currents, an over-simplified concept of a "neutral" civil service, for example. And these awkward conclusions were likewise supported by a parallel line of interpretation applied to business, involving a formal and strict separation of powers between stock holders, directors, and management. But the unreality of this doctrine as a definition of actual corporate behavior has become increas-

From Introduction to *Public Administration and Policy Development*, edited by Harold Stein, copyright, 1952, by Harcourt, Brace & World, Inc., and reprinted with their permission. Harold Stein, who died in 1966, taught at the Woodrow Wilson School of Public and International Affairs at Princeton University.

ingly obvious, and the appeal to the supposed example of business no longer carries weight when used in an attempt to interpret the nature of public administration.

There were various reasons why the establishment of water-tight compartments for "administration" and "politics" persisted so long. Perhaps the most important is to be found in the ambiguities of the word "politics" itself. Naïvely, but honestly, it has occasionally been assumed, for example, that to admit the political nature of public administration is to abandon faith in a non-partisan civil service. "Politics," "politician," "political" are all slippery words. In the United States all of them tend to be used in a pejorative sense, though the connotation of the phrase "political science," if not universally enlivening is at least honorable. In this situation the dictionary fails to enlighten.

Without attempting a formal definition, it can be said that the concept of public administration as politics as used here is designed particularly to refer to the administrator's understanding and pursuit of his objectives and his relations with the social environment outside his agency that affects or is capable of affecting its operations. This is obviously a rather special use of the phrase; the administrator also deals with the distribution of power and other political problems within his organization. But in this brief sketch, these matters are treated as part of public administration as process, so that the phrase "public administration as politics" in this particular context is given an essentially external orientation. The two concepts are, of course, complementary, and refer to two aspects of the same basic process.

It is in its political character that public administration tends to differ most decisively from private administration, and to vary most notably from one country, or even one jurisdiction within a country, to another. These differences are perhaps matters of degree not kind. All business is sensitive to a sort of constituency—its customers and prospective customers—and many businesses show an increasing tendency to give conscious thought to trade union, public, and governmental relations. Adaptations of this character are political in the sense in which the term is used here. Nevertheless, public administrators as a group are far more deeply affected than private administrators in making decisions by large, complex, often vaguely defined, social objectives and by the need for adjusting effectively to a highly complex environment composed of many forces, frequently conflicting—individuals, private associations, and the government itself.

A moment's reflection will show that variations in the tasks of public administrators are greatest in this area of external relations and final goals. While the British civil servant cannot be insensitive to public needs and desires, his formal line of responsibility is comparatively simple and direct, and his immediate relations with the outer world carefully defined. How different the problem of the administrator in our own national government. The Constitution, our customs and traditions, the size and complexity of our land and our society, produce cumulatively centrifugal pressures. Every executive agency, and many of its top administrators, have responsibilities to or toward the President, to a variety of control agencies either only partially or not at all under the President's discretionary supervision, ordinarily to at least four congressional committees, to Congress more generally, and to an indeterminate number of individual Congressmen and Senators; to the organized and unorganized constituencies of the agency; to pressure groups, public and private, local and national, powerful or merely persistent; frequently to the courts, and occasionally to a political party.

It is in this atmosphere that the administrator makes his decisions. It is perhaps arguable that all this is not as it should be, that while the administrator should be sensitive to public needs and desires, his direct line of responsibility should be reasonably clear and simple and he should be fairly free from the direct impact of the organized forces of American society. But that is another question. The individual administrator can do very little about changing the rules of the game; his task is to carry on his job under the rules as they exist, and the rules require him to deal with the forces that seek to deal with him.

Purely for purposes of discussion, it may be useful to distinguish two aspects of the administrator's adjustment to his political environment: the problem of survival and the problem of values. The problem of survival is omnipresent, though in fact the word "survival" tends to over-dramatize what occurs. In theory, an administrator who fails politically by antagonizing powerful groups may live to see the legislature repeal the law and thereby prevent the fulfillment of the public function he has been endeavoring to execute; but in practice this painful denouncement, or even the anticipation of this painful denouncement, is rare. Survival with disabilities is more usual. The administrator's job may be at stake—in some positions the job-holder may not even expect to be able to hold on very long—or some modification of the program (or curtailment of funds) may be involved, or both; on occasion the danger may lie in the possibility of transfer of function to another agency. And all these possible threats to what may be loosely called survival may come from a legislature such as Congress, for instance, or from an administrative superior such as the President, frequently acting on pressure from the general public or some specialized public.

Administrator, agency, program—all are subject to attack. But the reader should note that to phrase the question of survival in this way tends to assume the virtue of the administrator. For obvious reasons, most administrators normally assume their own virtue; but here the student must go his own way; for him, the virtue of the administrator cannot be assumed; it must be examined and evaluated.

Sometimes administrative survival is undermined by acts that clearly do the administrator no credit. There is no virtue in endangering person, agency, or program by clumsiness or tactlessness; there is no virtue (save perhaps for some special cases where the executive fulfills inescapable constitutional responsibilities in a way that incurs legislative disfavor) in cleaving to a policy that lacks any formal legislative sanction and meets with explicit legislative repugnance. But the usual case in this country is much harder: explicit legislative sanction and actual legislative repugnance—a law still on the books, but active objection to its energetic enforcement. What should the administrator do under such circumstances? (Throughout this discussion, opposition between administrator and superior can be substituted for the legislative-executive antithesis.)

No formula can provide the right answer to questions like this. Analysis and answer must follow two paths—tactics and values. Living with chief executive, legislature, pressure groups, and other elements in the political environment is a constant challenge to the administrator's tactical skill, and the components of that skill— timing, public relations, ability to mobilize friends, and the rest—are subject to analysis and evaluation.

The other aspect of survival—values—is also basic to the whole concept. For politics involves ethics and benefits and power; it is the resolution of the contending forces in society. In this light we see the administrator as an agent of society making choices that affect the well-being of society. With the increasing scope of government activity, the range of administrative discretion is enormously broadened. Pre-determined answers become increasingly less appropriate, and self-explanatory and self-executing standards more and more elusive. The administrator must rely on his own system of values— his feeling for what is right—his judgment of what to emphasize or what to play down—his sense of justice and fair play. The fundamental safeguard against an administrator's arbitrary and unethical conduct is the fact that public administration, especially in a democracy, circumscribes the range of values which the administrator can observe. For the making of value judgments by the administrator is part and parcel of the whole system; every act of political response that can be weighed in terms of its significance for survival has value connotations as well. In our society and particularly in our national government, it is doubtful that any administrator can long survive, no matter how adroit a manipulator, if his decisions reflect values that are sharply at variance with the general standards of society or the goals which society seeks.

The consideration of values in administrative behavior is thus no mere academic exercise. Students of public administration must be concerned with values. They are observers and they should be capable of dispassionate observation; but ultimate neutrality with respect to administrative decisions is self-defeating. A lack of concern for the values of public administration is indicative of a lack of sensitivity; and an insensitive observer can never attain to more than a limited insight.

THE ANALYSIS OF PUBLIC ADMINISTRATION

In the preceding pages, the reader has been given a brief indication of two ways of looking at public administration—as process and as politics. For the sake of simplicity, the two have been treated as if they dealt with separable matters: the internal functioning of public administration and its external goals and relations. This distinction is useful for purposes of explanation, but it has limited validity. The decision to assign a new function to a particular agency is on the surface an internal governmental matter; but different assignments can lead to strikingly different functional and political consequences. Nor, on the other side, can an administrator operate in his political environment without affecting the internal operations of his agency. Important decisions by public administrators characteristically can, and should, be analyzed simultaneously in terms of both process and politics.

Concepts like process and politics when used in the study of public administration do not lead to the formulation of rules and principles that can provide the administrator with automatic guides to the right answer and permit the student to grade administrative decisions on some mathematical scale. Rather their function is to suggest the kinds of questions that can usefully be asked and the kind that are self-defeating. By encouraging a search for the multitudinous factors that may enter into administrative decisions, and the multitudinous consequences that flow from them, they tend to preclude simple answers to complex questions. We can have no effective understanding of public administration unless we keep in mind the wide range of considerations that are relevant to the administrator's behavior.

This range of considerations is indeed very wide. The student will even find it necessary at times to concern himself with considerations that the administrator did not or could not take into account. The student's use of such considerations must be handled carefully. The student may observe, for example, that a thoroughly informed decision on a particular matter may not be possible in advance of the receipt of certain census data; but if the administrator is compelled by some legal or other overriding requirement to act sooner, criticism of the decision because of the failure to use the data is beside the point (though criticism of the requirement may be valid). Thus, for any decision, the appropriate considerations are not necessarily those one would like to apply in the abstract. The very fact that the administrator must apportion his time means that the amount of personal attention he can devote to questions will vary from one problem to another. We oversimplify if we make the assumption that all problems can receive equally careful thought.

Thus the student of public administration must ask not only many different questions, but many different kinds of questions. He can, for example, usefully ask the kinds of questions that the philosophers would have asked—Plato, Aristotle, Hobbes, Bentham, Dewey, for example—and analyze decisions by casuistic or utilitarian or ideal-istic or other modes of inquiry: was the decision conformable to the accepted rules and precedents? were the consequences of different al-ternatives duly weighed? was the decision based on some abstract principle of good conduct?

It is evident that ethical inquiries of this kind are intimately related to the modes of analysis that have been suggested earlier. The appli-cation of public law to a problem of decision is a form of casuistry; the utilitarian inqniry may relate to both survival and values; the appeal to an abstract ideal is one way of making, and justifying, a value judgment.

The different social sciences and disciplines make available another group of methods for the analysis of public administration. A lawyer may analyze a variety of illuminating matters, such as the powers and responsibilities of the administrator, of the chief executive, of the legislature. A social psychologist may explore the causes of public response to administrative action. A historian can reveal similarities and contrasts with events of the past. An economist may estimate the economic consequences of alternative administrative decisions. Others can express informed judgments on the effect of decisions by our government on friend and foe abroad. The relation of a particular decision to party structure in Congress can frequently be observed and occasionally predicted.

All these decisions and a host of others, are clearly relevant to the problem of the administrator and to the problem of the student of administration. Yet to balance these considerations wisely is ulti-mately as much a question of values as of technical knowledge. No scientists as such can give the reader a precise definition of a phrase like "civilian control of the military" or construct a scale on which this element is given a specific rating to be compared with "effi-ciency" or some other element. A considered judgment on "civilian control" requires knowledge, but knowledge does not constitute the judgment.

The administrator and the student are thus on their own in the final step of making and evaluating administrative decisions. They can, by experience or study or both, become competent judges of trends set in motion by organizational structure and procedure; they may acquire a more than superficial insight into the reactions of men and the part played in those reactions by intellectual and social backgrounds; they may acquire skill in observing and predicting world or domestic mass political reactions. Without insights of this character, and without knowledge thus acquired, sound judgment will be no more than an accident. But sound judgment in this field does not include the ability to make absolute (or quasi-absolute) predictions such as are made in the physical sciences, nor to propound absolute standards for administrative decisions. Thus there are obvious limits on what can be learned.

Within these limits, characteristic of all the social sciences, the study of public administration remains fruitful for both student and administrator. For the administrator, a recognition of the recurrent elements in the different problems that he faces makes it easier for him to distinguish what is novel in each new situation, concentrate on the novel element, and find a suitable solution; this kind of knowledge is obtainable by the study of public administration. So, too, as has been suggested above, is an awareness of the essential interrelationship of politics and process. If substantive decisions, as they are called—i.e., decisions on program—are arrived at by wise and informed use of the resources of administration and by intelligent appreciation of the political environment, they are far more likely to be sound than if they are arrived at in hit-or-miss or doctrinaire fashion. A realization of the nature of public administration leads to a clarification of objectives and to a more sophisticated approach to those objectives in the midst of the pressures generated by society.

For both professional students and lay citizens who seek to understand why government officials behave as they do and to learn how to judge their decisions, the same general conclusions apply. In our society, characteristically, we complain about our government, we question its very justification for being; we match it against an ideal. We look to government officials for qualities that we do not forcefully demand of others, including those with whom the government does important business. The private citizen in his dealings with government is held responsible only for common honesty (whatever other qualities may be desirable); but to the humblest administrator we look for some breadth of consideration, some penetration in analysis, some concern for the future. We cannot sensibly ask that public administrators be prophets or saints or geniuses; we can and do ask that they use foresight and decency and intelligence in reaching their decisions.

THE POLITICS OF ADMINISTRA- TION

MARSHALL AND GLADYS DIMOCK

All governmental administration operates in a political milieu. No matter what position is involved, from the least discretionary job in the civil service to the highest policy posts in appointive office, the political setting is a central fact of administrative life for the government official.

There are, of course, many fine shadings in the degree to which the influence of politics on administration is felt. Although politics cannot be defined in a single simple statement, the various connotations of the term must nevertheless be identified and finally integrated to show how, through the influence of politics on administration, governmental operations serve society's larger interests.

WHAT IS POLITICS?

As to any high-level abstraction such as state, society, economics, democracy, government, and public administration itself, so also to the term politics many definitions may be applied. The main problem is how to avoid a rigid dogmatism on the one hand and fuzzy think-

Condensed from Chapter 8, "The Politics of Administration," from *Public Administration*, 3rd edition, by Marshall E. Dimock and Gladys O. Dimock. Copyright 1953 by M. E. Dimock and G. O. Dimock. Copyright © 1958 by M. E. Dimock, G. O. Dimock, and Louis W. Koenig. Copyright © 1964 by Holt, Rinehart and Winston, Inc. Reprinted by permission of Holt, Rinehart and Winston, Inc. Marshall Dimock, whose wife collaborated with him on this work, retired in 1962 as head of the Government department at New York University.

ing on the other. If it is impossible to formulate a precise definition
—and often the attempt beclouds rather than elucidates practical
connotations—it is possible at least to analyze and describe what
actually occurs in various areas and at different levels of institutional
operation.

As a start, let us say that politics is problem solving in an attempt
to meet human needs. Politics is also choosing among alternatives,
making decisions where a choice is involved. Politics is deciding on
the content of policy and the values to be promoted; this is like
saying that politics is policy, which may and usually does involve
philosophies, value systems, and other high-level abstractions. Politics
is also partisanship, of course, meaning taking an active part in the
work of political parties, pressure groups, and other groups that
would influence public opinion for partisan purposes. As part of the
power struggle for preferment, access to dominance, and control,
politics is also competition for influence and position. And finally,
politics is a process involving a division of labor between legislation,
execution, and adjudication; but even so, in the large sense, discretion
and law making occur in all three of these branches of the political
process.

The foregoing rather impressionistic analysis shows that the range
of possible connotation of the term politics covers a spectrum extending all the way from personal partisan manipulation on the one hand,
to the ideas of political philosophers concerned with the public good
on the other.

In public administration, politics is a process that affects every
aspect of governmental operations, and because policy is a continuum, each aspect has an appropriate role to play that is interrelated with all the others. What these roles are depends on the
form of government in question. Thus, a monistic type of government
(one-party rule or a dictatorship) tends to concentrate power in
one place, whereas a democratic government widely distributes
power and decision making, creating fairly distinct roles in a system
of checks and balances. The democratic pattern is harder to describe
realistically than the monistic, the reason being that freedom is emphasized and hence citizens, public opinion, constitutions, law making, and popular control have a wider and more varied scope and
influence. The broad distribution of roles and authority makes possible a degree of freedom that allows public opinion to be the·arbiter
of policy.

Consequently, the problem of government and its administration
is to define roles precisely enough to avoid confusion and institutional
ineffectuality, but with enough flexibility to make it possible for
freedom and public opinion to pervade and control the whole of the
governmental machinery.

This proposition has been well stated by Paul Appleby, former dean of the Maxwell Graduate School of public administration at Syracuse University and a long-time federal official. "Public administration," said Appleby, "is policy-making." If this statement seems to exalt administration, the impression is false because an emphasis on politics actually subordinates the administrator, for it exalts the politician and thereby exalts the citizen as well. Thus, continued Appleby, "Public administration is policy-making. *But it is not autonomous, exclusive or isolated policy-making.* It is policy-making on a field where mighty forces contend, forces engendered in and by the society. It is policy-making subject to still other and various policy-makers." Indeed, public administration is one of several basic political processes by which a people achieves and controls governance. This statement comes only after Appleby has clearly shown that career and appointive officials alike share essentially the same responsibility for policy and leadership. Consequently, he is inclined to accentuate the policy role that professional administrators must play.

The best way to understand policy is to start with Appleby's statement that mighty forces contend. From that point, here is the way politics unfolds in a step by step progression: Society has certain needs. Government is the only modern social institution with sufficient scope to serve these needs. Some governmental functions, like the collection of taxes, are performed in order to maintain itself, but most of the others are the result of pressure from interested citizens and groups. Since people differ as to what government should and should not do, it is always the scene of active political controversy. Hence politics is the means by which society faces up to issues and decides how to resolve them. Politics involves a choice among alternatives that involve values, philosophies, ethical considerations. Politics is a quest for human betterment by public means. It is also, as Bismarck once noted, the art of the possible. In the ideal sense, politics is the purposeful activity by which men seek to live a better life.

Needs, pressures, policies: these eventually become law. Law takes many forms including constitutions, legislative enactments, administrative determinations, and judicial decisions. Administrators occupy the midway station in this process, often suggesting legislation in the first place and interpreting and adding to it once it is passed. In addition, administrators have a good deal more to do with the execution and enforcement of the law than the judicial branch itself. From this point of view, administration is the application of policy formulated by law in a constantly unfolding process, making the laws of legislatures and the courts increasingly more specific by means of policy formulations and determinations applied to particular publics, to smaller publics, and finally to individual cases. It has been rightly said that public administration is the intermingling of policy making and management that occurs between the levels of legislative, judicial, and popular-electoral policy determinations.

Where does partisan politics come in? So far, the discussion has centered on policy rather than partisanship. Although the question will be dealt with more fully at a later point, some reference to the role of political parties in administration is needed here. Much depends upon the form of government involved. In Britain, for example, where the party in power is responsible for carrying out the program promised the electorate, party policy is always government policy. By contrast, in the United States this responsibility is so much less that Appleby calls it marginal: "All administration and all policy-making within the government are political, being governmental, but only a small part of either, by mass, has identifiable partisan character." Moreover, he continues, not all partisan activity is concerned with policy and administration, for much is merely auxiliary, being concerned with keeping party machinery in readiness for the periodic selection and election of candidates for public office.

In summary, it must be understood that public administrators are always and inevitably concerned with politics in the sense of policy, but the extent to which they are affected by partisan political activity depends largely on whether political parties attempt to unify all of government through their policies and programs, as is the case in Britain, or whether their role is largely confined to electing candidates and winning elections, as is more characteristic of party activity in the United States.

There is, however, yet another aspect of politics with which every administrator must be concerned. This is what may be called political sense, and it depends on the personality and character of the individual. The qualities involved are intuition, tact, the ability quickly to size up a situation, the ability to get things done despite opposition, the skill to get people to cooperate and to make them content in their work.

As noted in an earlier chapter, government differs from business in certain aspects, but a high degree of political sense is a universal requirement in both cases. A group of Harvard professors, for example, made case studies of large corporations, and concluded that a main requirement of executive leadership in business is political sense. The reason, of course, is that as corporations become large they also become involved in competitions for power similar to those in government, and hence the same skills are needed in both cases. Again like government, corporations also have policy problems that have to do with survival, an area that continually grows in importance. The chairman of the board of a large public utility once remarked, for example, that he could see little difference between his company and Tammany Hall. Politics in this sense is a personal skill indispensable to administrative effectiveness. Indeed, the politician (in the best sense of that designation) and the administrator have certain skills that are interchangeable.

CHANGING ATTITUDES TOWARD POLITICS

Why is it then that during most of American political history, administration and politics have been considered as opposites rather than as two parts of a common experience? The reasons are various. For one thing, both before and after the passage of the Pendleton Act of 1883, civil service reform developed a fight-the-spoilsman psychology in which the foe was politics and politicians. For a long time the ideal goal set for administrators was political neutrality, until it was gradually recognized that to neglect policy, which inevitably involves politics, is to dull incentive and defeat the public good; that it is not policy that is objectionable but only certain kinds of partisan activity. Then, too, certain crass forms of political activity such as bossism and spoils were condemned by conscientious citizens who saw in them a threat to democratic survival. In addition, at a later point, more was expected of political parties in the form of leadership and responsibility than they have so far been able to supply.

Equally important, in its extreme form the theory of the separation of powers seemed to suggest that there should be watertight compartments in government, leading to the notion—now recognized as naïve—that administrators should be excluded from the making and interpretation of the law. Government itself was regarded with suspicion and "politics" was a smear word. There was a failure sufficiently to differentiate between policy, which was the cornerstone of Greek philosophy, and partisanship, by which the authors of The Federalist papers meant faction.

Early in the present century Congress and the President were still fighting over who should run the administrative branch (as they still are, of course) and the civil service was timid and demoralized. The role of Congress was ill defined and the Presidency not yet sufficiently institutionalized to make administration as effective as needed. Congress might have created a distinct career service, such as already existed in many western European nations, but decisive action was lacking. As a result, the administrative corps lacked the self-esteem, the self-confidence, and the freedom of scope that its duties required. As big government grew bigger, its structure became increasingly amorphous and confused. The original symmetry of a number of executive departments headed in each case by a Secretary as a member of the President's Cabinet was blurred when independent regulatory commissions and government corporations were created by Congress outside of the main lines of authority and responsibility leading up to the chief executive.

Fortunately, since the 1930s the situation has been changing: politics, which some blasé intellectuals regarded as merely a game, is now recognized as serious business. Government's role, once labelled by these same intellectuals as domination, is now seen as primarily a service to citizens and consumers. Administrators have always seen it this way, of course, but only recently have American political scientists generally begun to define politics broadly enough to include the service role of government and its organic relation to the rest of society.

It is irrelevant to speculate on which of the three branches of government is the most important, because all make and administer policy, as they should. Nevertheless, it has come gradually to be recognized that in practice the administrative branch is now relatively more influential than the other two and that its influence on policy is greater than was once supposed. Consequently there is a changing view as to the role of politics in administration and an attempt to make public administration a more effective instrument for the betterment of American society. Public opinion has come to see the need for more expertness, more sophisticated leadership, and more continuity for career officials in government employment. . . .

PRESSURE GROUPS, POLITICAL PARTIES, AND PUBLIC OPINION

Every government agency has a constituency for which it was largely created and whose interest and support are essential to its continued existence. In some cases the interest group involved is more obvious and tangible than in others. In the federal government, for example, the Departments of Commerce, Agriculture, and Labor reflect the existence of three major segments of the economy, although these agencies are also charged with serving the larger public interest as well. In each case the enabling legislation charges the department in question to "foster and promote the interest of" the particular economic interest involved. A similar link exists between educators and the Office of Education, physicians and the United States Public Health Service, and lawyers and the Department of Justice.

Depending on the program in question, however, agencies differ in the kind of interest evoked from special groups. Thus, a government agency may provide a special service (to farmers), wider economic service (in handling the mails), or a service to a particular group in the population (veterans, for example). Or the agency may offer a subsidy (to the aviation industry), or discharge a regulatory function (for television). Or it may attack some particular social problem (such as juvenile delinquency). Thus not all agencies directly serve a particular interest group, for many offer a more diffused public service to society as a whole, as in public health or public assistance.

But irrespective of the category or, as sometimes happens, the combination of categories under which an agency may be classified, the support of some portion of effective public opinion is always necessary—at least in a democracy—before its program can be created and remain in existence. Every agency has not only its supporters but in many cases also its opponents who for one reason or another would like to put it out of business or greatly reduce its role, a situation faced by even the largest and most powerful government bodies. Many conservative businessmen and an occasional farmer would like to see the Department of Agriculture's $5 billion budget reduced by abolishing price support and food storage programs, the two items that account for the largest single chunk of that agency's expenditures. Consequently every administrator is in politics, so to speak, for two good reasons: he needs the support of his clientele in order to promote his agency, and second, in many cases to protect it from its natural enemies.

The government agencies that cannot be classified under the foregoing are those with sovereign functions inherent in the very survival of government: the collection of taxes, the maintenance of police and military forces, the operation of the foreign office, the control of immigration and naturalization, the coining of money, the control of currency, and the operation of the courts, to mention only the most obvious ones. Such programs must rely on the interest of all citizens and lawmakers in protecting the life, liberty, and property of the entire population. Generally speaking, these agencies receive a wide popular support rather than a narrow interest group support, although many specific problems do arise especially in connection with civil liberties, fear of a police state, the incidence of taxes, and the like.

Because most public programs have a specific clientele, an administrator has a strong incentive to stay close to his interest group and reciprocally the interest group will stay close to the agency. For the administrator the relationship is sometimes a divided pleasure, however. Although it constitutes an opportunity to gain support for his program and to expand budget and services, unless he is careful he will be accused of being dominated by the interest group and thus of failing to serve the larger public interest, which also is his responsibility. The difficulty is especially present, of course, in the case of agencies concerned with labor, agriculture, commerce, regulation, subsidies, and tax policies, areas in which millions and even billions of dollars are often at stake. In such instances, therefore, the administrator needs not only a keen political sense but also a sense of ethics so as to avoid violation of the law, conflict of interest, or breach of the public sense of moral decency.

In American government, interest groups have a greater influence on legislation (and hence on policy) than do formal political parties, even though parties are more often brokers for interest groups than tight little oligarchies with ideas of their own. With the possible exception of an occasional lawmaker, an interest group feels closer to "its" agency than to any other aspect of government; hence it is only natural that administrators should have much to do with the inception of legislation. In the field of immigration prior to World War II, for example, there were some fifty private organized groups that singly or in concert pushed a liberal kind of legislation, while a half dozen or so favored more restrictive laws. Those on the liberal side were usually religious, nationality, welfare, or civil liberties groups, whereas those opposing were patriotic or labor organizations trying to keep "cheap" labor out of the country. For both the target was the executives of the Immigration and Naturalization Service, which, like most agencies in Washington, consequently had an internal committee on future legislation to sift the many proposals coming to it.

The procedure is usually like this: In most government agencies legislation emanating from an interest group or from the agency itself is constantly to the forefront of the attention of top officials. Some of these proposals would amend existing law and some express new programs and policies. Once the agency has decided what it favors, the proposal is reviewed by the Secretary of the department, then by a division in the Bureau of the Budget *where all proposals emanating from government agencies are required by presidential order to be cleared.*

At this point, if it has not already been done, the interest groups concerned will prevail upon some congressman to introduce a bill which then becomes either a private member or an administration bill. An administration bill bears the mark of the chief executive's prestige and reputation which makes it a part of "his" program. Something similar to the procedure in Washington occurs at the municipal level where a mayor or city manager, working through councilmen, pushes the adoption of ordinances and programs worked out in the executive department.

When a bill is introduced in Congress it is assigned to the appropriate committee which then holds hearings on it. The usual procedure is for spokesmen from the interested executive department to appear first, followed by representatives of interest groups and the public. If the bill is an important one a Cabinet officer may make the opening statement; if less so, a bureau chief or an assistant secretary (sub-Cabinet level) will testify. In either case, permanent career officials also are present, and committee members are generally at least as interested in their presentations as in those of the political executives. Indeed, career officials will often be asked to give independent testimony either in addition to or as a substitute for the testimony of political officials.

This confirms what was said earlier about the career legislator being closer to the career executive, as a rule, than to the political executive. One reason is the obvious fact of friendship; longtime legislators and career administrators each have something the other needs. Second, both feel that they have become tested veterans and that most political officials are neophytes. Third, the members of the legislature believe they understand the motivations of career executives while they are less certain—at least until some time has elapsed —about political executives.

What is the motivation of the career executive? Generally speaking it is his and his agency's mature view of what constitutes the good of the service. The good of the service is that which will make it stand high in public approbation, is best for the country, and is practical.

The legislator respects the judgment of the career man who must live with whatever proposal is offered, whereas he is less sure about political executives who are often here today and gone tomorrow. Consequently, if the political executive is wise, he will make certain where the career men in his department stand before he launches a campaign for new legislation. A private word from a career official to a seasoned veteran of the legislative process will often finish the chances of a bill before it gets started. In theory, perhaps, this should not be so but in fact it happens so often that the reality of it must be recognized.

The upshot is that administrators have much to do with the determination of public policy, whether it is conservative, traditional, progressive, liberal, or a compromise. If the tone of a particular bureau is lethargic its chief will usually follow the path of least resistance, which means that new policies and departures are discouraged. For this reason among others, career executives should be even better grounded in sociology and political economy—in recognizing the public interest—than in how to get along with political officials, which more often than not is something they learn very early.

In earlier chapters where reference was made to the new elite of government career executives, the financial and quantitative aspects of public programs were noted. Even more important is *the influence of career officials on public policy and decisions governing the fate of the nation.* The reason is that although career officials do not often appear in the political limelight, they do constitute the second level of organization where most of the work of the world is accomplished. Indeed, whether it be in large corporations, labor unions, universities, or some other institution, it is generally the practical man experienced in getting things done who guides the destiny of the enterprise and who therefore has the greatest influence on it. This is due partly to his continuity in office, partly to his objectivity, partly to his skill as an administrator who can produce results. In most organizations there is usually a man out front who meets the public and a second man who is the operator and on whom the enterprise depends.

This is not meant to depreciate the role of the political executive in government. On the contrary, in all decisions of any consequence his must always be the last word, for anything less would constitute a subversion of democracy and popular control. Unfortunately the American political official is not as professionalized as he should be, nor do he and his political party provide the continuity in policy and personnel needed for strong, responsible leadership. So long as this is true the relation of career official and career legislator will remain the dominant force in American politics, aided and abetted by the pressure groups that focus upon both of them. . . .

Public administrators generally consider pressure group support to be more an advantage than a handicap and wish they could secure the same kind of support from the legislature. While the current fashion is to castigate legislatures, especially Congress, those who believe in representative government realize that the legislature, being directly chosen by and speaking for the people, is the fulcrum by which government moves society.

Most of the difficulties encountered by legislatures are similar to those of administrators everywhere. As W. F. Willoughby so persuasively argued in his *Principles of Public Administration,* the work of a legislature differs from that of the executive or the judicial branches; nevertheless it is an organization and hence subject to the same principles and tools of analysis as they are. Few legislatures have ever done a proper job analysis inventory of themselves; even more rarely have they followed through with good effect. Like any organization, a legislature also must get the facts when there is a problem to be solved, analyze alternatives, organize so as to do its job effectively and responsibly, and concentrate on first things first. It must secure able personnel, arrange and oversee their responsibilities, and coordinate the whole effort to emphasize policy and accomplishment.

This is easy to say, harder to do. Legislatures make fundamental policy in the form of statute law. This law becomes the administrator's mandate, the legal basis on which he operates. Hence the quality of administration depends in no small part upon the quality of legislation. The main difficulty is that in terms of job analysis, legislators have so many other demands on their time that they have increasingly less to give to issues of high policy.

The Legislative Reorganization Act of 1946 made some improvements in the organization of Congress but for the obvious reason of vested institutional interests, failed to go far enough. There are still too many committees and not enough joint committees of the House and Senate. There are still too many congressional investigations, which sometimes turn out to be fishing expeditions, and not all of them are conducted by major standing committees. Although each major political party now has an internal policy committee, and although the major standing committees are sufficiently well staffed to be able to develop information independently and are no longer exclusively dependent in this matter on the executive departments, and although joint conferences between congressional leaders and the President are increasingly frequent, nevertheless Congress is still unable to develop reasonable priorities and timetables so as to take prompt and effective action in the solution of its own problems, to say nothing of problems relating to the needs of the nation. Legislatures should, of course, take time to air public issues and educate as well as heed public opinion in the process. But even for this function there seems to be less time each year.

There have been a number of proposals to remedy legislative weaknesses in the United States but since these go beyond the legitimate scope of public administration, only some of the more important ones will be mentioned here: Should there be further experimentation with unicameralism, which theoretically is more efficient than the two-chamber system? Are many legislatures too large to be effective? Should the majority political party, when it also controls the executive, be required to guarantee its program, in addition to trying to win the next election? Should there be a question period during which top administrators might regularly appear to explain and justify their policies and actions? Might not this procedure reduce the number of fishing expeditions? If a legislative-executive stalemate occurs, or if the legislative majority votes a lack of confidence in the chief executive, should new elections be held forthwith? Should the seniority system which currently thwarts the majority will be modified or even abolished so as more easily to secure key committee chairmen who favor the policies of the party in power? Should filibusters be controlled by changes in legislative rules? Should the power of the Rules Committee, which may refuse to allow a bill to be considered on the floor of the chamber, be modified so as to allow bills to be called up by a simple majority vote?

Such questions lie at the center of the average administrator's customary feeling of frustration at the hand of the legislature.

The basic conflict in the American system of government is the result of institutional jealousy between the legislative and executive branches. Institutions are naturally competitive. It is not the people in them that make it so; people are merely pawns in a kind of game. This fact becomes clear if one has served at different times as legislator and as administrator. In each case, one's psychology changes quite rapidly. The lawmaker finds himself thinking: How easy administrators have it. They are appointed but I must win an election. Their jobs are permanent but mine ends in two or four years unless I can be reelected. Their jobs are definite; mine is ambiguous and confusing. They have all the help they need; I feel powerless. They don't know who is boss. It is we who should be initiating legislation, but it is they who do it and ask us to serve as their agents. Their main interest is to spend more money and build new empires; I must stop them. They seem to think that they should automatically get whatever they need. They will not recognize that we are the boss.

As a result of this jealousy, even former legislators elected to executive office have as much trouble securing the legislation they want as one who has never had legislative experience at all.

Structural remedies must eventually be found to overcome these jealousies, but in the meantime there is much the administrator can do if he has the right understanding and attitude. He must recognize that the legislature is in fact the boss, and that if an administrator respects the members of the legislature, they will respect him. It must not be assumed that because they are politicians they are somehow different from him. He must act in a friendly manner toward the members of his committee. He must tell them of his difficulties and failures as well as of his triumphs, never try to cover up, hide behind a superior, or blow his own horn. And he must give credit where credit is due. When he is to appear before his legislative committee or the appropriations committee, he must anticipate their questions, make his statement logical and complete, be as specific as possible about statistics and figures, let them know that he would like, if possible, to accomplish the same work with less money and personnel. To make his committee management-minded he must first become legislative-minded. And finally, he must recognize that every legislative committee wants above all to make its independent judgment.

Although the foregoing admonitions do not constitute a sure formula for success, they will go a long way toward establishing a comfortable relationship between the administrator and his legislative boss. Handled with a sophisticated understanding of the situation, an appearance before a legislative committee can be a pleasure instead of an ordeal.

Finally, since for the administrator politics is primarily policy and only secondarily political parties, it is an advantage to have consciously thought about what constitutes the public interest in his own field of activity. The public interest is always broader than group interest, although that is the usual starting point. The public interest involves a series of questions familiar to philosophers and political economists in particular: What is the effect of a given course of action on people? On national strength? On economic well-being? On self-determination? On respect for the law? On equality of opportunity? On opportunity for self-growth? On long-range interests? On the reconciliation of public and private interest?

On any legislative committee the majority will sit up and take notice when an administrator talks sense about such issues. To talk this kind of sense, the administrator must start early in life to think about and study fundamental questions that have to do with political economy, and then profit from experience and reading. The administrator who keeps abreast of the issues and developments in his field will find most politicians not only challenging but compatible.

In the final analysis, what the administrator thinks of politics and how well he fares in it greatly depends on his attitudes toward the subject. Consequently the recent change in administrative thinking about politics is likely to push the solution of the still unresolved issues relating to better intragovernmental operation. Just as any administrative program is effective only when the parts combine smoothly, so in the wider reaches of government the cooperative relationship of legislature and administration is the key to the fostering of the public interest.

POWER AND ADMINISTRA-TION

NORTON LONG

There is no more forlorn spectacle in the administrative world than an agency and a program possessed of statutory life, armed with executive orders, sustained in the courts, yet stricken with paralysis and deprived of power. An object of contempt to its enemies and of despair to its friends.

The lifeblood of administration is power. Its attainment, mainte-nance, increase, dissipation, and loss are subjects the practitioner and student can ill afford to neglect. Loss of realism and failure are almost certain consequences. This is not to deny that important parts of public administration are so deeply entrenched in the habits of the community, so firmly supported by the public, or so clearly necessary as to be able to take their power base for granted and concentrate on the purely professional side of their problems. But even these islands of the blessed are not immune from the plague of politics, as witness the fate of the hapless Bureau of Labor Statistics and the perennial menace of the blind 5 percent across-the-board budget cut. Perhaps Carlyle's aphorism holds here, "The healthy know not of their health but only the sick." To stay healthy one needs to recognize that health is a fruit, not a birthright. Power is only one of the considerations that must be weighed in administration, but of all it is the most over-looked in theory and the most dangerous to overlook in practice.

From *Public Administration Review*, Vol. 9 (Winter 1949), pp. 257–264. Norton Long is Professor of Political Science, University of Illinois. Reprinted with per-mission of the author and the American Society of Public Administration.

The power resources of an administrator or an agency are not disclosed by a legal search of titles and court decisions or by examining appropriations or budgetary allotments. Legal authority and a treasury balance are necessary but politically insufficient bases of administration. Administrative rationality requires a critical evaluation of the whole range of complex and shifting forces on whose support, acquiescence, or temporary impotence the power to act depends.

Analysis of the sources from which power is derived and the limitations they impose is as much a dictate of prudent administration as sound budgetary procedure. The bankruptcy that comes from an unbalanced power budget has consequences far more disastrous than the necessity of seeking a deficiency appropriation. The budgeting of power is a basic subject matter of a realistic science of administration.

It may be urged that for all but the top hierarchy of the administrative structure the question of power is irrelevant. Legislative authority and administrative orders suffice. Power adequate to the function to be performed flows down the chain of command. Neither statute nor executive order, however, confers more than legal authority to act. Whether Congress or President can impart the substance of power as well as the form depends upon the line-up of forces in the particular case. A price control law wrung from a reluctant Congress by an amorphous and unstable combination of consumer and labor groups is formally the same as a law enacting a support price program for agriculture backed by the disciplined organizations of farmers and their congressmen. The differences for the scope and effectiveness of administration are obvious. The Presidency, like Congress, responds to and translates the pressures that play upon it. The real mandate contained in an Executive order varies with the political strength of the group demand embodied in it, and in the context of other group demands.

Both Congress and President do focus the general political energies of the community and are so considerably more than mere means for transmitting organized pressures. Yet power is not concentrated by the structure of government or politics into the hands of a leadership with a capacity to budget it among a diverse set of administrative activities. A picture of the Presidency as a reservoir of authority from which the lower echelons of administration draw life and vigor is an idealized distortion of reality.

A similar criticism applies to any like claim for an agency head in his agency. Only in varying degrees can the powers of subordinate officials be explained as resulting from the chain of command. Rarely is such an explanation a satisfactory account of the sources of power.

To deny that power is derived exclusively from superiors in the hierarchy is to assert that subordinates stand in a feudal relation in which to a degree they fend for themselves and acquire support peculiarly their own. A structure of interests friendly or hostile, vague and general or compact and well-defined, encloses each significant center of administrative discretion. This structure is an important determinant of the scope of possible action. As a source of power and authority it is a competitor of the formal hierarchy.

Not only does political power flow in from the sides of an organization, as it were; it also flows up the organization to the center from the constituent parts. When the staff of the Office of War Mobilization and Reconversion advised a hard-pressed agency to go out and get itself some popular support so that the President could afford to support it, their action reflected the realities of power rather than political cynicism.

It is clear that the American system of politics does not generate enough power at any focal point of leadership to provide the conditions for an even partially successful divorce of politics from administration. Subordinates cannot depend on the formal chain of command to deliver enough political power to permit them to do their jobs. Accordingly they must supplement the resources available through the hierarchy with those they can muster on their own, or accept the consequences in frustration—a course itself not without danger. Administrative rationality demands that objectives be determined and sights set in conformity with a realistic appraisal of power position and potential.

The theory of administration has neglected the problem of the sources and adequacy of power, in all probability because of a distaste for the disorderliness of American political life and a belief that this disorderliness is transitory. An idealized picture of the British parliamentary system as a Platonic form to be realized or approximated has exerted a baneful fascination in the field. The majority party with a mandate at the polls and a firmly seated leadership in the Cabinet seems to solve adequately the problem of the supply of power necessary to permit administration to concentrate on the fulfillment of accepted objectives. It is a commonplace that the American party system provides neither a mandate for a platform nor a mandate for a leadership.

Accordingly, the election over, its political meaning must be explored by the diverse leaders in the executive and legislative branches. Since the parties have failed to discuss issues, mobilize majorities in their terms, and create a working political consensus on measures to be carried out, the task is left for others—most prominently the agencies concerned. Legislation passed and powers granted are frequently politically premature. Thus the Council of Economic Advisers was given legislative birth before political acceptance of its functions existed. The agencies to which tasks are assigned must devote themselves to the creation of an adequate consensus to permit administration. The mandate that the parties do not supply must be attained through public relations and the mobilization of group support. Pendleton Herring and others have shown just how vital this support is for agency action.

The theory that agencies should confine themselves to communicating policy suggestions to executive and legislature, and refrain from appealing to their clientele and the public, neglects the failure of the parties to provide either a clear-cut decision as to what they should do or an adequately mobilized political support for a course of action. The bureaucracy under the American political system has a large share of responsibility for the public promotion of policy and even more in organizing the political basis for its survival and growth. It is generally recognized that the agencies have a special competence in the technical aspects of their fields which of necessity gives them a rightful policy initiative. In addition, they have or develop a shrewd understanding of the politically feasible in the group structure within which they work. Above all, in the eyes of their supporters and their enemies they represent the institutionalized embodiment of policy, an enduring organization actually or potentially capable of mobilizing power behind policy. The survival interests and creative drives of administrative organizations combine with clientele pressures to compel such mobilization. The party system provides no enduring institutional representation for group interest at all comparable to that of the bureaus of the Department of Agriculture. Even the subject matter committees of Congress function in the shadow of agency permanency.

The bureaucracy is recognized by all interested groups as a major channel of representation to such an extent that Congress rightly feels the competition of a rival. The weakness in party structure both permits and makes necessary the present dimensions of the political activities of the administrative branch—permits because it fails to protect administration from pressures and fails to provide adequate direction and support, makes necessary because it fails to develop a consensus on a leadership and a program that makes possible administration on the basis of accepted decisional premises.

Agencies and bureaus more or less perforce are in the business of building, maintaining, and increasing their political support. They lead and in large part are led by the diverse groups whose influence sustains them. Frequently they lead and are themselves led in conflicting directions. This is not due to a dull-witted incapacity to see the contradictions in their behavior but is an almost inevitable result of the contradictory nature of their support.

Herbert Simon has shown that administrative rationality depends on the establishment of uniform value premises in the decisional centers of organization. Unfortunately, the value premises of those forming vital elements of political support are often far from uniform. These elements are in Barnard's and Simon's sense "customers" of the organization and therefore parts of the organization whose wishes are clothed with a very real authority. A major and most time-consuming aspect of administration consists of the wide range of activities designed to secure enough "customer" acceptance to survive and, if fortunate, develop a consensus adequate to program formulation and execution.

To varying degrees, dependent on the breadth of acceptance of their programs, officials at every level of significant discretion must make their estimates of the situation, take stock of their resources, and plan accordingly. A keen appreciation of the real components of their organization is the beginning of wisdom. These components will be found to stretch far beyond the government payroll. Within the government they will encompass Congress, congressmen, committees, courts, other agencies, presidential advisers, and the President. The Aristotelian analysis of constitutions is equally applicable and equally necessary to an understanding of administrative organization.

The broad alliance of conflicting groups that makes up presidential majorities scarcely coheres about any definite pattern of objectives, nor has it by the alchemy of the party system had its collective power concentrated in an accepted leadership with a personal mandate. The conciliation and maintenance of this support is a necessary condition of the attainment and retention of office involving, as Madison so well saw, "the spirit of party and faction in the necessary and ordinary operations of government." The President must in large part be, if not all things to all men, at least many things to many men. As a consequence, the contradictions in his power base invade administration. The often criticized apparent cross-purposes of the Roosevelt regime cannot be put down to inept administration until the political facts are weighed. Were these apparently self-defeating measures reasonably related to the general maintenance of the composite majority of the Administration? The first objective—ultimate patriotism apart— of the administrator is the attainment and retention of the power on which his tenure of office depends. This is the necessary pre-condition for the accomplishment of all other objectives.

The same ambiguities that arouse the scorn of the naive in the electoral campaigns of the parties are equally inevitable in administration and for the same reasons. Victory at the polls does not yield either a clear-cut grant of power or a unified majority support for a coherent program. The task of the Presidency lies in feeling out the alternatives of policy which are consistent with the retention and increase of the group support on which the Administration rests. The lack of a budgetary theory (so frequently deplored) is not due to any incapacity to apply rational analysis to the comparative contribution of the various activities of government to a determinate hierarchy of purposes. It more probably stems from a fastidious distaste for the frank recognition of the budget as a politically expedient allocation of resources. Appraisal in terms of their political contribution to the Administration provides almost a sole common denominator between the Forest Service and the Bureau of Engraving.

Integration of the administrative structure through an over-all purpose in terms of which tasks and priorities can be established is an emergency phenomenon. Its realization, only partial at best, has been limited to war and the extremity of depression. Even in wartime the Farm Bureau Federation, the American Federation of Labor, the Congress of Industrial Organizations, the National Association of Manufacturers, the Chamber of Commerce, and a host of lesser interests resisted coordination of themselves and the agencies concerned with their interests. A Presidency temporarily empowered by intense mass popular support acting in behalf of a generally accepted and simplified purpose can, with great difficulty, bribe, cajole, and coerce a real measure of joint action. The long-drawn-out battle for conversion and the debacle of orderly reconversion underline the difficulty of attaining, and the transitory nature of, popularly based emergency power. Only in crises are the powers of the Executive nearly adequate to impose a common plan of action on the executive branch, let alone the economy.

In ordinary times the manifold pressures of our pluralistic society work themselves out in accordance with the balance of forces prevailing in Congress and the agencies. Only to a limited degree is the process subject to responsible direction or review by President or party leadership.

The program of the President cannot be a Gosplan for the government precisely because the nature of his institutional and group support gives him insufficient power. The personal unity of the Presidency cannot perform the function of Hobbes' sovereign since his office lacks the authority of Hobbes' contract. Single headedness in the executive gives no assurance of singleness of purpose. It only insures that the significant pressures in a society will be brought to bear on one office. Monarchy solves the problem of giving one plan to a multitude only when the plenitude of its authority approaches dictatorship. Impatient social theorists in all ages have turned to the philosopher king as a substitute for consensus. Whatever else he may become, it is difficult to conceive of the American president ruling as a philosopher king, even with the advice of the Executive Office.

The monarchical solution to the administrative problems posed by the lack of a disciplined party system capable of giving firm leadership and a program to the legislature is a modern variant of the dreams of the eighteenth century savants and well nigh equally divorced from a realistic appraisal of social realities.

Much of administrative thought, when it does not assume the value of coordination for coordination's sake, operates on the assumption that there must be something akin to Rousseau's *volonté générale* in administration to which the errant *volonté de tous* of the bureaus can and should be made to conform. This will-o'-the-wisp was made the object of an illuminating search by Pendleton Herring in his *Public Administration and the Public Interest*. The answer for Rousseau was enlightened dictatorship or counting the votes. The administrative equivalent to the latter is the resultant of the relevant pressures, as Herring shows. The first alternative seems to require at least the potency of the British Labour party and elsewhere has needed the disciplined organization of a fascist, nazi, or communist party to provide the power and consensus necessary to coordinate the manifold activities of government to a common plan.

Dictatorship, as Sigmund Neumann has observed, is a substitute for institutions which is required to fill the vacuum when traditional institutions break down. Force supplies the compulsion and guide to action in place of the normal routines of unconscious habit. Administrative organizations, however much they may appear the creations of art, are institutions produced in history and woven in the web of social relationships that gives them life and being. They present the same refractory material to the hand of the political artist as the rest of society of which they form a part.

Just as the economists have attempted to escape the complexities of institutional reality by taking refuge in the fictionless realm of theory, so some students of administration, following their lead, have seen in the application of the doctrine of opportunity costs a clue to a science of administration. Valuable as this may be in a restricted way, Marx has more light to throw on the study of institutions. It is in the dynamics and interrelations of institutions that we have most hope of describing and therefore learning to control administrative behavior.

The difficulty of coordinating government agencies lies not only in the fact that bureaucratic organizations are institutions having survival interests which may conflict with their rational adaptation to over-all purpose, but even more in their having roots in society. Coordination of the varied activities of a modern government almost of necessity involves a substantial degree of coordination of the economy. Coordination of government agencies involves far more than changing the behavior and offices of officials in Washington and the field. It involves the publics that are implicated in their normal functioning. To coordinate fiscal policy, agricultural policy, labor policy, foreign policy, and military policy, to name a few major areas, moves beyond the range of government charts and the habitat of the bureaucrats to the market place and to where the people live and work. This suggests that the reason why government reorganization is so difficult is that far more than government in the formal sense is involved in reorganization. One could overlook this in the limited government of the nineteenth century but the multi-billion dollar government of the mid-twentieth permits no facile dichotomy between government and economy. Economy and efficiency are the two objectives a laissez faire society can prescribe in peacetime as overall government objectives. Their inadequacy either as motivation or standards has long been obvious. A planned economy clearly requires a planned government. But, if one can afford an unplanned economy, apart from gross extravagance, there seems no compelling and therefore, perhaps, no sufficiently powerful reason for a planned government.

Basic to the problems of administrative rationality is that of organizational identification and point of view. To whom is one loyal —unit, section, branch, division, bureau, department, administration, government, country, people, world history, or what? Administrative analysis frequently assumes that organizational identification should occur in such a way as to merge primary organization loyalty in a larger synthesis. The good of the part is to give way to the reasoned good of the whole. This is most frequently illustrated in the rationalizations used to counter self-centered demands of primary groups for funds and personnel. Actually the competition between governmental power centers, rather than the rationalizations, is the effective instrument of coordination.

Where there is a clear common product on whose successful production the sub-groups depend for the attainment of their own satisfaction, it is possible to demonstrate to almost all participants the desirability of cooperation. The shoe factory produces shoes, or else, for all concerned. But the government as a whole and many of its component parts have no such identifiable common production which all depend. Like the proverbial Heinz, there are fifty-seven or more varieties unified, if at all, by a common political profit and loss account.

Administration is faced by somewhat the same dilemma as economics. There are propositions about the behavior patterns conducive to full employment—welfare economics. On the other hand, there are propositions about the economics of the individual firm— the counsel of the business schools. It is possible to show with considerable persuasiveness that sound considerations for the individual firm may lead to a depression if generally adopted, a result desired by none of the participants. However, no single firm can afford by itself to adopt the course of collective wisdom; in the absence of a common power capable of enforcing decisions premised on the supremacy of the collective interest, *sauve qui peut* is common sense.

The position of administrative organizations is not unlike the position of particular firms. Just as the decisions of the firms could be coordinated by the imposition of a planned economy so could those of the component parts of the government. But just as it is possible to operate a formally unplanned economy by the loose coordination of the market, in the same fashion it is possible to operate a government by the loose coordination of the play of political forces through its institutions.

The unseen hand of Adam Smith may be little in evidence in either case. One need not believe in a doctrine of social or administrative harmony to believe that formal centralized planning—while perhaps desirable and in some cases necessary—is not a must. The complicated logistics of supplying the city of New York runs smoothly down the grooves of millions of well adapted habits projected from a distant past. It seems naive on the one hand to believe in the possibility of a vast, intricate, and delicate economy operating with a minimum of formal over-all direction, and on the other to doubt that a relatively simple mechanism such as the government can be controlled largely by the same play of forces. . . .

If the advent of Keynesian economics and the erosion of laissez faire have created the intellectual conditions requisite for the formulation of over-all government policy, they do not by any means guarantee the political conditions necessary for its implementation. We can see quite clearly that the development of an integrated administration requires an integrating purpose. The ideals of Locke, Smith, Spencer, and their American disciples deny the need for such a purpose save for economy and efficiency's sake. Marx, Keynes, and their followers by denying the validity of the self-regulating economy have endowed the state with an over-arching responsibility in terms of which broad coordination of activities is not only intellectually possible but theoretically, at least, necessary. Intellectual perception of the need for this coordination, however, has run well ahead of the public's perception of it and of the development of a political channeling of power adequate to its administrative implementation.

Most students of administration are planners of some sort. Most congressmen would fly the label like the plague. Most bureaucrats, whatever their private faith, live under two jealous gods, their particular clientele and the loyalty check. Such a condition might, if it exists as described, cast doubt on whether even the intellectual conditions for rational administrative coordination exist. Be that as it may, the transition from a government organized in clientele departments and bureaus, each responding to the massive feudal power of organized business, organized agriculture, and organized labor, to a government integrated about a paramount national purpose will require a political power at least as great as that which tamed the earlier feudalism. It takes a sharp eye or a tinted glass to see such an organized power on the American scene. Without it, administrative organization for over-all coordination has the academic air of South American constitution making. One is reminded of the remark attributed to the Austrian economist Mises; on being told that the facts did not agree with his theory, he replied *"desto schlechter für die Tatsache."*

It is highly appropriate to consider how administrators should behave to meet the test of efficiency in a planned polity; but in the absence of such a polity and while, if we like, struggling to get it, a realistic science of administration will teach administrative behavior appropriate to the existing political system.

A close examination of the presidential system may well bring one to conclude that administrative rationality in it is a different matter from that applicable to the British idea. The American Presidency is an office that has significant monarchical characteristics despite its limited term and elective nature. The literature on court and palace has many an insight applicable to the White House. Access to the President, reigning favorites, even the court jester, are topics that show the continuity of institutions. The maxims of LaRochefoucauld and the memoirs of the Duc de Saint Simon have a refreshing realism for the operator on the Potomac.

The problem of rival factions in the President's family is as old as the famous struggle between Jefferson and Hamilton, as fresh and modern as the latest cabal against John Snyder. Experience seems to show that this personal and factional struggle for the President's favor is a vital part of the process of representation. The vanity, personal ambition, or patriotism of the contestants soon clothes itself in the generalities of principle and the clique aligns itself with groups beyond the capital. Subordinate rivalry is tolerated if not encouraged by so many able executives that it can scarcely be attributed to administrative ineptitude. The wrangling tests opinion, uncovers information that would otherwise never rise to the top, and provides effective opportunity for decision rather than mere ratification of pre-arranged plans. Like most judges, the Executive needs to hear argument for his own instruction. The alternatives presented by subordinates in large part determine the freedom and the creative opportunity of their superiors. The danger of becoming a Merovingian is a powerful incentive to the maintenance of fluidity in the structure of power.

The fixed character of presidential tenure makes it necessary that subordinates be politically expendable. The President's men must be willing to accept the blame for failures not their own. Machiavelli's teaching on how princes must keep the faith bears re-reading. Collective responsibility is incompatible with a fixed term of office. As it tests the currents of public opinion, the situation on the Hill, and the varying strength of the organized pressures, the White House alters and adapts the complexion of the Administration. Loyalties to programs or to groups and personal pride and interest frequently conflict with whole-souled devotion to the Presidency. In fact, since such devotion is not made mandatory by custom, institutions, or the facts of power, the problem is perpetually perplexing to those who must choose.

The balance of power between executive and legislature is constantly subject to the shifts of public and group support. The latent tendency of the American Congress is to follow the age-old parliamentary precedents and to try to reduce the President to the role of constitutional monarch. Against this threat and to secure his own initiative, the President's resources are primarily demagogic, with the weaknesses and strengths that dependence on mass popular appeal implies. The unanswered question of American government—"who is boss?"—constantly plagues administration. The disruption of unity of command is not just the problem of Taylor's functional foreman, but goes to the stability and uniformity of basic decisional premises essential to consequent administration.

It is interesting to speculate on the consequences for administration of the full development of congressional or presidential government. A leadership in Congress that could control the timetable of the House and Senate would scarcely content itself short of reducing the President's Cabinet to what in all probability it was first intended to be, a modified version of the present Swiss executive. Such leadership could scarcely arise without centrally organized, disciplined, national parties far different from our present shambling alliances of state and local machines.

A Presidency backed by a disciplined party controlling a majority in Congress would probably assimilate itself to a premiership by association of legislative leadership in the formulation of policy and administration. In either line of development the crucial matter is party organization. For the spirit of the party system determines the character of the government.

That the American party system will develop toward the British ideal is by no means a foregone conclusion. The present oscillation between a strong demagogic Presidency and a defensively powerful congressional oligarchy may well prove a continuing pattern of American politics, as it was of Roman. In the absence of a party system providing an institutionalized centripetal force in our affairs, it is natural to look to the Presidency as Goldsmith's weary traveler looked to the throne.

The Presidency of the United States, however, is no such throne as the pre-World War I *Kaiserreich* that provided the moral and political basis for the Prussian bureaucracy. Lacking neutrality and mystique, it does not even perform the function of the British monarchy in providing a psychological foundation for the permanent civil service. A leaderless and irresponsible Congress frequently makes it appear the strong point of the republic. The Bonapartist experience in France, the Weimar Republic, and South American examples nearer home, despite important social differences, are relevant to any thoughtful consideration of building a solution to legislative anarchy on the unity of the executive.

The present course of American party development gives little ground for optimism that a responsible two party system capable of uniting Congress and Executive in a coherent program will emerge. The increasingly critical importance of the federal budget for the national economy and the inevitable impact of world power status on the conduct of foreign affairs make inescapable the problem of stable leadership in the American system. Unfortunately they by no means insure a happy or indeed any solution.

Attempts to solve administrative problems in isolation from the structure of power and purpose in the polity are bound to prove illusory. The reorganization of Congress to create responsibility in advance of the development of party responsibility was an act of piety to principle, of educational value; but as a practical matter it raised a structure without foundation. In the same way, reorganization of the executive branch to centralize administrative power in the Presidency while political power remains dispersed and divided may effect improvement, but in a large sense it must fail. The basic prerequisite to the administration of the textbooks is a responsible two party system. The means to its attainment are a number one problem for students of administration. What Schattschneider calls the struggle for party government may sometime yield us the responsible parliamentary two-party system needed to underpin our present administrative theory. Until that happy time, exploration of the needs and necessities of our present system is a high priority task of responsible scholarship.

COMMENTARY

From these three selections it should be apparent that the focus of inquiry into administration assumes fundamentally different proportions when political phenomena are included as integral elements of the administrative decision-making process. Although numerous themes were advanced by Stein, the Dimocks, and Long, a basic premise shared by each was that efficiency is a secondary consideration. Indeed, the main thrust of the administration-as-politics approach was aimed at questioning the validity of the efficiency syndrome which stood as the central element in the management science school of thought. This is not to say that efficiency, *per se*, was deprecated by the "political," or "policy," or "power" oriented students of administration. Rather, the main objection to managerial efficiency rested on the premise that the primary function of government was to satisfy a wide range of subjectively held values and needs within the body politic, and the manner in which this function was performed simply could not be gauged in terms of a non-qualitative standard.

Thus, the public administrator had to become politically attuned because "politics involves a choice among alternatives that involve values, philosophies, ethical considerations" (Dimocks), and this meant that "the administrator must rely on his own system of values . . . his sense of justice and fair play" (Stein). The Dimocks' observation that "politics is problem-solving in an attempt to meet human needs," is a good example of how politics and administration were viewed synonymously by many scholars during the Roosevelt and Truman eras. But, interestingly enough, if this proposition was changed to read: *"administration* is problem-solving in an attempt to meet human needs," then certainly most management science advocates could readily concur. The essential difference between the two groups can be seen by posing the question: How is politics (or administration) to be utilized as a problem-solving device in meeting human needs? Here the management science school would respond, "In the most efficient and economical manner possible," which meant insuring the maintenance of a highly disciplined, well-organized, and totally dedicated internal managerial or bureaucratic apparatus. Stein, representing the administration-as-politics group, provided the administrator with an entirely different frame of reference. In this instance, the utilization of politics as a problem-solving mechanism in meeting human needs referred to "the administrator's understanding and pursuit of his objectives and his relations with the *social* environment *outside* his agency that affects or is capable of affecting its operation." Thus, administrative objectives were defined by the social and political forces manifested in an agency's external environment, and the function of the administrator was to respond to those forces in a manner consistent with the objectives of his organization. "If substantive decisions," wrote Stein, ". . . are arrived at by wise and informed use of the resources of administration, and by *intelligent appreciation of the political environment,* they are far more likely to be sound than if they are arrived at in hit-or-miss or doctrinaire fashion" (italics added).

The administrative system, therefore, was given meaning and substance, not by its internal organizational pattern but rather by the political sensitivity of those who controlled the decision-making process. An "intelligent appreciation of the political environment" was the pragmatic dogma of men like Dimock, for instance, who placed greater reliance on such traits as intuition, tact, personality, and character than on concepts such as efficiency, objectivity, facts, or certainty. Politics came to mean the result of feeding all the subjective values of man into the administrative process; this result was elevated, at times, to almost ethereal proportions. "Politics," according to the Dimocks, "is the quest for human betterment by public means," or it is "the purposeful activity by which men seek to live a better life." Administration *is* politics; man *is* a political animal; public policy *is* the vortex of social and political forces in society. In the final analysis, both Stein and the Dimocks seemed to suggest that the efficacy of the administrative system depended upon the extent to which the administrator, *per se,* was endowed with a compassionate sensitivity for the political and social temper of his external environment.

This holistic image of the public administrator, however, has to be kept in its proper perspective. True, the federal executive could direct the quest for human betterment through purposeful activity, but all four writers seemed to agree that the most purposeful activity was that designed to insure organizational self-preservation. Long was very clear in this regard; the lifeblood of administration was power and the "first object . . . of the administrator is the attainment and retention . . . of . . . power. . . ." But power for what purpose? Quite simply stated, power for the purpose of survival; power for the purpose of promoting and protecting the administrator's jurisdiction. To be responsible, an administrator had to be responsive to the needs and wants of his "constituency," but a close reading of Stein and the Dimocks suggests that administrative responsiveness was directly related to the extent that agency equilibrium was threatened by external forces.

Long provided the most relevant explanation for this pattern of administrative behavior. To him the atrophy of the political party structure in America made administrative involvement in policy promotion absolutely essential. The administrator assumed a vital function in organizing selected aspects of "the public interest," and, given the atrophy of the party system combined with the malapportionment of Congress, he also served as a major channel of representation for selected "publics" in the body politic.

The overall political system described by Stein, the Dimocks, and Long was one in which political power was diffused and highly decentralized. Effective administrative action depended not on formal authority, but on *de facto* power, ruthlessly acquired (if necessary), jealously guarded, and prudently utilized. The institutionalization of prudence implicit in Madison became the primary consideration of most writers of the "administrative politics" period.

Prudential politics places great emphasis on the tactical skills of the administrator. Thus, the "public interest," as defined in terms of public policy decisions, was the result of the skill of the administrator in reconciling competing forces in a manner which enhanced his own *de facto* power base. It is important to emphasize, however, that while a pragmatic administrative flexibility was assumed by most of these writers, the administrator was narrowly constrained by executive structure, congressional committees, statutory provisions, pressure group interests, and, occasionally, political party considerations. To a very real extent, politics—and hence, administration—became the Great Game, and, despite the Dimocks' disclaimer ("politics, which some blasé intellectuals regarded as merely a game, is now recognized as serious business"), Stein suggested that "the individual administrator can do very little about *changing the rules of the game*" (italics added). The politics of administration meant adhering to the rules of the game, and to improve his administrative competence, the prudent political executive sought to add to his tactical skills by cultivating support—i.e., mobilizing friends, manipulating political symbols, and most importantly, acting deferentially before his congressional patrons. "He must recognize the legislature is in fact the boss," the Dimocks noted, "and that if an administrator respects the members of the legislature, they will respect him."

The politics-of-administration approach reflected the American political system as it was, and not as it should be, and attempted to fashion a "public interest" focus within this political context. Stein, the Dimocks, and Long demonstrated the concept of political rationality at its best. They recalled the proposition advanced by Diesing that, "in a political decision . . . action is never based on the merits of the proposal but always on who makes it and who opposes it. . . . The best available proposal should never be accepted just because it is the best; it should be deferred, objected to, discussed, until major opposition disappears." Within this context, dissent had to be dissipated before action could be effected, and here the burden of responsibility rested almost exclusively with the individual administrator.

But it is not fair to conclude that in the politics approach, efficiency became an irrelevant consideration. To the extent that efficiency could be achieved (costs minimized and benefits maximized) within a political context (one in which threats to organizational equilibrium from external forces could be controlled), it became a valid operating criterion. But if agency equilibrium could be maintained only through inefficient operating procedures, economic and management principles had to be subordinated to the political realities of life. Hitch wrote that organizational objectives should never be used to obviate the canons of efficiency and economy; the administration-as-politics writers would be prepared to defend the proposition that the canons of efficiency and economy should never stand in the way of achieving the organization's objectives.

But what were the goals of the administrative branch as it functioned within this political system? The "public interest," human welfare, the betterment of society were, of course, logical goals to advance, but the main assumption of this school of thought, as represented by Long, was that the "public interest" would be served to the extent that the individual administrator was successful in promoting and protecting his agency's image. This meant, in effect, that the fundamental objective of every administrator was organizational survival, and survival could be enhanced only through the acquisition of power, the lifeblood of administration.

If this assessment is correct, then the concept of the politically attuned administrator as a man compassionately sensitive to the social needs and wants of his "constituents" should be reevaluated. In rejecting the doctrinaire rigidity of the management science approach, the political administrator was theoretically infused with operating discretion and flexibility. Public policy, consequently, was supposed to reflect the normative values of the body politic which had been drained dry by the qualitatively sterile management science doctrines. But if the administrator was to develop an "intelligent appreciation of the political environment"—i.e., become a political realist—then the basic objective of survival inevitably yielded a politics (and administration) of prudential pragmatism.

Pragmatism, of course, has long been considered an essential element of the American political system. However, it should also be recognized that in a truly pragmatic philosophy, the moral and ethical socio-political values become irrelevant. This is not to say that these values *per se* become irrelevant, as did Gulick, for instance, who sought to achieve a true science of administration. Instead, prudential pragmatism created a means-end relationship in which the security of the organization or agency became the all-important and compelling concern of the administrator, and any action taken short of illegal activities to insure that security constituted the administrative coda of the movement. Thus, although it is true that values did assume a prominent position in the political rationalism of these writers, it also seems fair to conclude that these were values present in the external environment and represented objects to be exploited rather than concepts to be respected.

An even more disturbing implication stems from this doctrine if it is realized that not all of the administrator's "clientele" demands were to be viewed as "free and equal." That is, every administrator would be confronted with demands, requests, and pleas from his environment for certain kinds of governmental support, but even if it were possible to satisfy all demands as they were presented, the prudent administrator would certainly disassociate himself and his agency from any demand which could jeopardize his agency's reputation. Conversely, the prudent pragmatist would not hesitate to respond affirmatively to the demands of any group which could enhance his agency's reputation—especially in the eyes of the Congress. Thus, as the amoral claims of the management science movement turned out to be sternly moral upon close examination, the proudly moral tenets of the administrative pragmatists turned out to be amoral at best, and, at worst, potentially quite immoral.

One final assessment should be noted. The management science group became excessively infatuated with the idea that the "good life" for the body politic was simply a product of a well-disciplined internal management structure, while the politics-as-administration supporters became equally convinced that the administrator was basically a politician whose major responsibility was to find harmony in the chaos of his external environment. For many students of administration, however, the political alternative to scientific management was as unacceptable as that which it sought to replace. Administration had to be more than a series of boxes neatly arranged on an organizational chart if it was to have life and form; and it had to be concerned with more than simply acquiring political power if it was to have meaning and substance. It was this search for the form and substance of administration that led another group of scholars in the post-World War II period to turn "back into" the organization, so to speak, and to focus their attention on interpersonal behavior. The Organization Man became the subject of close attention in both public and private administrative structures, and, administrative behavior (as opposed to management techniques) became the major object of the inquiry. More important, however, was the fact that organizational analysis became the object of attention of many sociologists and psychologists, and, as a consequence, administrative behavior came to be viewed as a composite of social, psychological, economic, and political forces. As can be seen in the selections which follow, the administrative behavior approach represented a logical extension of the science of administration theme as well as a natural rejection of the basic premises of that movement—i.e., hierarchical organization, centralized control and decision-making patterns, and unswerving individual loyalty to the organization.

ADMINISTRATION AS INTERPERSONAL BEHAVIOR

5

HIERARCHY AND HIERATICS

EARL LATHAM

This is an essay on the organization of a bureau. The subject deserves solemn respect. The bureau, in large measure, is the form of organization where most of the public business eventually centers. It is the place at which the major functions of government are organized and from which they are administered. For the purpose of this paper, the "bureau" is that size of administrative establishment larger than a division and not so large as a department. The observations about bureaus apply then to independent agencies also. The nomenclature is not entirely satisfactory but there are visible differences between bureaus on the one hand, and departments and divisions on the other. The department is usually a holding company of assorted services and functions organized by bureaus. Divisions perform activities designed to achieve the functions of the bureaus.

If these considerations are not strong enough to claim the attention of the gentle reader, let it be recalled that the word "bureau" is itself a reproach and a castigation. It is a word to be spoken with curled lip and a shudder of refined loathing, as when we say "bureaucrat." The words, "government by bureau" are a sneer and an insult that release explosions of apoplexy. The problems of a bureau then are obviously important since the bureau has come to bear the cross of all officialdom.

From "Hierarchy and Hieratics—A Note on Bureaus," *Employment Forum* (April 1947), pp. 1–6. Earl Latham is Professor of Political Science, Amherst College. Reprinted with permission of the author and the International Association of Personnel in Employment Security.

It is certainly not unusual to launch an exposition of such problems by scanning the ·literature, the hieratics or sacred writings of commentators, on the subject. There one can learn that bureaus should be organized by function or clientele, when they are not organized by accident or malice. When circumstance and accident beget bureaus, a light touch of coordination here and there is said to be important. Very nice things are also said about integration. Staff services almost always get favorable notices and a central place in the discussion, although the line may be mentioned sympathetically, as lords and ladies might refer with gracious pity to the "working classes," useful but dirty.

Such advices are no doubt well meant, like fathers' talk about the facts of life, but they are likely to be just as abstract. These propositions about public administration are often generalizations in which the affirmative is as true as the negative. Now generality is not an irreparable fault. At worst it is a weakness of professional habit. Referents can always be given to words of generality by relating them to their intended objects.

It is the principle behind the principle that starts curiosity, for a more fundamental difficulty than mere generality is involved. The innocent generalizations of the writers stand like pale flowers in a turbid bog of assumptions. There is a matrix that cradles each precept and gives it the family look. There is, in short, a system of beliefs about the nature of the administrative universe within which the general propositions are framed. Since cosmology is that branch of philosophy that deals with the nature of the physical universe, and a particular theory of creation is a cosmogony, this set of beliefs may be called a cosmogony of administration. When cosmology is overlaid with an epic myth about the role of divinity in the creation and maintenance of order in the physical universe, it becomes a theology. The theology of administration stands upon a familiar set of assumptions about the creation of administrative organizations.

What are the principle tenets of the theology of administration? (For latecomers, the subject is still the "bureau," considered as an administrative universe.) There are two principal tenets—an epic myth and a principle. The epic myth postulates a first cause in the person of a creator—in this case the chief of the bureau. It is the creator who fashions his particular bureaucratic world out of the void. As this godchief breathes the gift of life into his creation, there springs into being a structure of serried ranks, held in the confines of their accustomed bounds by his will and command. The mind of this secular divinity is the mind of the universe he begets, and his will is its will, his law, its law. In this mythic conception of the creation of the administrative universe, the creator may sometimes eat his children like Chronos in the Greek fable. For what the creator giveth, the creator may take away.

Having brought the administrative universe into being, the god-chief fixes its eternal form. The principle that maintains this form is the concept of hierarchy. Hierarchy is an ordered structure of inferior and superior beings in an ascending scale. The godchief dwells at the apex, from which, with his terrible eye, he can search out the hearts of his lowliest subordinates and mold their deed to his command. The graphic picture of this mythic form is the triangular shape associated with pyramids and pup tents. Hierarchy is the linchpin that locks the form. With the mythic creation to bring the bureau into being and the principle of hierarchy to fix its structure, the principal elements of the bureaucratic theology are complete. A vertical godchief fathers an orderly universe, and by his will, fixes the orbits of every star in his administrative galaxy.

Is this fanciful? Of course it is. But these assumptions are related to a science of administration, based upon observable data, as magic is to medicine. In fact our knowledge of what goes on in administration is roughly at about the stage medicine was in when the cure for typhoid was a ritual dance by a man with deer horns and a rattle. . . . But perhaps enough has been said to indicate that the parallel between standard theologies and the theology of administration is close. It is close enough to be fraternal, at least, if not filial.

What of it? To answer these three words it is necessary to ask at least twice three questions. What is the fact if the mythic conception is a fiction? What is organization? What is the grain of sense and truth in hierarchy as a frame of relations? What is the function of the chief, if not command? Are agency communications ever anything else than a "troublesome code of verbal signals, unintelligible to ordinary folk"? And, finally, what is the nature of the administrative universe, if not the extended will of the chief? These questions are the basic questions about bureaus, and they bring us to the subject, although in truth we have never left the subject. Because administration as a systematic body of knowledge is at the magic and not the medicine stage, it is more important to raise these first questions than to proceed on the basis of fictions and semantic exercises.

The following sections will discuss each of these questions and provide some answers, at least, if not conclusions.

TWO

First, as to organization. It is often stated to be the arrangement of men and materials for the accomplishment of some given purpose. That is one way of looking at organization, to be sure, but there is another way of stating it. Can you see it, feel it, taste it? Does it have weight, size, and density? Does it have personality? Where would you look to find an organization? The spectators at a baseball game are arranged by architects and engineers for the purpose of watching the game. Are they an organization? Clearly not, but why not? The answer, it may be suggested, is that the spectators don't think they are.

Organization is an idea, not a thing. It is an idea that men have about their relation to each in the accomplishment of common objectives. It does not exist anywhere but in the minds of people. It has no independent existence apart from the thoughts and understanding of men. Imagine two men, unknown to each other, trying to put out a brush fire. The first goes to a stream for a pail of water, returns and throws it on the flames. While he is at the fire, the second is at the stream. When the second is at the fire the first is at the stream. Each of them thinks that he is alone in the effort to put out the fire. Between them they extinguish it. They are nevertheless not an organization, for they have no idea of their relation to each other. Neither is combining his muscle with the other. There is no identification of each with respect to each, and together, with respect to the common object. Without this identification, organization does not exist.

Certain consequences follow from the view that organization basically is the idea that men have about their relationships to each other in joint undertakings. First, the common possession of such an idea helps to produce and maintain a sense of belonging. This sense of belonging tends to keep a group together. Second, it tends to develop a sense of not belonging that works to exclude "outsiders." The sum of these two senses is a sense of jurisdiction that is one of the elemental facts of bureaucratic life. In the establishment of a bureau or any larger or smaller unit of organization, this sense of jurisdiction has to be faced and dealt with. Within the organization, it tends to breed cults and factions. With respect to those outside the organization, it tends to breed rivalry and competition, both of the high order and the low order.

Consider the internal problem first. The bureau is going to need, say, lawyers and economists. Both of these groups show a remarkable clannishness. They exhibit a selective awareness of professional identity, and a tendency to exclude aliens to the craft. Unless regulated and controlled in the general interest, they may become clots in the blood stream of the agency. They must usually be so arranged with respect to the executive and the "line" that they serve without dominating. As staff technicians their function is to serve, not order. That is, they generally serve and do not order. Much depends upon whether the staff function is, as Pfiffner classifies them, general, technical, or auxiliary. Some of these, like the last, are "operations" themselves.

The propensity of the general and technical staff services to expand and control is a kind of internal imperialism that has to be limited else order is defeated and confusion prevails. In an excess of enthusiasm for their specialties, and a simple-minded belief that all men would be good and could be trusted if they were only lawyers, or economists, or whatever the private medicine is, they struggle for power in a high-minded way, for the good of the order. In so doing, and to the extent that they are successful, they split and diffuse the power of the agency, and prevent it from coming to a focus.

Consider next, the external problem. With respect to other agencies, the sense of jurisdiction (that is, of excluding others) produces most of the inter-bureau fights in Washington. A corollary of this attitude is the desire to become self-sufficient, the effect of which may be observed in both the internal and external relations of a bureau. The desire to be self-sufficient is based on the impulse to remain unique and to exclude others. Thus the War and Navy Departments have maintained separate procurement services for the same kinds of supplies and services. Bureaus and even divisions within bureaus recruit most of their personnel themselves, in effect maintaining their own personnel offices. The numerous housing agencies and housing services among the Federal agencies bespeak the urge to be self-sufficient in the matter of housing.

The key to organization is the understanding that each individual has of his relation to others in the achievement of the common purpose. But that understanding does not come to pass until the common purpose is defined. For what purposes are bureaus created? To fulfill some item of public policy stated in law, it may be said. But these statements of purpose are ordinarily very general and vague. These general purposes have to be defined more sharply, and that is where the bureau comes in. The bureau devises means to achieve these ends, techniques to fulfill these purposes. Bureaus exist to perform functions that will promote the realization of the general purposes of the agency of which it is a part. Within the bureau, the function may be broken into activities that will accomplish the function.

Purposes, functions, and activities then—this trinity contains the elements which must be understood by the members of a bureau if their relationship to each other is to be clear. Without this orientation of the parts to the whole, the members of an agency run the risk of acting at cross purposes and not as an efficient purposive unit. Without continuous orientation, the parts tend to break away from the hub. Technique becomes divorced from purpose and exists for its own sake. The bureau disintegrates and separates. Its divisions become independent satrapies. The work of the agency is done by treaty among the division chiefs. The cure for common ignorance about common purposes is instruction. Where the disintegration of a bureau's parts occurs because of common ignorance about the inter-connections of purpose, function, and activity, then it is clear there should be instruction on these points. This matter will be discussed further as an aspect of communications.

THREE

Organization, then, is an idea. If so, what is hierarchy? It also is an idea. It is the idea men have about whom they follow and whom they lead. Pfiffner's definition (he calls it the "scalar process") is as follows:

"There is supreme leadership represented by the person, or persons, at the apex of the hierarchical pyramid, but in order to exercise this leadership it is necessary to delegate both authority and responsibility to the sub-leaders on the various subordinate steps of the scale."

In so saying, he restates a belief and a manner of expressing it that has won the approval of Urwick, Fayol, Mooney and Reilley. It is held to be so self-evident that Urwick in his *Elements of Administration* remarks that it "is unnecessary to comment on this obvious requirement except to utter a warning against the common assumption that the necessity for a scalar chain of authority implies that every action must climb painfully through every link in the chain, whether its course is upwards or downwards." Here is all of the familiar symbolism of the theology of administration including the mystic sign of the pyramid. It is abstract and formalistic. It is metaphor, not science. It is a figure of speech, not a representation of observed characteristics.

Like an article of faith in a religious creed, hierarchy is a symbol of the belief in the mythic form of administrative organization. And again, like an article of religious faith it is believed in spite of the lack of evidence to support and confirm it and often in the face of evidence that disputes the truth of the article. At the most the notion of hierarchy is a symbol of relationships believed to be desirable, in which some impose themselves upon others in a serried order. . . .

It is a bold presumption to contradict so much piety. But the conventional expression of the organization of authority and the practice of leadership in administrative organizations is not always symbolically accurate or factually true. The grain of truth is the need for order in the administrative universe. But it need not be an authoritarian order. . . . The picturization need not be a pyramid of boxes.

If the pictographs of geometry are to be used, perhaps a circle would be more appropriate and relevant, with the parts arranged in an orderly way around the center. New knowledge about the structure of molecules, atoms, and electrons can supply other diagrams. Each of them is a cosmos, a microcosm that reproduces the solar system, in which the elemental parts are held in orderly relationship to the center. If metaphor is to color speech, perhaps the native form of administrative organization is to be found in nuclear physics instead of theology. . . .

To repeat, the germ of truth in the insistent use of the concept hierarchy is the need for order. But how is order contrived? The theology of administration makes it a function and by-product of the will of the godchief expressed in command. There is order because he wills order. His command proceeds from the top of the Olympian chart and rules the entire structure below him. But if hierarchy is the idea that each member of the organization has of whom to lead and whom to follow, it must be clear that order is rather a by-product of the leader-follower relationship. In short, it is the individuals that make up the organization who generate the will to order. Chester Barnard says the same thing in another way when he observes that authority "is the character of a communication (order) in a formal organization by virtue of which it is accepted by a contributor or 'member' of the organization as governing the action he contributes . . ." He concludes that "the decision as to whether an order has authority or not lies with the persons to whom it is addressed" and does not reside elsewhere. In brief, authority is the idea of him who receives orders and not him who makes them.

This notion turns upside down the administrative universe of bureaucratic theology. Hierarchic authority is a fiction and the gods are horizontal, not vertical. What is the fact? The fact is that human beings in a social group, be it government bureau or workshop, have a vitality and motive force which are independent of the speeches and advices of the nominal head. As individuals in a group they have an impulse or will to cooperate with the members of the group in common actions. They want to behave *socially*, that is, to act in concert with others. This impulse or will is not called into being by the godchief. It exists without him. In fact, the iron hand, the rigorous application of hierarchic notions, the frustration of social expression, produce tensions that may defeat the object of the group. The hierarchic conception assumes that the group innately is a rabble of unorganized individuals and that order, when it appears, is a reflection of the godchief's creative logic. But unless the administrator sees his group as a coherent social unity, he is likely to develop, not harmony and order, but disorder and discouragement.

FOUR

If hierarchic authority is a theological fiction, what is the function of the front office of the bureau? It is to provide leadership and judgment. Leadership is essentially guidance not command. The distinction is important. Guidance assumes an independent motion in the thing guided. This is the case with social groups including bureaus. As Elton Mayo has indicated, there is an internal motion of the members of a group toward joint action, an impulse to cooperate and work together. It exists whether it is oriented or not. Command on the other hand implies that independence of motion does not exist but that motion is provided originally by the commander. In this view, inert particles draw life and action from the moving cause, which is outside them. Leadership then directs the will to cooperate.

But, as indicated above, there is also a function of judging. What is the function of judging? It is the making of choices between alternative courses of policy or action. Where do these choices come from, and how are they stated? They come from within the organization. It has been suggested that one of the principal functions of bureaucratic organization is to restrict the number of alternative choices, so that the front office of the bureau or agency may choose from a few instead of many. In this conception the function of organization is to sift the available choices to reduce their number.

There is something to this view, although it needs qualification. It is objectionable in part because it concentrates unduly on the front office of the bureau at the expense of the rest of the bureaucratic group. It makes it appear as though the group existed for the front office when they should exist for each other. But it does point out that some of the work of the front office is that of judging. And it indicates further that the alternatives are worked over within the organization. In short, once the impulse to cooperate and work together is organized, its internal motion does not cease. There is a pressure upon the front office to act. This is certainly not the way the godchief's empire treats him, in the mythic fiction. Pressure is put on the front office by the organization to act or not to act. The pressure appears in the form of alternatives which the front office accepts or rejects. Whichever way it decides, it performs a function of judgment.

It is clear then that, once oriented by the front office, the bureau exhibits a velocity of its own. Under these circumstances, the front office, the leadership, serves another social function besides that of guiding and judging. The head is the symbol of the central idea that animates the group. Indeed after the functions of guiding and judging have been performed for a specific project, say, there is often nothing for the leader to do but let the group-in-motion take its course. And in enterprises of great complexity and vast interdependence, it may be impossible for the leader to divert the group-in-motion from its given course and object, once started. In the greatest over-the-water invasion in the history of the world, for example, Eisenhower, after giving the final assault command, was impotent for the duration of the assault.

FIVE

Several paragraphs ago, the subject of communications was taken up briefly and then deferred. It was there said that the cure for common ignorance about the common purpose of the bureaucratic group was instruction, and that instruction was an aspect of communications. . . . Being perpendicularly overhead at a vast distance, it is necessary to devise a "troublesome code of verbal signals, unintelligible to common folk, for the expression of mutual desires." In the conception of the bureau as a social group, however, communication is a functional process which moves throughout the whole body, like blood which carries food and air to the tissues. If any part of the social organism is shut off from the sources of its enrichment and nourishment, it quickly shows the signs of bureaucratic paralysis.

Communication should inform. If it is true that organization and hierarchy are ideas and that their location is not external to, but in the minds of men, it is important that these ideas reflect the common purpose. The only way that this can be accomplished is by a well designed system of communication. The system cannot be a one way street of orders, advices, instructions, rules, regulations, and commands. This is not communication but verbal archery, in which many of the arrows must fly wide of the mark. Successful orientation of the will of the group to cooperate depends upon the understanding of the common objective. Leadership involves constant guidance. The success of both depends upon the understanding men have of the purposes they are to share and the directions in which they are to move. Understanding needs to be kept informed. Communication is the very vitality of a living and moving organism.

Every employee in the public service can contribute some tale of the boss or supervisor or director who acted as though information was a scarce commodity to be rationed. Actually this possessive attitude is a mark of ecclesiastical castemindedness. Much of the early power of the churches was based upon the possession by clerics of the art and tools of writing. Monopoly of the printed word fortified the security of the institution. Ignorance created dependence. Clerics proverbially have acted as intermediaries between the generality of people and the gods they could not understand. In bureaus, socially considered, there is no room for these theological monopolies.

Free communication is closely associated with the achievement of the social and individual satisfactions of group existence, to use Mayo's terms. The identification of the self with the group is promoted when the sense of participation in the purposes of the group is fostered by free exchange of information. In the organization and establishment of a bureau it is certainly as important for the planners to provide complete forms of expression for the individual as it is to get green pile rugs for the brass hats. Lawrence Appley has said that the whole art of administration is the development of people. Free communication is a sovereign method to promote this end. . . .

SIX

. . . The theological coloration of the conception of hierarchy frequently tints speculation and practice where central office-field relationships are involved. There is a semi-religious sense in which it is often said that the central office is the top and the field is the bottom, the first "above" and the second "below." The relation of superior to inferior is here implied as when we say that a man is high-born or low-born. The military pattern exhibits this association of rank and status with regrettable fidelity. Many complications follow this habit of view where the field is involved. It is much easier for example to maintain the theological fiction of a godchief who never appears to his humble ministers in the line but whose will is interpreted to them by intermediary clerics. The difficulty of communication is enhanced by factors of time and distance. The very remoteness of the relationship breeds confusion.

It is important within the frame of a bureau, where all are within easy distance of each other, to devise arrangements of communication that inform. It is doubly important to do so when geography separates the center from the rest of the organization. The field and only the field can inform the headquarters of the problems of the bureau as they appear at the margin of deed and accomplishment where the agency meets the customers. The headquarters alone can provide the leadership that directs the internal motion of the group towards the common purpose. Even this division of labor is somewhat artificial for the headquarters has no monopoly of policy and the field no monopoly of action. The relationship is mutual and reciprocal and each area of competence shades imperceptibly into the other. The field should participate in the formulation of policy and both central office and field should share in the action.

The verbal archery conception of headquarters communications is utterly inadequate for the management of large enterprises in the field. The arrow makers in the central office satisfy a certain lust in fondling lethal missiles and there is pleasure in flexing the bow that drives them out of sight. But the arrow makers and bow benders are acting a fantasy. Frequently they commit the group to ill considered and rash enterprises because of insufficient knowledge of the facts in the field. Or, as has often happened, the field first learns about important policy changes by reading the newspapers. The fault is a failure of communications. The remedy is in the hands of the central office. A bureau which sets up a field establishment without heeding this need vitiates the strength and effectiveness of the group.

SEVEN

The sum of these observations can be quickly stated. The theology of administration is a less satisfactory explanation of what goes on in the bureau form of group life than the sociology of administration. Not structure but people are the stuff of which a bureau is made. And its motive force is not mechanics but dynamics. Because bureaus are groups of people, they exhibit the common patterns of behavior of groups of people. There is no science of "bureau" administration, narrowly conceived, that is different from the science of group behavior in other forms of administrative groups. What is relevant and true about the behavior of bureaus is relevant and true about the behavior of departments and divisions, the next larger and the next smaller forms of administrative organization.

The people of these groups are not an unrelated rabble, wholly unorganized and formless. It is a mere manner of speaking to assert that they possess only the imprinted will of the chief. The persistent use of the concept hierarchy is a way of looking at people as members of a rank or order without personal individuality. People unfortunately tend to lose their human identity when bracketed in this fashion. There is no objective evidence that hierarchy is descriptive of anything that happens naturally among people. In fact there is evidence to the contrary. The willful use of the conception then can be explained as an expression of relationships deemed to be desirable. If so, a little airing of the alleged desirability might be in order.

Elton Mayo believes that one consequence of the hypothesis that people are a rabble of unrelated individuals is authoritarian control. Where the nature of people in groups is misunderstood, it is easy to deal with them as though they weren't people. They can be treated instead as layers of matter supporting what one writer has called "an apex of super-intelligences." Assume that they are disorderly unless confined, and it is logical to confine them. The unnaturalness of such impositions is abundantly testified to by the struggles they invariably provoke to throw off the restraints. In administrative groups, the reaction may show up as excessive turnover, or absenteeism, or inefficient production. In factories, the reaction to oppressive imposition may take the form of trade unionism although there are other causes. The Second World War came to a close with a clangorous protest from the soldiery against military authoritarianism. Nuremberg marked the end of the road for one brand of authoritarianism.

It is not an over-calculation of the relevant factors to suggest that new approaches to bureaucracy, both public and private, need to be considered. Empirical study of the ways in which human beings behave in shop, factory, and office is needed to counteract the pernicious effect of the slogans and mottoes which pass as explanations of how people act. Society at this moment in history is neurotic and disintegrated. Before we return to the arboreal life, we should try once to see if we can be as smart about people as we have been about engines, if indeed it isn't too late.

AUTHORITY IN ORGANIZA-TIONS

ROBERT V. PRESTHUS

The concept of authority provides a useful tool to help us understand organizational behavior because it asks and suggests answers to the question of how the organization achieves its objectives. How are the energies of its members directed along desired channels? While organizations are designed to gain certain large ends, they must enlist instruments of motivation and direction to overcome the individual goals of their members. Authority is a crucial element in this equation, particularly if it is defined to include the ideas of reward and reciprocity.

One view of the relations between organizational leaders and their followers assumes that compliance with authority is in some way rewarding to the individual and that each participant plays an active role in defining and accepting authority—not merely in some idealistic sense but in operational terms. This might be called a "transactional" view of authority.[1] Organizational behavior, in this view, consists of individual bargaining. But it is not bargaining in the static

[1] This conception of authority is similar to Barnard's permissive concept, but it incorporates more limitations on the individual's influence over those who exercise authority, and it attempts to set down the bases upon which authority will be accepted. C. I. Barnard, *Functions of the Executive* (Harvard University Press, 1938).

From *Public Administration Review*, Vol. 20 (Spring 1960), pp. 86–91. Robert Presthus is Professor of Political Science, York University, Toronto. Reprinted with permission of the author and the American Society for Public Administration.

sense of equilibrium theory, which explains participation as the result of a rough balance between the individual's contributions to the organization and the psychic and economic compensations he receives in return. This theory implies that the organization and the individual independently decide what kinds of concessions each is willing to make in sharing authority or in determining the work contract. In the transactional view, the individual is intrinsically involved in the authority process. One can have equilibrium in an organization without having this kind of reciprocity among individuals at different levels in the hierarchy.

WHAT AUTHORITY IS

Authority can be defined as the capacity to evoke compliance in others. We are here concerned with formal organizations as systems in which interpersonal relations are structured in terms of the prescribed authority of the actors. Of course positions of authority develop even in so-called informal organization, as William F. Whyte and others have shown.[2]

One major proposition of the transactional view of authority is that it is reciprocal. This idea stems in part from the psychological theory of perception, which tells us that reality is not some fixed entity but is defined by each individual's perception; it is relative. The way B defines the cues he has received from A determines their meaning for him and his reply. How close B comes to A's intended meaning depends on chance and how many related values A and B share, as well as how precisely they express themselves. Individuals impute different meanings to the same situations, reflecting their own personality structures.

Authority, too, is not a static, immutable quality that some people have while others do not. Rather, it is a subtle *interrelationship* whose consequences are defined by everyone concerned. The process is reciprocal because each actor tries to anticipate the reaction of all participants before he acts. A gaming process occurs in which each actor asks himself, "If I do this, what will X's reaction be, and in turn, what will my response to his assumed reaction be?"

In organizations, one's perceptions of the authority enjoyed by others as well as by oneself is thus a critical variable. Experimental evidence supports this conclusion: As Lippitt found:

1. a group member is more likely to accept direct attempts to influence him from a person he defines as powerful, and

[2] Whyte, *Street Corner Society* (University of Chicago, 1958, revised edition). Those interested in field research will find Whyte's appendix on the research methods used in this study fascinating.

2. the average group member will tend to initiate deferential, approval-seeking behavior toward persons seen as more powerful than himself.[3]

We may conclude that in the highly structured authority system of the typical big organization such reactions to authority are especially likely. This proposition will be developed further after the process of validating authority is considered.

THE LEGITIMATION PROCESS

The process by which authority is accepted may be called legitimation, which is roughly synonymous with "sanctioned" or "validated." It usually occurs when the individual is integrated into a society or a group, when he accepts its norms and values.

That authority must be legitimated is explicit in Barnard's conclusion that it can rarely be imposed from above but becomes viable only through the acceptance of those exposed to it.[4] Obviously, the social context including the mission and traditions of the organization, its program, the relative influence of the actors, and the way each behaves affects the process of legitimation. However, the *specific conditions* under which authority will be accepted or rejected remain to be isolated by careful research. Superficially, we can assume that in highly disciplined organizations such as the Marine Corps, the legitimation process becomes virtually automatic, reflecting the Corps' traditions, volunteer character, and the high degree of commitment among its members. Turning to the other end of the continuum, the university or the research organization, the process becomes highly diffused and unstructured, with professional values competing for legitimation with hierarchical authority.[5]

Personality is another variable that affects legitimation. One suspects that in most cases it reinforces legitimation as a result of the socialization process mentioned above. A recent study[6] illustrates the effects of this element. Personality tests[7] were given 54 male university students to determine their attitudes toward authority. Then the students were asked to perform a simple task, with the instruction that they could stop whenever they wished. However, when the stu-

[3] R. Lippitt, N. Polansky, and S. Rosen, "The Dynamics of Power," 5 *Human Relations* 44–50 (No. 1, 1952).

[4] *Op. cit.*, pp. 163–169.

[5] N. Kaplan, "The Role of the Research Administrator," 4 *Administrative Science Quarterly* 20–42 (June, 1959).

[6] J. Block and J. Block, "An Interpersonal Experiment on Reactions to Authority," 5 *Human Relations* 91–98 (1952).

[7] Both thematic apperception tests and the Berkeley ethnocentrism scale were used.

dent did stop, the researcher immediately asked, "Don't you want to do some more?" Some gave in to what the researcher seemed to want and continued; others refused to go on. By and large, the personality tests of those who went on revealed a general tendency to accept authority, and vice versa.

Such variations in the legitimation process in different organizations and among different individuals complicate its analysis. Moreover, the values of the observer also interfere. As Herbert Simon concludes, "Authority that is viewed as legitimate is not felt as coercion or manipulation, either by the man who exercises it or by the man who accepts it. Hence, the scientist who wishes to deal with issues of manipulation that are sometimes raised in human relations research must be aware of his own attitudes of legitimacy. . . . If he regards the area of legitimate authority as narrow, many practices will appear to him coercive or manipulative that would not seem so with a broader criterion of legitimacy."[8]

These variations are further complicated by the fact that authority has several bases of legitimation. While authority may appear to rest upon his formal role, an executive's reliance upon this formal position for legitimation of his leadership is usually a confession of weakness. Authority seems more likely to be a contingent grant, received initially as part of formal position but requiring nourishment from other kinds of legitimation as well.

FOUR BASES OF LEGITIMATION

Four bases of legitimation may be suggested: technical expertise, formal role, rapport, and a generalized deference to authority. They are, of course, intermixed in most situations. Each ramifies the other, although the relative weight of each varies among types of organizations. My purpose here is not an exhaustive analysis of each basis of legitimation but rather a brief, exploratory outline which may be useful in conceptualizing authority in an operating situation.

LEGITIMATION BY EXPERTISE

For a variety of historical and cultural reasons technical skill and professional attitudes are perhaps the most pervasive criteria for validating authority in the United States, i.e., many persons accept the authority of competent persons simply because they are competent. In this country, equality of opportunity has always been an ideal; ability to do the job has been widely accepted as the only

---

[8] "Authority" in C. Arensberg (ed.), *Research in Industrial Human Relations* (Harper & Brothers, 1957), p. 106. Simon posits four bases for accepting authority: confidence (technical skill); social approval; sanctions; and legitimation. Legitimation is thus used in a different, and more restricted sense than here.

moral basis for selection. Our pragmatic approach to getting a job done, never impeded by a rigid class system, reinforces this moral conviction.

Respect for the superior's expertise as a source of validating his authority is particularly effective where his expertise is the same as that of his subordinate's only greater. This source of legitimation has been strengthened by specialization, which, in turn, has been reinforced by the professionalization process.[9]

LEGITIMATION BY FORMAL POSITION

There are some indications that formal role is becoming more significant as a basis for the legitimation of authority. In big organizations, authority is structured to insure control by limiting information, centralizing initiative, restricting access to decision-making centers, and generally controlling the behavioral alternatives of members. The formal allocation of authority is also reinforced by various psychological inducements, including status symbols, rewards, and sanctions. Such differential allocations of status, income, and authority have important objectives and consequences other than as personal rewards for loyal and effective service. They provide a battery of cues or signals for the entire organization; they provide the framework for personal transactions; they communicate appropriate behavior and dramatize its consequences. In brief, such signals define and reinforce authority.

In addition to these structural and psychological instruments, the traditions and the mission of the organization are important conditioning factors. Business organizations exhibit a high potential for validating authority mainly in terms of hierarchy; military organizations are similar, although there is some evidence that technical expertise is assuming a larger role as warfare and weapons become more scientific and complex.[10] There is also some evidence that the great size and specialization of modern organizations are forcing a greater reliance upon legitimation by formal role, even in research and educational organizations where legitimation by expertise has been traditional. The bureaucratization of research which attends the huge grants of government and the big foundations provides some evidence.[11]

Still, in most organizations a conflict usually exists between formal position and expertise as bases for authority. In organizations with many functional areas this conflict is aggravated because the generalist

[9] For an inquiry into this problem see Robert V. Presthus, "The Social Bases of Organization," 38 Social Forces 103–109 (December, 1959).

[10] See Morris Janowitz, "Changes in Organizational Authority: The Military Establishment," 3 Administrative Science Quarterly 473–493 (March, 1959).

[11] C. Wright Mills, The Sociological Imagination (Oxford University Press, 1959); Dwight MacDonald, The Ford Foundation (Reynal & Co., 1956).

at the top can rarely be expert in more than one or two functional areas. Thus he will be denied the legitimation of expertise by those in other fields. He may also experience conflict between his generalist role and his identification with a functional area. In universities, for example, it is well known that the department which represents the substantive field of an incoming president is bound to rise. When the inevitable occurs, other departments emphasize legitimation by expertise in an effort to buttress their claims for equality.

We can safely conclude that the problems of authority are aggravated by the tendency of individuals to validate authority on the basis of competence in their own fields and to thus look to different reference groups for models for their own behavior. This condition has important consequences for loyalty to the organization, acceptance of its rules and traditions, and for the direction of professional energy. Gouldner has divided individuals into two role types, "cosmopolitans" and "locals," according to the bases upon which they grant authority.[12] As the term suggests, "cosmopolitans" have an outward orientation; their major loyalty and energy are directed toward their profession, and their activities are aimed at gaining national prominence in their field. "Locals," on the other hand, are oriented toward the organization with which they happen to be associated; they express great loyalty toward it, accept its major values, justify its policies, and expect to carve out a career within it.

Authority that attempts to rely solely upon formal role is thus challenged by the conflicting values and assumptions of the groups that comprise large organizations. Legitimation by expertise suffers from a similar conflict as each self-conscious group strives to make its own skills and values supreme. Both the size and specialization of modern organizations aggravate this conflict. Indeed, one could probably construct a useful "index of anticipated conflict" on the basis of the number of discrete functional groups contained within a given organization.

The resulting stalemate among conflicting professions results in a power vacuum which the generalist soon fills, again reinforcing the hierarchical basis of authority. Thus, in the main, modern organizations are controlled by generalists, reflecting their monopoly of information and initiative, extended tenure allowing freedom for tactical maneuver, control of procedural and judicial matters within the organization, absence of any legitimate, internal opposition (the common one-party system) to the "official" policies enunciated by leaders, and mastery over external relations with other elites.[13]

12 A. Gouldner, "Cosmopolitans and Locals: Toward an Analysis of Latent Social Roles," 2 *Administrative Science Quarterly* 281–306; 440–480 (December, 1957–March, 1958).

13 Robert Michels, *Political Parties: A Study of Oligarchical Tendencies in Modern Democracy* (The Free Press, 1949).

LEGITIMATION BY RAPPORT

Democratic political theory, the conflicts between generalists and specialists, and, one fears, the desire to rationalize human personality in the service of management, have combined to emphasize human relations in organization. This emphasis also serves to blunt the impersonality and routinization of big organization. Authority, then, often will be legitimated on the basis of interpersonal skill and the work climate that executives and supervisors maintain. This process may be called legitimation by rapport. Our bureaucratically inclined economy reinforces this mechanism by standardizing work conditions, pay, and career opportunities. Sympathetic human relations tend to become the major distinction among jobs. As a result, expert and hierarchical criteria of legitimation are challenged by the warm personality of the boss. Research supports this proposition. We know that executives rarely fail for lack of technical skill but rather for inadequate personal relations. More important, the acceptance of authority has been shown to be positively related to affection for the person exercising it:

1. The amount of influence or authority that a leader *attempts* to exert increases with increased acceptance of him by the recipients;

2. The leader's actual influence over the group increases with increasing acceptance of him as a person.[14]

The same study verified the existence of legitimation by expertise. The more one's subordinates recognized him as an expert in their own specialized field, the more effective he was. Influence was also positively related to the formal role of leader.

The administrator, then, not only must be aware of these several bases of legitimation, he also must accommodate himself to the particular basis that an individual or a group seems most likely to use in validating his authority in a given situation.

LEGITIMATION BY A GENERALIZED DEFERENCE TO AUTHORITY

Individual needs for security often result in a generalized deference to authority. Indeed, one is tempted to suggest that other sources of legitimation are often used as rationalizations for this form of legitimation. This deference, which often reflects distorted perceptions of authority, seems to fall in the category of nonrational behavior, or at least it seems less rational than legitimations based upon objective indexes such as technical skill and formal position. However, definitions of rationality must rest upon an explicit statement of the objectives sought. If an individual derives security and less strained interpersonal relations by deferring to authority, his behavior is rational from his standpoint.

[14] R. P. French and R. Snyder, "Leadership and Interpersonal Power," in D. Cartwright (ed.), *Studies in Social Power* (University of Michigan Institute for Social Research, 1959), pp. 118–149.

This basis of legitimation assumes that individual behavior in complex organizations may usefully be conceptualized as a series of reactions to authority. Its theoretical framework reflects Harry Stack Sullivan's view that personality is the result of an individual's characteristic mode of accommodating to authority figures over a long period of time. His belief that anxiety-reduction is the basic mechanism in such accommodations is also accepted here: "I believe it fairly safe to say that anybody and everybody devotes much of his lifetime and a great deal of his energy to . . . avoiding more anxiety than he already has, and if possible, to getting rid of some of this anxiety."[15]

Sullivan also insists that anxiety is the major factor in learning by both children and adults. They learn to trade approval and the resulting reduction of anxiety for conformity with authority. We thus assume that individual reactions to organizational authority are a form of learning. Moreover, as in all learning, the mechanisms of perception and reinforcement are operating. Complex organizations, then, may be regarded as educational institutions whose systems of authority, status, and goals provide clear stimuli for their members.[16]

Pavlov was among the first to note that anxious people acquire conditioned responses with unusual speed. Eysenck reports a study in which normal individuals required 25 repetitions of a nonsense syllable accompanied by a buzzer before a conditioned response was established, while anxiety neurotics required only 8 repetitions.[17] Research on the effects of different anxiety loadings would require further specification of organizational role types in terms of their reactions to authority. It seems reasonable to assume that a certain amount of anxiety is conducive to organizational socialization, while too heavy a load may result in dysfunctional reactions to authority.[18]

These considerations suggest some limitations of the permissive concept of authority which holds that subordinates play the major role in legitimating organizational authority. Basically, this concept seems to overstate the amount of discretion enjoyed by the recipient of a superior's order. It underestimates the disparities in power between any given individual and the organization's leaders. But more important, it neglects the behavioral effect of a lifetime of learned deference to authority and the psychological gains attending such be-

15 "Tensions, Interpersonal and International" in H. Cantril (ed.), *Tensions That Cause Wars* (University of Illinois, 1950), p. 95.

16 For a detailed analysis of organizational behavior in a psychological context, see my *The Organizational Society*.

17 H. J. Eysenck, *The Psychology of Politics* (Praeger, 1954), pp. 260–261; O. H. Mowrer, "Anxiety Reduction and Learning," 27 *Journal of Experimental Psychology* 497–516 (1940).

18 See footnotes 3 and 6, T. Leary, *Interpersonal Diagnosis of Personality* (Ronald Press Co., 1957).

havior. If Sullivan is correct, the individual is trained from infancy to defer to the authority of parents, teachers, executives, and leaders of various kinds. He develops over time a *generalized* deference to authority, based upon such socialization and its compensations.

Legitimation by deference appears exceptionally compelling in an organizational milieu where the location of authority and the symbols that define it are clear. Unlike many groups, big organizations are authoritative milieux; influence—evoking compliance without the backing of sanctions—is not really the primary ingredient in interpersonal affairs. As Wright Mills says, organizations are systems of roles graded by authority. Titles, income, accessibility, size and decor of office, secretarial buffers, and degree of supervision are the stimuli that validate such authority. They provide cues that define interpersonal relations, limit alternatives, and inhibit spontaneity. The degree to which authority is institutionalized is suggested by the fact that whereas the individuals who occupy the formal roles may change, the *system* of authority relationships persists, again reinforcing deference toward the holder of the formal position.

It is a safe generalization, too, that most individuals tend to accept group judgments in return for the psychic satisfaction of being in the majority and winning the group's approval.[19] Organizations are composed of a congeries of such groups and subhierarchies, each bound together by authority, mission, and interest to form a microcosm of the larger system. Each has its own power structure in which its leaders enjoy considerable discretion in dealing with their own subordinates although they are often nonleaders when viewed from a larger perspective.[20] This devolution of power has important consequences for legitimation. Discipline is insured since the life chances of those in each group are determined largely by the representations made on their behalf by their leaders. Organizational authority is transmitted downward by the subleaders, reinforcing their own authority and status by the opportunity to demonstrate the loyalty and dispatch with which they carry out higher policy.

Role conflict may occur here between the leader's personal and his organizational role. He simultaneously must promote the larger goals of the organization yet maintain equilibrium in his group by defending those group objectives which are not the same as the organization's. He will sometimes be caught between the conflicting demands of hierarchy and technical skill; here, his own identification with a pro-

[19] See, for example, the well-known experiments of Sherif and Asch, reported in M. Sherif, *Outline of Social Psychology* (Harper & Brothers, 1952) and S. E. Asch, *Social Psychology* (Prentice-Hall, 1952).

[20] E. Stotland, "Peer Groups and Reactions to Power Figures," in D. Cartwright (ed.), *Studies in Social Power*, pp. 53–68; W. G. Bennis and H. A. Shepard, "A Theory of Group Development," 9 *Human Relations* 415–437 (November, 1956).

fessional field may aggravate such conflicts, making it more difficult to meet the organizational claims implicit in his formal position.[21] For example, formal budget requirements which seem to impede the work of a research group may nevertheless be important to the goal of the larger organization. At other times conflicting goals or policies within the larger organization make role conflict almost certain. This problem is nicely demonstrated in prison administration where rehabilitation and custodial goals may be pursued in the same prison at the same time, resulting in role conflict among those dealing directly with the prisoners.[22] But where the organization's policies are consistent, we may safely assume that its groups will often play an active role in legitimating them, particularly when their leaders have been "sold" on their rationality.

CONCLUSIONS

In sum, authority seems to grow out of a dynamic, reciprocal relationship between leader and led, in which the values, perceptions, and skills of followers play a critical role in defining and legitimating the authority of organizational leaders. Acceptance of authority rests essentially upon four interlocking bases: the technical expertise of the leader; his formal role or position in the organization's hierarchy; his rapport with subordinates or his ability to mediate their individual needs for security and recognition; and the subordinates' generalized deference toward authority, reflecting in turn the process of socialization.

[21] A. Etzioni, "Authority Structure and Organizational Effectiveness," 4 *Administrative Science Quarterly* 43–67 (June, 1959).

[22] D. R. Cressey, "Contradictory Directives in Complex Organizations," *Ibid.*, pp. 1–19.

HEURISTIC SYSTEMS OF ACTION

WILLIAM J. GORE

Rational systems of action are productive mechanisms. They are marvelously efficient devices for meeting the proliferation of societally defined needs. Because these needs are so much in the center of our concerns, and because so much of our time and energy is invested pursuing them, we sometimes overlook the importance of heuristic strategies.* From investigations underlying this formulation it appears that heuristic processes are an alternative to rational systems and are activated when for some reason the aspired-to objects of activity are not forthcoming or are unlikely to be forthcoming.

One of the most direct ways of avoiding frustration and the possibility of failure is to find a way around the barrier blocking realization of the preferred goal. To do this usually requires some reinterpretation of the goal, which will delineate an alternative path. If the existing goal has been rationalized into a system of action, logical analysis is likely to reinforce the commitment of the organization to this goal and to its accompanying pattern of action. And as we just noted, this may push the level of frustration so high, it may pierce the barriers

* Editorial note: A heuristic is a problem solving process that may be employed when no single, objectively correct solution can be obtained. Under these circumstances additional variables must be introduced which reflect the value assumptions of the decision-maker. Thus, a heuristic process incorporates the utilization of implicit value assumptions about what is or is not important, good, or correct, or about what is more (or less) important, good, or correct.

From *Administrative Decision-Making: A Heuristic Model* (New York: John Wiley & Sons, Inc., 1964), pp. 8–14. William Gore is Professor of Political Science, University of Washington. Reprinted with permission of the publisher.

179

behind which the organization's stresses are contained, threatening disintegration. (It may also provide an increase in effort sufficient to realize the goal.)

Goal substitution is a term which means replacing one aspired-to object with another. To the researcher interested in the dynamics of organization the statement that one goal has been substituted for another may carry little or no emotional impact. To those who bring about these adjustments in goals there is inevitably a sense of loss, a feeling that, having sought something selfishly desired and altruistically valued, they have been inadequate to its attainment. If the culture of an organization is such that the expression of these feelings is repressed, the incidence of goal substitution may manifest itself in the inexplicable flaring-up of a once quiescent conflict. Where collective inhibition is less relied upon, the forms of self-expression that individuals use to dissipate their feelings may be only too apparent. Whatever the case, disengaging an organization from a goal is much more complicated than formally declaring the goal no longer attainable.

Heuristic processes are important for another, more substantial reason. Western man has had a good deal to say about the non-material benefits generally represented as a kind of bonus accruing to those who follow the dictates of rationality. (This might be considered an intellectual equivalent to some religious sect's storing up points in the hereafter.) Those tough-minded enough to follow this strategy will find that those environmental restraints binding others in a kind of environmental determinism are relaxed in their own case.

In my view this claim can be justified only if it is qualified, for the traditional position that science is objective is no longer fully accepted by any knowledgeable social science discipline. That science is essentially a heuristic strategy with a built-in self-correcting capacity is gaining some impressive adherents.

If science contains some significant limitations; if, for example, science cannot provide an objective, myth-free foundation for a rational system of action supplying an explication of those causes that can release the desired consequences; if, in short, science alone cannot support the rational systems of action we require, the need for an alternative basis for collective action arises.

I think that the limitations of the rationalistic strategy (and only these limitations are under discussion here) are larger than this. Rational systems presuppose not only an understanding of causes and effects but also a stability of goals. National resource development programs illustrate this point. America has eliminated the environmental threat of floods in some areas and reduced it in others through the development of dam systems built one or two at a time, year after year during the last generation. If people had not been led to what they considered an irreversible commitment to this policy, some other outlet for these resources would have claimed them before the minimal number of dams were completed. Our flood control programs have had a stable base of public support partly because they have been pursued through multipurpose installations involving hydroelectric power, river navigation, and flood control. The rational justification for these projects will shortly receive a heavy blow, for atomic-powered generators mounted on railroad cars will soon be able to produce electricity at comparable rates.

Rational systems of action depend upon another quality inherent in collective goals—their consistency or lack of it. Specifically, rational systems of action require a minimal logical consistency among the multiple goals that are the hallmark of today's corporate activity. . . .

The Lawrence, Kansas, Fire Department has three functions—putting out fires, preventing fires, and sustaining its capacity to execute both of these activities through training. These functions are implemented through two administrative units, the fire-fighting crews and the fire-prevention teams, each unit being responsible for training its own personnel. Though the city manager, the city fathers, and the public see these activities as logically related—who but a fireman knows what does and does not constitute a fire hazard?—the fire chief is well aware that a fully effective program of fire prevention will do away with the need for his fire department as presently constituted. Since most men who join fire departments do so because, among other things, they seek opportunities to express their physical bravery, fire prevention raises the prospect that this opportunity may eventually be taken from them.

Above all, rational systems of action presuppose differential perception in terms of logically prescribed cues. This is in painful opposition to the traditional or folk custom of identifying cues by their emotional appeal. In plain language, the manager of a baseball team must train himself to make choices in terms of the odds instead of in terms of his anxieties. . . .

This suggests that rational systems of action are powerful social mechanisms for the satisfaction of collective needs. However, contrary to what a few have claimed and many have assented to, such systems are not appropriate to every situation. Probably the full power of a system can be realized only in a situation so socially constructed above as well as others are provided for.

People in organizations seem to develop complementary strategies which they use as an alternative in dealing with a single complex of objectives. Through a heuristic process a scheme embodying a series of routinized programs of action is devised. These schemes specify the kinds and quantities of resources required. They contain a carefully delineated pattern of collective activity which will realize sought-after goals and avoid threatening consequences. Once activated these systems of action become self-energizing since they include reward and penalty components which tap the emotional strivings of the individual. Often, contrary to traditional doctrine, they manifest a capacity not only to sustain themselves but also to regenerate and extend themselves. The feeling that most rational systems become expansive once they have "shaken themselves down" is now so widely held that it is common to assume that rational systems have considerable stability and the capacity to maintain themselves almost indefinitely. It is probable that once a rational system of action is translated into a viable organization, it has the potentiality of becoming more and more vital through appropriate heuristic processes. These processes themselves are more effective, because the structuring embodied in the organization as a rational system of action means that the power of the heuristic process can be focused on a smaller area.

Whether a rational system of action becomes expansively self-regenerative, proliferating with facility, or whether it finds increasing difficulty in maintaining itself and finally passes from the scene is only partly a function of the properties of the system. Here is reflected the contrast between the capabilities of the rational system and the claims people mount against it. Equally important is the disparity between the resources available from the agency's environment and the resources it requires. When some resource becomes so scarce that its cost is more than the agency's capacity to pay, a substantial adjustment may become necessary.

These two factors are often simple to deal with in comparison with the socio-psychological difficulties stemming from the people who constitute the agency. Firemen want to fight fires, not to prevent them. Soldiers sign up to undertake another kind of fighting. Professors want to spend their time in the laboratory instead of the classroom. Workers seek higher and higher wages for less and less work. That such a list has no end is probably symptomatic of the extent of the difficulty. And it is a difficulty that does not lend itself to either rational analysis or logical resolution.

Whereas the rational system of action evolves through the identification of causes and effects and the discovery of ways of implementing them, the heuristic process is a groping toward agreements seldom arrived at through logic. The very essence of the heuristic process is that the factors validating a decision are internal to the personality of the individual instead of external to it. Whereas the rational system of action deals with the linkages between a collective and its objectives and between a collective and its environment, the heuristic process is oriented toward the relationship between that private core of values embedded in the center of the personality and its public counterpart, ideology. The dynamics of personality are not those of logic but rather those of the emotions. Personality may be tamed to the imperatives of logic, but that is not its natural inclination.

The essential function of the heuristic process is to induce a several-sided, commonly held set of understandings consisting of a shared conception of the world in general, the problem at hand, and the conditions under which the problem can be acceptably resolved from the jumble of conceptions that constitute the normal state of affairs. Mostly the activities undertaken in the name of heuristic decision-making are indigenous and extra-formal. They are therefore largely volitional. As a result the agreements more or less voluntarily arrived at usually represent some form of consensus. Since the consensus of a collective is arrived at through indigenous practices largely undisciplined by logic and untrammeled by scientific knowledge, it may have a primitive quality. As the understandings grow and mature they become more elaborate, usually somewhat more complex, and less internally consistent. In either case the base upon which the rational system is erected has a folk quality embodying the emotional investment of the individual in some collectively defined object, collectively imbued with value.

One of the things that sets the heuristic process off from the rational system of action is its verbal character. Although the rational system of action may move forward through discussion including from time to time vaguely defined values or loosely cast projections of the future, it ultimately involves concrete, here-and-now arrangements that pertain to collective action. Conversely, the heuristic process may be activated as a result of some event that is a part of the immediate experience of people on the scene, but it soon becomes an almost completely verbal process reaching backward into the memory and forward into the future, returning to that completely emotional climate where individuals retain a private place for their own uncollectivized life. This is not the only place touched by the heuristic process as it meanders through the light as well as the dark places of the social system, but it must touch these private worlds. Through the heuristic process the private world of one individual is linked both to others and to the collectively constituted world which supports and nourishes individual existence.

If there is to be meaning and reward in cooperative activity they must be based on the interpenetration of these two social spaces; the vehicle of interpenetration is the heuristic process. The stuff that links them together is the verbal element common to both. A cognitive structure cannot be designed through logic for the simple reason that some of the linkages between people involve unconscious urges, felt but all but impossible to define. Although they can be accommodated by ideological terms rich with inchoate meaning projected into them, these invisible but frequently potent emotional forces may be misdirected if subjected to rational manipulation. When the surge of emotional energy behind these forces is blocked, it erupts into frustration and tension. If these tensions are not dissipated, they burst past the threshold of disintegration and begin to destroy some of the relationships constituting the social system. Then disorganization sets in.

The central presupposition underlying this presentation can now be restated. Modern societies have developed a highly efficient, massively powerful social mechanism—the rational system of action. The accumulation of effort formed by harnessing talent, resources, and facilities to operations designed to take advantage of scientifically defined chains of cause and effect is the central dynamic of this system. Although there has sometimes been the implication that formal organizational mechanisms are built and maintained as independent entities, these mechanisms are in fact mounted on rather elaborate foundations which remain mostly unseen below the surface of social experience once an organization is operative. Whether seen or unseen, the vital emotional motivations that energize the organizational system are released by the heuristic process.

HUMAN
BEHAVIOR
AND
ORGANIZATION

HERBERT
SIMON,
DONALD
SMITHBURG,
AND
VICTOR
THOMPSON

We have now examined at some length the influences on the employee's behavior that lie outside the organization. We have seen that what he does and what decisions he makes are to a very considerable extent determined by the personality, character structure, knowledge, and attitudes that have been impressed upon him before he comes into the organization and by influences that operate upon him outside the sphere of his organizational life. If this were all that could be said about human behavior, we would not need special books about administration. If these outside influences completely determined behavior, people would behave in organizations just as they did everywhere.

But in fact, individuals placed in organizational situations—employed as stenographers, or laborers, or recreation directors, or foresters, or department heads—do behave differently than they would if they were outside organization, or if they were in different organizational situations. The organizational system itself brings to bear upon them strong influences that modify and redirect their behavior tendencies. . . .

From *Public Administration* (New York: Alfred A. Knopf, Inc., 1950), pp. 79–91. Herbert Simon is Professor of Computer Science and Psychology, Carnegie-Mellon University; Donald Smithburg is Professor of Political Science, University of Alabama; and Victor Thompson is Professor of Political Science, University of Illinois, Urbana. Reprinted with permission of the publisher. Footnotes renumbered.

185

CHARACTERISTICS OF BEHAVIOR IN ORGANIZATION

To the extent that a person's participation in an organization subjects him to psychological influences, we find that his behavior tends to take on the following characteristics:[1]

VALUE PREMISES

The value premises (goals, objectives) upon which the employee bases his decisions tend to be the objectives of the organization or organizational unit in which he works. When the forest ranger is advised that a fire has started in his district he immediately makes decisions and takes actions that are directed toward the objective of putting out the fire. If he were merely a camper in the woods his main concern about a fire would probably lie in not being trapped and burned. Even if he possessed social attitudes that led him to try to do something about the fire, he certainly would not feel the same responsibility, the same single-minded purpose to extinguish it, that would be felt by the ranger.

To be more accurate, the value premises that the individual employee incorporates into his behavior are not usually the goals of the organization as a whole, but intermediate goals—means to the larger organization ends—that define his particular job in the organization. The forest ranger acts not in terms of extinguishing fires in general, but of extinguishing those in his fire district. Hence, behavior in organization is characterized by the division of the complete task of the organization into partial tasks that serve as goals for particular employees or groups of employees.

ACCEPTANCE OF INFLUENCE

The employee tends to accept influences that are "legitimately" imposed upon him by other members of the organization. If the ranger's supervisor instructs him to clear the brush from a particular forest trail, he is more likely to accept the instruction than if it came from a visitor in the forest. . . .

To the extent that this acceptance develops in the employee, he derives many of the premises of his behavior from his communication with other organization members. This communication may be in the form of orders, information and advice, and training. To a very considerable extent, these various forms of communication can be de-

[1] We are describing here what the sociologist would call the assumption of an organizational *role*—an organizationally and socially defined standardized pattern of behavior. For an analysis in these terms, see Samuel A. Stouffer, *et al., The American Soldier: Combat and Its Aftermath* (Princeton: Princeton University Press, 1949), p. 101.

liberately designed so as to bring the employee within a planned environment of organizational influence. Examples of such planned influences are formal "lines of authority," report forms and instructions for their preparation and routing, formally established "consultant" positions, and the assignment of employees to participate in formal training programs. For this reason, the definition and enforcement of these channels of influence has always been a central concern of organization planning.

EXPECTATIONS

The employee tends to form stable expectations about his relations with other people, and how they will behave under particular circumstances. When the ranger receives from his lookout a report of a fire in the adjoining district, he does not take direct action, but phones his fellow ranger with full confidence that the latter will take charge of the situation. He likewise has confidence that if a lookout in the adjoining district detects a fire in his district, he will be informed about it promptly.

ORGANIZATIONAL MORALE

The employee tends to assume not just a passive but an active attitude toward the furtherance of the organization's objectives. He does not merely accept the organization goals in deciding those questions that come to him, or accept the instructions he receives, but he exericses more or less initiative in finding ways of furthering those goals. In most cases the ranger would see that the brush was cleared from an overgrown trail long before anyone gave him instructions to do so— often long before anyone besides himself knew that the problem existed.

Active rather than merely passive participation and cooperation is almost essential if an organization is to attain even moderate efficiency. If the organization must drive its employees every step of the way, if they stop and await new instructions each time a specific task is completed, if they contribute little of their own thought and spontaneous effort, then the largest part of the organization's energies will be swallowed up and consumed in overcoming their inertia. The power that operates an automobile comes from the motor, not from the driver. So in an organization the energy that accomplishes its tasks must be secured from the spontaneous contributions of employees who are actively working toward the organization goal. For those who are directing the organization to attempt to supply it with energy would be as effective as for the driver of a car to get out and push instead of starting the motor.

The willingness of employees to participate in a truly active way and to devote their full energies to the organization's task is what is usually meant by high *morale*.[2] If the playground director has high morale—if he is sold on the recreation department's goals and willingly and enthusiastically contributes his mind and energies toward realizing them—then the organization's influences upon him will serve to channel and direct these energies toward effective activity. Lacking such morale, the organization will be burdened with the almost hopeless task of supplying initiative as well as direction.

OTHER CHARACTERISTICS

The science of economics makes great use of a mythical individual known as "economic man"—an individual who goes about his business singlemindedly maximizing his profits. The behavior tendencies we have been describing of individuals in organization might be combined into a picture of an equally mythical individual whom we could call "administrative man." Administrative man accepts the organization goals as the value premises of his decisions, is particularly sensitive and reactive to the influences upon him of the other members of his organization, forms stable expectations regarding his own role in relation to others and the roles of others in relation to him, and has high morale in regard to the organization's goals. What is perhaps most remarkable and unique about administrative man is that the organizational influences do not merely cause him to do certain specific things (e.g., putting out a forest fire, if that is his job), but induce in him a habit pattern of doing *whatever* things are appropriate to carry out in cooperation with others the organization goals. He develops habits of cooperative behavior.

It should not be thought, however, that all the influences operating upon the employees of an organization further cooperation. There may be, for example, conflicting interpretations of the organization goals, or various units of the organization may have inconsistent goals. Incompatibility among members of the organization may lead to friction and may increase, rather than reduce, resistance to organizational influence. Certain methods of supervision may curb rather than stimulate initiative. Nevertheless, the first set of influences —those encouraging cooperation—predominate most of the time in most organizations. If they did not, organized behavior would not be an effective way of carrying out tasks, members would receive no inducement toward continued participation, and the organization itself would disappear. Hence only those organizations survive for any length of time whose net influence upon their members is to preserve and develop habits of cooperation.

[2] The term "morale" is defined in many ways in books on administration. The definition given here will prove most useful for our purposes.

CHARACTER OF ORGANIZATIONAL INFLUENCES

We may next inquire into the nature of the influences that impinge upon a person who becomes a member of an organization. All of them derive from the fact that his participation in the organization brings him into frequent communication with other members. He talks to them and observes them, and they talk to him. In the course of this communication, they induce him to behave in particular ways by convincing or persuading him, by attaching pleasant consequences for him to desired behaviors and unpleasant consequences to undesired ones (rewards and punishments), and by providing him with social satisfactions and dissatisfactions from his association with them. Social satisfactions and dissatisfactions may, of course, be regarded as particular kinds of rewards and punishments, but they are of such central importance that they deserve special treatment.

Influencing people by convincing and persuading them are processes that are obviously not peculiar to organization. Organization, by multiplying the occasions for communication, does however greatly reinforce these processes. They are further reinforced by the habits of cooperation that the individual gradually acquires.

Rewards and punishments are important and obvious means of influence. The threat of dismissal, the promise of higher wages or promotion, praise and reprimand are examples of commonly used rewards and punishments. Less obvious, but at least as important, are social satisfactions and dissatisfactions derived from association with other organization members. In particular, most persons are sensitive to the approval or disapproval of those persons with whom they are in close association.

The division of the organization's work and the assignment of particular duties to individuals and groups of individuals bring certain employees into close contact and association with certain others. These associations provide the fertile soil upon which social relations and group loyalties can grow. Organizational loyalties are of particular importance because many of the values that motivate any individual are values that derive from the face-to-face work group with which he identifies and to which he is loyal. The attitudes of an employee toward the organization goals and toward the authority exercised over him are very closely related to the attitudes of the persons who work with him. If his fellow-employees are dissatisfied with their jobs, or think the supervisors are unfair, or evidence low morale in other ways, the typical employee, whatever his original disposition, is likely to develop similar dissatisfactions.

The structure of loyalties in a typical organization is highly complex, embracing loyalties to *groups* as well as loyalties to *goals*. Because of the individual's sensitivity to the social group in which he finds himself, influences upon these loyalties must be primarily influences upon the employee as a member of a face-to-face group rather than as an individual "atom." . . .

REINFORCEMENT OF THE INFLUENCES

The ability of organizations to develop in their members habits of cooperation is greatly increased by the attitudes and habits that these members bring to organizations. . . . The mores of the society in which the new member has lived have predisposed him to accept authority, to recognize differences in status, to consider efficiency and group loyalty as positive values. He has acquired certain desires—for example, the desire for a higher income—that give the organization a means of rewarding or punishing him. Moreover, he may have had specific training for the kinds of tasks he will be asked to perform in the organization.

To be sure, not all the habits he has acquired before joining the organization will reinforce the influences that are imposed upon him. In many cases his prior habits will conflict with the new influences. He may have habits of tardiness, of carelessness, of rudeness, or training in methods different from those employed by the organization. Nevertheless, the patterns of cooperation in an organization will generally reflect to a very considerable degree the patterns of cooperation that are incorporated in the mores and training procedures of the larger society. The organization will receive further reinforcement from pre-existing attitudes by selecting those persons as employees who appear most susceptible to its influence.

FORMAL ORGANIZATION

By *formal organization* is meant the pattern of behaviors and relationships that is deliberately and legitimately planned for the members of an organization. Two words in the definition of formal organization need explanation: "deliberately" and "legitimately." In some simple situations an organization may be wholly unplanned. When a car gets stuck in the mud of a country road, the passengers may get out and push without anyone "deliberately" planning their behavior. On the other hand, in most organizations, and certainly in all governmental organizations, there are some employees who spend part or all of their time planning the system of organization behavior—the division of work and allocation of duties, authority relationships, lines of communication, and so forth.

Now of course anyone in an organization (or outside it, for that matter) may make such a plan. Several plans may be made, and these may conflict. Formal organization comes into existence when there is an agreed-upon and accepted procedure for giving "legitimacy" to one of these plans. In the case of governmental organizations, this legitimacy flows ultimately from the action of the legislature in creating the organization (or the larger structure of which it is part) by statute, and providing a procedure by which an executive or board is appointed to direct it. The legally constituted executive, in turn, authorizes more detailed plans for the structure of his organization, and appoints principal subordinates to positions of formal authority in it. This process may be several times repeated down through the structure of the organization. As a result of a series of steps of this kind, we may find that Mr. A has been "legitimately" appointed to a position of section chief, and that he in turn has "legitimately" (i.e., in accordance with the terms of the formal plan of the larger organization) made assignments of duties to the members of his section.

How plans of formal organization are established and made legitimate may be illustrated from the history of the Economic Cooperation Administration. On April 3, 1948, the Economic Cooperation Act of 1948 was adopted by the Congress. This Act established (i.e, promulgated a legitimate plan for) an Economic Cooperation Administration, and provided for the appointment of an Administrator to direct it. Within a few days, Paul Hoffman had been appointed Administrator by the President. From this point on, the administrative orders and regulations of Mr. Hoffman, his appointments of subordinates and his plans for the allocation of duties were legitimate plans—for formal organization—in that they were included in, and contemplated by, the formal organization plan laid down by Congress in the Act itself, and by the President in his appointment of Mr. Hoffman.

But still this does not give us a basis for distinguishing formal organization plans from plans that have not been legitimatized. We have merely found the source of one set of formal plans—those of Mr. Hoffman—in another set of underlying formal plans—those of the Congress. Why do we consider the statute "legitimate"? The answer lies in the attitudes of those persons to whom the plans are directed (e.g., the employees of ECA). The only reason why it is important that Congress places its blessing upon a plan by enacting it into law, is that people in this country behave differently toward plans that have been so blessed than toward plans that have not. Acceptance of the legitimacy of Congress and its actions is an acceptance of the legitimacy of the American governmental system. It is an essential and important part of mores of the society in which the employee lives, and which he has accepted long before he becomes a member of the organization. It defines for him the conditions under which the general mores of authority come into play—the situations in which, according to his mores, he feels that he *ought* to accept authority.

We cannot pursue further at this point the subject of legitimacy and the acceptance of authority except to warn against certain misconceptions. First, legitimacy is at root not a legal but a psychological matter. A legal or any other system of authority is legitimate only to the extent that those persons to whom it is directed feel that they ought or must accept it. Second, the legitimacy of an organizational plan is seldom accepted as absolute by those whom it seeks to govern. There are always limits—often fairly narrow limits—which, if exceeded, will cause refusal to accept the plan or even to admit its legitimacy. Third, legitimacy need not be hierarchical in its structure, resulting from successive acts of delegation. Although the examples we have cited were of a hierarchical character, we shall see that legitimacy can arise in many other ways. . . .

INFORMAL ORGANIZATION

Almost always the actual pattern of behaviors and relationships of the members of an organization will depart slightly or widely from the formal plan of organization. The actual pattern may differ from the formal plan in two ways: (1) the formal plan may be incomplete— it may not include the whole pattern of behavior as it actually develops; and (2) some portions of the actual pattern of behavior may be in contradiction to the plan. By *informal organization* is meant the whole pattern of actual behaviors—the way members of the organization really do behave—insofar as these actual behaviors do not coincide with the formal plan.

Incompleteness of Formal Organization

There are wide differences in the degrees to which various organizations attempt to plan formally the behavior of their employees. In some organizations the plan is very sketchy. It consists of little more than a few verbal or written instructions that assign tasks to employees, and perhaps specify the principal lines of legitimate authority. The formal plans of small organization units, with a dozen employees, say, seldom amount to more than this. In other organizations the plan is very elaborate—for example, the regulations in an army or navy specify the manner in which an enlisted man shall address an officer, the occasions on which he is permitted to initiate a contact with an officer, and the exact occasions and manner of saluting.

The incompleteness of the formal plan provides a vacuum which, like other vacuums, proves abhorrent to nature. The members of an organization gradually develop patterns of behavior and relationships with each other, and the unplanned aspects of their behavior may come to be as structured, as stable, and as predictable as the planned aspects. Well defined "habits" will almost inevitably develop defining how the boss is to be greeted when he enters the office in the morning (which we have seen is an element of formal organization in a military unit), who is to lunch with whom, and who is to be consulted when a decision of a particular kind is to be reached.

CONFLICTS BETWEEN FORMAL AND INFORMAL

Not only is the formal plan always supplemented by informally-developed patterns, but it is almost always contradicted in some respects by the actual pattern of behavior. These failures to carry out the formal plan may be deliberate or non-deliberate. Refusal to obey legitimate orders—either outright refusal or refusal through "misunderstanding" of intent—is a common phenomenon in almost every organization. Attempts to exercise authority beyond that legitimately assigned are equally common. In extreme instances we may find cliques within the organization attempting to wrest control of it from those to whom control has been formally assigned, and to use this control either to change the goals of the organization, or to benefit the clique members, or both. Such "illegal" activities, which are of the same kind as revolutionary behaviors, are of considerable importance. . . .

Non-deliberate departures from the formal organization plan are probably of even more frequent occurrence, and of equal significance. Organization members who possess strong qualities of leadership will almost inevitably find themselves, even without deliberate purpose, exercising far more influence than is contemplated in the organization plan. Where the plan conflicts with deep-seated habits or attitudes it may be forgotten or ignored, even without deliberate intent, and often at the expense of considerable guilt-feelings of those who ignore it. This occurs very frequently when the formal plans are overelaborate —for example, where elaborate paper-work processes are established whose meaning and usefulness is not apparent to the employees. When employees find that it is too complicated to do things "through channels," new and often explicitly forbidden informal channels are employed to supplement and by-pass the formal ones.

MUTUAL INFLUENCE OF THE FORMAL AND INFORMAL

From our discussion of informal organization we can draw two generalizations: (1) when human beings are brought together into frequent contact they will develop more or less definite patterns of relationship even in the absence of a formal plan, and certainly in supplementation to any formal plan that is promulgated; (2) the influence of legitimacy, and the other influences that those who authorize formal plans can bring to bear upon behavior are only a few among the numerous influences, organizational and non-organizational, that determine the behavior of organization members. To the degree that these other influences work at cross purposes to the plan of organization, the actual pattern of behavior is likely to depart from the planned pattern.

It is not easy to distinguish those instances where the behavior of an employee reflects the influence of the formal organization from those instances where it reflects the influence of the informal organization—in most cases these influences parallel and reinforce each other. A forest ranger may take great care to maintain the fire trails in his forest because he has been formally assigned this job. On the other hand, he may do this because he wants his fellow rangers to regard him as a good forest manager. Most likely both these motives, and perhaps others as well, enter into his behavior, and it would be almost impossible to determine the separate importance of each.

Nor is it easy to distinguish between the formal or informal influences of the organization and the responses of the employee to influences that have been internalized and have become part of his own personality. The efficiency criterion is one example. Most people accept employment in an agency with a full expectation that they will attempt to carry out their responsibilities in an efficient manner. The typist knows, even before she receives specific orders, that she is expected to type as rapidly and accurately as possible, not as slowly and carelessly as possible.

We see, then, that the environment in which an employee finds himself in an organization is usually a closely intertwined composition of formal and informal influences. In the first place, many of the informal relationships grow directly out of the formal structure. The planned arrangement of offices, for example, may throw two employees into frequent contact with each other, and as a result they may often converse, have lunch together, and develop social contacts outside office hours. Similarly, the hierarchical relationships tend to bring together employees who are at about the same status level and to create a great social distance between those at high levels and those at low levels. In civilian organizations, where the contacts between subordinates and superiors are not usually formally regulated, this social distance may be almost as great as in an army, where it is embodied in formal instructions.[3]

In the second place, formal and informal are intertwined because relationships that initially grow up on an informal basis may be "ratified" and incorporated in the formal structure by subsequent

[3] Observation of a group of executives sitting down at a conference or at lunch where the seats are not assigned ahead of time almost always reveals something of the status system of the group. At a long table, the persons of high status will usually tend to cluster at the middle or one end, with the persons of lowest status occupying the seats farthest from them.

regulations. For example, most public personnel systems provide for a formal position classification—a detailed statement of the duties and responsibilities of each position. When an employee "works out of classification"—i.e., performs duties not listed in his job description—the procedures usually provide that his job may be redescribed and re-classified to bring about consistency between the formal description and what he is actually doing.

The early months of the Economic Cooperation Administration provide a striking example of the ratification of informal relations. Between April, 1948, when the agency was established, and about July 15, when it already had some six hundred employees, it operated without any formal plan for its internal structure even so elaborate as an organization chart showing its principal divisions. To be sure, certain formal organization decisions had been made by appointing and giving titles to key employees, and by specifying certain procedures for paper flow (which were frequently informally violated), and by settling certain disputes about self-assumed jurisdiction. But the real core of this organization, which was in full operation before May 1, lay in a complex set of behaviors and understandings that had grown up almost spontaneously. The formal plans that were finally issued in July and subsequently were in very large part ratifications of this informal scheme.

SUMMARY: THE INDIVIDUAL AND THE ORGANIZATION

. . . We have examined the tangled scheme of relationships that ties an individual to an organization and makes his behavior a part of the system of organization behavior. Being an employee of an organization alters an individual's behavior by altering the factual premises and the value premises that underlie his choices and decisions. As a result of his employment he works toward different goals, and he has different conceptions as to how to achieve these goals, than if he were in some other environment.

But the individual employee is by no means putty in the organization's hands. His behavior is controlled and controllable only within rather narrow limits. A wide range of influences, past and present, lying outside the organization, and especially outside its formal plans, all have their part in accounting for his actual behavior.

The organization encounters not only individual resistance, but also group resistance to its influences. To the degree that employees are sociable, they are highly responsive to their immediate work groups, which thus become important channels of organization influence. Only in recent years has adequate attention been paid to the role of such face-to-face groups and their importance for administration. . . .

COMMENTARY

The administrative behavior approach represented a resurgence of scientific inquiry into administrative systems. It focused on "administrative man" as a social organism and not solely a political animal; and it viewed organizations as informal social networks of interpersonal relationships, as opposed to formal structures endowed with punitive and suppressive powers. In short, it offered as a generalized thesis the proposition that the organization was just as much controlled by its members as it was able to control them. Starting with this basic premise, the focus of administrative analysis was extended to include the sociological and psychological motivations of the Organization Man. For the most part, the inquiries conducted in conjunction with this approach focused on explaining how and why man behaved as he did in an administrative setting. Normative values were considered valid concepts for scientific inquiry, but the explicit thrust of the administrative behavior approach was descriptive, not prescriptive. However, these writers implicitly fostered a quasi-scientific ideology which strengthened a fundamental weakness in the tenets of political rationality. It is in this context that the selections of the preceding authors should be examined.

At the outset it seems clear that all the preceding writers viewed organizational efficiency and effectiveness as products of certain forces internalized by the individual member. Thus, Latham's point that organization is a state of mind was repeated by Presthus (authority relates to one's perception of authority), Gore (the organization is energized by the vital emotional motivations of the personality), and Simon-Smithburg-Thompson (internalized expectations of social

196

satisfactions and dissatisfactions are at least of equal importance in controlling individual behavior as formal sanctions and rewards). Elsewhere, it was Latham who stated that "people are the stuff of which a bureau is made" and, indeed, the basic focus of this approach was directly on the individual and his relationships with his superiors, his subordinates, and his peers. From this interaction of forces emerged the administrative patterns, or habits, which, on an informal and unofficial level, provided the amalgam which held the organization together. In a sense, the formal structure became a facade which deceptively covered the true energy of the system. As Presthus noted, "While authority may appear to rest upon a formal role, an executive's reliance upon this formal position for legitimation of his leadership is usually a confession of weakness."

As noted in Chapter Three, leadership was an integral feature of the management science authority structure. In formal, hierarchical terms, the organization was a composite of the leaders and the led—those who could suppress and those who were suppressed. For Latham, however, hierarchical authority was a "theological fiction" which in actual fact was a distorted picture of reality. Or, as seen by Simon-Smithburg-Thompson, "The individual employee is by no means putty in the organization's hands. His behavior is controlled and controllable only within rather narrow limits. A wide range of influences, past and present, lying outside the organization, and especially outside its formal plans, all have their part in accounting for his actual behavior." In short, the management science school revealed a Hobbesian view of man which assumed that effective and efficient operations could only be the by-product of a highly structured, immutable set of superior-subordinate relationships. The administrative behavior school, on the other hand, assumed a much more optimistic view of man as one who, according to Latham, wanted "to behave socially" even without authoritative direction.

This is not to suggest that these writers were a utopian group who saw "administrative man" existing in an idyllic state of perfect order and harmony. On the contrary, conflict was seen as an inherent part of all human relations. But the difference between this approach to conflict and that of the management science advocates was that for the latter conflict was to be controlled by formal organizational forces, while the former sought to control conflict through interpersonal forces. As Latham noted, "It is the individuals that make up the organization who generate the will to order." In this regard, the key factor in controlling conflict, and indeed in regulating all administrative behavior, was, as seen by Presthus, the psychological element of anxiety.

The formal organization could increase individual anxiety through the use of threats and the imposition of sanctions. By the same token it could decrease individual anxiety by bestowing rewards, indicating approval of behavior, and generally increasing the occupational security of the individual. In addition, anxiety could be directly affected by one's informal relationships with those with whom he interacted regularly on a face-to-face basis. Thus, according to Presthus, anxiety was an emotional element which all normal human beings attempt to minimize as much as possible.

An increase in anxiety as a result of either formal organizational actions or informal actions developing within one's social context could prove to be quite dysfunctional insofar as operating effectiveness was concerned. By the same token, however, the writers of the administrative behavior approach recognized that dysfunctional consequences for the organization could very well result if individual anxiety was completely eliminated. Absolute security, psychologically speaking, could yield complacency, which, in turn, could adversely affect operating effectiveness. Thus, the challenge for the organization was to locate an optimum anxiety-reward balance for each individual which, through the astute manipulation of material and symbolic rewards, would permit the individual to endure varying degrees of anxiety.*

The concept of anxiety reduction advanced by Presthus offered an important insight into the nature of Organization Man as viewed by the administrative behaviorists. The administrative man of this approach was a utilitarian man who quite clearly sought pleasure and avoided pain. Thus, the authoritarian Hobbesian figure of the management science literature was in the administrative behavior approach replaced by a Benthamite utilitarian concept which, as will be seen, provided a natural link between administrative behavior doctrines and political rationalism.

If the utilitarian interpretation of the administrative behaviorists is recognized as valid, then the easiest way for the Organization Man to maximize his security (pleasure) and minimize his anxiety (pain) was to become totally socialized by his overall organization, as well as by his immediate peer group. Or, as Simon-Smithburg-Thompson noted, "Administrative man accepts the organization's goals as the value premises of his decisions, is particularly sensitive and reactive to the influences upon him of the other members of his organization, forms stable expectations regarding his own role in relation to others and the roles of others in relation to him, and has high morale in regard to the organization's goals." The former Democratic Speaker of the U.S. House of Representatives, Sam Rayburn, said essentially

* The anxiety-reward balance concept is a slight modification of Presthus' evaluation of anxiety. For a more detailed elaboration of anxiety-reward balance see Gawthrop, *Bureaucratic Behavior in the Executive Branch* (New York: The Free Press, 1969), pp. 137ff.

the same thing in his famous dictum to freshman congressmen, "If you want to get along, go along." The individual administrator, as seen by the behaviorists, wanted to behave in a socially acceptable manner and wanted to cooperate with his superiors, his subordinates, and most especially with his peers. Under these circumstances, the primary function of leadership was to direct and coordinate the inherently cooperative nature of man, according to Latham. And, as seen by Simon-Smithburg-Thompson, "Only those organizations survive for any length of time whose net influence upon their members is to preserve and develop habits of cooperation."

What the administrative behaviorists were describing was a personality-type which closely resembled Riesman's other-directed man —that person who was anxious to accommodate his will to the will of others, who was willing to compromise, and who was quick to seek consensus in the face of conflict in order to minimize his own personal anxiety as well as the anxiety of others. This behavioral characteristic bears a very close resemblance to what Herbert Simon has classified as "satisficing" when applied to administrative decision-making. That is, no administrator has either the time or the intellectual capacity (and one might add, the desire) to explore all possible alternatives in an effort to determine the *best possible* solution to a given problem. His only recourse, therefore, is to seek a satisfactory solution, or one which is "good enough"—i.e., he must "satisfice." This other-directed, "satisficing" attitude was presented in no better behavioral context than in Gore's discussion on heuristic systems of action.

Heuristic thought is that branch of logic which deals with discovery and invention. Thus, when Gore stated that the heuristic process was a groping toward agreements seldom arrived at through logic, he was referring to logic in the rational sense. The heuristic process is one in which the individual either seeks to discover or invents his own solutions to immediate problems. It is, indeed, a groping process of trial-and-error which involves a high degree of pragmatic planning as opposed to the comprehensive characteristic of rational planning. In addition, heuristics imply values (i.e., security, stability, continuity, consistency), which may or may not be internalized as part of the human psyche. For Gore, "The very essence of the heuristic process is that the factors validating a decision are internal to the personality of the individual instead of external to it." Thus, the personality of the individual becomes a critical variable in the administrative process, especially in view of the assertion by Gore that the "dynamics of personality are not those of logic but rather those of the emotions." Heuristic strategies are those aimed at the coordination and accommodation of diverse and conflicting emotional energies, which—for the most part—are not amenable to rational manipulation. When a small rural community is informed that its "little red schoolhouse" is to be abolished in favor of a new, modern, consolidated school district, the decision may be incontrovertible on the basis of rational analysis. But a heuristic strategy may very well have to be devised to win agreement of the people of this community who may have strong emotional feelings over the loss of their own school building. For example, an appeal based on the prestige to be gained by the community in having a modern structure in its area might be effective. The possibility of drawing the district's boundaries in such a way as to exclude clusters of minority groups might be very appealing in certain sections of the country. Gore's point was simply that because emotions were quite resistant to logical analysis the organization had to direct the vital emotional energies of the personality in a positive, functional manner if it was to survive.

In other words, the administrative behaviorists thought that the health of any organization depended on the extent to which the rational decision-making structure was capable of accommodating the emotional energy contained in each individual's personality. For the most part, this accommodation was accomplished most effectively through the use of heuristic strategies aimed at achieving heuristic agreements. Heuristic strategies, according to Gore, were mainly indigenous, extra-formal, and volitional. Heuristic agreements, "usually represent some form of consensus." In short, the search for consensus among conflicting and diverse sets of normative values was the essence of the heuristic process.

Thus, the Benthamite man of the administrative behaviorists, supplemented by an other-directed personality characteristic, moved in the same direction as the politically-attuned administrator of the previous chapter. Stein, the Dimocks, and Long explained the public administrator's pragmatic, prudent behavior in political terms: the atrophy of the party system, the fragmented and decentralized nature of our political process, the inherent jealousy between the executive and legislative branches. The writers of the administrative behavior approach explained the same pragmatic, prudent behavior in sociopsychological terms. The essential weakness of the political power-oriented writers was that they could provide no fundamental justification for the behavior of their "administrative man" other than one presented in politically pragmatic terms. The "rules of the game" were set; the successful administrator played the game according to the rules. "This may not be the way it should be," wrote Stein, "but that is another question." This question was left unanswered by Stein and his colleagues, but the main thrust of the literature of the behavioral approach was aimed at filling just this void. According to this approach the public administrator had to adapt to the dynamics of his politically-sensitive environment not because he had to play by the rules of the game to survive, but, rather, because the vital emotional motivations inherent in his personality inevitably caused him to seek socially-satisfying and anxiety-reducing agreements.

In reacting against the economics-oriented management science dogmas built around the twin pedestals of economy and efficiency, administrative theory turned first in the direction of politics for a satisfactory alternative model to "administrative man," and then in the direction of sociology and psychology. As has been suggested, the political and the socio-psychological models blended well to provide a coherent explanation *and justification* of why the administrative structure of the executive branch of government had to operate in a consensus-oriented context. This evolving alternative model was nevertheless vulnerable. Hardheaded economists remained unconvinced that the inequitable and inefficient allocation of governmental resources was required by the necessities of prudential pragmatism, anxiety-reduction, or heuristic strategies. They based their judgment on the observation of private executives who psychologically behaved no differently than their public counterparts, but who, nonetheless, were able to maximize operating efficiency.

For years, the absence of the profit motive in government was invoked as the economic justification for the distinction between public and private attitudes toward efficiency. However, in the post-World War II period, the traditional, or classical liberal, notion of profit was altered drastically in the world of private business and industry primarily as a result of the emphasis that came to be placed on corporation growth, research and development, advertising, and quality control. Thus, a new justification was needed to replace the outdated profit differentiation theory, but the challenge was formidable since the new theory had to satisfy two essential requirements. First, like the theory it was to replace, it had to explain in current and relevant terms why the allocation of governmental resources could not be accomplished economically and efficiently as a matter of course. Second, the explanation advanced to satisfy the first requirement had to complement and supplement the political and socio-psychological explanations that were already established. In other words, figuratively speaking, the search was for a composite politico-economic/socio-psychological model which could be used to differentiate public administration from the criteria used to judge operating effectiveness in private organizations. The model which finally emerged is presented and evaluated in the following chapter.

ADMINISTRATION AND INCREMENTALISM 6

THE SCIENCE OF MUDDLING THROUGH

CHARLES E. LINDBLOM

Suppose an administrator is given responsibility of formulating policy with respect to inflation. He might start by trying to list all related values in order of importance, e.g., full employment, reasonable business profit, protection of small savings, prevention of a stock market crash. Then all possible policy outcomes could be rated as more or less efficient in attaining a maximum of these values. This would of course require a prodigious inquiry into values held by members of society and an equally prodigious set of calculations on how much of each value is equal to how much of each other value. He could then proceed to outline all possible policy alternatives. In a third step, he would undertake systematic comparison of his multitude of alternatives to determine which attains the greatest amount of values.

In comparing policies, he would take advantage of any theory available that generalized about classes of policies. In considering inflation, for example, he would compare all policies in the light of the theory of prices. Since no alternatives are beyond his investigation, he would consider strict central control and the abolition of all prices and markets on the one hand and elimination of all public controls with reliance completely on the free market on the other, both in the light of whatever theoretical generalizations he could find on such hypothetical economies.

From *Public Administration Review*, Vol. 19 (Spring 1959), pp. 79–88. Charles Lindblom is Professor of Economics and Political Science, Yale University. Reprinted with permission of the author and The American Society of Public Administration.

Finally, he would try to make the choice that would in fact maximize his values.

An alternative line of attack would be to set as his principal objective, either explicitly or without conscious thought, the relatively simple goal of keeping prices level. This objective might be compromised or complicated by only a few other goals, such as full employment. He would in fact disregard most other social values as beyond his present interest, and he would for the moment not even attempt to rank the few values that he regarded as immediately relevant. Were he pressed, he would quickly admit that he was ignoring many related values and many possible important consequences of his policies.

As a second step, he would outline those relatively few policy alternatives that occurred to him. He would then compare them. In comparing his limited number of alternatives, most of them familiar from past controversies, he would not ordinarily find a body of theory precise enough to carry him through a comparison of their respective consequences. Instead he would rely heavily on the record of past experience with small policy steps to predict the consequences of similar steps extended into the future.

Moreover, he would find that the policy alternatives combined objectives or values in different ways. For example, one policy might offer price level stability at the cost of some risk of unemployment; another might offer less price stability but also less risk of unemployment. Hence, the next step in his approach—the final selection—would combine into one the choice among values and the choice among instruments for reaching values. It would not, as in the first method of policy-making, approximate a more mechanical process of choosing the means that best satisfied goals that were previously clarified and ranked. Because practitioners of the second approach expect to achieve their goals only partially, they would expect to repeat endlessly the sequence just described, as conditions and aspirations changed and as accuracy of prediction improved. . . .

Accordingly, I propose in this paper to clarify and formalize the second method, much neglected in the literature. This might be described as the method of *successive limited comparisons.** I will contrast it with the first approach, which might be called the rational-comprehensive method.[1] More impressionistically and briefly—and therefore generally used in this article—they could be characterized as the branch method and root method, the former continually build-

---

* Editorial note: As explained in the following Commentary, this method is synonomous with the bargaining-incremental approach.

[1] I am assuming that administrators often make policy and advise in the making of policy and am treating decision-making and policy-making as synonymous for purposes of this paper.

ing out from the current situation, step-by-step and by small degrees; the latter starting from fundamentals anew each time, building on the past only as experience is embodied in a theory, and always prepared to start completely from the ground up.

Let us put the characteristics of the two methods side by side in simplest terms.

Rational-Comprehensive (*Root*)	*Successive Limited Comparisons* (*Branch*)
1a. Clarification of values or objectives distinct from and usually prerequisite to empirical analysis of alternative policies.	1b. Selection of value goals and empirical analysis of the needed action are not distinct from one another but are closely intertwined.
2a. Policy-formulation is therefore approached through means-end analysis: First the ends are isolated, then the means to achieve them are sought.	2b. Since means and ends are not distinct, means-end analysis is often inappropriate or limited.
3a. The test of a "good" policy is that it can be shown to be the most appropriate means to desired ends.	3b. The test of a "good" policy is typically that various analysts find themselves directly agreeing on a policy (without their agreeing that it is the most appropriate means to an agreed objective).

4a. Analysis is comprehensive; every important relevant factor is taken into account.	4b. Analysis is drastically limited:
	  i) Important possible outcomes are neglected.
	  ii) Important alternative potential policies are neglected.
	  iii) Important affected values are neglected.

5a. Theory is often heavily relied upon.	5b. A succession of comparisons greatly reduces or eliminates reliance on theory.

INTERTWINING EVALUATION AND EMPIRICAL ANALYSIS (1b)

The quickest way to understand how values are handled in the method of successive limited comparisons is to see how the root method often breaks down in *its* handling of values or objectives. The idea that values should be clarified, and in advance of the examination of alternative policies, is appealing. But what happens when we attempt it for complex social problems? The first difficulty is that on many critical values or objectives, citizens disagree, congressmen disagree, and public administrators disagree. Even where a fairly specific objective is prescribed for the administrator, there remains considerable room for disagreement on sub-objectives. Consider, for example, the conflict with respect to locating public housing, described in Meyerson and Banfield's study of the Chicago Housing Authority[2]—disagreement which occurred despite the clear objective of providing a certain number of public housing units in the city. Similarly conflicting are objectives in highway location, traffic control, minimum wage administration, development of tourist facilities in national parks, or insect control.

Administrators cannot escape these conflicts by ascertaining the majority's preference, for preferences have not been registered on most issues; indeed, there often *are* no preferences in the absence of public discussion sufficient to bring an issue to the attention of the electorate. Furthermore, there is a question of whether intensity of feeling should be considered as well as the number of persons preferring each alternative. By the impossibility of doing otherwise, administrators often are reduced to deciding policy without clarifying objectives first.

Even when an administrator resolves to follow his own values as a criterion for decisions, he often will not know how to rank them when they conflict with one another, as they usually do. Suppose, for example, that an administrator must relocate tenants living in tenements scheduled for destruction. One objective is to empty the buildings fairly promptly, another is to find suitable accommodation for persons displaced, another is to avoid friction with residents in other areas in which a large influx would be unwelcome, another is to deal with all concerned through persuasion if possible, and so on.

How does one state even to himself the relative importance of these partially conflicting values? A simple ranking of them is not enough; one needs ideally to know how much of one value is worth sacrificing for some of another value. The answer is that typically the administrator chooses—and must choose—directly among policies in which these values are combined in different ways. He cannot first clarify his values and then choose among policies.

A more subtle third point underlies both the first two. Social objectives do not always have the same relative values. One objective may be highly prized in one circumstance, another in another circumstance. If, for example, an administrator values highly both the

[2] Martin Meyerson and Edward C. Banfield, *Politics, Planning and the Public Interest* (The Free Press, 1955).

dispatch with which his agency can carry through its projects *and* good public relations, it matters little which of the two possibly conflicting values he favors in some abstract or general sense. Policy questions arise in forms which put to administrators such a question as: Given the degree to which we are or are not already achieving the values of dispatch and the values of good public relations, is it worth sacrificing a little speed for a happier clientele, or is it better to risk offending the clientele so that we can get on with our work? The answer to such a question varies with circumstances.

The value problem is, as the example shows, always a problem of adjustments at a margin. But there is no practicable way to state marginal objectives or values except in terms of particular policies. That one value is preferred to another in one decision situation does not mean that it will be preferred in another decision situation in which it can be had only at great sacrifice of another value. Attempts to rank or order values in general and abstract terms so that they do not shift from decision to decision end up by ignoring the relevant marginal preferences. The significance of this third point thus goes very far. Even if all administrators had at hand an agreed set of values, objectives, and constraints, and an agreed ranking of these values, objectives, and constraints, their marginal values in actual choice situations would be impossible to formulate.

Unable consequently to formulate the relevant values first and then choose among policies to achieve them, administrators must choose directly among alternative policies that offer different marginal combinations of values. Somewhat paradoxically, the only practicable way to disclose one's relevant marginal values even to oneself is to describe the policy one chooses to achieve them. Except roughly and vaguely, I know of no way to describe—or even to understand—what my relative evaluations are for, say, freedom and security, speed and accuracy in governmental decisions, or low taxes and better schools than to describe my preferences among specific policy choices that might be made between the alternatives in each of the pairs.

In summary, two aspects of the process by which values are actually handled can be distinguished. The first is clear: evaluation and empirical analysis are intertwined; that is, one chooses among values and among policies at one and the same time. Put a little more elaborately, one simultaneously chooses a policy to attain certain objectives and chooses the objectives themselves. The second aspect is related but distinct: the administrator focuses his attention on marginal or incremental values. Whether he is aware of it or not, he does not find general formulations of objectives very helpful and in fact makes specific marginal or incremental comparisons. . . .

As to whether the attempt to clarify objectives in advance of policy selection is more or less rational than the close intertwining of marginal evaluation and empirical analysis, the principal difference established is that for complex problems the first is impossible and irrelevant, and the second is both possible and relevant. The second is possible because the administrator need not try to analyze any values except the values by which alternative policies differ and need not be concerned with them except as they differ marginally. His need for information on values or objectives is drastically reduced as compared with the root method; and his capacity for grasping, comprehending, and relating values to one another is not strained beyond the breaking point.

RELATIONS BETWEEN MEANS AND ENDS (2b)

Decision-making is ordinarily formalized as a means-ends relationship: means are conceived to be evaluated and chosen in the light of ends finally selected independently of and prior to the choice of means. This is the means-ends relationship of the root method. But it follows from all that has just been said that such a means-ends relationship is possible only to the extent that values are agreed upon, are reconcilable, and are stable at the margin. Typically, therefore, such a means-ends relationship is absent from the branch method, where means and ends are simultaneously chosen.

Yet any departure from the means-ends relationship of the root method will strike some readers as inconceivable. For it will appear to them that only in such a relationship is it possible to determine whether one policy choice is better or worse than another. How can an administrator know whether he has made a wise or foolish decision if he is without prior values or objectives by which to judge his decisions? The answer to this question calls up the third distinctive difference between root and branch methods: how to decide the best policy.

THE TEST OF "GOOD" POLICY (3b)

In the root method, a decision is "correct," "good," or "rational" if it can be shown to attain some specified objective, where the objective can be specified without simply describing the decision itself. Where objectives are defined only through the marginal or incremental approach to values described above, it is still sometimes possible to test whether a policy does in fact attain the desired objectives; but a precise statement of the objectives takes the form of a description of the policy chosen or some alternative to it. To show that a policy is mistaken one cannot offer an abstract argument that important objectives are not achieved; one must instead argue that another policy is more to be preferred.

So far, the departure from customary ways of looking at problem-solving is not troublesome, for many administrators will be quick to agree that the most effective discussion of the correctness of policy does take the form of comparison with other policies that might have been chosen. But what of the situation in which administrators cannot agree on values or objectives, either abstractly or in marginal terms? What then is the test of "good" policy? For the root method, there is no test. Agreement on objectives failing, there is no standard of "correctness." For the method of successive limited comparisons, the test is agreement on policy itself, which remains possible even when agreement on values is not.

It has been suggested that continuing agreement in Congress on the desirability of extending old age insurance stems from liberal desires to strengthen the welfare programs of the federal government and from conservative desires to reduce union demands for private pension plans. If so, this is an excellent demonstration of the ease with which individuals of different ideologies often can agree on concrete policy. Labor mediators report a similar phenomenon: the contestants cannot agree on criteria for settling their disputes but can agree on specific proposals. Similarly, when one administrator's objective turns out to be another's means, they often can agree on policy.

Agreement on policy thus becomes the only practicable test of the policy's correctness. And for one administrator to seek to win the other over to agreement on ends as well would accomplish nothing and create quite unnecessary controversy.

If agreement directly on policy as a test for "best" policy seems a poor substitute for testing the policy against its objectives, it ought to be remembered that objectives themselves have no ultimate validity other than they are agreed upon. Hence agreement is the test of "best" policy in both methods. But where the root method requires agreement on what elements in the decision constitute objectives and on which of these objectivies should be sought, the branch method falls back on agreement wherever it can be found.

In an important sense, therefore, it is not irrational for an administrator to defend a policy as good without being able to specify what it is good for.

NON-COMPREHENSIVE ANALYSIS (4b)

Ideally, rational-comprehensive analysis leaves out nothing important. But it is impossible to take everything important into consideration unless "important" is so narrowly defined that analysis is in fact quite limited. Limits on human intellectual capacities and on available information set definite limits to man's capacity to be comprehensive. In actual fact, therefore, no one can practice the rational-comprehensive method for really complex problems, and every administrator faced with a sufficiently complex problem must find ways drastically to simplify.

An administrator assisting in the formulation of agricultural economic policy cannot in the first place be competent on all possible policies. He cannot even comprehend one policy entirely. In planning a soil bank program, he cannot successfully anticipate the impact of higher or lower farm income on, say, urbanization—the possible consequent loosening of family ties, possible consequent eventual need for revisions in social security and further implications for tax problems arising out of new federal responsibilities for social security and municipal responsibilities for urban services. Nor, to follow another line of repercussions, can he work through the soil bank program's effects on prices for agricultural products in foreign markets and consequent implications for foreign relations, including those arising out of economic rivalry between the United States and the U.S.S.R.

In the method of successive limited comparisons, simplification is systematically achieved in two principal ways. First, it is achieved through limitation of policy comparisons to those policies that differ in relatively small degree from policies presently in effect. Such a limitation immediately reduces the number of alternatives to be investigated and also drastically simplifies the character of the investigation of each. For it is not necessary to undertake fundamental inquiry into an alternative and its consequences; it is necessary only to study those respects in which the proposed alternative and its consequences differ from the status quo. The empirical comparison of marginal differences among alternative polices that differ only marginally is, of course, a counterpart of the incremental or marginal comparison of values discussed above.[3]

RELEVANCE AS WELL AS REALISM

It is a matter of common observation that in Western democracies public administrators and policy analysts in general do largely limit their analyses to incremental or marginal differences in policies that are chosen to differ only incrementally. They do not do so, however, solely because they desperately need some way to simplify their problems; they also do so in order to be relevant. Democracies change their policies almost entirely through incremental adjustments. Policy does not move in leaps and bounds.

The incremental character of political change in the United States has often been remarked. The two major political parties agree on

---

[3] A more precise definition of incremental policies and a discussion of whether a change that appears "small" to one observer might be seen differently by another is to be found in my "Policy Analysis," 48 *American Economic Review* 298 (June, 1958).

fundamentals; they offer alternative policies to the voters only on relatively small points of difference. Both parties favor full employment, but they define it somewhat differently; both favor the development of water power resources, but in slightly different ways; and both favor unemployment compensation, but not the same level of benefits. Similarly, shifts of policy within a party take place largely through a series of relatively small changes, as can be seen in their only gradual acceptance of the idea of governmental responsibility for support of the unemployed, a change in party positions beginning in the early 30's and culminating in a sense in the Employment Act of 1946.

Party behavior is in turn rooted in public attitudes, and political theorists cannot conceive a democracy's surviving in the United States in the absence of fundamental agreement on potentially disruptive issues, with consequent limitation of policy debates to relatively small differences in policy.

Since the policies ignored by the administrator are politically impossible and so irrelevant, the simplification of analysis achieved by concentrating on policies that differ only incrementally is not a capricious kind of simplification. In addition, it can be argued that, given the limits on knowledge within which policy-makers are confined, simplifying by limiting the focus to small variations from present policy makes the most of available knowledge. Because policies being considered are like present and past policies, the administrator can obtain information and claim some insight. Non-incremental policy proposals are therefore typically not only politically irrelevant but also unpredictable in their consequences.

The second method of simplification of analysis is the practice of ignoring important possible consequences of possible policies, as well as the values attached to the neglected consequences. If this appears to disclose a shocking shortcoming of successive limited comparisons, it can be replied that, even if the exclusions are random, policies may nevertheless be more intelligently formulated than through futile attempts to achieve a comprehensiveness beyond human capacity. Actually, however, the exclusions, seeming arbitrary or random from one point of view, need be neither.

ACHIEVING A DEGREE OF COMPREHENSIVENESS

Suppose that each value neglected by one policy-making agency were a major concern of at least one other agency. In that case, a helpful division of labor would be achieved, and no agency need find its task beyond its capacities. The shortcomings of such a system would be that one agency might destroy a value either before another agency could be activated to safeguard it or in spite of another agency's efforts. But the possibility that important values may be lost is present

in any form of organization, even where agencies attempt to comprehend in planning more than is humanly possible.

The virtue of such a hypothetical division of labor is that every important interest or value has its watchdog. And these watchdogs can
protect the interests in their jurisdiction in two quite different ways;
first, by redressing damages done by other agencies; and, second, by
anticipating and heading off injury before it occurs.

In a society like that of the United States in which individuals are
free to combine to pursue almost any possible common interest they
might have and in which government agencies are sensitive to the
pressures of these groups, the system described is approximated. Almost every interest has its watchdog. Without claiming that every interest has a sufficiently powerful watchdog, it can be argued that our
system often can assure a more comprehensive regard for the values
of the whole society than any attempt at intellectual comprehensiveness.

In the United States, for example, no part of government attempts a
comprehensive overview of policy on income distribution. A policy
nevertheless evolves, and one responding to a wide variety of interests.
A process of mutual adjustment among farm groups, labor unions,
municipalities and school boards, tax authorities, and government
agencies with responsibilities in the fields of housing, health, highways, national parks, fire, and police accomplishes a distribution of
income in which particular income problems neglected at one point
in the decision processes become central at another point.

Mutual adjustment is more pervasive than the explicit forms it takes
in negotiation between groups; it persists through the mutual impacts
of groups upon each other even where they are not in communication.
For all the imperfections and latent dangers in this ubiquitous process
of mutual adjustment, it will often accomplish an adaptation of
policies to a wider range of interests than could be done by one group
centrally.

Note, too, how the incremental pattern of policy-making fits with
the multiple pressure pattern. For when decisions are only incremental—closely related to known policies, it is easier for one group
to anticipate the kind of moves another might make and easier too for
it to make correction for injury already accomplished.[4]

Even partisanship and narrowness, to use pejorative terms, will
sometimes be assets to rational decision-making, for they can doubly
insure that what one agency neglects, another will not; they specialize
personnel to distinct points of view. The claim is valid that effective
rational coordination of the federal administration, if possible to

---

[4] The link between the practice of the method of successive limited comparisons
and mutual adjustment of interests in a highly fragmented decision-making
process adds a new facet to pluralist theories of government and administration.

achieve at all, would require an agreed set of values[5]—if "rational" is defined as the practice of the root method of decision-making. But a high degree of administrative coordination occurs as each agency adjusts its policies to the concerns of the other agencies in the process of fragmented decision-making I have just described.

For all the apparent shortcomings of the incremental approach to policy alternatives with arbitrary exclusion coupled with fragmentation, when compared to the root method, the branch method often looks far superior. In the root method, the inevitable exclusion of factors is accidental, unsystematic, and not defensible by any argument so far developed, while in the branch method the exclusions are deliberate, systematic, and defensible. Ideally, of course, the root method does not exclude; in practice it must.

Nor does the branch method necessarily neglect long-run considerations and objectives. It is clear that important values must be omitted in considering policy, and sometimes the only way long-run objectives can be given adequate attention is through the neglect of short-run considerations. But the values omitted can be either long-run or short-run.

SUCCESSION OF COMPARISONS (5b)

The final distinctive element in the branch method is that the comparisons, together with the policy choice, proceed in a chronological series. Policy is not made once and for all; it is made and re-made endlessly. Policy-making is a process of successive approximation to some desired objectives in which what is desired itself continues to change under reconsideration.

Making policy is at best a very rough process. Neither social scientists, nor politicians, nor public administrators yet know enough about the social world to avoid repeated error in predicting the consequences of policy moves. A wise policy-maker consequently expects that his policies will achieve only part of what he hopes and at the same time will produce unanticipated consequences he would have preferred to avoid. If he proceeds through a *succession* of incremental changes, he avoids serious lasting mistakes in several ways.

In the first place, past sequences of policy steps have given him knowledge about the probable consequences of further similar steps. Second, he need not attempt big jumps toward his goals that would require predictions beyond his or anyone else's knowledge, because he never expects his policy to be a final resolution of a problem. His decision is only one step, one that if successful can quickly be fol-

[5] Herbert Simon, Donald W. Smithburg, and Victor A. Thompson, *Public Administration* (Alfred A. Knopf, 1950), p. 434.

lowed by another. Third, he is in effect able to test his previous predictions as he moves on to each further step. Lastly, he often can remedy a past error fairly quickly—more quickly than if policy proceeded through more distinct steps widely spaced in time.

Compare this comparative analysis of incremental changes with the aspiration to employ theory in the root method. Man cannot think without classifying, without subsuming one experience under a more general category of experiences. The attempt to push categorization as far as possible and to find general propositions which can be applied to specific situations is what I refer to with the word "theory." Where root analysis often leans heavily on theory in this sense, the branch method does not.

The assumption of root analysis is that theory is the most systematic and economical way to bring relevant knowledge to bear on a specific problem. Granting the assumption, an unhappy fact is that we do not have adequate theory to apply to problems in any policy area, although theory is more adequate in some areas—monetary policy, for example—than in others. Comparative analysis, as in the branch method, is sometimes a systematic alternative to theory. . . .

SUCCESSIVE COMPARISON AS A SYSTEM

Successive limited comparisons is, then, indeed a method or system; it is not a failure of method for which administrators ought to apologize. None the less, its imperfections, which have not been explored in this paper, are many. For example, the method is without a built-in safeguard for all relevant values, and it also may lead the decision-maker to overlook excellent policies for no other reason than that they are not suggested by the chain of successive policy steps leading up to the present. Hence, it ought to be said that under this method, as well as under some of the most sophisticated variants of the root method —operations research, for example—policies will continue to be as foolish as they are wise.

Why then bother to describe the method in all the above detail? Because it is in fact a common method of policy formulation, and is, for complex problems, the principal reliance of administrators as well as of other policy analysts.[6] And because it will be superior to any

[6] Elsewhere I have explored this same method of policy formulation as practiced by academic analysts of policy ("Policy Analysis," 48 *American Economic Review* 298 [June, 1958]). Although it has been here presented as a method for public administrators, it is no less necessary to analysts more removed from immediate policy questions, despite their tendencies to describe their own analytical efforts as though they were the rational-comprehensive method with an especially heavy use of theory. Similarly, this same method is inevitably resorted to in personal problem-solving, where means and ends are sometimes impossible to separate, where aspirations or objectives undergo constant development, and

other decision-making method available for complex problems in many circumstances, certainly superior to a futile attempt at super-human comprehensiveness. The reaction of the public administrator to the exposition of method doubtless will be less a discovery of a new method than a better acquaintance with an old. But by becoming more conscious of their practice of this method, administration might practice it with more skill and know when to extend or constrict its use. (That they sometimes practice it effectively and sometimes not may explain the extremes of opinion on "muddling through," which is both praised as a highly sophisticated form of problem-solving and denounced as no method at all. For I suspect that in so far as there is a system in what is known as "muddling through," this method is it.)

One of the noteworthy incidental consequences of clarification of the method is the light it throws on the suspicion an administrator sometimes entertains that a consultant or adviser is not speaking relevantly and responsibly when in fact by all ordinary objective evidence he is. The trouble lies in the fact that most of us approach policy problems within a framework given by our view of a chain of successive policy choices made up to the present. One's thinking about appropriate policies with respect, say, to urban traffic control is greatly influenced by one's knowledge of the incremental steps taken up to the present. An administrator enjoys an intimate knowledge of his past sequences that "outsiders" do not share, and his thinking and that of the "outsider" will consequently be different in ways that may puzzle both. Both may appear to be talking intelligently, yet each may find the other unsatisfactory. The relevance of the policy chain of succession is even more clear when an American tries to discuss, say, anti-trust policy with a Swiss, for the chains of policy in the two countries are strikingly different and the two individuals consequently have organized their knowledge in quite different ways.

If this phenomenon is a barrier to communication, an understanding of it promises an enrichment of intellectual interaction in policy formulation. Once the source of difference is understood, it will sometimes be stimulating for an administrator to seek out a policy analyst whose recent experience is with a policy chain different from his own.

This raises again a question only briefly discussed above on the merits of like-mindedness among government administrators. While much of organization theory argues the virtues of common values and agreed organizational objectives, for complex problems in which the

---

where drastic simplification of the complexity of the real world is urgent if problems are to be solved in the time that can be given to them. To an economist accustomed to dealing with the marginal or incremental concept in market processes, the central idea in the method is that both evaluation and empirical analysis are incremental. Accordingly I have referred to the method elsewhere as "the incremental method."

root method is inapplicable, agencies will want among their own personnel two types of diversification: administrators whose thinking is organized by reference to policy chains other than those familiar to most members of the organization and, even more commonly, administrators whose professional or personal values or interests create diversity of view (perhaps coming from different specialties, social classes, geographical areas) so that, even within a single agency, decision-making can be fragmented and parts of the agency can serve as watchdogs for other parts.

THE BUDGETARY PROCESS RECONSIDERED

AARON WILDAVSKY

COMPREHENSIVENESS

One prescription offered by the critics for "rationally" solving problems of calculation is to engage in comprehensive and simultaneous means-ends analysis. But budget officials soon discover that ends are rarely agreed upon, that they keep changing, that possible consequences of a single policy are too numerous to describe, and that knowledge of the chain of consequences for other policies is but dimly perceived for most conceivable alternatives. The result, as Charles Lindblom has demonstrated, is that although this comprehensive approach can be described, it cannot be practiced because it puts too great a strain by far on man's limited ability to calculate.[1] What budget officials need are not injunctions to be rational but operational guides that will enable them to manage the requisite calculations. Commands like "decide according to the intrinsic merits," "consider everything relevant," "base your decision on complete understanding," are simply not helpful. They do not exclude anything; unlike the aids to calculation, they do not point to operations that can be performed to arrive at a decision.

[1] Charles Lindblom, "The Science of 'Muddling Through'" *Public Administration Review*, XIX, 1959, pp. 79–88.

From "Toward a Radical Incrementalism," in *Congress: The First Branch of Government*, Alfred de Grazia (ed.) (Washington: American Enterprise Institute, 1966), pp. 126–140, 146–147. Aaron Wildavsky is currently Dean of the Graduate School of Public Affairs, University of California, Berkeley. Reprinted with permission of the publisher. Footnotes renumbered.

All that is accomplished by injunctions to follow a comprehensive approach is the inculcation of guilt among good men who find that they can never come close to fulfilling this unreasonable expectation. Worse still, acceptance of an unreasonable goal inhibits discussion of the methods actually used. Thus, responsible officials may feel compelled to maintain the acceptable fiction that they review (almost) everything; and yet when they describe their actual behavior, it soon becomes apparent that they do not. The vast gulf between the theories espoused by some budget officials and their practice stems, I believe, from their adherence to a norm deeply imbedded in our culture, which holds the very definition of rational decision is comprehensive and simultaneous examination of ends and means. In this case, however, the rational turns out to be unreasonable. Sad experience warns me that even those who agree with the analysis thus far are prone to insist that governmental officials must "take a look at the budget as a whole," even though neither they nor anyone else has any idea of what that might mean or how it might be accomplished. Surely, considering "the budget as a whole" does not mean merely putting it between the covers of one volume, or letting one's eyes run over the pages, or merely pondering the relationship between income and expenditure. Yet, if (to take current examples) evaluating the most important relationships between the space program, the war on poverty, and aid to education appears to be extraordinarily difficult, what is the point of talking about reviewing "the budget as a whole" in the real sense of analyzing the interrelationships among all the important programs. The perpetuation of myth is an old story. What is unfortunate is that insistence on an impossible standard takes our attention away from real possibilities for change.

Failure to consider the contributions toward calculation of the existing budgetary process distorts the magnitude of the problem. New programs and substantial increases and decreases in old programs do not receive close attention when interest groups, politicians, or bureaucrats, anxious to make an issue, demand an investigation. What escapes intensive scrutiny is not the whole but only certain parts, which carry on as before. The fact that some activities do not receive intensive scrutiny is hardly sufficient reason to do everything over every year. In my recommendations, I shall deal with the problem that remains.

COORDINATION

The fact that the budgetary process is not comprehensive has given rise to charges that it is uncoordinated. Indeed, the very terms that we have used to describe budgetary practices—specialized, incremental, fragmented, sequential, non-programmatic—imply that at any one time the budget is not effectively considered as a whole so as to systematically relate its component parts to one another. As long as the lack of coordination is the result of ignorance of other people's activities or the complexity of organization, there is a good chance of overcoming it by dedicated staff work or some formal coordinating mechanism. But, in many cases, lack of coordination is a result of conflicting views about policy that are held by men and agencies that have independent bases of influence in society and in Congress. The only way to secure coordination in these cases is for one side to convince or coerce or bargain with the other. When it is understood that "coordination" is often just another word for "coercion," the full magnitude of the problem becomes apparent. For there is no one, the President and congressional leaders included, who is charged with the task of dealing with the "budget as a whole" and who is capable of enforcing his preferences. Vesting of formal power to coordinate the budget effectively would be tantamount to a radical change in the national political system, requiring the abolition of the separation of powers and a federally controlled party system, among other things.

What may be said about coordination, then, if we take the existing political system as not subject to drastic change? By taking as our standard of coordination the existence of a formal structure charged with the task and capable of executing it, we come up with an obvious answer: there is very little coordination excepting what the President can manage through the Budget Bureau. By accepting the possibility of informal coordination, of participants who take into account what others are doing, we can say there is a great deal of coordination that has escaped the notice of observers. . . .

To some critics the procedure by which the agencies (as well as the appropriations committees and the Budget Bureau to a lesser extent) try to gauge "what will go" may seem unfortunate. They feel that there must be a better justification for programs than the subjective interpretation of signals from the environment. Yet we live in a democracy in which a good part of the justification for programs is precisely that they are deemed desirable by others. What is overlooked is that these informal procedures are also powerful coordinating mechanisms: when one thinks of all the participants who are continuously engaged in interpreting the wishes of others, who try to feel the pulse of Congress, the President, interest groups, and special publics, it is clear that a great many adjustments are made in anticipation of what other participants are likely to do. This, it seems to me, is just another term for coordination, unless one insists that coordination be redefined to require conscious control by a single individual or group. . . .

NEGLECT OF CONSEQUENCES

The budgetary process is sometimes attacked for its apparent neglect of consequences, and there can be no doubt that lack of comprehensiveness in budgeting means that a participant making a specific decision will often neglect important values affected by that decision. However, Lindblom has proposed that consequences neglected by one participant may be considered by another, or by the same participant working on another problem.[2] To the extent, therefore, that all significant interests tend to be represented in a fragmented political system, decision makers may reduce their information costs, by neglecting many alternatives, in the confidence that they will be picked up by others or by themselves at another time. Thus, the budgetary process as a whole may be considered rational even though the actions of individual participants may not seem to be because they omit from their calculations consequences important for others.

The political process in a democracy has a built-in feature that assures that some presently neglected values will be considered. This mechanism exists because politicians and interest-group leaders are motivated, by their hope of retaining or winning office, to find needs that have not been met and proposing to fulfill them in return for votes.

No doubt the neglect of some values (say those dear to Negroes) could be better avoided by increasing the weight of the appropriate interests in the political process. There is no point, it seems to me, in faulting the budgetary process for the lamentable failure of some groups to be properly represented in the political life of the nation. Political mobilization of Negroes will obviously do much more to protect their neglected interests than any change in the mechanism for considering budgets.

The most powerful coordinating mechanisms in budgeting undoubtedly are the various roles adopted by major participants in the budgetary process. Because the roles fit in with one another and set up a stable pattern of mutual expectations, they do a great deal to reduce the burden of calculations for the individual participants. The agencies need not consider in great detail how their requests will affect the President's overall program; they know that such criteria will be introduced in the Budget Bureau. The appropriations committee and the Budget Bureau know that the agencies are likely to put forth all the programs for which there is prospect of support and can concentrate on fitting them into the President's program or on paring them down.

[2] See his *Decision-Making In Taxation and Expenditures, Public Finances, Needs, Sources and Utilization* (Princeton: National Bureau of Economic Research, 1961), pp. 295–336.

The Senate committee operates on the assumption that if important items are left out through House action the agency will carry an appeal. If the agencies suddenly reversed roles and sold themselves short, the entire pattern of mutual expectations might be upset, leaving the participants without a firm anchor in a sea of complexity. If the agency were to refuse the role of advocate, it would increase the burden on the congressman; they would not only have to choose among desirable items placed before them with some fervor, but they would also have to discover what these items might be. This is a task ordinarily far beyond the limited time, energy, information, and competence of most congressmen. . . .

Some critics suggest that appropriations committee members should adopt a different role. In this "mixed" role, the congressman would be oriented toward neither cutting nor increasing but to doing both in about equal proportions. Each case would have to be considered on its own merits. To some extent, of course, this balance occurs under the present system. The difference is one of degree, but not less important for being so. For where they are in doubt or do not care to inquire in detail, the congressmen may now follow their prevailing orientation—usually to cut at the margin—expecting to receive feedback if something drastic happens. Under a "mixed" role, however, an exhaustive inquiry into all or most items would be called for. The resulting increase in amounts of calculation required would be immense. And to the extent that other participants adopted a mixed role, the pattern of role expectations upon which participants are now dependent as a calculating device would no longer prove stable. The calculation of preferences, essential in a democratic system, would become far more burdensome since inquiries would have to be instituted to find out what the various groups wanted in specific cases.

Furthermore, the adoption of a mixed role would be likely to lead to a greater neglect of values affected by decisions. Unless the ability of each participant to calculate the consequences of his actions is much more impressive than the evidence suggests, he is bound to neglect more if he attempts to do more. Yet this is precisely what a mixed role would force him to do. Instead of concentrating on a limited range of values within his jurisdiction, as his present role requires, he would have to consider the widest possible range of values in order to make a mixed role work. In place of the reasonable certainty that each participant does a good job of looking after the relatively narrow range of values entrusted to his care, there would be little certainty that any particular value would be protected because no one had been especially directed to look after it. Let us explore this question further as a fundamental problem in normative political theory.

INTERESTS

Why, it may be asked, should the various participants take a partial view? Why should they not simply decide in accordance with what the public interest requires? Actually, this is the principle that participants think they are following now; they all believe that their version of the public interest is correct. It is their differing institutional positions, professional training, and group values that lead to perspectives producing somewhat different interpretations of the public interest. Let us, then, rephrase the question and ask whether it is better for each participant to put first the achievement of his own goals (including the goals entrusted to him by virtue of his position) when he considers what is meant by "public interest," or whether he should view the goals of others as of prime or at least equal importance to this consideration?

I am prepared to argue that the partial-view-of-the-public-interest approach is preferable to the total-view-of-the-public-interest approach, which is so often urged as being superior. First, it is much simpler for each participant to calculate his own preferences than for each to try to calculate the preferences of all. It is difficult enough for a participant to calculate how the interests he is protecting might best be served without requiring that he perform the same calculation for many others who might also be affected. The "partial" approach has the virtue of enabling others to accept as an input in their calculations the determination of each participant as to his preferences, which is not possible under the total approach. The danger of omitting important values is much greater when participants neglect the values in their immediate care in favor of what seem to them a broader view. How can anyone know what is being neglected if everyone speaks for someone else and no one for himself?

The partial approach is more efficient for resolving conflicts, a process that lies at the heart of democratic politics. Because the approach is partial, it does not require its practitioners to discover all or most possible conflicts and to work out answers to problems that may never materialize. It permits each participant to go his own way until he discovers that the activities of others interfere. Effort can then be devoted to overcoming the conflicts that arise. The formation of alliances in a political system requiring them is facilitated by the expression and pursuit of demands by those in closest touch with the social reality from which they issue. It is not, then, *noblesse oblige* but self-interest that assures that all demands insist on being heard and find the political resources to compel a hearing. A partial adversary system in which the various interests compete for control of policy (under agreed upon rules) seems more likely to result in reasonable decisions—that is, decisions that take account of the multiplicity of values involved—than one in which the best policy is assumed to be discoverable by a well-intentioned search for the public interest for all by everyone.

STRATEGIES

If it is granted that budgetary practices based on a partial view of the public interest are desirable, then it would appear necessary to accept the use of strategies designed to secure appropriation goals. It is not surprising, however, that critics find something basically underhanded, even undemocratic, in the maneuvering of "special interests" for strategic advantage. Would not a straightforward approach based on the "merits" of each program be preferable?

Requiring that an individual commit suicide for the public good may at times have an acceptable rationale; suggesting that it become a common practice can hardly claim as much. I shall take it as understood, then, that asking participants in budgeting consistently to follow practices extremely disadvantageous to themselves and their associates is not reasonable. The participants must be able to maintain themselves in the environment.

The notion that administrators go around telling each other (or believing in secret) that the purposes for which they request funds are not valid but that they want the money anyway in order to advance themselves and build empires is not worthy of consideration. It would be exceedingly difficult to keep people in an organization if they could not justify its purposes to themselves. Such an attitude would be bound to come to the attention of other participants, who would take appropriate action. It would be bad strategically as well as morally. Attempts to reduce a complex distributive process like budgeting to the terms of a western melodrama—the good men ride white horses and advance on their merits; the bad men wear black masks and rely on strategies—do away with the great problem of deciding upon expenditures advocated by officials who are sincere believers in their proposals, and who know that all demands can be satisfied.

Budgetary strategies may generally be characterized as attempts to make the best case for the agency at the best time and thus to get as large an appropriation as possible. This behavior follows from the role of the agency as advocate. As a practical matter, we would expect any agency head worth his keep to respond to opportunities for increasing appropriations and warding off cuts. The contrary position—making the worst case at the worst time—is not likely to be greeted with enthusiasm by either congressmen or agency staff.

Seizing on the opportune moment for advancing the agency's budgetary goals has much to commend it. The nation is served by initiative in meeting the needs of the time. An element of flexibility is generated that helps ensure that opportunities for action will be taken. "Crisis" strategies belong in this category. What is the difference, we may ask, between using a crisis to increase appropriations and acting to meet the nation's requirements in an hour of need? The desire to present the agency's requests in the best light can be used in a positive sense to improve the thinking of the operating units. The budget office can play an important mediating role because it must explain and justify agency actions to the outside world. By playing devil's advocate to agency personnel, by pointing out that justifications are not clear or persuasive, by saying that the program heads have to do better to convince the Budget Bureau or the appropriations committees, the Budget office may compel or encourage thinking from diverse perspectives. In this way, a wider range of interests and values receive consideration.

Clientele and confidence strategies are desirable as well as inevitable in a democratic society. The feedback that clientele give to the participants is essential political information about who wants what programs, at what level, and with what degree of intensity. The establishment of confidence in an agency and its officers provides the trust necessary for congressmen who must live with complexity; the sanctions upon that agency that follow from lack of congressional confidence represent a great safeguard against duplicity. That morality is to some extent the handmaiden of necessity does not make it any less real or valuable.

A naked recital of strategies is bound to suggest that a certain amount of trickery is involved. Some strategies that appear to be deceitful represent amoral adjustments to an environment that does not give the participants much choice. Consider the kind of duplicity that appears to be involved in the game wherein agency people make believe that they are supporting the President's budget while actually encouraging congressmen to ask questions that will permit them to talk about what they would really like to have. Is this behavior immoral or does the immorality belong to the Executive Office directive that tries to compel agency personnel to say things that they do not believe in order to support the President? Congress has the power of the purse and it is difficult to argue that it should not have the kind of information about what the people in charge of the program think they ought to get that might help it to arrive at decisions. If one wants to get rid of Congress, then the problem solves itself. But if one accepts the separation of powers, then it may well be that it would be destructive to deny Congress information it would like to have, especially when for Congress to have it is manifestly in the interests of administrators. The Biblical injunction against excessive temptation is appropriate here.

MERITS

Despite all that has been said, the very idea that strategies are employed may still appear disturbing. Why cannot programs be presented on their merits and their merits alone? The most obvious answer is that the question presupposes popular, general agreement on what constitutes merit when the real problem is that people do not agree. That is why we have politics. To lay down and enforce criteria of merit in budgeting would be, in effect, to dispense with politics in favor of deciding what the government shall do in advance.

Much of what is meant by merit turns out to be "meets my preferences" or "serves my interests" or "the interests of those with whom I identify." It would be most peculiar for a nation calling itself a democracy to announce that only the most meritorious policies were carried out despite the fact that they were not preferred by any significant group in the population. The degree to which widespread preferences are met not only *is* but *ought* to be *part* of why policies are deemed meritorious.

We all know that people do not always realize what is good for them. They are occupied with many things and may not recognize the benefits flowing from certain policies. They may find it difficult to support policies that are meritorious but not directly related to their own immediate needs. Here is where strategies come in. Where support is lacking, it may be mobilized; where attention is unfocused, it may be directed by advertising; where merits are not obvious, they may be presented in striking form. Ability to devise strategies to advance the recognition of merit is immensely more helpful than cries of indignation that political artistry should be necessary.

Merit consists, in part, of the effectiveness with which programs are formulated and carried out. No one should doubt that this criterion is recognized in the budgetary process; estimates, justifications, and presentations are directed to this end. Though effectiveness is indispensable—confidence would be lacking without it, for one thing; clientele would be dissatisfied, for another—agencies find that it does not take them far enough. An agency may be wonderfully effective in formulating and carrying out its programs and yet see its fortunes suffer because of the need for Congress to cut that year or to shift funds to some other vital area. Defense appropriations are often a function of domestic concerns; stabilization policy may be constrained by military needs; the complexity of a project or the difficulty of demonstrating immediate results may militate against it. Consequently, the agency invariably finds that in some areas its good works and best efforts are not being rewarded. Prizes are simply not distributed for good deeds alone. The agency's mode of adapting to this circumstance is to use demonstration of good works as one among a number of strategies. Forbidding agencies to use strategies designed to give its good requests a better chance, because bad requests can also be dressed up, seems inadvisable as well as unlikely to succeed.

MOTIVATION

Instead of bewailing the use of strategies, it would be immensely more fruitful to arrange incentives within the system so as to insure that good strategies and good programs will go together as often as possible. Budgeting would be conceived of in this sense as constituting a problem in human motivation. When motivation is disregarded, it is no wonder that unsatisfactory results ensue. In order to demonstrate that this problem is by no means peculiar to the national budgetary process let us take a brief look at budgeting in Soviet and American industrial firms.

Rewards to managers in Soviet industrial firms depend on their meeting production quotas assigned in economic plans. But necessary supplies—skilled labor and financial resources—are often lacking. The first consequence of this is that the quota is not set from above but becomes the subject of bargaining as the managers seek to convince the ministries that quotas should be as low as possible. Yet the managers find it prudent not to hugely exceed their quota, for in that case next year's quota will be raised beyond attainment. The second consequence is that production is not rationalized to produce the greatest output at the lowest cost, but is geared instead to meeting specific incentives. Heavy nails are overproduced, for example, because quotas are figured by weight. Maintenance may be slighted in favor of huge effort for a short period in order to meet the quota. Funds are hidden in order to provide slack that can be used to pay "pushers" to expedite the arrival of supplies. The list of essentially deceitful practices to give the appearance of fulfilling the quota is seemingly endless: producing the wrong assortment of products, transferring current costs to capital accounts, shuffling accounts to pay for one item with funds designated for another, declaring unfinished goods finished, lowering the quality of goods, and so on.[3] The point is that the budgetary system arranges incentives in such a way that managers cannot succeed with lawful practices. When similar incentives are applied in American industrial firms, similar practices result, from running machines into the ground, to "bleeding the line," to meeting a monthly quota by doctoring the accounts.[4]

[3] Joseph S. Berliner, *Factory and Manager in the USSR* (Cambridge: Harvard University Press, 1957).

[4] Frank Jasinsky, "Use and Misuse of Efficiency Controls," *Harvard Business Review*, XXXIV, 1956, p. 107; Chris Argyris, *The Impact of Budgets on People* (New York: Controllership Foundation, Inc., 1952), pp. 12ff.

As in the Soviet Union, American firms often use budgets not to reflect or project reality but to drive managers and workers toward increased production. Budgets are conceived of as forms of pressure on inherently lazy people[5] so that (to paraphrase Mao Tse-tung) the greater the pressure the better the budget. Inevitably, managers and workers begin to perceive budgets as "perpetual needlers" or as "the hammer that's waiting to hit you on the head."[6] In some cases, this leads to discouragement because it is apparent that whatever the effort, the budget quota will be increased. Since accounting is separate for sub-units in the firm, it is not surprising that fierce negotiations take place to assign costs among them. As a result, top officials find it necessary to engage in campaigns to sell budgets to the units. Otherwise, sabotage is likely.[7] While some attention has been given to human relations in budgeting,[8] only Stedry[9] has attempted to explore the essential motivational problems of budgeting within an organizational framework. Yet, without an understanding of the impact of different goals and incentive systems on human activity, reliable statements about the likely consequences of different budgetary incentives can hardly be made. . . .

SUMMARY

In appraising the budgetary process, we must deal with real men who know that, in this real world, the best they can get is to be preferred to the perfection they cannot achieve. Unwilling or unable to alter the basic features of the political system, they seek to make it work for them rather than against them in budgeting. Participants in budgeting not only work within the specified constitutional rules, they also make active use of them. Problems of calculation are mitigated by the division of labor in the separation of powers; morality is enforced by substantial external checks as well as by inner motives; a wider range of preferences is taken into account by making the institutional participants responsible for somewhat different ones. A great deal of informal coordination takes place as participants adjust to their expectation of other's behavior. An incremental approach guards against radical departures most of the time, whereas agency

[5] Argyris, *op. cit.*, pp. 6ff.

[6] *Ibid.*, pp. 12–13.

[7] *Ibid.*, *inter alia;* Bernard H. Sord and Glenn A. Welsch, *Business Budgeting: A Survey of Management Planning and Control Practices* (New York: Controllership Foundation, Inc., 1958), pp. 140–50.

[8] Arnold A. Bebling, "A Look at Budgets and People," *Business Budgeting*, X, 1961, p. 16.

[9] Andrew C. Stedry, *Budget Control and Cost Behavior* (Englewood Cliffs, N.J.: Prentice-Hall, 1960).

advocacy and strategies designed to take advantage of emergent needs help ensure flexibility. A basic conclusion of this appraisal is that the existing budgetary process works much better than is commonly supposed.

There is, however, no special magic in the *status quo*. Inertia and ignorance as well as experience and wisdom may be responsible for whatever problems exist in the present state of affairs. Improvements of many kinds are undoubtedly possible and desirable. The heart of the problem of budgetary reform lies in the inevitable tension between the practice of incrementalism and the ideology of comprehensiveness. The assumption of all previous proposals for reform has been that incrementalism must be sacrificed to comprehensiveness. But as this section has suggested formal coordination and comprehensive calculation of budgets are unfeasible, undesirable, or both. If comprehensiveness is rejected, however, there turn out to be other significant directions for reform that have not yet been tried. My view is that the present budgetary process should be taken as far as it will go and then corrected for its worst deficiencies. Proposals for reform should advocate a more thoroughgoing incremental approach, not its opposite—a more comprehensive one. There should be greater use of aids to calculation rather than less. Agencies should not be told to give up advocacy, but should be motivated to make their best case even more persuasive. There should be even less formal unity and more conflict in budgeting than there is today.

STRATEGIC PROGRAMS AND THE POLITICAL PROCESS

SAMUEL P. HUNTINGTON

The Joint Chiefs of Staff, except when the Secretary of Defense participates, is exclusively military. The National Security Council, except for its military adviser, is exclusively civilian. At stake in the deliberations of both, however, are personal and organizational interests, values, and perspectives. Both resort to the same methods for resolving or disposing of controversial issues. These are the traditional means of the congressional legislative process. They may be grouped into four categories.

AVOIDING CONTROVERSIAL ISSUES, DELAYING DECISION ON THEM, REFERRING THEM TO OTHER BODIES FOR RESOLUTION
If an issue appears highly controversial, members of the strategic committees, like members of Congress, attempt to avoid considering it. Since "one dissenting Chief can prevent action on an issue for long periods," General Taylor has written, "it is difficult to force consideration of matters unpalatable to one or more of the services." If the strategic legislature is unable to avoid formal responsibility for the issue, it may still avoid facing it directly by postponing consideration of it or by devolving responsibility for it to other agencies. Decision delayed is disagreement avoided. Unless serious differences exist, little reason exists to delay decision on an issue, and yet delay has

From *The Common Defense* (New York: Columbia University Press, 1961), pp. 162–174. Samuel Huntington is Professor of Government, Harvard Uuniversity. Reprinted with permission of the publisher. Footnotes deleted.

been an oft-commented-upon aspect of JCS operations. Some issues simply invite delay. "Even under the stress of war," General Marshall remarked, "agreement has been reached in the Joint Chiefs of Staff at times only by numerous compromises and after long delays ..."

The proliferation of committees is a useful political device to facilitate and, in some cases, legitimate the avoidance of decision. Issues can be referred from committee to committee, up and down the hierarchy, and since the same service and departmental interests are usually represented on all the committees, agreement in one is just as unlikely as agreement in another. The hope always exists, however, that further study may illuminate new avenues of agreement. The tendency is to "sweep controversial issues under the rug, where they lie dormant for indefinite periods."

Controversial decisions may also be avoided by devolving them from the Joint Chiefs back upon the services. Thus, while the Chiefs authorize force levels, they do not specify particular types of forces and weapons. The number of attack carriers comes before the JCS; whether they are nuclear powered or conventional powered, large or small, is left for the Navy and the Budget officials to decide. The advantages of a live-and-let-live philosophy on weapons development were underlined by the B-36 controversy of 1949. In formulating the force levels for FY 1960 the Joint Chiefs did not specifically consider "whether the Army should be maintained at 870,000 or 900,000, whether funds should be sought for a Navy carrier, and what should be done with reference to the B-52 bomber program." Agencies are naturally reluctant to bring programs of great importance to themselves before the NSC or JCS for consideration.

Decision on major issues also may be avoided by devoting more time to minor ones. The relations among the services tend to inflate relatively unimportant administrative questions into major interservice political issues. Even so, the resolution of those issues undoubtedly is considerably easier than the resolution of the major ones on strategy, missions, and budgets. One-third of JCS decisions in 1951 and 1952 dealt with administrative matters other than strategy. The JCS "dips into matters it should avoid," Vannevar Bush complained, "it fails to bring well-considered resolution to our most important military problems, and it fritters away its energy on minutiae." Departmental representatives in the NSC machinery, a Senate study said, aim "to bypass the committees while keeping them occupied with less important matters." The Chiefs and the NSC, however, were treading a well-worn legislative path. In almost identical terms, political scientists have for years accused Congress of refusing to grapple with major issues of public policy and of wasting time and energy on minor matters of administrative detail.

COMPROMISE AND LOGROLLING, THAT IS, TRADING OFF
SUBORDINATE INTERESTS FOR MAJOR INTERESTS

If an issue cannot be avoided, recourse is frequently had to the classic political processes of compromise and logrolling. In the executive as in the legislature, different interests can agree upon the disposition of the immediate issue before them without agreeing upon the long-range goals of policy. Where the framework of decision is authoritatively set from the outside, the logic of compromise demands service equality. As the $14 and $13 billion ceilings firmly succeeded each other in the late 1940s, the tendency to divide the funds equally among the three services became more and more pronounced. If, however, the limits permitted by superior executive authority are broad or undefined, logrolling enables each service to obtain what it considers most important. In "Operation Paperclip," Army, Navy, and Air Force proposals are added together and called a joint plan. In 1947, for instance, the President's Air Policy Commission criticized the duplication between the Air Force and naval aviation and asked the Chiefs to prepare an integrated plan. In the paper which the Chiefs submitted, however, "agreement was reached between them by avoiding that issue [of overlap], for the paper merely approved the statement of requirements each service presented—14,500 aircraft for Naval aviation and a 70-group Air Force." During the Korean War General Vandenberg reportedly secured support for additional Air Force wings by agreeing to the Navy's program for Forrestal class carriers. A "tacit agreement" developed among the Joint Chiefs that no one chief would oppose the purchasing program of another. Interservice conflicts over the control of weapons systems inevitably tended toward duplication: Thor and Jupiter, Nike and Bomarc. Duplication is simply the price of harmony. It is hardly surprising that JCS should be referred to as "a trading post." As one congressman remarked to his colleagues:

If you are concerned, you politicians, with getting unanimity of action, I refer you to the Joint Chiefs of Staff. There is a classic example of unanimity of action on anything: You scratch my back and I will scratch yours. "Give me atomic carriers," says the Navy, "and you can have your B-52s in the Air Force." I do not know why General Taylor is going along, because I have never been able to find anything that the Army is getting out of the deal.

EXPRESSING POLICIES IN VAGUE GENERALITIES REPRESENTING
THE "LOWEST COMMON DENOMINATOR" OF AGREEMENT
IN WHICH ALL CAN ACQUIESCE

If jurisdiction over an issue cannot be avoided and if trading or logrolling is impossible, policy may still be defined in vague words and phrases lacking operational meaning. Referring to the annual NSC statement of national security policy, General Taylor has declared:

The end product . . . has thus far been a document so broad in nature and so general in language as to provide limited guidance in practical application. In the course of its development, the sharp issues in national defense which confront our leaders have been blurred in conference and in negotiation. The final text thus permits many different interpretations. The protagonists of Massive Retaliation or of Flexible Response, the partisans of the importance of air power or of limited war, as well as the defenders of other shades of military opinion, are able to find language supporting their divergent points of view. The "Basic National Security Policy" document means all things to all people and settles nothing.

Similarly, when the Secretary of Defense compels the Joint Chiefs to consider a disagreeable issue, their answer often "may be 'waffled,' i.e., made ambiguous or incompletely responsive to the fundamental question." In effect, this frequently means that the decision is referred back to the services or subordinate committees, for it is they who must make the policy in the process of executing it. Decisions become more of a way of producing agreement among equals than of producing action by subordinates.

What may seem to be insignificant struggles over semantics and phraseology thus assume importance as methods of securing general endorsement of a policy by the interested parties. The Joint Chiefs, as Hanson Baldwin declared in 1951, "often argue over phraseology, instead of substance, and try to reach agreement by compromises in semantics." In formulating a statement of China policy, for instance, the NSC's predecessor, the State-War-Navy Coordinating Committee, carefully interlarded words and phrases from the State Department, on the one hand, and the military, on the other hand, to produce a balance which became national policy, a process no different in its essentials from that by which a congressional committee produces a statute.

BASING POLICIES UPON ASSUMPTIONS
WHICH MAY OR MAY NOT BE REALISTIC
An alternative to agreement on the vague generality is agreement upon specific policies or programs which are based upon unrealistic assumptions. Usually these are assumptions that the domestic situation will permit larger forces than would actually be the case or that the international situation will permit weaker forces than appear to be warranted. In 1948 the Joint Chiefs easily agreed on a budget on the assumption that the Administration would make $23 billion available to the military. In the late 1950s the mid-range plans of the Chiefs

(the Joint Strategic Objectives Plans) reflected assumptions that $48 to $58 billion would be available. On this basis the Chiefs could agree. In actuality, the Administration was attempting to hold military spending at about $40 billion and rejected the Chiefs' "Blue Sky planning." The mid-range plans were also criticized on the grounds that they set goals for the pre-D-day procurement of mobilization reserves which were totally unrealistic in terms of the national fiscal limitations on the military budget.

Agreement on strategic programs may also be based upon tenuous assumptions about the state of the world. Thus, General Ridgway agreed to the three-year New Look program with the understanding that it was based on the assumptions: "1) that there would be no new outbreak of war in Korea, 2) that the political situation in Korea would become stabilized, 3) that the build-up of the German, Korean and Japanese armed forces would proceed on schedule, 4) that the war in Indo-China would be ended and the political situation there stabilized, 5) that the European Defense Community plan would be ratified, and 6) that there would be no further deterioration in international political conditions." In the final New Look paper, however, some of these assumptions were transmuted into "implementing actions," that is, the paper recommended that the German and Japanese rearmaments be hastened rather than assuming that they would be hastened. The approval which Ridgway gave the paper was apparently contingent upon the realization of the assumed conditions, not merely upon their encouragement. Until the assumptions clearly were not realized, however, presumably the New Look commanded the unanimous support of the Chiefs.

Curiously enough, the location of the point of decision on strategic programs in the executive rather than in Congress has occasioned only sporadic criticism from American commentators. Instead, dissatisfaction has focused upon the importation into the executive branch of the processes and characteristics of policy-making common to the legislative branch. The most common criticisms are: 1) National security policy has lacked unity, coherence, and a sense of direction; decisions have been made upon an *ad hoc* basis, uninformed and unguided by a common purpose; 2) National security policies have been stated largely in terms of compromises and generalities; clear-cut alternatives have not been brought to the highest level for decision; 3) Delay and slowness have characterized the policy-making process; 4) The principal organs of policy-making, particularly the NSC, have not been effective vehicles for the development of new ideas and approaches; they tend to routinize the old rather than stimulate the new; 5) The procedures of policy-making tend to magnify the obstacles and difficulties of any proposed course of action; 6) The above deficiencies are primarily the product of government by committee, particularly when the members of the committee necessarily represent the interests of particular departments and services.

To remedy these deficiencies, the critics urge reducing the role of committees and enhancing the role of individual executive decision-makers, developing more effective, farsighted, and more powerful executive leadership, imbuing the executive branch with a greater sense of purpose and direction, and, in general, rationalizing the structure of the executive to achieve a greater correspondence between organization and purpose.

Almost all these allegations of fact are accurate. The strategy-making process *is* slow, prone to compromise, given to generalities, strewn with reefs and shoals, and unlikely to produce clear-cut, coherent, and rational policies. Judgments of the effectiveness of a policy-making process, however, must be based upon at least two criteria. In strategy, as elsewhere, meaningful policy requires both content and consensus. Strategic policies, like statutes or treaties, are both prescriptions for future action and ratifications of existing power relationships. A strategy which is so vague or contradictory that it sets forth no prescriptions for action is no strategy. So also, a strategy whose prescriptions are so unacceptable that they are ignored is no strategy. Consensus is a cost to each participant in the policy-making process, but it is a prerequisite to any policy.

Critics raise two issues. First, is the "better" policy, however defined, more likely to be the product of a single responsible official of agency or the product of negotiation and compromise among a number of officials and agencies? The answer depends largely upon whether one thinks that the policy views of the single responsible official or agency will coincide with one's own policy views. The Framers of the Constitution, believing that it was wiser not to take chances, devised a remarkably complex system of dividing power and responsibility. Bagehot, on the other hand, argued that the American Constitution was based "upon the principle of having many sovereign authorities, and hoping that their multitude may atone for their inferiority." The question of who was right need not be answered here. The second issue raised by the critics is the more relevant one: To what extent is policy made through a single responsible official or agency feasible in the American system of government? Madison not Bagehot wrote the Constitution. In the course of a century and a half, constitutional pluralism has been supplemented by socio-economic pluralism and bureaucratic pluralism. One can accept the premise of the critics that greater purpose, unity, and direction are needed for a good policy, but one must also accept the fact of American politics that agreement among a number of groups and agencies is needed for any policy. One perceptive critic, for instance, has argued that ". . . the conclusions of both the Joint Chiefs of Staff and the National

Security Council reflect the attainable consensus among sovereign departments rather than a sense of direction." Some measure of departmental consensus, however, is essential to any policy. If it is a good policy, it will also have direction and purpose. But the direction can only be a product of the consensus, not an alternative to it. Professor Morgenthau has struck directly to the heart of the problem and argued that:

> The policy decisions of the Executive Branch of the Government, like the decisions of the business executive or any decision an individual must make in his private affairs, are fundamentally different from the legislative decision. The latter is supposed to represent divergent interests brought to a common denominator or one interest which has won out over the others. The executive decision is supposed to be, first of all, the correct decision, the decision which is more likely than any other to bring forth the desired result.

> The committee system is appropriate for the legislative process, and it is not by accident that it originated and was institutionalized there. The executive decision requires the mind and will of one man who, after hearing the evidence and taking counsel, takes it upon himself to decide what is the right action under the circumstances.

"Divergent interests," however, exist within the executive as much as within Congress. Lower taxes, domestic welfare programs, balanced budgets, massive retaliation, limited war, foreign assistance—these are only a few of the foreign and domestic goals and needs represented by executive agencies. That the conflict among them takes place within the executive branch of government does not make that conflict any less real or the values at stake any less important.

Committees have proliferated within the executive branch precisely because the "committee system is appropriate for the legislative process." At times, of course, the President does act against the advice of his associates. Major decisions on strategic programs, however, can seldom be the result of the "mind and will of one man." Like major decisions on domestic programs in Congress, they require the participation and consent of many men representing many interests. If the negotiation and bargaining do not take place in committees, they take place outside them. On the principal issues which come up within the executive branch, there is no single "correct decision." There may, indeed, be no decision at all if the interests involved cannot discover some basis of agreement; the form which that agreement may take is as unpredictable as the final version of a bill in the legislative process in Congress. In the executive as in Congress, the major problem is not to discover rationally what is required to bring forth "the desired result" but rather to reconcile conflicting views of what results are desirable. The problem of consensus always exists, and there are costs involved in winning support for any policy proposal or decision. Many practices which critics properly deplore because they weaken the content of policy contribute directly to the development of a consensus for policy.

The political and legislative character of the strategy-making process also casts a different light on the argument that the NSC and JCS have failed to initiate new policy proposals. As one observer of the domestic legislative process has commented, "Very little legislation ever originates within a legislature." Hence, it is to be expected that original contributions and policy proposals would come from the service staffs rather than the Joint Staff, which functioned as a negotiating agency. In view of the significance of this function for the NSC, the JCS, and their subordinate bodies, the absence of originality among them hardly seems so crucial. Similarly, as the critics argue, the committee system facilitates the raising of objections to any particular proposal. If a function of the committee, however, is to elicit consent, to devise the policy upon which all can agree, the airing of all major objections to that policy becomes an essential part of the process.

Just as much of the early criticism of Congress stemmed from failure to appreciate the political roles of that body, so much of the criticism of the NSC and JCS stems from the application to these bodies of nonpolitical standards. In the past, it has been assumed that through investigation and debate all members of a legislative body should arrive at similar conclusions as to where the public interest lay. More recently, conflict within a legislature has been viewed as normal rather than reprehensible, and policy thought of as the result, not of a collective process of rational inquiry, but of a mutual process of political give and take. Analyses of Congress seldom criticize it now because of the conflicts and disagreements among its members. To a considerable extent, however, the JCS and the NSC are judged by the earlier theory: in them disagreement is still considered inherently evil. As one naval officer wryly commented: "How curious it is that the Congress *debates*, the Supreme Court *deliberates*, but for some reason or other the Joint Chiefs of Staff just *bicker!*"

Significantly, next to the supposed lack of agreement among the Joint Chiefs, those aspects of their operation which receive the greatest criticism are precisely their mechanisms for reaching agreement: delay, devolution, referral, platitudinous policies, compromise, logrolling. Assuming agreement among the Chiefs to be natural and rational, the critics have almost as little use for artificially produced agreement as they have for the inherent tendencies toward disagreement. At the same time the Chiefs are criticized because they can not resolve major issues, they are also criticized because they do resolve them through the classic means of politics.

Much criticism of strategic decision-making fails to appreciate the tenuous and limited character of hierarchical authority in American government. Reacting against the prevalence and visibility of horizontal bargaining, the critics almost unanimously advocate the abolition of committees and the strengthening of executive controls. In temporary periods of emergency and crisis presidential coordination may partially replace the normal bargaining processes. But no presidential laying on of hands can accomplish this on a permanent basis. Decisions on strategic programs are simply too important to be fitted into a symmetrical and immaculate model of executive decision-making. Clarifications of the chain of command and legal assertions of formal authority may reduce bargaining, but they can never eliminate it. Each of the three reorganizations of the military establishment after 1947 purported to give the Secretary of Defense full legal authority to control his department and yet each succeeding Secretary found his control circumscribed. The existence of counterparts to the NSC and JCS in almost every other modern state suggests that the causes which have brought them into existence may be pervasive and inherent in the problems with which they deal.

The problem of legislating strategy is the dual one of producing both content and consensus. The problem can be solved neither by denying its complexity nor by looking for relief in institutional or administrative reforms which are not based upon underlying political realities. The abolition of committees or a reduction in their importance, for instance, may not necessarily strengthen executive leadership. What strength the administrative hierarchy does retain is at least partially derived from the fact that it does not have to bear the entire burden of bargaining, that much of the responsibility for developing a consensus within the executive establishment has been transferred to horizontal mechanisms such as the NSC and the JCS. The emergence of these committees in the executive branch was, in part, an effort to avoid the problems and difficulties of bargaining along the vertical axis. Abolition of the committees would transfer many questions now resolved by negotiation among bureaucratic equals back to the administrative hierarchy to be resolved by negotiations between an administrative superior and a multiplicity of subordinates. The result could overload the hierarchy, increase the ambiguities and misunderstandings resulting from the confusion of hierarchical and bargaining roles, and dissolve still further the authority of the superior over his subordinates.

"Nobody stands sponsor for the policy of the government," one critic has written. "A dozen men originate it; a dozen compromises twist it and alter it; a dozen offices whose names are scarcely known outside of Washington put it into execution." These words sum up the case against the strategy-making process. They were written, however, by Woodrow Wilson in 1885. The new criticism of strategy-making falls into a classic pattern of criticism of American governmental processes. The ideas, fears, goals, and even phrases of the strategic reformers echo those not only of Wilson, but those of the progressives in the first part of the twentieth century, the devotees of economy and efficiency of the 1920s, and, most particularly, the complaints of the liberal reformers of the 1930s and 1940s on domestic policy and economic planning. In each case, the critics concluded that certain critical policy needs demanded prompt, coherent action, and that the governmental machinery was incapable of giving these needs the priority which they deserved. The targets of the liberal reformers and the strategic critics were thè same: the dispersion of power, the absence of sharply defined alternatives, the dangers of stalemate. The liberal critics saw policy as the product of compromise among pressure groups with narrow interests; the strategic critics see it as the product of compromise among agencies and departments with narrow purposes. The liberal criticism complained that political parties cohered only long enough to produce an electoral majority at the polls; the strategic criticism argues that the policy-making committees cohere only long enough to produce a unanimous report. The old criticism argued that the absence of disciplined and responsible parties prevented the voters from making a clear choice between sharply different policy proposals; the new criticism argues that the proliferation of committees prevents executive officials from making a clear choice between sharply different policy proposals.

The liberal criticism wanted to organize the majority so that it could work its will despite interest groups, local bosses, and the constitutional separation of powers; the strategic criticism wants to organize the executive so that presidential leadership can override semi-autonomous departments, parochial interests, and bureaucratic inertia. The principal reforms advocated by the old critics were responsible parties, modification of the separation of powers, and presidential leadership. The principal reforms advocated by the new critics are elimination of committees, vitalization of the chain of command, and presidential leadership. What the old criticism found inadequate in Congress, the new criticism finds inadequate in the executive.

The prophecies of economic calamity by the old critics proved erroneous and their demands for reform superfluous. The American people moved out of the depression without resorting to constitutional reform, disciplined parties, or cabinet government, and even in the face of a gradual decline in the effectiveness of presidential leadership from its high point of 1933–1935. This was due more to fortuitous circumstance, which moderated and redirected the challenge, than to the demonstrated ability of the governmental system to meet the challenge. The economic challenge disappeared in World War II and was replaced by the strategic challenge. The likelihood of fortuitous circumstance's moderating or eliminating the latter appears reasonably remote.

Criticism of strategy-making is thus the latest phase in a prolonged confrontation or dialogue between American intellectuals and reformers and American political institutions. It is directed at the appearance in the strategy-making process of characteristics pervasive in American government. On the one hand, the critics express the need to recognize new policy imperatives, to establish priorities, and to reflect felt needs in an adequate manner and with a sense of timeliness. On the other hand, the persistent and pervasive dispersion of power and authority in American government insures the representation of all claims but the priority of none. The criticisms of the strategic reformers go to the very roots of the governmental system. In many ways they are much more profound than the critics themselves seem to realize. The condition which they protest is not a passing one, the product of particular men or events. The defects which they highlight are not easily remedied by exhortations to unity, assertions of executive authority, or changes in personnel or administration. They are endemic to the political system.

COMMENTARY

The preceding chapters have attempted to describe the fundamental dichotomy of administrative thought in America from several different historical and conceptual perspectives. The focus of this and subsequent chapters will be to analyze the scope and nature of this continuing conflict as it is currently manifested in the theory and practice of public administration. The selections in this chapter deal with the incremental allocation of governmental resources and the application of an incremental decision-making approach to administrative problems. In contrast to the incremental model, the rational-comprehensive allocative and problem solving method will be defined and analyzed in the following chapter. Both approaches to decision-making and resource allocation can be viewed as diverse sets of operating techniques designed to achieve administrative effectiveness. But both approaches to the administrative process must be viewed as more than mere sets of technical operating details as both represent integral elements of clearly defined, socio-political theories. The relevance of each to contemporary social and political problems is presented in the two concluding chapters.

Both theories are integrally related to specific procedural details in such a way that the theoretical tenets are meaningless without a clear understanding of the operating techniques. Thus, the primary purpose of this and the following chapter is to insure that the operating techniques, approaches, and concepts of the incremental and rational-comprehensive models are made perfectly clear.

The successive-limited-comparison method described and advocated by Lindblom represents the core of what he later named "disjointed incrementalism."* The terms are synonymous and in basic contrast to the rational comprehensive approach. Incrementalism, as defined by Lindblom, is a slow, gradual, step-by-step extension of the present into the future. It is a process which administrators are forced to use, according to Lindblom, since "the root method [the rational comprehensive approach] is in fact not workable for complex policy questions." The justification for this assertion is presented by Lindblom in a series of interrelated propositions which form a basic set of premises behind the entire bargaining-incremental model.

At the outset, it is necessary to understand clearly the distinction between policy and program. Public policies represent broadly defined statements of goals and, as such, include certain value premises, stated either implicitly or explicitly. Policy statements, in other words, provide normative justifications for governmental action in a particular area of the public sector. By contrast, a program is a public policy decision translated into detailed specifics. It is a statement of how a particular policy decision is to be actually implemented. A government program is normally a totally objective statement; policy statements are used to justify programs but programs are devoid of explicit normative content. Programs, not policies, are presented to Congress by the executive branch, and it is programs, not policies, which are formally and legally enacted into law. Thus, in reviewing the Federal School Lunch Program, for instance, one might ask why the federal government *should* provide certain school children with free lunches. The answer to this question is to be found in the policy statement associated with the program.

This distinction between policy and program represents a vitally important aspect of Lindblom's thinking. If agreement among diverse individuals and groups is the *sine qua non* of the democratic process, then, given the nature of our pluralist political system, it follows that there is a higher probability that agreement can be obtained on specific, objective operating plans or programs than on abstract, normative policy objectives. In other words, it is easier to agree on a plan in which policy goals are implicitly built-in than to agree on

---

* Lindblom's thinking on incrementalism is expanded and refined in much of his subsequent writings. See *The Strategy of Decision*, with David Braybrooke (New York: The Free Press, 1963); and *The Intelligence of Democracy* (New York: The Free Press, 1965). Perhaps the primer for bargaining-incrementalism was done by Lindblom and Robert Dahl, *Politics, Economics and Welfare* (New York: Harper & Row, Publishers, 1953). Dahl and Lindblom are, in fact, the two leading academic figures who developed and articulated a coherent and concise bargaining-incremental conceptual model. For this reason, Dahl's writings are equally as important as Lindblom's. These include, *A Preface to Democratic Theory* (Chicago: The University of Chicago Press, 1956); and *Pluralist Democracy in the United States* (Chicago: Rand McNally & Company, 1967).

explicitly stated policy goals and then proceed to devise an implementing program.

From this it follows that the normal distinction between policy and program as an ends-means relationship is no longer meaningful. If the plan-with-the-built-in-objective approach is used, then means-ends become indistinguishable; indeed, the means may become the end—the plan or program becomes the objective.

On what basis, then, can a choice be made between alternative solutions to any given problem? As Lindblom observes, a "correct," or "good" choice cannot be made among alternative policies. Agreement cannot be obtained simply because no standard of correctness can be applied to judge policy goals and values. On the other hand, if discussion is focused exclusively on the specific, alternative program proposals—i.e., the means and not the ends—then fruitful discussion and debate are more likely to result, and agreement will be more easily obtained. The "standard of correctness" therefore is agreement; the plan which wins agreement is the "correct" plan, and as Lindblom warns, "for one administrator to seek to win the other over to agreement on ends as well would accomplish nothing and create quite unnecessary controversy." Given Lindblom's premise that no goal, or end, or objective has a natural or immutable validity, it follows that the primary function of every administrator is to obtain agreement over means, not ends. For this reason, "it is not irrational for an administrator to defend" a plan-with-a-built-in-objective "as good without being able to specify what it is good for."

Having set forth the above propositions as basic hypotheses, Lindblom then proceeds to explain how his "administrative man" must obtain agreement on particular program proposals. What follows is the basic core of the incremental decision-making approach.

The administrator is restricted by some very real limitations; he has neither unlimited intellectual capabilities nor unlimited research resources, including most importantly, the element of time. Thus he must devise a decision-making scheme which takes these limitations into account *and also* permits him to obtain agreement. Two suggestions are advanced.

First, if an existing program is taken as a given, agreement on changes from the status quo is more likely to result if discussion is limited *only* to those proposed programs which differ slightly from the existing program. And furthermore agreement is more likely to result if discussion is limited *only* to those aspects of the proposed program which differ slightly from the status quo. Proposals for radical changes are thus ignored, general, overall program reviews are avoided, and the zone of potential disagreement is substantially narrowed. Thus, incremental decision-making maximizes predictability since the future is built into the present, which is an extension of the past.

The second suggestion for obtaining agreement is for the administrator to ignore the wide range of possible consequences that may emerge from a proposed change. In other words, if one can assume that the political system is self-correcting insofar as unforeseen consequences are concerned, then the necessity to anticipate these consequences is virtually eliminated. This optimism is an inherent part of Lindblom's analysis: ". . . it can be argued that our system often can assure a more comprehensive regard for the values of the whole society than any attempt at intellectual comprehension." Elsewhere he writes, the incremental approach "arranges for each group alert enough to make its interests felt to evaluate the advantages and disadvantages of the various policies from its own point of view."*

Thus, the successive limited comparison approach involves both the incremental allocation of tangible economic resources *and* the incremental allocation of intellectual resources. The public policy process becomes a never-ending flow chart of continuous approximations toward some built-in objective which is, itself, constantly redefined by the incremental plans. In the final analysis, ". . . the administrator knows that the best available theory will work less well than more modest incremental comparisons."

This is the essence of the incremental approach, and while Lindblom's short treatment of this topic obviously leaves many penetrating questions unanswered, it is only fair to note that his subsequent writings provide a much more elaborate and fully developed theory of incrementalism than is revealed in the preceding article. However, certain observations can be drawn from "The Science of Muddling Through." For example, it is apparent that the incremental approach takes a totally pragmatic view of the political universe. The search for agreement can lead in many different directions, but, given a highly diverse and heterogeneous political system, a natural inclination is to move toward the lowest common denominator. Of course, "agreement" is really never defined by Lindblom except in a rather indirect fashion when he states that only a waste of time and unnecessary controversy would result if one administrator sought to win another over to agreement on ends as well as means.

But an abundance of social science research data presents solid evidence to support the hypothesis that agreement among individuals on socio-political values and policy goals is related to a wide range of variables including the number of individuals involved, their cohesiveness, their socio-economic status, education, occupations, and so forth. In other words, the intrinsic factor of disagreement which Lindblom advances as a reason to avoid discussion of ends and focus on means is much more accurately applied to a large, heterogeneous

* *Strategy of Decision*, p. 235.

group of individuals, such as the Congress of the United States, than to the disagreement that may develop between two administrators in the executive branch. The incremental design is, in fact, aimed at explaining how legislative agreement to executive proposals for change can most effectively and efficiently be obtained. It is, in effect, a scheme designed to accommodate the diverse, fragmented nature of our legislative process, and, as such, it searches not merely for agreement but for agreement *and* stability.

The maintenance of political stability in the framework of our pluralist political system is, in fact, the ultimate objective of the incrementalists, and, as such, it is a heavily laden normative goal objective which they seek. Internal stability must be maintained. The demands for governmental resources emanating from the vast multitude of diverse groups from within the body politic invariably exceed the supply of resources which are available for allocation. It follows, therefore, that not all demands can be satisfied fully. The choice, then, is whether the demands of certain selected groups should be satisfied fully, or whether the demands of as many groups as possible should be satisfied partially. Widespread conflict and disorder are more likely to be avoided if many groups are partially satisfied than if some groups are totally dissatisfied. Thus, the incremental allocation of resources is advanced as the only effective means by which order and stability in a pluralistic society can be assured.

It is important to note that several basic assumptions serve as linchpins for this whole theory. In the first place, the "self-correcting future" syndrome is definitely at work here. That is to say, the demands of every single group in the body politic do not have to be taken into account year-in and year-out. The limited available resources may be incrementally allocated but only among those groups *"alert enough"* to make their interests *felt*. This, of course, automatically eliminates a large portion of the population from the competition for a share of the available resources. The assumption is that any group that is not alert enough to make its interests felt either does not have intense feelings about its needs, or, even if intensity is high, the group is not cohesive enough to make its influence felt. In either case, although dissatisfaction may result, such dissatisfaction is not likely to manifest itself in a way which would threaten public order and political stability. The best current example of this situation is the continued plight of the American consumer. Thus, conflict can never be eliminated completely, but if through the strategic incremental allocation of resources it can be limited and isolated, threats to the stability of the political system can be effectively contained.

The second basic assumption behind the incremental design is that certain "rules of the game" will be observed. Ideally, the optimum result of the incremental approach is to achieve a "no-lose" situation for everybody (or, at least, for all groups who are alert enough to have their interests felt). As Lindblom notes, "The policies that survive are typically presented as benefiting everybody or everybody in a certain group, without affecting anyone outside it adversely."* Given the nature of public policy conflict, the idea of winning and losing, or gains and losses, is by no means an uncommon concern. The key to the successful implementation of the incremental strategy is to avoid zero-sum situations which are based on the "winner-take-all" principle. Thus, partial gains as well as *partial losses* may have to be allocated incrementally with the understanding that incremental losses *must* be offset by subsequent incremental gains. In other words, the integrity of the entire system rests on the basic presumption that losses will not become cumulative for any single influential group in the body politic. Thus, labor-management relations over the years have seesawed back and forth between partial gains and losses, with incremental losses always being offset by subsequent incremental gains. Lindblom describes this situation quite clearly: ". . . any given state of affairs or combination of policies is viewed as only temporary. . . . As long as the policy-making situation is fluid . . . there will always be a tomorrow where inequities can be righted. . . ."† In the event that inequities are not corrected—i.e., losses do become cumulative to the point where they can never be offset by future *incremental* gains—the rationale for continuing to observe the rules of the game is destroyed, and the stability of the political system which is dependent upon maintaining agreement is jeopardized. The manner in which system stability can be seriously threatened will be examined more fully in Chapter Nine. However, if system stability depends upon maintaining agreement on public policy decisions, and especially agreement on the manner in which available resources are to be allocated, it seems reasonable to ask at this point, "Agreement among whom?"

It has been suggested that legislative agreement is an important element of the incremental strategy, but a more precise elaboration of this point is necessary. An essential aspect of incrementalism as developed fully by Dahl and Lindblom in their *Politics, Economics and Welfare* and by Lindblom in *The Intelligence of Democracy* is the bargaining or partisan mutual adjustment process. By focusing attention on only those aspects of a proposed program which differ slightly from the status quo, the range of potential disagreement is considerably narrowed, and, conversely, the range for the accommodation of differences is widened. The essence of achieving agreement in the incremental strategy is through accommodation and compromise. Accommodation and compromise, in turn, are the result of the bar-

* *Strategy of Decision*, p. 190.
† *The Intelligence of Democracy*, p. 215.

gaining or mutual adjustment process. The efficacy of the bargaining process depends on the attitudes and values of the individuals who are involved, and, in this regard, the principal virtue of a successful bargaining agent is the willingness to compromise his own interests in order to accommodate the interests of other involved agents. Reasonableness of demands and the willingness to respect the demands of others are the key factors which are most likely to yield agreement and stability.

Thus it should be apparent that bargaining and incrementalism are simply two sides of the same coin. However, it should also be apparent that the efficacy of the bargaining-incremental process is dependent upon the extent to which it is operated by "professionals"—i.e., those full-time political actors (such as legislators, career administrators, lobbyists, and party officials) who have developed a high degree of expertise in the intricacies of the political and bargaining processes. When "professionals" who share common rules of the game are in control of the allocation process, stability, order, and agreement are most likely to prevail. The important factor is the almost absolute requirement that the bargaining arena remain uncluttered—i.e., operated *only* by the professional bargainers. Only if this condition is realized can compromise and accommodation be accomplished within a context of maximum stability and order. Once amateur political advocates enter into the bargaining arena and become involved in the final outcome of a particular conflict, the professional bargainer may find his usually wide freedom of maneuver severely restricted. Furthermore, the political "transient" not only diminishes the freedom of maneuver of the professional, but the intensity of his commitment usually eliminates the possibility that his perceived needs will be satisfied by an incremental reward. Thus the stability of the system is dependent upon the agreements reached among professional bargainers as to how available and limited resources are to be incrementally allocated within the body politic. Moreover, system stability is dependent upon the extent to which groups not directly involved in the allocation process are prepared to accept these decisions either as satisfactory or with low-intensity dissatisfaction. If dissatisfaction intensity increases, conflict expands, and amateur advocates become involved in the public policy process. When this occurs the grand strategy of the bargaining-incrementalist scheme is upset.

The manner in which the bargaining-incremental strategy is, actually applied in the public policy process is the subject which Huntington and Wildavsky deal with in their respective selections. As described by Huntington, the Joint Chiefs of Staff and the National Security Council follow the bargaining-incremental strategy quite closely. Agreement in the form of consensus is a necessary prerequisite to any policy. Huntington clearly echoes Lindblom when he writes that the major problem of the JCS "is not to discover rationally what is required to bring forth the desired result but rather to reconcile conflicting views of what results are desirable." Wildavsky makes essentially the same point: "To lay down and enforce criteria on merit in budgeting would be, in effect, to dispense with politics in favor of deciding what the government should do in advance." One does not decide what to do in advance; one must decide first on what results are desirable. The JCS, we are told by Huntington, avoid controversial issues ("decision delayed is disagreement avoided . . ."), bargain over immediate specific plans without attempting to confront long-range policy goals, and cloak policy statements in the broadest and vaguest generalities to obtain acquiescence.

For Wildavsky, comprehensive review of the annual budget requests poses an impossible intellectual task while formal, overall coordination of the entire budgetary process poses an impossible political task. As a result, what is needed is "a more thoroughgoing incremental approach, not its opposite—a comprehensive one."

At least for Lindblom and Wildavsky, the bargaining-incremental strategy represents more than an administrative technique to allocate available resources in an effective and efficient manner. It is a key to stability and order; it is a device to maintain a balance of power among the diverse segments of our political system; it provides the best insurance for agency and individual survival. Incrementalism is, in fact, a state of mind which influences one's entire outlook on the socio-political process. As with Madison, security—i.e., stability and order—is the prime consideration for Lindblom, while Wildavsky, like Stein, the Dimocks, and Long, assumes that agency and individual survival are the key motivating factors behind bureaucratic behavior. The good administrator for Dawes was one who sought only enough money to get along; Wildavsky's successful administrator is the one who can get as large an appropriation as possible.

The lure of the sea must affect all sensitive, reflective minds. The interesting point is how different men with different perspectives prepare for their mythical journeys across the oceans of the body politic. Charles Dawes placed himself "in the stokehold of the ship of state, and we are concerned simply with the economical handling of fuel. The President and Congress determine which way the ship sails, for that is a matter of policy, but we in the hold of the ship have something to do with how far she can sail through the way in which, in our humbler place, we apply common sense business principles." Lindblom may not be as humble as Dawes but certainly he is equally sententious as he assumes the position of the helmsman.

We must acknowledge that the [incremental] strategy does not remove [the possibility that ignoring certain consequences may cause unanticipated adverse effects]. It is beyond human power to remove it. . . . No one can tell what reefs and breakers lie ahead or where the icebergs are that may be drifting in the fog. The voyage into future seas must continue, but how can anyone pretend to set a safe course?*

Lindblom is content to troll cautiously in the tidewaters in a good ship that he need not explain what it is good for and in a direction that is dictated by the tides and the winds. Under these circumstances uncertainty as to what barriers lie ahead is bound to prevail. If a wet finger raised in the air is the only navigational instrument to be employed by the incrementally-oriented administrator, then Latham is indeed correct: "In fact our knowledge of what goes on in administration is roughly at about the stage medicine was in when the cure for typhoid was a ritual dance by a man with deer horns and a rattle."

If one thinks only in terms of absolutes there is no safe course in life. For others, however, to wait until the future becomes the present is to place it already in the past insofar as effective action is concerned. In an attempt to alter this situation, the efforts of many individuals are now being directed to the coordination of the fragmented sources of executive power toward projected future public policy objectives. Comprehensive planning, coordination, and integration are the essential elements of this administrative movement but in a way quite unlike the management science approach of an earlier decade. Total systematic analysis is a catchall which can be used to designate this approach, although the inadequacy of selecting any single designation for what Lindblom would refer to as the "root method" should become apparent in the chapter which follows.

* *Strategy of Decision*, pp. 236–37.

ADMINISTRATION AND ANALYTIC METHODS 7

THE ROLE OF ANALYTICAL AIDS

ROLAND N. McKEAN

It should go without saying that all decision-making persons or groups attempt to economize, in the true sense of the word. That is, they try to make the "most," as they conceive of the "most," of whatever resources they have. Business firms may have a comparatively clear-cut notion of what they mean by the most, while consumers and governmental units have much more difficulty in defining it. But all of them, unless they make their decisions by drawing straws, are trying to do something in the best way possible with the resources that are available. Even the church, in offering spiritual guidance, is concerned with economy, but economy at a high level. The attitude of the clergy is that while we are good at getting the most in day-to-day lower-level problems, we sometimes define "most" incorrectly by choosing the wrong high-level goals. Incidentally, it will be convenient, from time to time, to make this rough distinction between broad or high-level problems and narrower or lower-level problems.[1]

---

[1] This distinction is the basis for another one that is often made. It is sometimes said that "economic problems" are concerned with picking the best allocation of given resources among *competing* uses, while "technological or engineering problems" are concerned with finding the best way of using given resources to achieve a single end [e.g., G. Stigler, *The Theory of Price* (New York: The Macmillan Company, 1946), p. 15]. But most engineering problems really involve the allocation of resources among competing uses, and thus are "economic problems," or else there is no choosing to be done. To find the best way to use a given

From *Efficiency in Government Through Systems Analysis* (New York: John Wiley & Sons, Inc., 1958), pp. 3–16. Roland McKean is Professor of Economics, University of Virginia. Reprinted with permission of the publisher.

THE USEFULNESS OF ANALYTICAL AIDS

In tackling problems of choice, people have always found it advantageous to think about the consequences of alternative policies rather than to choose among them by, say, flipping coins alone. To assist them in predicting those consequences, they use models of the real situation. These may be small-scale representations, such as a model airplane in a wind tunnel or a pilot industrial plant. They may be representations on paper—mathematical models which grow out of laboratory experiment, reasoning, or the observation of small-scale physical models. Or, finally, these models may be simple sets of relationships that are sketched out in the mind and not formally put down on paper. If a schoolboy considers different ways to throw a basketball, he figures that the ball, if thrown with a certain type of English and at a particular angle to the backboard, will probably rebound into the basket. If a sales manager compares different advertising campaigns, he uses certain relationships to help him estimate the consequences. If a person tries to gauge the effects of tariffs, price controls, or monopoly, he makes use of some model of the economy. Or, to refer once more to the church's concern about high-level economy, if your minister advises you to mend your ways, he definitely has a model in mind.

Now in no case are these models photographic reproductions of reality. If they were, they would be so complicated that they would be of absolutely no use to us. So they abstract from a great deal of the real world. This does not mean that they are "bad" models, nor does it mean that they are "good." Whether or not one is better than another depends upon whether or not it gives better predictions (and, therefore, helps us to make better decisions) than another. This may be hard to determine, but it is the acid test of a model's quality.

The notion of models has been stressed because the term is widely used and because systematic thought about any problem of choice necessarily involves models, naive or otherwise. The alternative is to flip coins, draw straws, or rely on conjecture. Sometimes, of course, these are the only things one can do, but by and large good solutions to problems have been reached by means of thoughtful analysis, and that means through the use of models. All history shows—which means "I think," according to a rough translation by Frank H. Knight —that this is so. But seriously, most history *does* indicate that thought-taking is better than chance in solving problems.

---

stock of machine tools within a firm means to allocate them among competing uses. And the allocation involves the valuation of those competing uses. The distinction, and it is a convenient one, is really between problems of choice at different levels.

THE DEVELOPMENT OF ANALYTICAL AIDS

Some of the most fundamental analytical aids have long been available, and could have been used in the past to much greater advantage than they were. Although refinements have occurred, e.g., in the handling of uncertainty, the main elements of the theory of choice have existed for a long time, in economic theory, mathematics, and certain branches of philosophy, for example. This sort of aid indicates at least what questions should be asked in comparing alternative courses of action, and even without other tools, raising the right questions can generate simple models that are powerful problem solvers.

The spectacular advances over the past fifty years, however, have pertained to other tools. One thing that has happened has been the rapid development of all the sciences so that it has become possible to say much more about the relationship of one event to another—about the effects, for example, of using prestressed concrete or higher octane fuel, or about the relationship between smog and combinations of sunshine, ozone, and gasoline fumes. As missing links in the chains of relationship were filled in, it became possible to predict more accurately the consequences of various actions. This development has sometimes necessitated, in problems of sufficient importance, the collaboration of teams of scientists and analysts in order to bring the knowledge of specialists to bear.

Along with the better understanding of scientific relationships has come more and better data. Or perhaps the data might be described as one facet of that better understanding. In any event, more facts are available about plastics, rainfall, markets, disease, national income, and so on. Also there have been refinements in the methods of statistical inference—for instance, in the use of small samples, sequential sampling, and experimental designs—and in techniques of computation and model-building, such as linear programming. Finally, electronic computers have come along to make it practicable to utilize all the other refinements. More complex models, which in some cases yield more useful predictions, can be employed; more numerous calculations to show results in a wider range of situations have become feasible. In fact, some persons believe that modern computers mark a massive technological breakthrough, so far as analysis is concerned, somewhat as the microgroove recording was a crucial breakthrough in the high-fidelity reproduction of music. However, it should be recognized that much of the most useful quantitative analysis of today is still done with a hand computer or even on the back of an envelope.

At the same time that these tools were being developed, new applications, or types of analysis, were emerging, and new terminology was being used to describe them. Originally, thoughtful analysis may have been called just that, or possibly "problem solving." In connection with problems which have attracted the attention of economists[2]— such as those pertaining to the balance of payments, price level fluctuations, and possible improvements in general resource allocation— the comparison of alternative policies has been labeled simply "economic analysis." In the early decades of this century, there was a period of "scientific management" or "efficiency engineering" when F. W. Taylor focused attention on factory layout and time-motion studies. Through the years, the stop watch of the early studies has been supplemented by high-speed cameras and by other instruments for measurement and techniques for looking at problems. During roughly the same period, "financial analysis" caught on rapidly, as executives turned to accounting data and short-cut models to predict the effects of alternative management policies. Another development was "consumers' research," in which simple models spelled out some of the characteristics of competing products. For example, lawn sprinklers have been compared with respect to "evenness" by finding out how much water fell into various tin cans evenly spaced around the sprinklers. Also, in the comparison of possible locations, new products, or sales policies, "market research" became widely used.

During World War II, modern statistical techniques and knowledge from different sciences were used, sometimes with striking effectiveness, in the comparison of military tactics, such as various deployments of aircraft or ships. As these studies were used to assist in operational decisions, they became known as "operations research." Since the war,

2 It is surprising, incidentally, how litt'e attention has been given by economists, especially by public-finance specialists, to efficiency in government. A good deal of work has been done to compare alternative means of getting revenue and alternative ways of handling the government's liabilities. With respect to expenditures it is sometimes suggested that, in principle, the government should allocate outlays so that the gains from an incremental dollar's expenditure are the same in every direction (including tax reduction). For the most part, however, economists have been *relatively* uninterested in the optimal allocation of government expenditures or (the same problem at a practical level) in comparisons of alternative purchases by government. This was noted several years ago by V. O. Key, Jr., who remarked that in their textbooks, public-finance experts ". . . generally dispose of the subject of expenditures with a few perfunctory chapters and hurry on to the core of their interest—taxation and other sources of revenue." ("The Lack of Budgetary Theory," *American Political Science Review*, December, 1940, p. 1139.) In recent years, a few economists have stressed the importance of looking at expenditures: e.g., see Arthur Smithies, *The Budgetary Process in the United States*, Committee for Economic Development Research Study (New York: McGraw-Hill, 1955), and James M. Buchanan, "The Pure Theory of Government Finance: A Suggested Approach," *Journal of Political Economy*, December, 1949, pp. 496–505; and there were exceptions before World War II, such as Mable L. Walker, *Municipal Expenditures* (Baltimore: The Johns Hopkins Press, 1930).

this general approach has been applied also to military development and procurement problems, which has meant peering further into the future, including a greatly expanded number of variables, examining a wider range of possible actions, and taking higher-level alternatives into account. The comparison of such enlarged systems of interrelated elements has often been called "systems analysis." For analysis to help business firms increase their profits, a variety of names, from operations research to capital budgeting, have been used during this past decade.[3]

For the most part, these various titles do reflect somewhat different types of analysis, the differences stemming largely from the character of the problems attacked. Yet at the same time these types exhibit a marked similarity: all of them are attempts to trace systematically at least part of the effects of alternative courses of action. Consequently, many of the methodological difficulties that are encountered in any one of these types are common to all.

Despite the encouraging developments of analytical tools and of new applications, it is clear that the role of such analysis must be that of an *aid* to the decision-maker, not that of a substitute for him. In the face of uncertainty about outcomes, for instance, operations research and kindred activities can assist, but not supplant, the exercise of judgment as to which policy is best. Perhaps it should also be mentioned that such analysis is no serious rival of the price mechanism and free enterprise in the organization of the private economy for technical reasons alone (quite apart from the merits of the price system as a decision-making process). Indeed, the best medicine for well-meaning central planners is perhaps a stiff dose of down-to-earth operations research on complex problems of the Federal government; such an experience would lay bare, more vividly than does meditation alone, the awesome difficulties that would be encountered (and the grim mistakes and concentration of power that would surely occur) in detailed central direction of the economy. But where the price mechanism and the action of competing firms do not attend to problems of choice—in *internal* decisions of a consumer, government unit, or firm—it is operations analysis that often has no practicable rival.

THE APPLICATION OF ANALYTICAL AIDS IN GOVERNMENT

In recent years, governmental units have turned increasingly to the quantitative comparison of the alternative policies that are open

---

[3] See various issues of *The Journal of the Operations Research Society of America;* Joel Dean, *Capital Budgeting: Top-Management Policy on Plant, Equipment, and Product Development* (New York: Columbia University Press, 1951).

to them. For example, the military services have internal operations analysis sections or evaluation groups, and, in addition, the Departments of the Army, Navy, and Air Force hire independent organizations to perform such research.[4] As another case in point, some agencies have made progress in the use of work-measurement systems to help select the administrative policy that achieves a fixed task at lowest cost or the maximum output for a given cost. This type of analysis involves the selection of "work-units" (such as hearings completed, parcels shipped, applications examined) in terms of which to measure the output of accounting divisions, legal divisions, wrapping and shipping departments, licensing offices, and so on.[5] Private firms, such as mail-order houses, have long used work-measurement systems to help project personnel requirements in different departments at various times of the day, thus enabling them to shift some employees from time to time in such a way as to maximize the value of their services. In the last few years, the Department of Agriculture has turned to such a system to compare output at various regional offices and under various circumstances,[6] enabling officials to reduce the manpower required to perform a given task, to make sure that manpower is reduced when the task or workload declines, or to consolidate regional offices in response to altered workloads. State and local governments and numerous other agencies have also made use of work-measurement systems.

Another instance, the one to which much of our attention will be devoted in this study, is the use of "cost-benefit analysis" in the evaluation of water-resource developments, such as navigation, flood control, and soil-conservation measures. Even in the thirties the Bureau of Reclamation and Corps of Engineers worked up estimates of benefits and costs for numerous water-resource projects in order to facilitate their comparison. Since World War II, however, interest in cost-benefit analysis has heightened; the Department of Agriculture has completed similar analyses of several watershed-treatment programs, and the Federal Inter-Agency River Basin Committee has been

---

[4] See Florence N. Trefethen, "A History of Operations Research," in *Operations Research for Management*, ed. J. F. McCloskey and F. N. Trefethen (Baltimore: The Johns Hopkins Press, 1954), pp. 3–35.

[5] See the bibliography contained in *A Work Measurement System: Development and Use (A Case Study)*, Management Bulletin, Bureau of the Budget, March, 1950. For a good clear discussion of the main problems, see *Techniques for the Development of a Work Measurement System*, Bureau of the Budget, March, 1950.

[6] "Work-Measurement and Work-Status Reporting System: PMA Commodity Offices," unpublished working papers, loaned by Mrs. Robert P. Beach, Budget Officer, Production and Marketing Administration, Department of Agriculture.

reviewing current procedures and drawing up recommendations concerning future measurement of benefits and costs.[7]

NEED FOR SUCH ANALYSIS IN GOVERNMENT

But surely a great deal more can be done. The trend toward the greater use of quantitative analysis is a response to a very real need, one that is intensified by (a) the absence of any built-in mechanism which would lead to greater efficiency, and (b) the spectacular growth in the size of government.

Absence of Price Mechanism, Profit Lure, "Natural Selection." For one thing, there is no price mechanism within government which points the way to high-level efficiency, that is, to the correct allocation of resources among "industries" or broad governmental functions. For another, there is no competitive force that induces lower-level efficiency—the adoption of methods and equipment which carry out each function at minimum cost. Because of the lure of profits and the threat of bankruptcy, private firms are under pressure to seek out profitable innovations and efficient methods. In this search they have often used, and are now using to an increasing extent, formal quantitative analysis.[8] But even if they do not, continued progress and increased efficiency still tend to come about, though less rapidly. After all, *some* firm is likely to discover more efficient methods through trial and error even if systematic analysis is absent, indeed even if the right questions are not asked. Subsequently, other firms copy the innovation; those that fail to do so (those who make inferior choices of methods) begin to suffer losses, and the process of "natural selection" tends to eliminate them.[9]

In government, however, there is no profit lure, and promotions or salary increases do not depend on profits. Most of the cost of poor decisions does not fall on those who make them. The incentive to seek profitable innovations and efficient methods is not a strong one. Experience in the Post Office Department may illustrate this point: a few postmasters with exceptional drive or motivation have introduced cost-cutting innovations even though this action brought no personal

[7] *Proposed Practices for Economic Analysis of River Basin Projects,* Report to the Federal Inter-Agency River Basin Committee Prepared by the Subcommittee on Benefits and Costs, May, 1950.

[8] See various articles in *Operations Research for Management.*

[9] A. Alchian, "Uncertainty, Evolution, and Economic Theory," *Journal of Political Economy,* June, 1950, pp. 211–221. The prevention of mistakes by systematic analysis would be a cheaper path to progress than their correction by natural selection—*if* the former procedure were as effective as the latter.

gain; yet there are no lures sufficient to cause these innovations to be imitated in other post offices of similar size and setup.[10]

Finally, the process of "natural selection," whose working depends upon the degree and type of rivalry, operates only weakly, if at all, to eliminate wasteful governments. The Federal government, for instance, competes only with the political party that is out of office, and survival in this competition depends upon many things other than efficiency in the use of resources. Thus, there are no forces which operate to reveal the cheapest methods of performing public functions and to induce or compel the government to adopt such methods.

It should be mentioned that in a few government activities, for example, the Military Sea Transport Service, simulation of the market mechanism is attempted. These activities are set up as businesses, provided with working-capital funds, and instructed to charge market prices for the output and to achieve maximum profits—often in the light of special constraints. At present, this institutional arrangement is not widespread, and one is justified in referring to the absence of the price mechanism in government. However, such simulation of the market is a policy which should be explored and evaluated.

Adoption of "Requirements Approach." In the absence of such forces and, to a considerable extent, of systematic analyses in terms of gains and costs, a procedure that might be called the "requirements approach" is used throughout much of the government. Officials inspect a problem pertaining to, say, defense, water usage, or medical care, and set up a "required" task, piece of equipment, or performance characteristic. Cost, i.e., whatever has to be sacrificed in order to obtain the requirement, is given little or no explicit consideration at this point: the requirement is somehow drawn up in the light of the need or payoff alone.[11] (Of course, some notion of cost, however imprecise, is implicit in the recognition of any limitation.) Then feasibility is checked: Can the performance characteristic, such as some designated speed or degree of reliability, be achieved? Can the necessary budget be obtained? Does the nation have the necessary total resources? If the program passes the feasibility tests, it is adopted; if it does not, some adjustments must be made. But the question—what are the payoffs *and the costs* of alternative programs? —may not be explicitly asked during the process of setting the requirement or deciding upon the budget.

[10] For evidence on this point, see Paul Douglas, *Economy in the National Government* (Chicago: University of Chicago Press, 1952), p. 127; and the *Task Force Report on the Post Office* prepared for the Commission on Organization of the Executive Branch of the Government, January, 1949, p. 17.

[11] Indeed, the situation is still worse; . . . "requirements" are often drawn up in the light of little or no idea of true potential payoffs.

The procedure is illustrated by the way in which programs are developed in the Department of Interior. Each of the seven Field Committees (for example, there is one for the Colorado River-Great Basin Region) is instructed to prepare an "optimum program" which is ". . . formulated on the basis of regional needs. It takes into account all practical limitations (such as availability of manpower, laboratory facilities, etc.), *except limitations on funds* [italics added]. This program presents the optimum schedule which should be undertaken in the first year of the six-year program to meet the goals described in the narrative part of each functional chapter."[12] Other programs which relate to alternative budget levels are also prepared in advance (a highly commendable procedure), but the "optimum" program, the one that is regarded as the requirement, is derived by disregarding fund limitations. In the end, higher officials *may* consider alternative programs in the light of their costs. But in all likelihood, major problems of choice will already have been disposed of before costs enter the picture.

The defects of this approach can be seen clearly if an analogy from the life of the consumer is introduced. Suppose the consumer mulls over his transportation problem and decides, "I need a Cadillac," without any information about the cost—that is, about the required outlay and hence about the goods and services that could be had for the same amount. An alternative purchase is a more modest automobile plus other items that could be purchased with the amount saved. But thousands of additional possibilities exist. There is ordinarily a wealth of choice, and to ignore the cost of a course of action is to ignore the possible worth of all these other actions.

This requirements approach appears to be prevalent at various levels of decision-making. Requirements are often set by looking at "need" without regard to cost not only when selecting broad programs but also when choosing the means of carrying them out. With this approach, it is not unnatural for a military service to procure, for example, all-hair wrestling mats even though they cost about twice as much as the half-hair-half-wool mats that are used in most gymnasiums.[13] Specifications for ping-pong balls that take up five and a half pages of single-spaced typing may also stem from too much emphasis on "requirements" and too little on cost.[14]

Importance of Economy in Government. All of this—the absence of the price mechanism and competitive forces, and the prevalence of

[12] Instructions on the Preparation of Regional Program Reports," attached to a memorandum to all Field Committee Chairmen from the Office of the Secretary, U.S. Department of the Interior, January 7, 1953.

[13] Douglas, *op. cit.*, p. 175.

[14] *Ibid.*, p. 173.

the requirements approach—was comparatively unimportant thirty years ago when Federal expenditures were about three billion dollars, but it is an extremely serious matter now that the national government alone disburses more than 70 billion dollars per year. The point is sometimes emphasized by the following type of comparison: during the two years 1953–1954, the Federal government disbursed roughly the same amount (about 140 billion dollars) that was spent in the entire 140-year period from 1789 to 1929. (And during the 15 years from 1939 to 1954, Federal outlays have amounted to almost 800 billion dollars.) Such comparisons are meaningful only in a very limited sense, for changes in the price level are left out of account, but they certainly show that our national government uses and transfers a lot of resources. . . .

NEED FOR BETTER ANALYSIS

Thus, because of government's lack of a competitive market mechanism and because of its tremendous expansion, formal analysis of alternative actions may be especially rewarding in the public sphere. But mere quantity of analysis is unlikely to be particularly rewarding. Although the potential gains from "good" operations analysis may be greater in government than in private industry, the likelihood of social losses from "bad" analysis is also greater, chiefly for two reasons: (1) the process of "natural selection" does not penalize the government that bases decisions on inferior analyses—e.g., comparisons which, however systematic in other respects, use inappropriate criteria or conceal crucial uncertainties ; (2) the problem of choosing appropriate criteria, which will be examined later, is even more difficult in the analysis of many governmental operations than in the analysis of business operations. In the latter, one can usually take the ultimate objective to be the maximization of the present value of expected profits, and then judge whether criteria in particular problems are consistent with the over-all objective. For these reasons, firms can often use relatively poor criteria, such as the minimization of unit costs, in a way that leads them to genuine economies. In the analysis of government operations, however, the over-all objective is so complex, and the "firm" so big and compartmentalized, that it may be more difficult to select appropriate criteria that are consistent with over-all objectives or to use poor criteria judiciously. Therefore it is not mere analysis, but *careful* analysis, that is so urgently needed to assist decision-making in government.

Indeed the bulk of this inquiry is devoted to pitfalls and the means of avoiding them. If these pitfalls are not avoided, quantitative comparisons can do more harm than good: ". . . there is an arguable case for the view that it is better than spurious definiteness, that final decisions actually use judgment rather than implicitly following benefit-cost ratios calculated by different agencies in different ways."[15] This comment (which could apply equally well to types of analysis other than cost-benefit) is surely an understatement if careless estimates are to be carelessly used. Hence it is *better* quantitative analysis which holds the promise of greater economy.

It is also worth noting that additional criticism and independent analysis are especially needed. It would be helpful if outside researchers (for example, those in universities) devoted more time to the painstaking comparison of alternative government actions at various levels. It would be a good thing, so far as quality of analysis is concerned, if staff agencies within government engaged in mutual criticism to a greater extent. In fact, without competition and criticism, staff agencies may not do much good, for they labor under certain handicaps: they have special allegiances,[16] they may develop goals of their own, and they may confuse lines of authority.[17] "Agencies which are under the necessity of competitive survival, with high principles but with equally high desires to develop in size and in significance, cannot be expected to appraise the validity of undertakings in the most abstract and impartial manner."[18]

OUTLOOK FOR THE USE OF ANALYTICAL AIDS

Questions are often, and quite properly, raised about the practical usefulness of analytical aids in the solution of government problems. First, *would* their use have any impact, given the welter of political considerations? Despite the pessimistic views that are sometimes expressed, there is every reason to believe that more and better analysis would influence policy-makers. Pork-barrel aims, local pressures, logrolling, empire-building—in short, political considerations both good and bad—are obviously powerful forces, often decisive ones, in the shaping of decisions at all levels. Yet one reason that these forces are so powerful is that decision-makers are rarely presented with analyses in terms of economic criteria. If these are unavailable (or unreliable), then why not press for a special interest, or flip a coin, or adopt some "off-beat" criterion? If, however, the effects of different policies on economic efficiency are made apparent, it becomes at least a little harder to neglect this consideration. The pressures shift; the cost of making uneconomic choices becomes real.

[15] J. M. Clark, E. L. Grant, and M. M. Kelso, "Secondary or Indirect Benefits of Water-Use Projects," Report of Panel of Consultants to Michael W. Straus, Commissioner, Bureau of Reclamation, June 26, 1952 (mimeographed), p. 12.

[16] Douglas, *op. cit.* pp. 68–69.

[17] See Herbert A. Simon, "Staff and Management Controls," *Annals of the American Academy of Political and Social Science,* March, 1954, pp. 95–103.

[18] *Principles of a Sound National Water Policy,* Prepared under the Auspices of the National Water Policy Panel of Engineers Joint Council, July, 1951, p. 22.

This is not to say, of course, that cogent analysis would promptly carry the day or that it ought to do so if this implied the nullification of independent judgments or of checks and balances. The point here is merely that sound analyses are seldom completely disregarded by policy-makers. Wherever specific studies have had something to contribute, they have usually (not always, to be sure) had some impact on policy. A reading of Congressional hearings on appropriations suggests to me that by and large the departments *do* struggle to achieve something more than, say, departmental security, and Congress and the Agencies *do* grope for sensible allocations of the budget among programs. The trouble is mainly that proper criteria are slippery and the problems difficult.[19] The risk that log-rolling officials will ignore "good" analysis is not too great, probably not as great as the risk that they will be receptive to "bad" analysis or mere assertion.

A second question that arises is the following: could such analysis really play a substantial role? The answer is certainly yes. It could play a most important role because many government operations appear to be susceptible to this sort of analysis. (It should be recalled that quantitative analysis, such as operations research, is referred to; there is obviously a vital role for thought-taking in general as opposed to mere hunch, in every problem of choice.) . . . opportunities for quantitative analysis are numerous in activities that account for over three-quarters of current disbursements. In order for such opportunities to exist, there must be (a) alternative ways to carry out task or programs, and (b) meaningful quantitative indicators of gain and of cost. . . . these conditions are fulfilled in most defense activities and in at least half of the non-defense programs. Indeed, in programs accounting for perhaps one-fifth of the non-defense budget, gains can probably be given meaningful price tags and measured in terms of dollars so that activities which carry out rather dissimilar functions can be compared directly. To be sure, there are some activities, such as those pertaining to foreign policy, which appear to offer little opportunity for the measurement of gains and costs. But other sectors of the Federal budget—such as the natural-resource programs, the Post Office Department, transportation programs, and the provision of health services—are promising from the standpoint of applying quantitative analysis.

[19] For a revealing account of the headaches of budget allocation, see *The Forrestal Diaries*, ed. W. Millis (New York: Viking Press, 1951), pp. 492–530.

PPBS: RATIONALE, LANGUAGE, AND IDEA-RELATIONSHIPS

SAMUEL M. GREENHOUSE

An understanding of what the Planning-Programming-Budgeting System (PPBS) purports to be and to do for the U.S. Government rests, I believe, upon recognizing the primacy and interplay of two PPBS ingredients. These two "molecules"—as they stand individually, contribute proportionately, interact, and interdepend—compose the vital core of PPBS.

Let me begin by identifying the two ingredients, as a prelude to defining and discussing them.

A single concept, dealing with the accountability of the Federal agency apparatus, forms the philosophic base of the PPBS structure.

The main structural members of PPBS are eight terms with definitions so special that, in effect, PPBS has a "language all its own." True, none of the words and phrases in this language is really new. But each is used so very differently in the PPBS context that earlier-entrenched images (which our minds seem to conjure up whenever the terms are heard) may in some cases prevent comprehension. The eight terms are: objectives, programs, program alternatives, outputs, progress measurements, inputs, alternative ways to do a given job, and systems analysis. A true understanding of PPBS cannot derive from reliance upon the traditional definitions of these terms. Each has a

From *Public Administration Review*, Vol. 26 (December 1966), pp. 271–277. Samuel Greenhouse is a member of the Administrator's Advisory Council, Veterans Administration, Washington, D.C. Reprinted with permission of the author and the American Society of Public Administration.

particular meaning and significance in the *rearrangement of established ideas* which PPBS represents.

The fresh design which emerges from this rearrangement, rather than the individual ideas themselves, is what is new about PPBS.[1] But in rearranging, in linking and relating the ideas, a trimming and fitting had to take place. Through this tailoring process, the terms remained unchanged while the ideas (which the terms had so long and effectively stood for) took on subtle differences of flavor and shade. Given these new meanings, the terms have become coordinates with distinct functions, hierarchical placements, and highly significant relationships within the flow and overall framework of PPBS.

THE BASIC CONCEPT: ACCOUNTABILITY

PPBS is a multi-purpose system. If it is implemented and instrumented soundly, it should have a variety of uses. Only one of these—and perhaps not the most important one, although it is receiving predominant attention at this stage—is the improvement of individual Federal agency operations. Whether the regulation of Federal agency activities is a key purpose or not, the careful installation of PPBS in the individual agencies is of surpassing importance, because the agencies are indispensable building blocks in the overall system. That is to say, PPBS could not exist disembodied from the individual agencies, even if the main purpose of PPBS were, say, to accelerate the economic growth of the United States rather than to introduce a new technique of agency management. This may help to explain why the bedrock concept of PPBS concerns the matter of Federal agency accountability.

Now, what is the PPBS concept, and how is it different?

The PPBS concept is that each Federal agency is accountable to the President[2] for the production of goods and services, and more particularly, *for the distribution of these goods and services to the American people.*

This is a considerable departure indeed, for, until PPBS, the Federal agency apparatus, was considered to be held accountable by, and to, the President for providing the Presidency with "administrative support." Application of this vague concept has become more difficult as the Federal apparatus has grown and diversified. Our Presidents have

[1] In this regard, PPBS is not surprisingly like many conceptual "innovations." It is often said that there is "nothing new under the sun." That many discoveries consist in rearranging and regrouping ideas which are, individually, already known, does not diminish the usefulness of the results. The important question is whether and in what directions PPBS may prove useful.

[2] And to the Congress.

become too busy to locate, identify in specifics, and hold direct reins of responsibility.

The PPBS accountability concept focuses the attention of each agency on the question: What is our business? The PPBS concept provides a basis for particularizing the answers to the question: Accountable for specifically what products (goods or services), delivered to whom?

The PPBS concept matches the reality of today's Federal agency operations, demonstrating once again that "theory interprets established fact." The agencies *are* producing goods and services, and distributing them to the American people.[3] What PPBS *adds* to this reality is the assumption that product delivery to the American public is the *central* purpose of agency operation rather than merely a happenstance or a by-product of other, more characteristic purposes.

Of course, all Federal agencies perform other functions besides distributing goods and services to the public. For example, each agency generates goods and services for purely internal uses; for the use of other agencies; or for the President and Congress. However, an understanding of PPBS depends upon recognizing that all "inside-the-government" efforts and interchanges are considered subordinate to the central purpose. Inside-government activities are not pertinent for PPBS accountability. Unless this is recognized, the ideas which underlie the terms "objective," "program," "output," and "input" cannot be clearly discerned nor can the interplay of these terms be comprehended. The discussions of output and input allude in greater detail to this crucial matter.

If the agencies are to be held accountable for discharging the central purpose of distributing agency-produced goods and services to the American public, the public becomes, conceptually speaking, the market for the agencies' products and services. Thus, the explicit business of each Federal agency is to satisfy the public's actual and potential market demands for the agency's particular product/service lines. Accountability discharge becomes subject to evaluation in terms of each agency's success in (1) gauging the nature and proportions of the market demands, and (2) fulfilling these demands.

OBJECTIVES

With this background, it becomes clear that the apex-term of the PPBS idea-structure is "objectives." As the preceding discussion indicates, a more precise way to visualize the idea here denoted is to

---

[3] In some cases, the agencies contract for goods and services, and perform the distribution themselves. So long as the production is government financed, and performed under government auspices, it can be regarded the same way, for PPBS purposes, as in government production.

expand the term to "market objectives." Each agency is supposed to generate *explicit* market objectives, to make possible a genuine agency-wide understanding and a common agency approach toward their achievement. Satisfactory market objectives would, one supposes, provide specific grounds upon which to base the answers to three questions[4] about *each* main class of items produced by a given agency:

What class of goods or services is contemplated for production? (Each agency has at least one main class of items, or product line; most agencies have more than one.)

What market group is each product line (good or service) intended to satisfy? (Some agencies have readily identifiable groups of customers, e.g., veterans; other agencies serve fluid and only temporarily associated groups, such as air travelers.)

What specific needs, of the market group served, is the product designed to satisfy? (For example, if the American Indian, say, were assumed to need help in achieving economic well-being comparable to the "national average," what indications of this need might be cited in support of programmatic intentions?)

If this theme correctly interprets PPBS, customer-oriented market objectives are destined to become key standards for agency self-appraisal and accountability. Such standards are quite common for private industry, except that total sales volume is a more readily obtainable index of market needs and satisfactions than will be available in government.

Allowing for the absence of various profit mechanisms in government, the effect of PPBS will be to bring governmental practice to a somewhat closer approximation of common industrial practice than has been possible before.

PROGRAMS

What idea underlies the term "program"? In PPBS language, a program is a package which encompasses each and every one of the agency's efforts to achieve a particular objective or set of allied objectives.[5] If the objective were to provide economic assistance to the

---

[4] These questions appear useful to the author to illustrate the concept of market demand which PPBS implies. They are not to be found in the available PPBS literature.

[5] Whenever the term "objectives" is used hereafter, it should be read as "customer-oriented market objectives."

American Indian, the program would be composed of all agency activities and expenditures put to that purpose.

Bear in mind that *this* idea of program is very different from the traditional governmental usage. Prior to PPBS, all agencies used the term to characterize functions and professional disciplines. Hence, "procurement," "data management," "engineering," and many other activities were called programs. The habit persists even now, because PPBS has not yet succeeded in making its point.

Those agencies which did not understand the new meaning of the term in advance of generating their initial PPBS "program structures," will certainly need to redo program structures if PPBS is ever to gain solid ground. Individual activities, functions, and professional disciplines are the very antitheses of programs in the PPBS sense. The whole PPBS idea is to facilitate the drawing together, the summation of all agency efforts to meet particular objectives, so that the validity of each program may be assessed in terms of overall approach, dimension, and costs and may be compared with other competing programs, potential or existing. It should be recognized, then, that in the future, a program which mirrors (corresponds with) a given agency's established organization structure will be a rarity, unless the agency happens to have only one program. An agency with a functional-type organization must break down functional efforts and apportion them among programs, in order to successfully sum each program.[6]

As the foregoing discussion may have indicated, there is a strong conceptual relationship between objective(s) and program. In "PPBS language," there are no objectives recognized except those which suggest a program designed specifically to fulfill them; and there can be no recognized entity describable as a program unless it is designed to accomplish explicit objectives (customer-oriented market objectives).

PROGRAM ALTERNATIVES

The term "program alternatives" is next in the PPBS hierarchy.[7] Within any one agency, this term means other possible programs besides those already decided upon. Consequently, it suggests a comparison of two or more programs (i.e., two or more possible approaches) toward fulfilling the *same market objective(s)*. For example, as in the hypothetical case mentioned earlier, suppose that an agency

[6] However, it is not required that there be change in the established organization structure; merely a change in the accounting will do.

[7] Of course, these PPBS terms may be considered in any order, but the author finds the order of presentation given here easiest to work with for definition purposes.

wanted to accomplish the objective of raising the economic well-being of the American Indian to some mythical level such as the national average. Presumably, any one of several programs, existing or new, might succeed in bringing this about. The agency would wish to choose the "best" program for the purpose, and to disregard other program alternatives.[8] Or, it might simply wish to evaluate a number of program alternatives so that, having selected one, it could demonstrate the wisdom of the selection by revealing the inadequacies (in the discarded programs) which the comparative evaluation had uncovered.[9]

OUTPUT

In PPBS language, an output must have, conceptually speaking, all of the following properties:

It is a product (either a good or a service).

It is produced by a Federal agency, or is produced under the agency's auspices.

It is a tangible outgrowth of a particular program (i.e., it is the result of a calculated program effort).

It is the sort of product which can be appropriately singled-out as an indicator of program results. (Logically, therefore, it must be a program end-product, and an important one, at that.)

It is considered by the agency as satisfying an explicit market objective (or related set of objectives).

The foregoing list of properties should serve to illustrate the connective tissue which runs all the way through PPBS. That is, the idea of output is inseparably linked to the earlier discussed ideas of market objectives and program(s). And this idea-connection is highly significant for interpreting the PPBS notion of output. It means that many

[8] The term "systems analysis" will be defined later, at which point the mechanics for selecting a "best" program from among the possible program alternatives will be suggested.

[9] There are two other types of alternatives in PPBS language. One is "alternative ways to do a given job," to be defined later. At that time, the distinction between "program alternatives" and "alternative ways to do a given job" should become manifest. The other, which could be termed "comparison of all agencies' programs" is not discussed in this paper because it is not a prominent part of PPBS as applied in the individual agencies. It is applied, however, by the President and his executive staff.

types of products which the agencies have been accustomed to regard as outputs can no longer be so regarded. PPBS has preempted the word, so to speak, for a much narrower, sharper-focused usage than the traditional one. In order to be considered an output in PPBS language, the good or service produced must satisfy an explicit market objective *and* must be an indicator of program results.

Let us appraise a few items traditionally considered outputs, in light of these definitional criteria. Suppose that an agency decides upon a program to build schools. The agency's procurement division places a series of contracts with construction firms. One month later, the agency's statistical division prepares and forwards to the agency director a "construction progress report." Are the contractual documents properly countable as outputs? No! Is the statistical report an output? No! Why? Neither the documents nor the report satisfies a customer-oriented market objective, and neither represents an indicator of program achievement (although both of them do represent divisional, that is, internal, achievements).

They are intermediate, or contributory products, rather than outputs in the PPBS sense.

What would constitute *program* achievement, and thus be an output in the PPBS sense of the word, could in the example cited above be the number of schools built, number of new classrooms available, or number of new classroom seats set into place.

The distinction between intermediate or contributory products and output is a very critical matter, insofar as understanding PPBS is concerned. If we would follow the logic-structure of PPBS, we must reconstitute our thinking. We must consider many of the things we are accustomed to producing (and claiming output-credit for) as mere intermediates. This is not so illogical as it may at first appear to be. Coal is the output of a miner, but is only a contributing factor for the completion of industrial processes, rather than an output of any of those processes. In turn, the processes' outputs are, or may be, salable commodities. One man's output is, to another man, merely a contribution to *his* output. The logic of how to classify an item, such as coal, depends entirely upon the intent and purpose of the classification, rather than upon some immutable principle. For purposes of PPBS output, the government's many agencies may be regarded as analogous to the separate divisions of any large corporation. The corporate outputs, in any such enterprise, are only those items produced to reach the public. Neither those items consumed by and for the production processes themselves, nor those exchanged between the corporate divisions, are regarded by the corporation as outputs.

Given the realization that this is the output focus of PPBS, we can now get a clearer fix on the PPBS idea of progress measurement.

PROGRESS MEASUREMENT

The notion that progress should be measured in some fashion is not likely to trouble many people. The question that may be vexing some students of PPBS is: What does PPBS want us to measure? Or, put in another way: What does PPBS regard as *progress* in a given program?

If output means only those programmatic end-products which satisfy explicit market objectives, then program *fulfillment* must imply that *both* of two conditions have occurred:

The output which had been planned has materialized, *and*

The output distribution which had been intended has been completed.[10]

If that is fulfillment, then progress must imply one of two questions, depending upon what stage the program happens to be in at the time when progress is measured:

Either, how closely does the production progress match planned progress?

Or, how well is the output distribution proceeding, as compared with the distribution plan?

INPUT

Of all the words in the special language of PPBS, input is probably the easiest to grasp, because the PPBS definition is fairly close to the traditional usage of the term. If all of the inputs to a given program were expressed in dollars, the sum would comprise the total costs incurred by the program (during the time-period that the program had been in effect). In other words, the total quantity of manpower, facilities, equipment, and materials applied to the program, expressed in either units or dollars, is the program input. Note, however, that the facilities, equipment, and materials applied may, in a given program, include some intermediate or contributory products.[11]

---

[10] At this early stage in the evolution of PPBS, with the distribution aspect not yet generally recognized, few agencies' plans give distribution intentions any prominence. Where on-going programs are concerned, particularly, the agencies have tended to disregard distribution considerations altogether. If PPBS "makes it," this situation will change.

[11] In which case, we may be classifying as *inputs,* for PPBS purposes, some items which would have been classified, in pre-PPBS days, as *outputs.* But remember: don't duplicate inputs—that is, whether summarizing input units or input dollar costs, don't count both the intermediate/contributory products *and* the manpower, facilities, equipment, or materials that were used *in their production.* Count either one or the other as input, but not both.

ALTERNATIVE WAYS TO DO A GIVEN JOB

The concept of "alternative ways to do a given job" is input-related, insofar as PPBS is concerned. The "given job" notion means that the output to be produced and the distribution pattern for that output have already been decided upon. The question, at any phase of the program subsequent to that decision-point, becomes: Can we alter the production or distribution *technique* and by so doing improve either:

The timing of the production or delivery, or

The quantity or quality of the item(s) being produced, or

The unit or total cost of the production or delivery?

Every one of the three questions above is input-oriented. That is why defining the term program alternatives separately (as was done earlier) is advantageous. True, the word "alternatives" appears in both "program alternatives" and "alternative ways to do a given job." The first is output-related; it suggests substituting an entirely different program (and therefore a different output or outputs) for a program already planned or in progress. On the other hand, "alternative ways to do a given job" takes the program as given, and raises possibilities for changing the mix of inputs, and thereby redirecting the program.

Viewed in another way, the first involves policy questions, while the second involves operational matters. It is quite useful to distinguish between these two, as an aid in placing responsibility. That is to say, any single group of executives need not, sometimes should not, and often cannot answer both types of questions. However, the agency head, able in a given case to distinguish the PPBS situation as either policy or operations, is well on the way toward getting appropriate action taken, because he will know which group of his executives to contact.

SYSTEMS ANALYSIS

Of the eight terms characterized as important for understanding PPBS, only systems analysis remains to be discussed.

In the foregoing, the attempt has been to establish a distinct identity for PPBS. If this has succeeded, the reader already knows that systems analysis isn't PPBS, and that PPBS isn't systems analysis. The number of people who appear to regard these two things as one and the same is astounding.

Purely for purposes of differentiating the two, PPBS may be captioned as a bag of promises, concepts and relationships; whereas systems analysis may be captioned as a bag of techniques attached to a way of approaching problems. No disparagement of the latter is intended. To the contrary. The cause of technique is not advanced by confounding it with the very content to which it can be most profitably applied.

If systems analysis isn't synonymous with PPBS, what is it? More particularly, what is it insofar as PPBS is concerned?

A capsule definition would be: systems analysis is the application of "benefit-cost" analytical techniques to several areas of the PPBS anatomy.[12]

From the standpoint of the individual Federal agencies, two PPBS areas are especially amenable to benefit-cost techniques. One is the posing and evaluation of program alternatives, i.e., ascertaining the benefit-cost advantage (if any) of shifting to different outputs and/or distribution patterns so as to satisfy market objective(s) better. The other is the measurement of progress in a given program, i.e., ascertaining the benefit-cost advantage (if any) of changing the input mix so as to produce and/or distribute the output more efficiently.[13] In either case, the function of the systems analyst is to diagnose the benefit-cost situation as it exists, so that the agency head may have the opportunity to make his decision on a benefit-cost basis if the circumstances suggest to him that such is the appropriate basis. If other considerations suggest to the agency head that the decision should be predicated upon different or broader criteria than simply benefit and cost, that remains his prerogative. He should have the benefit-cost data in any case, so that he can know what sacrifice, if any, the exercise of the prerogative entails.

The preceding only skims the surface of systems analysis. A more complete treatment is beyond the scope of an essay on the nature of PPBS.

SUMMARY

What is PPBS? It is a structure with a base unusual for government, and with key structural members so interdependent that comprehension must extend to all, or true perception of the "building" is impeded. The base is accountability in the citizen market. Therefore, the objectives must be product supply and distribution. Accordingly, programs are conceived and executed as production/distribution entities. Consequently, program alternatives are different production/distribution entities which might offer better benefit-cost ratios than

---

[12] In the broader context represented by economic theory, benefit-cost techniques have been described for a century as "marginal utility" analysis.

[13] A special and very useful application of systems analysis, which overlaps both foregoing cases, is the benefit-cost evaluation of program expansion/contraction.

existing ones. End-products become the only items construed as outputs. And, progress is viewed and measured in terms of output/distribution timing and effectiveness vs. planned timing and effectiveness. Hence, the inputs are "whatever resources it takes to get the production-distribution job done." As a result, alternative input-mixes become important comparison bases within any given program. Finally, systems analysis contributes diagnosis and appraisal to the whole.

Those familiar with PPBS will have noted the omission of many details. The workaday requirements in planning, programming, and budgeting; the preparation and time-phasing of "program memoranda" and "program and financial plans"; the problems and reasoning associated with below-the-first-tier program structuring; the many different ways in which the cost-benefit approach and techniques (marginal utility theory) may be applied—all of these have been omitted or touched lightly, in large part because they have been treated thoroughly and in depth by many. Hopefully, the details will take on greater meaning within the framework of the "larger architecture" which this essay has sought to delineate.

THE SYSTEMS ANALYSIS APPROACH

ALAIN C. ENTHOVEN

It is a great pleasure for me to appear before you this morning and to have the opportunity to make a contribution to the use of Systems Analysis on problems of State and local governments. I believe that this is a most worthwhile objective and that there are clear possibilities for making major contributions to the public welfare through the broader use of Systems Analysis at all levels of government.

What I have to say will be based on our experience in the Department of Defense. But, I want to emphasize at the outset my conviction that the problems of State and local government and the problems of education, natural resource management, pollution of the environment and public health and welfare are no more complex and no less amenable to systematic, rational analysis than are the problems of defense. I need only mention our current problems in NATO and in defeating aggression in Southeast Asia to illustrate the point that we have our share of complex problems. While I would not want to suggest that Systems Analysis has "solved" these problems, I think that it is fair to say that a systematic and integrated approach to the gathering and presentation of information on the alternatives available to our Government has made the work of our responsible decision-makers easier and more productive than it might otherwise be.

From *Planning-Programming-Budgeting: Selected Comments,* Government Operations Subcommittee on National Security and International Operations, U.S. Senate, 90th Congress, 1st Session, 1967, Committee Print, pp. 1–10. Alain Enthoven is Vice President of Economic Planning, Litton Industries, Inc.

There is a great deal that might be said about the Systems Analysis approach. In this statement, I would like to pick out a few of the aspects that seem to me to be especially relevant and to make these points largely by the use of excerpts from A Modern Design for Defense Decision.[1]

In my statement, I would like to expand on the following points:

1. Systems Analysis is a reasoned approach to problems of decision, accurately described as "quantitative common sense."

2. Systems Analysis is an application of scientific method, using that term in its broadest sense.

3. There are limitations in the application of Systems Analysis, although these have often been overstated.

4. In 1961, the Defense planning and budgeting system had to be changed to permit the application of Systems Analysis.

5. Systems Analysis is a regular working contributor to the annual Defense decision-making cycle.

6. Two necessary conditions for the successful application of Systems Analysis as a working part of an operating organization are that it be used by decision-makers, and that it be fed with ideas by a broadly based interdisciplinary research program.

7. Systems Analysis can be applied to the problems of State and local government, including programs for social welfare.

SYSTEMS ANALYSIS APPROACH

Systems Analysis is nothing more than quantitative or enlightened common sense aided by modern analytical methods. What we seek to do in the systems analysis approach to problems is to examine an objective in its broadest sense, including its reasonableness or appropriateness from a national policy point of view, and then develop for the responsible decision-maker information that will best help him to select the preferred way of achieving it. This process of selection requires that we first identify alternative ways of achieving the objective and then estimate, in quantitative terms, the benefits (effectiveness) to be derived from, and the costs of, each alternative. Those aspects of the problem that cannot easily be quantified are explicitly stated. In principle, we strive to identify the alternative that yields a specified degree of effectiveness for the least cost or, what is the same thing, the greatest effectiveness for a given cost. In essence, it is a way of dealing with the basic economic problem—how best to use our limited national resources. So much for what systems analysis is. A few words on what it is not.

[1] Industrial College of the Armed Forces. A Modern Design for Defense Decision—A McNamara-Hitch-Enthoven Anthology, edited by Samuel A. Tucker. Washington, D.C., 1966.

Systems Analysis is not synonymous with the application of computers. There is no essential connection between the two. Certainly the development of the former in no way depends on the latter. Some researchers, working within the limits of the systems analysis approach, try to do their analyses by means of large-scale computer simulations. Actually, the computer simulation approach so far has not been particularly fruitful as a method of weapon systems analysis. However, the potential advantages offered by high-speed electronic computers are very great. One of the primary advantages of the computer to the systems analysis function is to permit us to examine a much larger number of alternatives in a shorter period of time than would be otherwise possible. This is especially important in the case of very complex and interrelated systems where hand calculations would limit the time available for the more important work of analysis. I intend to try to exploit more fully the potential of high speed computers. But I would like to make it clear that I view the computer as a mechanical aid in my work and not as the substance of my work.

Moreover, systems analysis is not mysterious or occult. It is not performed with the help of a mysterious black box. A good system analyst should be able to give a clear nontechnical explanation of his methods and results to the responsible decision-makers.

APPLICATION OF THE SCIENTIFIC METHOD

I would like now to turn to what I believe are some of the basic characteristics of the Systems Analysis method. Systems Analysis is at once eclectic and unique. It is not physics, engineering, mathematics, economics, political science or military operations and yet it involves elements of all of the above disciplines. But regardless of its make-up, the art of systems analysis—and it is an art—like the art of medicine, must be based on the scientific method, using this term in its broadest sense.

What are the relevant characteristics of scientific method as applied to the problem of choosing strategies and selecting weapon systems, or, for that matter, to the analysis of any problem of public policy involving allocation of the nation's scarce resources. I would like to answer this by quoting a passage from an address I gave before the Naval War College in 1963.

"First, the method of science is an open, explicit, verifiable self-correcting process. It combines logic and empirical evidence. The method and tradition of science require that scientific results be openly arrived at in such a way that any other scientist can retrace the same steps and get the same result. Applying this to weapon systems and to strategy would require that all calculations, assumptions, empirical data, and judgments be described in the analysis in such a way that they can be subjected to checking, testing, criticism, debate, discussion, and possible refutation. Of course, neither science nor systems analysis is infallible. But infallibility is not being claimed; it would be worse than unscientific to do so. However, scientific method does have a self-correcting character that helps to guard science from persistence in error in the long run.

"Second, scientific method is objective. Although personalities doubtless play an important part in the life of the Physics profession, the science itself does not depend upon personalities or vested interest. The truth of a scientific proposition is established by logical and empirical methods common to the profession as a whole. The young and inexperienced scientist can challenge the results of an older and more experienced one, or an obscure scientist can challenge the findings of a Nobel Prize winner, and the profession will evaluate the results on the basis of methods quite independent of the authority of the contenders, and will establish what is the correct conclusion. In other words, the result is established on the objective quality of the Physics and not on the reputations of the persons involved. . . .

"Third, in scientific method in the broadest sense, each hypothesis is tested and verified by methods appropriate to the hypothesis in question. Some are tested and verified logically, some experimentally, some historically, etc. Some sciences, of course, can reproduce experiments cheaply and they tend to emphasize experiment. This is notably the case with the Physical Sciences. In others, particularly some branches of Medicine and the Social Sciences, one cannot experiment readily, if at all, and the detailed analysis of available historical data is most appropriate. In this respect, they resemble Military Science very closely. In choosing weapon systems some experimentation is possible but a great deal of analysis is also required. In fact, in the development of weapon system analysis, one is more handicapped than in most of the sciences, for fully realistic tests come only at infrequent intervals in war, while the development of new weapon systems also takes place in peacetime. But this argues for better analysis and more heavy reliance on analysis where fully relevant experience is not generally available.

"Fourth, quantitative aspects are treated quantitatively. This is not to say that all matters can be reduced to numbers, or even that most can be, or that the most important aspects can be. It is merely to say that the appropriate method for dealing with some aspects of problems of choice of weapon systems and strategies requires numbers. Nonquantitative judgment is simply not enough. What is at issue here really is not numbers or computers versus words or judgments. The real issue is one of clarity of understanding and expression. . . .

"Numbers are a part of our language. Where a quantitative matter is being discussed, the greatest clarity of thought is achieved by using numbers instead of by avoiding them, *even when uncertainties are present.* This is not to rule out judgment and insight. Rather, it is to say, that judgments and insights need, like everything else, to be expressed with clarity if they are to be useful.

"Let me emphasize the point about uncertainties. Many people seem to feel that quantitative analysis is not possible if there are any uncertainties. But this view is incorrect. In fact there is substantial literature on the logic of decision-making under uncertainty going back at least as far as Pascal, Bernoulli, and Bayes in the 17th and 18th centuries. Moreover, there are simple practical techniques for dealing with uncertainty which make it possible to do analyses that point up the uncertainties for the decision-maker and indicate their significance. In fact, rather than conceal uncertainties, a good analysis will bring them out and clarify them. If it is a question of uncertainties about quantitative matters such as operational factors, it is generally useful to examine the available evidence and determine the bounds of the uncertainty. In many of our analyses for the Secretary of Defense, we carry three estimates through the calculations: an 'optimistic,' a 'pessimistic,' and a 'best' or single most likely estimate. If there are uncertainties about context, at least one can run the calculations on the basis of several alternative assumptions so that the decision-maker can see how the outcome varies with the assumptions."

THE LIMITATIONS OF SYSTEMS ANALYSIS

I have frequently been asked about the shortcomings and limitations of the systems analysis approach. Let me refer to an article I wrote for the Naval Review, 1965, reprinted in *A Modern Design for Defense Decision.*

"What's wrong with systems analysis? What are its particular limitations and biases?" One criticism I have heard is that emphasis on quantitative analysis risks ignoring those factors that cannot be reduced to numbers, or at least over-emphasizing those that can.

"Suppose, for example, that the problem is to choose between two alternative ways of destroying a certain set of targets. The less costly way is to base short-range missiles on the territory of an ally; the more costly way is to cover the targets with long-range missiles based in the United States. But suppose basing the missiles on the ally's territory would lead to political difficulties, to the embarrassment and possible fall of a friendly government. How does one take account of such political aspects in a quantitative analysis? The answer is that one doesn't. There is no way of 'grinding in' the potential political difficulties of an ally. The most the analysis can do is to make clear to the decision-maker the differences in cost and effectiveness between the two approaches so that he can make an informed judgment about their weight in relation to the political problems.

"I would not want to deny that there is potential danger here, even though there is nothing about the systems analysis approach that prevents an assessment of the political or other nonquantitative factors from being included in the staff work. I am confident that the top-level leaders of the Department of Defense who use systems analyses as one of their sources of information are careful to give balanced consideration to all factors, whether quantitative or not.

"Another criticism sometimes made is that application of the 'flat of the curve' argument to force or performance requirements may lead people to ignore the decisiveness of a narrow edge in superior performance. There is a danger here if an unwary analyst confuses *performance* and *effectiveness*. There is no question but that, in some cases, a narrow edge in performance may have a very great impact on effectiveness. The performance advantage of the Japanese Zero fighter over American aircraft at the beginning of World War II is a good case in point. But there are other cases in which even a substantial increase in performance, purchased at a high price, may have a small impact on effectiveness. For example, many Navy aviators believe that under today's conditions, a substantial speed advantage in attack aircraft may mean rather little in terms of increased effectiveness. It is easy to confuse performance and effectiveness. But this mistake is clearly not peculiar to the systems analysis approach. The only way to avoid it, and to relate performance to effectiveness properly, is with the help of good analysis.

"Next, it is argued that the systems analysis approach may be biased against the new and in favor of the old. I am sometimes concerned that our analyses may be subject to such bias, but I think that the method of open explicit analysis is much less likely to be so biased than is reliance on judgment or intuition or experience unsupported by analysis. The reason for the bias is that we all tend to compare the old and the new in the current mission that happens to have been optimized for the old. . . .

"Finally, sometimes it is said that systems analyses oversimplify complex problems. Of course, we have to simplify the complex problems we face; no one could possibly understand most problems of modern weapon systems and strategy in all their complexity. And it is a natural human failing to oversimplify. But I believe the facts are that the systems analysis approach is much less prone to oversimplification than any alternative approach. For it is part of systems analysis to bring to bear all of the best of modern analytical techniques for organizing data and summarizing clearly its most relevant aspects. Moreover, reliance on the method of open, explicit analysis is our best guarantee against persistence in harmful oversimplification. For if I must lay out clearly all of my assumptions, objectives, factors, and calculations, my critics can see what I have done and point out where I have oversimplified, if indeed I have done so. But if I am allowed to keep it all in my head and appeal to experience or judgment, others have no way of knowing whether or not I have oversimplified the problem."

INTRODUCTION OF SYSTEMS ANALYSIS IN THE DEFENSE DEPARTMENT

Although systems analysis is a reasonable and straightforward concept, it was not an easy one to implement in the Department of Defense. In conducting a sound cost-effectiveness study you must be able to associate both the benefits and costs with the alternatives to be examined. The Defense management system as it existed five years ago did not permit this. Assistant Secretary Hitch described the problems he encountered as follows:

"In 1961, the chief, in fact the Secretary's only systematic and comprehensive vehicle for the allocation of resources in the Defense Department, was the annual budget. For the task which it was being asked to perform, it was deficient in several respects. The budget focused on the financial problems of a single upcoming fiscal year, thereby discouraging adequate consideration of decisions whose near term dollar impact was slight but whose impact in later years was very large, to the point of becoming an important constraint on Defense managers. The structure of the budget, which portrays the Defense program in terms of broad functional purposes (e.g., personnel, procurement and construction) and organizational components also limited its usefulness as a management tool. Rational military strategies and force requirements have to be planned and expressed in terms of the final products of the military program such as numbers of combat ready divisions and deployed missiles, rather than in terms of the basic resource ingredients of the budget. Moreover, in the Department of Defense at that time there was an almost complete dichotomy between military planning, which was long range, expressed in terms of outputs, and performed by military planners in the Joint Staff and the Military Departments; and budgeting, which was short range, expressed in terms of inputs, and performed by the Comptroller organization.

"It was to bridge the gap between these two functions that we designed and installed the 'programming' system. By linking military planning and budgeting in a unified planning-programming-budgeting decision-making process we are able to produce a single department-wide blueprint for the future known as the 'Five Year Force Structure and Financial Program.' The program projects not only the military forces needed to meet the requirements of our long-range military plans but also the personnel, equipment, supplies and installations required to support them. In addition, the program projects the full costs of these resources, thereby permitting responsible decision-makers to assure themselves that the program they are planning is financially feasible and is providing a sound basis for the development of our annual budget requests to Congress.

"The Five Year Program is organized by forces and weapon systems grouped by mission. At the broadest level of aggregation, there are ten major military programs—the Strategic Retaliatory Forces, the Continental Air and Missile Defense Forces, the General Purpose Forces, Airlift and Sealift Forces, and Research and Development Program, etc. These major military programs are made up of subaggregations. These, in turn, are made up of 'program elements' which we consider the basic building blocks as well as the decision-making level of the programming process. A 'program element' is an integrated force or activity—a combination of men, equipment and facilities whose effectiveness can be directly related to national security objectives. The B-52 bomber force, together with all of the supplies, bases, weapons, and manpower needed to make it militarily effective is such a program element. Other examples would be attack carriers or infantry divisions. There are in all about 1,000 program elements. Groupings of program elements are based on a common mission or set of purposes, with elements either complementing each other or being close substitutes which should be considered together when making major program decisions."

The Programming System thus allows the reader to see at a glance how much of the Department of Defense Budget is going to strategic retaliatory forces and how much of that is going to each of the major weapon systems included in that category. This is clearly a far more meaningful way of subdividing the Defense Budget from the point of view of determining its overall shape. But even more importantly, the programming system permits us to relate both benefits and costs to the forces and activities that must be compared and planned. This feature is essential to any agency that hopes to apply the Systems Analysis approach to its problems.

THE WORK OF SYSTEMS ANALYSIS

The primary function of Systems Analysis in the Pentagon is to assist the Secretary of Defense by developing information that will be useful to him in making key decisions on force levels and resource requirements. For this reason the work of the staff is tied very closely to the annual Defense decision-making cycle which is based on detailed continuing requirements studies. Carefully formulated, detailed analytical studies are basic to sound decisions on force and resource requirements. We develop each year a program of studies that we believe should be conducted during the coming year. These proposed studies are submitted to the Secretary who reviews them, decides which ones he feels are required, and requests the Joint Chiefs of Staff and the Service Secretaries to have their staffs conduct them. My staff works closely with the groups that are actually conducting the studies to advise them on methodology, selecting assumptions, and to insure that the study is focused on the questions the Secretary feels need answering. When the studies are completed and submitted to the Secretary we assist him by reviewing them, indicating weaknesses, summarizing them for his use, etc.

The completed studies normally serve as the basis for proposed changes to the Five Year Defense Program. These changes may be submitted by one of the military departments or by the Joint Chiefs of Staff. Proposed changes to the Force Structure are then reviewed in depth by the staff of the Office of the Secretary of Defense. We in Systems Analysis emphasize "cost-effectiveness" studies of the proposals, comparing each with the previously approved force and other alternative ways to accomplish the mission. The Secretary then makes tentative decisions on the Force Structure. These tentative decisions are reviewed by the Joint Chiefs of Staff and the Military Departments, who have the opportunity to make further recommendations. After further discussions with his principal military and civilian advisers, the Secretary of Defense makes his final decisions, and these decisions serve as the basis for the annual budget. The budget is reviewed by the Secretary in the fall of each year and, of course, submitted to Congress in January. By this point we are well into the next cycle and new requirements studies are being initiated.

Throughout the decision-making cycle, Systems Analysis emphasizes integration of the various elements of the defense program and focuses on the broad national security objectives. This should be a primary objective of any Systems Analysis staff, at the Federal, State, or local governmental level, as it is an area in which most government organizations are weak. This was particularly true in Defense five years ago.

A 1961 organization chart of the Department of Defense would show the advisers to the Secretary of Defense on forces and military strategy, the Joint Chiefs of Staff; the adviser on research and engineering matters, the Director of Research and Engineering; the adviser on financial matters, the Comptroller; the adviser on production matters, the Assistant Secretary for Supply and Logistics; the adviser on international matters, the Assistant Secretary for International Security Affairs; etc. Each adviser was concerned primarily with his own specialty rather than the Defense program in its entirety. The Secretary of Defense, virtually alone, was expected to integrate all of these diverse facets personally and to do so without systematic assistance.

The Programming System was developed to provide one mechanism for integrating the diverse parts of the Defense program, especially to integrate force planning with budgeting and support programs. The Systems Analysis Office was established to gather and display information associated with these different areas in a manner that would show the Secretary of Defense how the pieces fit together. Its work cuts across these various specialties. Of course, the information that we provide the Secretary of Defense is only one of many inputs available to him, and the integrating functions that we perform in no way reduce the very great importance the Secretary attaches to the advice and information provided by the Joint Chiefs of Staff and his other civilian advisers.

SOME IMPORTANT PRECONDITIONS FOR SUCCESS

Two conditions seem to me to be necessary to the successful development and functioning of a Systems Analysis group within a policy-making organization. The first is that the responsible decision-makers make use of Systems Analysis and take it seriously. Without this, the professional personnel will recognize in time that their work is not influencing the course of events and their motivation is likely to be destroyed. By using Systems Analysis and taking it seriously, I do not mean that the decision-makers must accept the results of the analyses uncritically or that they must rely exclusively on the Systems Analysis input. Far from it. Every analysis must be based on many assumptions, and a responsible decision-maker may not choose to accept the assumptions that his analysts have made. What is important is that the analyses be given a fair hearing and be acted upon if they successfully stand up under reasonable debate and criticism; or, if they are not acted upon, that the analysts are told why so that they can correct their work in the future. The analysts must have this "feedback" from the decision-makers if they are to know which issues are considered relevant or significant, which objectives the decision-makers wish to pursue, and which assumptions appear to them to be plausible. A Systems Analysis capability installed as "window dressing" is not likely to develop into a good one.

The second necessary condition is that the Systems Analysis operation be fed with ideas growing out of a broadly based interdisciplinary research program. A research program is necessary in order to develop analytical tools, to define criteria and objectives for programs, and to invent new alternatives for achieving the objectives. Certainly, in Defense, the research program must be interdisciplinary, because the scope and complexity of Defense problems is too great to be encompassed with any single discipline. I am sure that this would also be true of Systems Analysis applied to major social problems outside of Defense.

One practical implication of this is that, generally speaking, research funds in these fields are likely to be better spent supporting research institutes containing groups of scholars from a variety of relevant disciplines oriented toward the problems, rather than on individual scholars who are more likely to be oriented toward the exercise of their academic specialties.

SYSTEMS ANALYSIS NON-DEFENSE APPLICATIONS

Finally, let me repeat my conviction that Systems Analysis can be applied fruitfully to social problems. I feel certain that good analysis can assist in the design, development and consideration of alternative approaches to education, health, urban transportation, justice and crime prevention, natural resources, environmental pollution and numerous other problems. In fact, there is already a great deal of useful research going on in these areas.

It is often suggested that these problem areas will be resistant to systematic analysis because they do not lend themselves to quantification. In commenting on that, I would like to point out that we, in the Defense Department, also have our own imponderables to deal with. We try to measure those things that are measurable, and insofar as possible, to define those things which are not, leaving to the responsible decision-makers the job of making the difficult judgments about the imponderables. It has been our experience that in those areas most difficult to quantify, years of research and the application of a good deal of ingenuity will often yield ways of measuring and making comparisons that were not available at the outset.

Ultimately, policy decisions will be based on judgments about relative values, the likelihood of uncertain future events, which risks we should and should not run, et cetera. But, in Defense, and in these other areas as well, good analysis can do a great deal to sharpen the issues, clarify the alternatives available to the decision-makers, and narrow substantially the range of uncertainty, thus freeing the responsible officials to concentrate their attention on the crucial judgments.

COST EFFECTIVE- NESS

CHARLES J. HITCH

Midway in my second lecture I alluded, in connection with the first phase of the planning-programming-budgeting process, to the need for military-economic studies which compare alternative ways of accomplishing national security objectives and which try to determine the way that contributes the most for a given cost or achieves a given objective for the least cost. The extensive and comprehensive use of these "cost-effectiveness" studies or systems analyses was the second major innovation introduced into the decision-making process of the Defense Department.

Although the introduction of the programming function was generally well received, considerable controversy arose over this extensive use of cost-effectiveness studies in the decision-making process, and some of this controversy continues. Why this is so is something of a mystery to me. We have made repeated efforts to explain the essential nature of these studies and the contribution that they make to the achievement of greater military effectiveness as well as economy in the defense establishment. But the suspicion still persists in some influential quarters that, somehow or other, cost-effectiveness studies put "dollars before national security," or will result in our going to war with "cut-rate, cut-quality, cheapest-to-buy weapons."[1] Virtually every

[1] From an editorial in the *Army–Navy–Air Force Register,* March 7, 1964.

From *Decision-Making for Defense* (Berkeley: University of California Press, 1965), pp. 43–49, 53–58. Charles Hitch is President of the University of California. Reprinted by permission of The Regents of the University of California.

attempt we have made to explain the inexorable logic of relating cost
to military effectiveness seems to shatter itself on the argument—
"Nothing but the best will do for our boys." And the "best" usually
refers to some particular characteristic of physical performance, such
as speed, altitude, or firepower, or even unit cost!

Implicit in this challenge is the deeply rooted feeling that national
defense is far too important a matter to be inhibited by cost. If one
weapon system performs better than another, then we should buy the
higher performance system, regardless of cost; the country can afford
it. Indeed, the people who hold this view feel that it is somehow
sinful, or at least unpatriotic, to try to relate performance or military
effectiveness to costs; that considerations of military effectiveness and
cost are antithetical.

To anyone trained in economics, this is a most puzzling attitude. We
know that the very act of making a choice—and that is all we are
doing when we choose weapons—involves weighing the utility or
benefit to be gained against the cost which must be incurred. Why is
that so? It is so because benefits *cost* resources and we live in a world
in which resources are limited. If we use more for one purpose, less
remains for other purposes—even in as rich a nation as the United
States.

Certainly, most of us are continuously being forced to make such
choices in our personal lives. Although explicit calculations may be
rare in these personal choices, they are common, if not quite universal,
in business affairs. Indeed, the weighing of benefits against costs is
one of the imperatives of any good business decision. The fact that one
machine can produce twice as much or twice as fast as another must
obviously be weighed against its additional cost in order to determine
which is the more profitable. The principle is exactly the same in defense, except that in private business the manager is guided by the
profit goal and the market prices of what he buys and sells; whereas in
government the decision-maker, since he is not selling in a market,
must determine the worth of his "product," e.g., of added performance, by careful analysis and the application of experienced judgment. In this respect, cost-effectiveness analysis is more difficult in
defense than in a private firm operating in a market economy, and
even more important.

Contrary to the suspicion in some quarters, the scarcity of resources
and the consequent necessity for economic choice is not the invention
of economists or defense comptrollers, or even of the Democratic
administration. The Hoover Commission in its report of June 1955
pointed out that:

The question of "quantity" cannot be considered except in conjunction
with that of "cost." Just as in a business, one cannot make a decision to buy

material or equipment without simultaneous consideration of price, so the Government cannot intelligently consider the wisdom of embarking on any program without a similar consideration of its cost. A decision to increase or decrease the number of air wings is intimately connected with consideration of the cost at which an air wing can be equipped and operated.[2]

The role of the cost-effectiveness study is to assist management in making just such decisions by bringing into clearer focus the impact on overall military effectiveness of an increase or decrease in the number of air wings and the specific cost implications of such changes.

I was somewhat startled about a year ago to read a statement by a leading member of the Congress:

There is no hard evidence that the Soviet Union is applying cost-effectiveness criteria in its planning for future weapons systems. In fact, many knowledgeable students of Soviet thinking believe that the opposite is quite probably the case.[3]

It reminded me of a statement made some years earlier by Hanson Baldwin to the effect that:

In the Western World—though not in Russia—costs are a more decisive factor in shaping defense than is military logic.[4]

The idea that the Soviets pay little attention to cost is a very common misconception in this country. At the risk of opening up a new controversy on the "cost-effectiveness gap," let me assure you that the Soviet leaders are most sensitive to the need for applying cost-effectiveness principles in all of their economic planning, and there is no reason to doubt that they follow the same approach in the military area. For example, here is a statement from the program adopted by the 22nd Congress of the Communist Party of the Soviet Union in 1961:

Chief attention in all links of planning and economic management must be focused on the most rational and effective use of material, labor, financial and natural resources, and on the elimination of excessive expenditures and losses. It is an immutable law of economic construction to achieve, in the interests of society, the greatest results at the lowest cost.[5]

[2] *Task Force Report on Budget and Accounting in the United States Government,* Commission on Organization of the Executive Branch of the Government, U.S. Government Printing Office, Washington, D.C., June 1955, pp. 11ff.

[3] *Congressional Record,* Vol. 110, No. 77, April 21, 1964, p. 8287. Statement of Representative Melvin Laird.

[4] "Arms and the Atom—I," *New York Times,* May 14, 1957, p. 21.

[5] "Program of the Communist Party of the Soviet Union," *The Current Digest of the Soviet Press,* Vol. XIII, No. 46, p. 8.

The formulation is not elegant, or even accurate, but the sense of it shines through.

That military expenditures were not excluded from this consideration was made evident by Mr. Khrushchev's explanation of the cutback in the Soviet military forces announced in January 1960. At that time he said:

> The elimination of nonproductive expenditures and the search for additional possibilities for economic development are tasks that constantly confront not only us but any state. I repeat that this matter is always urgent and will always attract unflagging attention. . . . The proposal to reduce the Soviet Armed Forces . . . will yield an annual saving of approximately 16,000,000,000 to 17,000,000,000 rubles [old rubles]. This will be a very tangible saving for our people and our country. It represents a powerful reinforcement for fulfilling and over-fulfilling our economic plans.[6]

And as further evidence, the U.S.S.R. has now translated *The Economics of Defense in the Nuclear Age* into Russian, with a first printing of 10,000 copies (but no royalties!).

Thus it seems plain that the Soviets, too, realize that they are not immune to the laws of economics, that they are not exempt from having to choose among the various alternative claims on the limited resources available to them. Nor do they appear reluctant to make use of the most modern methods and techniques to assist their managers in making these choices. Clearly, the Soviets have also realized that the modern world is far too complex to rely solely on intuitive judgment and that their decision-makers must be supported by quantitative analysis.

But opposition to cost-effectiveness studies stems not only from a suspicion of quantitative analysis but also from the conviction—completely unsubstantiated but nevertheless firmly held—that these studies inevitably lead to decisions favoring the cheapest weapon. Nothing could be further from the truth. Cost-effectiveness analysis is completely neutral with respect to the unit cost of a weapon. What it is concerned with is: Which strategy (or force, or weapon system) offers the greatest amount of military effectiveness for a given outlay? Or looking at the problem from another direction: How can a given level of military effectiveness be achieved at least cost?

In some cases the most "economical" weapon may be the one with the highest unit cost; in other cases, it may be the one with the lowest unit cost—it will depend on the relative military worth of quality and quantity in the particular circumstances. Unit cost, by itself, is simply an index—an inverse index—of quantity. There have been many cases

[6] Khrushchev, N. S., "Speech to the Supreme Soviet, January 15, 1960," *The Current Digest of the Soviet Press*, Vol. XII, No. 2, p. 13.

in history where the cheaper and technically less efficient weapon proved to be the "best," simply because its lower cost permitted it to be acquired in much greater numbers.

I am indebted to Joseph Alsop for one of the earliest reported cases of this phenomenon. In his book on the Greek Bronze Age, which he calls *From the Silent Earth*,[7] Mr. Alsop puts forth his theory on the collapse of the Mycenaean Greek civilization in about the twelfth century before Christ. The destruction of that civilization was so complete that even the written language was lost and the Greeks remained illiterate until the arrival of the new alphabet about 750 B.C.

The speed and completeness with which the Mycenaeans were virtually wiped off the face of the earth he attributes to the fact that the Dorians invading from the northwest used primitive iron swords against the highly developed bronze weapons of the Mycenaeans. The first of the Mycenaean centers to be destroyed was Pylos on the west coast of Greece, the nearest to the Dorians. Pylian society was much more highly developed than that of the Dorians, and the two evidently engaged in trade. Thus the Pylians were probably aware of iron weapons. Why then did they not make the obvious conversion from bronze to iron? Mr. Alsop suggests two reasons: One, the more advanced Pylians would have been reluctant to believe that a great advance in weaponry could possibly be achieved by their Dorian poor relations; and two, and I quote Mr. Alsop directly:

. . . unless the Pylian fighting men were very different from any subsequent soldiers, they would have been inclined to pooh-pooh the ugly, gray, innovating blades of the Dorians. . . .

. . . the earliest iron weapons may not have been immensely better, sword for sword, than the good bronze blades of late Mycenaean times. Some students of the subject have even suggested that at this early stage in iron technology a swordsman must have had to stop and bend his sword back into shape after a few hacks at his enemy. One can all but hear the Pylian senior officers snorting with complacent disdain because of the defects of iron. But . . . the Pylian senior officers would then have failed to notice the essential point—that iron, being common, could be used to arm everyone, instead of being restricted, like bronze, to the armament of a military elite. Whole hordes of iron-armed soldiers would soon overwhelm a smaller, elite, bronze-armed force, even if the individual bronze swords were better than the iron swords.[8]

Bronze, as Mr. Alsop pointed out, was a semi-precious metal at that time, and, as we know from other sources, bronze weapons were relatively expensive to produce. Thus, cost alone could explain why all

[7] Alsop, Joseph, *From the Silent Earth,* Harper and Row, New York, 1954.
[8] *Ibid.,* p. 136.

Bronze Age armies, not only the Pylians, were generally small and based on an elite corps. Here we see how a technically inferior weapon, simply because it is cheaper and therefore can be acquired in larger numbers, can beat the superior weapon which is dear and can only be acquired in small numbers.

But there were other times in history when "quality" appeared to have carried the day. For example, after the Persians, using relatively large armies, carved a major empire for themselves in the fifth century B.C., the Spartans, by concentrating on the training of an elite corps called hoplites, by refining their offensive and defensive weapons, and by using advanced tactical formations—in other words, by emphasizing "quality"—proved the worth of their small but highly effective army against a larger Persian army. The greater effectiveness of the Spartan hoplite over his Persian counterpart lay not only in his training but in his equipment and support as well. Each hoplite was provided with some seventy-two pounds of equipment and was supported by seven helots or serfs who formed the rear ranks, making the phalanx eight deep. Although the investment per hoplite was very high, his great combat effectiveness crowned Spartan arms with success.[9]

After the fall of the Roman Empire, the picture becomes less clear. But by the early Middle Ages, "quality" again emerged as a decisive factor, first with the development of intricate armor plates as a means of protecting the horseman and his horse, and second, with the appearance of the fortified castle. Both of these innovations required tremendous investments, made the individual far more effective for both offense and defense, and led again to reliance on an expensive elite corps. The cost of the armored knight was staggering for those times. By the end of the Middle Ages each knight required upwards of two hundred pounds of hammered plate for himself and his horse, plus a large retinue to keep him in the field. But the armored knight was a highly effective weapon system. It is said that in the eleventh century a force of about seventy knights conquered the ancient and civilized kingdom of Sicily.[10]

Then the pendulum swung to quantity when a new, relatively inexpensive weapon successfully challenged the knight and helped to end the age of feudalism. The Battle of Crécy during the Hundred Years' War pitted the longbowman against the knight and over 1,500 French lords and knights fell as compared to a few dozen English archers.[11]

---

[9] Fuller, Maj. Gen. J. F. C., *The Age of Valor*, Scribner's Sons, New York, 1945, pp. 25ff.

[10] Kenworthy, Lt. Comdr. (R.N.) John M., *New Wars: New Weapons*, Elkin, Mathews and Marrot, London, 1930, p. 28.

[11] Fuller, *op. cit.*, pp. 57ff.

And then the musket and black powder challenged the bow, not because the musket was superior to the bow and arrow; it wasn't. The musket had less range and accuracy than the bow and a much lower rate of fire. But let my colleague Eugene Fubini tell that story:

The main advantage of the musket was that it was much cheaper to equip troops with musket and powder than with the bow and arrow. Moreover, in the early days, the musket did not require much actual training, because accuracy was not a factor. Massed gunfire was what was wanted. This in turn led to virtually all modern infantry tactics, from standardized unit organization to close order drill. And all this came about mainly because arrows were expensive to manufacture and archers difficult to train.[12]

With the gradual introduction of the musket and the rifle, the swing toward emphasis on quantity was in full force. It brought the revitalization of the infantry, the return to mass armies. Gunpowder, as Carlyle said, "makes all men alike tall."[13] More than the iron sword, more than the barbarian on horseback, more than the longbow, it proletarianized war. This process reached its culmination during the French Revolution in the *levée en masse* of 1793. After this, the "nation at arms" was a constant of European politics for 150 years, reaching its full flower in the two World Wars.

With the advent of nuclear power, the pendulum swung back sharply toward "quality." Notwithstanding the missile's enormous unit cost—$40 million per ATLAS or TITAN on a launcher plus $1 million per year per missile to keep them ready to fire—its tremendous destruction potential and, therefore, the relatively small numbers required well justified its development, production, and deployment.

Thus, the lesson of history is clear—neither cost nor effectiveness alone is a sufficient basis upon which to choose a weapon system. Both must be considered simultaneously and in relation to each other.

• • •

But let me hasten to say that systems analysis or cost-effectiveness studies are by no means a panacea for all the problems of defense. Costs in general can be measured quantitatively, although not always with the degree of precision we would like. Measuring effectiveness or military worth poses a much more difficult problem. Reliable quantitative data are often not available. And even when such data are available, there is usually no common standard of measurement. This is particularly true with regard to systems analyses involving

---

[12] Fubini, Eugene, "Down-to-Earth Research," *Ordnance*, March–April, 1964, Vol. 48, pp. 522ff.

[13] Fuller, *op. cit.*, p. 77.

complex new technologies. Here, even reliable cost data are seldom available. Accordingly, the preferred alternative can rarely, if ever, be determined simply by applying a formula.

It has long been my contention:

that economic choice is *a way of looking at problems* and does not necessarily depend upon the use of any analytic aids or computational devices. Some analytic aids (mathematical models) and computing machinery are quite likely to be useful in analyzing complex military problems, but there are many military problems in which they have not proved particularly useful where, nevertheless, it is rewarding to array the alternatives and think through their implications in terms of objectives and costs. Where mathematical models and computations are useful, they are in no sense alternatives to or rivals of good intuitive judgment; they supplement and complement it. Judgment is always of critical importance in designing the analysis, choosing the alternatives to be compared, and selecting the criterion. Except where there is a completely satisfactory one-dimensional measurable objective (a rare circumstance), judgment must supplement the quantitative analysis before a choice can be recommended.[14]

I am the last to believe that an "optimal strategy" can be calculated on slide rules or even high-speed computers. Nothing could be further from the truth. Systems analysis is simply a method to get before the decision-maker the relevant data, organized in a way most useful to him. It is no substitute for sound and experienced military judgment, and it is but one of the many kinds of information needed by the decision-maker.

It is my experience that the hardest problems for the systems analyst are not those of analytic techniques. In fact, the techniques we use in the Office of the Secretary of Defense are usually rather simple and old-fashioned. What distinguishes the useful and productive analyst is his ability to formulate (or design) the problem; to choose appropriate objectives; to define the relevant, important environments or situations in which to test the alternatives; to judge the reliability of his cost and other data; and finally, and not least, his ingenuity in inventing new systems or alternatives to evaluate. My friend and former colleague, Albert Wohlstetter, used to insist that the systems analyst could contribute much more by inventing new systems than by comparing proposed systems; his own inventions are eloquent testimony to the validity of this view.

The analysis of rapid deployment of forces to trouble spots around the world illustrates many of these points. Early analyses (you may find one in *The Economics of Defense in the Nuclear Age*) concentrated on the question: what is the most economical type of aircraft

14 Hitch, Charles J. and McKean, Roland N., *The Economics of Defense in the Nuclear Age,* Cambridge: Harvard University Press, 1960, p. 120.

to procure for the purpose? Sealift was regarded as much too slow to be a competitor. From an early date, extensive prepositioning of men and equipment, or of equipment only, was recognized as an alternative, or a partial alternative, and included in the analysis.

Then a systems analyst made an invention. A great problem with prepositioning is the difficulty of acquiring real estate for the purpose in foreign countries and the likelihood that the real estate, if acquired, and the prepositioned stocks will turn out to be in the wrong country (or even the wrong continent) when hostilities actually threaten or break out. So this analyst thought: why not preposition on ships? A pregnant thought. We now have many "forward floating depots"—Victory ships stocked with Army equipment—in the Western Pacific, ready to steam to any threatened area and substantially augmenting our airlift rapid deployment capability.

At about the same time a more straightforward design development or "invention" produced the Roll-on/Roll-off, or "Ro-Ro," ship which can rapidly load and unload Army vehicular equipment at even primitive ports.

Then a third invention was made by an ingenious systems analyst who simply combined the characteristics of the forward floating depot and the Ro-Ro ship and developed an appropriate operational concept for the combination. This definitely made sealift competitive with airlift for rapid deployment in many situations, and we have asked Congress in the 1966 budget for four specially designed Ro-Ro's to be used as forward floating depots.

Meanwhile some design inventions stimulated by airlift analyses promise us much more efficient airlift aircraft. The most important enables us to combine the marked economies of a very large aircraft with a landing gear and power plant which permit operations from short, primitive forward air bases. This combination promises to reduce or even eliminate the ground line of communication in the combat theater, with substantial savings in time, troops, and equipment. We are starting full-scale development of such an aircraft—the C-5A—this year.

Our analytic problem now is to determine the best mix of this better sealift and this better airlift. In many situations (e.g., close to the shore in SE Asia and Korea), the ships can win handily on cost-effectiveness criteria. In other hypothetical situations (e.g., farther inland), the C-5A wins handily. Each system has capabilities the other has not. And problems the other has not. And different and difficult-to-analyze vulnerabilities to enemy action. No computer will automatically provide the answer to this problem of optimum mix, although a carefully formulated computer program can, under specified conditions, give valuable insights about break-even points and regions of sensitivity.

Typically in major systems comparisons this is the situation. There are multiple objectives or payoffs—not just one which is well defined and clear-cut. There are multiple circumstances in which the system may be called upon to function. And there are usually great uncertainties about costs, enemy intentions and capabilities, and other factors. This kind of systems analysis makes great demands on the analyst's ingenuity, his experience, and above all his judgment and common sense. When Ellis Johnson called it "quantified common sense," he was not far off the mark.

Finally, we must recognize that if the objectives or the costs or the measurements of military effectiveness are wrong, the answers will also be wrong. The SKYBOLT air-to-ground missile is a case in point. A gross underestimate of costs in 1961 led to a decision to carry that project into the production stage. When the full dimensions of the ultimate cost later became apparent, the decision was made to drop the project since it was not worth the increased cost in the light of the other alternatives available, namely, expanding the MINUTEMAN force and retaining more of the HOUND DOG air-to-ground missiles which were already in the inventory. You may recall that this decision led to some very painful moments with our British colleagues as the United Kingdom had also planned to use the SKYBOLT missile with its bombers. Our decision to drop the project created some very difficult problems for the British Government at the time and led to a meeting at Nassau between President Kennedy and Prime Minister Macmillan.[15] Yet, no responsible military or civilian official in our Defense Department or, I believe, in the British Defense Ministry, would argue in favor of the SKYBOLT today.

But notwithstanding all of these dangers I have mentioned, the need for systematic quantitative analysis in defense is much more important than in the private sector of the economy. Almost never do we find one person who has an intuitive grasp of all the fields of knowledge that are relevant to a major defense problem. We may be able to assemble a group of experts, each of whom has a good intuitive grasp of the factors relevant for answering one of the many subquestions and after discussion emerge with a fairly unequivocal answer. But in general, and especially when the choice is not between two but among many alternatives, systematic analysis is essential.

Moreover, in contrast to the private sector where competition provides an incentive for efficiency, efficiency in government depends on the conscious and deliberate selection of techniques and policies. And wherever the relevant factors are diverse and complex, as they usually

---

[15] See text of joint communiqué and "Statement on nuclear defense systems" issued by President Kennedy and Prime Minister Macmillan, December 21, 1962, at Nassau, The Bahamas, *New York Times*, December 22, 1962, p. 3.

are in defense problems, unaided intuition is incapable of weighing them and reaching a sound decision.

The need for systems analysis exists not only in the Office of the Secretary of Defense, that of the Joint Chiefs of Staff, and the headquarters of the military departments, but also at the other levels of the management structure in the defense establishment. After all, the purpose of this function is to help reduce the uncertainties involved in making choices among alternatives, and such choices have to be made at many different echelons. The areas of interest, the problems, and the subject matter will be different at these different levels, but the general approach—the way of looking at a problem—and the techniques will be basically the same.

Our objective, therefore, has been to build an integrated and mutually supporting structure of systems analysis throughout the defense establishment, with the broadest kind of exchange of information and techniques at and between various levels. This arrangement provides the checks and balances so essential to minimizing parochial viewpoints and organizational bias. The systems analyst, like any other scientist, must always be prepared to submit his work to critical scrutiny, and not just by other systems analysts. This is one of the great merits of the scientific method—it is an open, explicit, verifiable, and self-correcting process. . . .

From a small beginning, systems analysis has now become a vital and integral part of the Defense Department decision-making process. The new programming function provides the link between planning and budgeting, relating both the forces and their resource costs to major military missions. Systems analysis provides the analytical foundation for the making of sound objective choices among the alternative means of carrying out these missions. Thus, the Secretary of Defense now has the tools he needs to take the initiative in the planning and direction of the entire defense effort on a truly unified basis.

COMMENTARY

The preceding selections depart significantly from Gore's heuristic decision-making approach and Lindblom's "branch method." Systematic analysis, regardless of the precise form it may take, is a clear and radical alternative to the traditional incremental allocation of governmental resources through bargained agreements among professional political actors. It offers, instead, the promise of a more rational allocation of resources through the comprehensive analysis of pertinent and relevant data, systematically collected. As McKean notes, regardless of the specific type of analysis that can be applied to the decision-making process, each bears a basic common concern, that of examining systematically the effects of alternative courses of action. Preferably this systematic evaluation of alternatives is accomplished quantitatively, but, as Enthoven explains, this may not always be possible, and other—i.e., historical, logical, empirical—methods may be applied. In any case, given this basic approach, the difference between the rational-comprehensive and the incremental models is dramatic.

As McKean explains, the application of a more systematic decision-making approach in government is progressing at a rapid, albeit somewhat disorganized, pace. The reason for this is clear. Given the magnitude of the resources of the federal government, an increasing number of individuals are convinced that the future growth and health of the nation are sorely jeopardized by the continued application of the bargaining-incremental strategy. Efficiency in government has become a major concern for McKean, Hitch, Enthoven, and others. Unlike the absolute pragmatism of the incrementalists which permits them to view the future with a high degree of cynical optimism, the rationalists—as they shall be referred to here—are much more pessimistic about a future limited by the present and based on the past. The future, as seen by the rationalists, must be anticipated if effective public policy decisions are to be made. Needs must be anticipated as well as the resources to meet those needs. The rationalists view this attitude as a common-sense approach to public policy; as viewed by the incrementalists, this attitude is purely utopian.

As indicated in Chapter One, in 1965 the executive branch of the federal government was mandated by a presidential directive to adopt an allocative decision-making system referred to as planning-programming-budgeting (PPB). As Greenhouse notes, PPB is a multi-purpose system that is really a collection of premises, concepts, and relationships, but for our purposes it is sufficient to note that the key concepts of PPB are objectives, outputs, and program alternatives. The role of objectives in PPB stands in clear contrast to the position assumed by the incrementalists in this regard. In the incremental framework ends and means became indistinguishable; the program became the policy; objectives or goals became implicitly built into the operating plan. In PPB, however, policies *must* precede programs; objectives *must* be made explicit and operationally valid; goals *must* be considered ends.

The concept "operationally valid" is an important aspect of goal attainment under PPB. Goals cannot be so narrowly defined as to create agency exclusiveness no matter how operationally valid they may be. Thus, if the goal of the federal highway program, for instance, is simply bigger and more highways, then the operating agency has created its own exclusive administrative niche and cannot be integrated into other related federal transportation programs. On the other hand, the danger is ever-present that goals may be defined so broadly and generally as to become devoid of any substantive content. PPB cannot operate successfully unless these twin dangers are removed, simply because, unlike the bargaining-incremental strategy, plans and programs must flow *from* objectives and goals.

The significance of the role of objectives in PPB can best be demonstrated by discussing the relationship between objectives and outputs. As Greenhouse notes, an output is a tangible outgrowth or product of a particular program which can be singled-out as an indicator of program results. This means, obviously, that if objectives are operationally valid, then program outputs should provide direct measures of program effectiveness and goal attainment. Objectives and outputs become integrally related. If the effective and efficient interstate movement of goods and people is one objective of the U.S. Department of Transportation, then the number of travel hours eliminated becomes an output which is directly related to this objective. As such it can be applied as a tangible measure of a particular program—the federal highway program, for example. The construction of interstate highways, on the other hand, provides no valid measure of output which can be directly related to the basic goal. Highway construction may triple in the next twelve months, while the movement of goods and people across the nation may in fact become less efficient as a result. Highway construction must be viewed as an input if the role of the federal highway agency is to be properly integrated in the PPB framework.

Indeed, one is inclined to disagree with Greenhouse that the number of new schools built becomes an output measure which can be directly related to our federal educational policy. Actually, if our educational objectives are, among others, the decrease of illiteracy, social integration, occupation retraining, etc., then the construction of new schools, more classrooms, more classroom seats must properly be viewed as inputs.

In addition to linking program performance to goals, outputs serve as a measurement of comparability among competing agencies and bureaus. For example, if the effective and efficient movement of goods and people is one basic objective of the Transportation Department, then the extent to which the Department's aviation, highway, and railroad programs comparatively contribute to this goal can be determined by applying the same output criterion, i.e., travel hours eliminated. Comparability is an essential element of PPB since it permits different agencies and bureaus to be drawn together on the basis of a common performance indicator. As a consequence, the Secretary of Transportation would be in a position to assess intelligently the performances of his three agencies or bureaus on the basis of a common factor. In addition, and probably more importantly, he would be in a much stronger and better position to make intelligent and rationally sound decisions concerning the intra-departmental allocation of resources. As noted in the discussion on objectives, exclusiveness is a characteristic to be avoided within the PPB framework. In terms of outputs, a common measure of performance effectively strips the affected administrative units of any such pretense.

The third key element of PPB—program alternatives—is integrally related to objectives and outputs. Moreover, it is in the development of alternatives that systems analysis enters into PPB. Enthoven describes the essence of systems analysis clearly. Analysts examine a given objective in its broadest sense. They then generate a range of alternative approaches, each designed to accomplish the given objective. Finally, they estimate, in quantitative terms, the benefits to be derived from and the costs of each alternative. This final step is what is variously referred to as cost-benefit, cost-effectiveness, or cost-efficiency analysis—the terms are synonymous. This process is the basic aspect of systems analysis, and it is a critical feature of PPB.

Having estimated the costs and benefits of the proposed alternative approaches to a given objective, the analytical process technically ends and the political process takes over. In other words, the final choice of which alternative, or combination of alternatives, to pursue rests with political officials, not the systems analysts.

As far as the method of systems analysis is concerned, it is apparent that a wide range of assumptions, both scientific and normative, are included in what Enthoven describes as the "the scientific method." The development of alternatives, admittedly, imposes no special scientific demands other than imaginative, innovative, and logical minds. Systems analysis is simply systematic problem solving, and the first step is to engage a group of analysts to think up a series of alternative solutions to a given problem. The scientific method comes into play when the costs and benefits of each alternative are calculated. Cost-benefit analysis as related to PPB is conducted on a multi-year basis which means that each proposed alternative must be calculated, for example, on a five year projected schedule. Costs also must be presented in terms of *total* costs, including not only capital and operating costs but intangible socio-cultural costs as well. What are the costs of a proposed new housing project? Land acquisition and contractor services can be easily calculated, and loss of tax revenue and relocation of displaced residents are also tangible costs that can easily be taken into account. But major housing projects trigger a whole series of consequences which result in what may be described as a social congestion syndrome, and the multiplicity of costs associated with this characteristic must also be calculated. The same process is applied in the calculation of benefits. In other words, the method of systems analysis is to investigate, analyze, and calculate in quantitative terms the ramifications of a proposed public policy decision to the fullest extent possible for a given number of years into the future.

Having completed this process for a series of alternatives to a given problem, the analysts are then in a position to advise public officials which alternative or combination of alternatives would yield the most favorable cost-benefit ratio—i.e., yield a specified level of benefits for the least cost or yield the greatest benefits for a specified cost. This approach should be able to suggest whether a high-rise apartment building or a garden apartment project would yield a more favorable ratio of benefits over costs, or whether the most favorable ratio could be obtained by simply rehabilitating the existing neighborhood. In any event this analysis is presented in such a manner that top-level executive officials can compare it with other similar analyses dealing, for example, with educational, health, public safety, and recreational proposals. At that point, ultimate decisions have to be made as to which proposals would yield the most favorable cost-benefit ratio for the total community. The political decision-makers may very well decide that the projected composite (political-social-economic) pay-offs in the proposals involving public health and public safety far exceed those projected for public housing, and the latter may be passed over in favor of the former. But even if the housing project is given top priority on the basis of certain pressing political considerations, the responsible public officials at least have had the benefit of examining what the estimated consequences of their decision may yield.

Basically, the end sought by PPB and systems analysis is greater control over future uncertainty, and in this respect the rationalists depart fundamentally from the incrementalists. Such statements as the one by Lindblom that an administrator may defend a program as good without having to state what it is good for would be incomprehensible to the systems analyst. For the incrementalists the present defines the future, but for the rationalists it is the future which controls the present.

Uncertainty in dealing with the future cannot, of course, be completely eliminated from the area of public policy planning, but, according to Enthoven, the application of the scientific method over an extended time period can gradually shrink the zone of the unknown. Nevertheless, given the inevitability of some degree of uncertainty, the rationalists see a major contribution in simply making explicit these uncertainties. Enthoven writes, ". . . rather than conceal uncertainties, a good analysis will bring them out and clarify them." To be forewarned is to be forearmed is the motto of the rationalists, while the incrementalists are quite prepared to leave unanticipated future consequences to the self-correcting mechanisms which they feel are an inherent part of our political system.

Although the differences between the rationalist and incremental approaches are fundamental, a line of continuity between systematic analysis and the management science approach of an earlier era does appear. A close examination of the two, however, should reveal that even here their differences are much more significant than their similarities. For example, economy, efficiency, and effectiveness are three terms which are employed by each approach but which are given an entirely different emphasis by each. The internal operating efficiency of the management science approach must be contrasted to the planning efficiency sought by the rationalists. Dawes, for example, was primarily concerned with the manner in which the organization manipulated its inputs to achieve efficiency, while Enthoven, McKean, and Hitch are much more concerned with how an organization is to relate its outputs to its goal objectives.

The difference between the two approaches appears further magnified if one considers how each deals with the concept of costs. The rationalists view costs in a teletic fashion—the more data that can be collected the sounder the analysis. The management science approach revealed a much more restricted view of costs—labor, capital, and equipment. Efficiency during the earlier period meant cost reduction; at the present stage it means cost effectiveness.

The technical differences between the rational-comprehensive, bargaining-incremental, and management science approaches are, in fact, quite significant, but what about the normative differences which distinguish, particularly, the rationalist and incrementalist? Are systems analysis and PPB, for example, value-enhancing or value-destroying schemes? The technical or scientific bias of the rationalist is obvious; Hitch, McKean, and Enthoven make no effort to hide their commitment to the systematic analysis of quantitative data. But what are their value biases? What are the politics of PPB and systems analysis? Or, do these men follow in the footsteps of Wilson, who sought to insulate administration from politics, and Gulick, who sought a value-free science of administration? Is the analytical method a part of, or apart from, the political process? The purpose of the following chapter is to resolve these questions.

THE POLITICS OF ANALYSIS 8

THE POLITICAL ECONOMY OF EFFICIENCY

AARON WILDAVSKY

There was a day when the meaning of economic efficiency was reasonably clear.

An objective met up with a technician. Efficiency consisted in meeting the objective at the lowest cost or in obtaining the maximum amount of the objective for a specified amount of resources. Let us call this "pure efficiency." The desirability of trying to achieve certain objectives may depend on the cost of achieving them. In this case the analyst (he has graduated from being a mere technician) alters the objective to suit available resources. Let us call this "mixed efficiency." Both pure and mixed efficiency are limited in the sense that they take for granted the existing structure of the political system and work within its boundaries. Yet the economizer, he who values efficiency most dearly, may discover that the most efficient means for accomplishing his ends cannot be secured without altering the machinery for making decisions. He not only alters means and ends (resources and objectives) simultaneously but makes them dependent on changes in political relationships. While he claims no special interest in or expertise concerning the decision apparatus outside of the market place, the economizer pursues efficiency to the heart of the political system. Let us call this "total efficiency." In this vocabulary, then, concepts of efficiency may be pure or mixed, limited or total.

From *Public Administration Review*, Vol. 26 (December 1966), pp. 292–310. Aaron Wildavsky is currently Dean of the Graduate School of Public Affairs, University of California, Berkeley. Reprinted with permission of the author and the American Society of Public Administration.

A major purpose of this paper is to take the newest and recently most popular modes of achieving efficiency—cost-benefit analysis, systems analysis, and program budgeting—and show how much more is involved than mere economizing. *Even at the most modest level of cost-benefit analysis, I will try to show that it becomes difficult to maintain pure notions of efficiency. At a higher level, systems analysis is based on a mixed notion of efficiency. And program budgeting at the highest levels leaves pure efficiency far behind its over-reaching grasp into the structure of the political system. Program budgeting, it turns out, is a form of systems analysis, that is, political systems analysis.*

These modes of analysis are neither good for nothing nor good for everything, and one cannot speak of them as wholly good or bad. It is much more useful to try to specify some conditions under which they would or would not be helpful for various purposes. While such a list could not be exhaustive at this stage, nor permanent at any stage (because of advances in the art), it provides a basis for thinking about what these techniques can and cannot do. Another major purpose of this paper, therefore, is to describe cost-benefit and systems analysis and program budgeting as techniques for decision-making. I shall place particular stress upon what seems to me the most characteristic feature of all three modes of analysis: the aids to calculation designed to get around the vast areas of uncertainty where quantitative analysis leaves off and judgment begins.

COST-BENEFIT ANALYSIS

. . . One can view cost-benefit analysis as anything from an infallible means of reaching the new Utopia to a waste of resources in attempting to measure the unmeasurable.[1]

[1] A. R. Prest and R. Turvey, "Cost-Benefit Analysis: A Survey," *The Economic Journal,* Vol. LXXV, December, 1965, pp. 683–75. I am much indebted to this valuable and discerning survey. I have also relied upon:

Otto Eckstein, "A Survey of the Theory of Public Expenditure Criteria," in *Public Finances: Needs, Sources, and Utilization,* National Bureau of Economic Research (New York, Princeton University Press, 1961), pp. 439–504.

Irving K. Fox and Orris C. Herfindahl, "Attainment of Efficiency in Satisfying Demands for Water Resources," *American Economic Review,* May, 1964, pp. 198–206.

Charles J. Hitch, *On the Choice of Objectives in Systems Studies* (Santa Monica, The RAND Corporation, 1960).

John V. Krutilla, "Is Public Intervention in Water Resources Development Conducive to Economic Efficiency," *Natural Resources Journal,* January, 1966, pp. 60–75.

John V. Krutilla and Otto Eckstein, *Multiple Purpose River Development* (Baltimore, Johns Hopkins Press, 1958).

Roland N. McKean, *Efficiency in Government Through Systems Analysis with Emphasis on Water Resources Development* (New York, 1958).

The purpose of cost-benefit analysis is to secure an efficient allocation of resources produced by the governmental system in its interaction with the private economy. The nature of efficiency depends on the objectives set up for government. In the field of water resources, where most of the work on cost-benefit analysis has been done, the governmental objective is usually postulated to be an increase in national income. In a crude sense, this means that the costs to whomever may incur them should be less than the benefits to whomever may receive them. The time streams of consumption gained and foregone by a project are its benefits and costs.

The aim of cost-benefit analysis is to maximize "the present value of all benefits less that of all costs, subject to specified restraints."[2] A long view is taken in that costs are estimated not only for the immediate future but also for the life of the project. A wide view is taken in that indirect consequences for others—variously called externalities, side-effects, spillovers, and repercussion effects—are considered. Ideally, all costs and benefits are evaluated. The usual procedure is to estimate the installation costs of the project and spread them over time, thus making them into something like annual costs. To these costs are added an estimate of annual operating costs. The next step involves estimating the average value of the output by considering the likely number of units produced each year and their probable value in the market place of the future. Intangible, "secondary," benefits may then be considered. These time streams of costs and benefits are discounted so as to obtain the present value of costs and benefits. Projects whose benefits are greater than costs may then be approved, or the cost-benefit ratios may, with allowance for relative size, be used to rank projects in order of desirability.

UNDERLYING ECONOMIC AND POLITICAL ASSUMPTIONS

A straightforward description of cost-benefit analysis cannot do justice to the powerful assumptions that underlie it or to the many conditions limiting its usefulness. The assumptions involve value judgments that are not always recognized and, when recognized, are not easily handled in practice. The limiting conditions arise partly out of the assumptions and partly out of severe computational difficulties in estimating costs, and especially benefits. Here I can only indicate some major problems.

Cost-benefit analysis is based on superiority in the market place,[3] under competitive conditions and full employment, as the measure of

---

[2] Prest and Turvey, *ibid.*, p. 686.

[3] In many important areas of policy such as national defense it is not possible to value the product directly in the market place. Since benefits cannot be valued in the same way as costs, it is necessary to resort to a somewhat different type of analysis. Instead of cost-benefit analysis, therefore, the work is usually called cost-effectiveness or cost-utility analysis.

value in society. Any imperfection in the market works against the validity of the results. Unless the same degree of monopoly were found throughout the economy, for example, a governmental body that enjoys monopolistic control of prices or outputs would not necessarily make the same investment decisions as under free competition. A similar difficulty occurs where the size of a project is large in comparison to the economy, as in some developing nations. The project itself then affects the constellation of relative prices and production against which its efficiency is measured. The assumption based on the classical full employment model is also important because it gives prices special significance. Where manpower is not being utilized, projects may be justified in part as putting this unused resource to work.

The economic model on which cost-benefit analysis depends for its validity is based on a political theory. The idea is that in a free society the economy is to serve the individual's consistent preferences revealed and rationally pursued in the market place. Governments are not supposed to dictate preferences nor make decisions.

This individualist theory assumes as valid the current distribution of income. Preferences are valued in the market place where votes are based on disposable income. Governmental action to achieve efficiency, therefore, inevitably carries with it consequences for the distribution of income. Projects of different size and location and composition will transfer income in different amounts to different people. While economists might estimate the redistributive consequences of various projects, they cannot, on efficiency grounds, specify one or another as preferable. How is this serious problem to be handled?

Benefit-cost analysis is a way of trying to promote economic welfare. But whose welfare? No one knows how to deal with inter-personal comparisons of utility. It cannot be assumed that the desirability of rent supplements versus a highway or dam can be measured on a single utility scale. There is no scientific way to compare losses and gains among different people or to say that the marginal loss of a dollar to one man is somehow equal to the gain of a dollar by another. The question of whose utility function is to prevail (the analyst versus the people involved, the upstream gainers versus the downstream losers, the direct beneficiaries versus the taxpayers, the entire nation or a particular region, and so on) is of prime importance in making public policy.

The literature on welfare economics is notably unable to specify an objective welfare function.[4] Ideally, actions would benefit everyone

[4] A. Bergson, "A Reformulation of Certain Aspects of Welfare Economics," *Quarterly Journal of Economics*, February, 1938; N. Kaldor, "Welfare Propositions and Interpersonal Comparisons of Utility," *Economic Journal*, 1939, pp. 549–52; J. R. Hicks, "The Valuation of Social Income," *Economica*, 1940, pp.

and harm no one. As an approximation, the welfare economist views as optimal an action that leaves some people better off and none worse off. If this criterion were applied in political life, it would result in a situation like that of the Polish Diet in which anyone who was damaged could veto legislation. To provide a way out of this impasse, Hicks and Kaldor proposed approval of decisions if the total gain in welfare is such that the winners could compensate the losers. But formal machinery for compensation does not ordinarily exist and most modern economists are highly critical of the major political mechanism for attempting to compensate, namely, log-rolling in Congress on public works projects.[5] It is a very imperfect mechanism for assuring that losers in one instance become winners in another.

Another way of dealing with income distribution is to accept a criterion laid down by a political body and maximize present benefits less costs subject to this constraint. Or the cost-benefit analyst can present a series of alternatives differing according to the individuals who pay and prices charged. The analyst must not only compute the new inputs and outputs, but also the costs and benefits for each group with whom the public authorities are especially concerned. No wonder this is not often done! Prest and Turvey are uncertain whether such a procedure is actually helpful in practice.[6]

Income redistribution in its most extreme form would result in a complete leveling or equality of incomes. Clearly, this is not what is meant. A more practical meaning might be distributing income to the point where specific groups achieve a certain minimum. It is also possible that the operational meaning of income redistribution may simply be the transfer of some income from some haves to some have nots. Even in the last and most minimal sense of the term it is by no means clear that projects that are inefficient by the usual economic criteria serve to redistribute income in the desired direction. It is possible that some inefficient projects may transfer income from poorer to richer people. Before the claim that certain projects are justified by the effect of distributing income in a specified way can be accepted,

---

105–24; I. M. D. Little, *A Critique of Welfare Economics* (Oxford, 1950); W. J. Baumol, *Welfare Economics and the Theory of the State* (Cambridge, 1952); T. Scitovsky, "A Note on Welfare Propositions in Economics," *Review of Economic Studies*, 1942, pp. 98–110; J. E. Meade, *The Theory of International Economic Policy*, Vol. II: *Trade and Welfare* (New York, 1954).

[5] For a different view, see James M. Buchanan and Gordon Tullock, *The Calculus of Consent: Logical Foundations of Constitutional Democracy* (Ann Arbor, University of Michigan Press, 1962).

[6] Prest and Turvey, *op. cit.*, p. 702. For a contrary view, see Arthur Maas, "Benefit-Cost Analysis: Its Relevance to Public Investment Decisions," Vol. LXXX, *The Quarterly Journal of Economics*, May, 1966, pp. 208–226.

an analysis to show that this is what actually happens must be at hand.

Since the distribution of income is at stake, it is not surprising that beneficiaries tend to dominate investment decisions in the political arena and steadfastly refuse to pay for what they receive from government tax revenues. They uniformly resist user charges based on benefits received. Fox and Herfindahl estimate that of a total initial investment of three billion for the Corps of Engineers in 1962, taxpayers in general would pay close to two-thirds of the costs.[7] Here, greater use of the facilities by a larger number of beneficiaries getting something for nothing inflates the estimated benefits which justify the project in the first place. There may be a political rationale for these decisions, but it has not been developed.

In addition to redistributing income, public works projects have a multitude of objectives and consequences. Projects may generate economic growth, alleviate poverty among some people, provide aesthetic enjoyment and opportunities for recreation, improve public health, reduce the risks of natural disaster, alter travel patterns, affect church attendance, change educational opportunities, and more. No single welfare criterion can encompass these diverse objectives. How many of them should be considered? Which are susceptible of quantification? The further one pursues this analysis, the more impassable the thicket.

LIMITATIONS IN THE UTILITY OF COST-BENEFIT ANALYSIS

One possible conclusion is that at present certain types of cost-benefit analysis are not meaningful. In reviewing the literature on the calculus of costs and benefits in research and development, for example, Prest and Turvey comment on "the uncertainty and unreliability of cost estimates . . . and . . . the extraordinarily complex nature of the benefits. . . ."[8]

Another conclusion is that one should be cautious in distinguishing the degree to which projects are amenable to cost-benefit analysis.

. . . When there are many diverse types of benefits from a project and/or many different beneficiaries it is difficult to list them all and to avoid double counting. This is one reason why it is so much easier to apply cost-benefit analysis to a limited purpose development, say, than it is to the research and development aspects of some multi-purpose discovery, such as a new type of plastic material. . . . It is no good expecting those fields in which benefits are widely diffused, and in which there are manifest divergences between accounting and economic costs or benefits, to be as cultivable as

[7] Irving K. Fox and Orris C. Herfindahl, "Attainment of Efficiency in Satisfying Demands for Water Resources," *American Economic Review*, May, 1964, p. 200.

[8] Prest and Turvey, *op. cit.*, p. 727.

others. Nor is it realistic to expect that comparisons between projects in entirely different branches of economic activity are likely to be as meaningful or fruitful as those between projects in the same branch. The technique is more useful in the public-utility area than in the social-services area of government.[9]

If the analysis is to be useful at all, calculations must be simplified.[10] The multiple ramifications of interesting activities can be taken into account only at the cost of introducing fantastic complexities. Prest and Turvey remark of one such attempt, that "This system . . . requires knowledge of all the demand and supply equations in the economy, so is scarcely capable of application by road engineers."[11] They suggest omitting consideration where (1) side effects are judged not terribly large or where (2) concern for these effects belongs to another governmental jurisdiction.[12]

If certain costs or benefits are deemed important but cannot be quantified, it is always possible to guess. The increasing use of recreation and aesthetic facilities to justify public works projects in the United States is disapproved by most economists because there can be a vast, but hidden, inflation of these benefits. For example, to attribute the same value to a recreation day on a reservoir located in a desert miles from any substitute source of water as to a day on an artificial lake in the heart of natural lake country is patently wrong. Economists would prefer to see recreation facilities listed in an appendix so that they can be taken into account in some sense, or, alternatively, that the project be presented with and without the recreation facilities, so that a judgment can be made as to whether the additional services are worth the cost.[13]

Economists distinguish between risk, where the precise outcome

[9] *Ibid.*, pp. 729, 731.

[10] David Braybrooke and Charles Lindblom, *A Strategy for Decision* (New York, 1963).

[11] Prest and Turvey, *op. cit.*, p. 714.

[12] *Ibid.*, p. 705.

[13] See Jack L. Knetch, "Economics of Including Recreation as a Purpose of Water Resource Projects," *Journal of Farm Economics*, December, 1964, p. 1155. No one living in Berkeley, where "a view" is part of the cost of housing, could believe that aesthetic values are forever going to remain beyond the ingenuity of the quantifier.

There are also costs and benefits, such as the saving and losing of human life, that can be quantified but can only be valued in the market place in a most peculiar (or ghoulish) sense. See Burton Weisbrod, *The Economics of Public Health; Measuring the Economic Impact of Diseases* (Philadelphia, 1961), for creative attempt to place a market value on human life. Few of us would want to make decisions about public health by use of this criterion, not at least if we were the old person whose future social value contribution is less than his cost to the authorities.

cannot be predicted but a probability distribution can be specified, and uncertainty, where one does not even know the parameters of the outcomes. The cost-benefit analyst must learn to live with uncertainty, for he can never know whether all relevant objectives have been included and what changes may occur in policy and in technology.

It is easy enough to cut the life of the project below its expected economic life. The interest rate can be raised. Assumptions can be made that costs will be higher and benefits lower than expected. All these methods, essentially conservative, are also highly arbitrary. They can be made somewhat more systematic, however, by sensitivity analysis in which length of life, for instance, is varied over a series of runs so that its impact on the project can be appraised.

Lessening uncertainty by hiking the interest or discount rate leads to greater difficulties, for the dominance of "higher" criteria over economic analysis is apparent in the frustrating problem of choosing the correct interest rate at which to discount the time streams of costs and benefits essential to the enterprise. Only an interest rate can establish the relationship between values at different periods of time. Yet people differ in preferences for the present versus the intermediate or long-run value. Moreover, the interest rate should also measure the opportunity cost of private capital that could be used to produce wealth elsewhere in the economy if it had not been used up in the form of tax income spent on the project under consideration. Is the appropriate rate the very low cost the government charges, the cost of a government corporation like TVA that must pay a somewhat higher rate, the going rate of interest for private firms, or an even higher rate to hedge against an uncertain future? As Otto Eckstein has observed, ". . . the choice of interest rates must remain a value judgment."[14]

If the efficiency of a project is insensitive to interest costs, then these costs can vary widely without mattering much. But Fox and Herfindahl discovered that if Corps of Engineer projects raised their interest (or discount) rate from 2⅝ to 4, 6, or 8 percent, then 9, 64, and 80 percent of their projects, respectively, would have had a benefit-cost ratio of less than unity.[15] This single value choice among many has such large consequences that it alone may be decisive.

THE MIXED RESULTS OF COST-BENEFIT ANALYSIS

Although cost-benefit analysis presumably results in efficiency by adding the most to national income, it is shot through with political and social value choices and surrounded by uncertainties and difficulties of computation. Whether the many noneconomic assumptions and consequences actually result in basically changing the nature of a

[14] Otto Eckstein, op. cit., p. 460.

[15] Fox and Herfindahl, op. cit., p. 202.

project remains moot. Clearly, we have come a long way from pure efficiency, to verge upon mixed efficiency.

Economic analysts usually agree that all relevant factors (especially nonmarket factors) cannot be squeezed into a single formula. They therefore suggest that the policy maker, in being given the market costs and benefits of alternatives, is, in effect, presented with the market value he is placing on nonmarket factors. The contribution of the analyst is only one input into the decision, but the analyst may find this limited conception of his role unacceptable to others. Policy makers may not want this kind of input; they may want *the* answer, or at least an answer that they can defend on the basis of the analyst's legitimized expertise.

The dependence of cost-benefit analysis on a prior political framework does not mean that it is a useless or trivial exercise. Decisions must be made. If quantifiable economic costs and benefits are not everything, neither would a decision-maker wish to ignore them entirely. The great advantage of cost-benefit analysis, when pursued with integrity, is that some implicit judgments are made explicit and subject to analysis. Yet, for many, the omission of explicit consideration of political factors is a serious deficiency.

The experience of the Soil Conservation Service in lowering certain political costs may prove illuminating. For many years the Service struggled along with eleven major watershed projects involving big dams, great headaches, and little progress. Because the watersheds were confined to a single region, it was exceedingly difficult to generate support in Congress, particularly at appropriations time. The upstream-downstream controversies generated by these projects resulted in less than universal local approval. The SCS found itself in the direct line of fire for determining priorities in use of insufficient funds.

Compare this situation with the breakthrough which occurred when SCS developed the small watershed program. Since each facility is relatively inexpensive, large numbers can be placed throughout the country, markedly increasing political support. Agreement on the local level is facilitated because much less land is flooded and side payments are easier to arrange. A judicious use of cost-benefit analysis, together with ingenious relationships with State governors, places the choice of priorities with the States and yet maintains a reasonable level of consistency by virtue of adherence to national criteria. Errors are easier to correct because the burden of calculation has been drastically reduced and experience may be more easily accumulated with a larger number of small projects.

Consider the situation in which an agency finds it desirable to achieve a geographical spread of projects in order to establish a wider base of support. Assume (with good reason) that cost-benefit criteria will not permit projects to be established in some states because the value of the land or water is too low. One can say that this is just too bad and observe the agency seeking ways around the restriction by playing up benefits, playing down costs, or attacking the whole benefit cost concept as inapplicable. Another approach would be to recognize that federalism—meaning, realistically, the distribution of indulgences to State units—represents a political value worth promoting to some extent and that gaining nation-wide support is important. From this perspective, a compromise solution would be to except one or two projects in each State or region from meeting the full requirement of the formula, though the projects with the highest benefit-cost ratio would have to be chosen. In return for sacrificing full adherence to the formula in a few instances, one would get enhanced support for it in many others.

Everyone knows, of course, that cost-benefit analysis is not the messiah come to save water resources projects from contamination by the rival forces of ignorance and political corruption. Whenever agencies and their associated interests discover that they cannot do what they want, they may twist prevailing criteria out of shape: Two projects may be joined so that both qualify when one, standing alone, would not. Costs and benefits may be manipulated, or the categories may be so extended that almost any project qualifies. On the other hand, cost-benefit analysis has some "good" political uses that might be stressed more than they have been. The technique gives the responsible official a good reason for turning down projects, with a public-interest explanation the Congressman can use with his constituents and the interest-group leader with his members.

This is not to say that cost-benefit analysis has little utility. Assuming that the method will continue to be improved, and that one accepts the market as the measure of economic value, it can certainly tell decision makers something about what they will be giving up if they follow alternative policies. The use of two analyses, one based on regional and the other on national factors, might result in an appraisal of the economic costs of federalism.

The burden of calculation may be reduced by following cost-benefit analysis for many projects and introducing other values only for a few. To expect, however, that the method itself (which distributes indulgences to some and deprivations to others) would not be subject to manipulation in the political process is to say that we shall be governed by formula and not by men.

Because the cost-benefit formula does not always jibe with political realities—that is, it omits political costs and benefits—we can expect it to be twisted out of shape from time to time. Yet cost-benefit analysis may still be important in getting rid of the worst projects. Avoiding the worst where one can't get the best is no small accomplishment.

SYSTEMS ANALYSIS

The good systems analyst is a "chochem," a Yiddish word meaning "wise man," with overtones of "wise guy." His forte is creativity. Although he sometimes relates means to ends and fits ends to match means, he ordinarily eschews such pat processes, preferring instead to relate elements imaginatively into new systems that create their own means and ends. He plays new objectives continuously against cost elements until a creative synthesis has been achieved. He looks down upon those who say that they take objectives as given, knowing full well that the apparent solidity of the objective will dissipate during analysis and that, in any case, most people do not know what they want because they do not know what they can get.

Since no one knows how to teach creativity, daring, and nerve, it is not surprising that no one can define what systems analysis is or how it should be practiced. E. S. Quade, who compiled the RAND Corporation lectures on systems analysis, says it "is still largely a form of art" in which it is not possible to lay down "fixed rules which need only be followed with exactness."[16] He examined systems studies to determine ideas and principles common to the good ones, but discovered that "no universally accepted set of ideas existed. It was even difficult to decide which studies should be called good."[17]

Systems analysis is derived from operations research, which came into use during World War II when some scientists discovered that they could use simple quantitative analysis to get the most out of existing military equipment. A reasonably clear objective was given, and ways to cut the cost of achieving it could be developed, using essentially statistical models. Operations research today is largely identified with specific techniques: linear programming; Monte Carlo (randomizing) methods; gaming and game theory. While there is no hard and fast division between operations research and systems analysis, a rough separation may perhaps be made. The less that is known about objectives, the more they conflict, the larger the number of elements to be considered, the more uncertain the environment, the more likely it is that the work will be called a systems analysis. In systems analysis there is more judgment and intuition and less reliance on quantitative methods than in operations research.

Systems analysis builds models that abstract from reality but represent the crucial relationships. The systems analyst first decides what questions are relevant to his inquiry, selects certain quantifiable factors, cuts down the list of factors to be dealt with by aggregation and by eliminating the (hopefully) less important ones, and then gives

---

[16] E. S. Quade, *Analysis for Military Decisions* (Chicago, 1964), p. 153.
[17] *Ibid.*, p. 149.

them quantitative relationships with one another within the system he has chosen for analysis. But crucial variables may not be quantifiable. If they can be reduced to numbers, there may be no mathematical function that can express the desired relationship. More important, there may be no single criterion for judging results among conflicting objectives. Most important, the original objectives, if any, may not make sense.

It cannot be emphasized too strongly that a (if not the) distinguishing characteristic of systems analysis is that the objectives are either not known or are subject to change. Systems analysis, Quade tells us, "is associated with that class of problems where the difficulties lie in deciding what ought to be done—not simply how to do it—and honors go to people who . . . find out what the problem is."[18] Charles Hitch, the former Comptroller of the Defense Department, insists that:

> . . . learning about objectives is one of the chief ·objects of this kind of analysis. We must learn to look at objectives as critically and as professionally as we look at our models and our other inputs. We may, of course, begin with tentative objectives, but we must expect to modify or replace them as we learn about the systems we are studying—and related systems. The feedback on objectives may in some cases be the most important result of our study. We have never undertaken a major system study at RAND in which we are able to define satisfactory objectives at the beginning of the study.[19]

Systems analysts recognize many good reasons for their difficulties in defining problems or objectives. Quade reaches the core: "Objectives are not, in fact, agreed upon. The choice, while ostensibly between alternatives, is really between objectives or ends and nonanalytic methods must be used for a final reconciliation of views."[20] It may be comforting to believe that objectives come to the analyst from on high and can be taken as given, but this easy assumption is all wrong. "For all sorts of good reasons that are not about to change," says Hitch, "official statements of national objectives (or company objectives) tend to be nonexistent or so vague and literary as to be non-operational."[21] Objectives are not only likely to be "thin and rarified," according to Wohlstetter, but the relevant authorities "are likely to conflict. Among others there will be national differences within an alliance and within the nation, interagency, interservice, and intraservice differences. . . ."[22]

[18] *Ibid.*, p. 7.

[19] Charles J. Hitch, *op. cit.*, p. 19.

[20] E. S. Quade, *op. cit.*, p. 176.

[21] Charles J. Hitch, *op. cit.*, pp. 4–5.

[22] Albert Wohlstetter, "Analysis and Design of Conflict Systems," in E. S. Quade, *op. cit.*, p. 121.

Moreover, even shared objectives often conflict with one another. Deterrence of atomic attack might be best served by letting an enemy know that we would respond with an all-out, indiscriminate attack on his population. Defense of our population against death and destruction might not be well served by this strategy,[23] as the Secretary of Defense recognized when he recommended a city-avoidance strategy that might give an enemy some incentive to spare our cities as well. Not only are objectives large in number and in conflict with one another, they are likely to engender serious repercussion effects. Many objectives, like morale and the stability of alliances, are resistant to quantification. What is worth doing depends on whether it can be done at all, how well, and at what cost. Hence, objectives really cannot be taken as given; they must be made up by the analyst. "In fact," Wohlstetter declares, "we are always in the process of choosing and modifying both means and ends."[24]

Future systems analysts are explicitly warned not to let clients determine objectives. A suggestive analogy is drawn with the doctor who would not ignore a patient's "description of his symptoms, but . . . cannot allow the patient's self diagnosis to override his own professional judgment."[25] Quade argues that since systems analysis has often resulted in changing the original objectives of the policy-maker, it would be "self-defeating to accept without inquiry" his "view of what the problem is."[26]

I have stressed the point that the systems analyst is advised to insist on his own formulation of the problem because it shows so closely that we are dealing with a mixed concept of efficiency.

Adjusting objectives to resources in the present or near future is difficult enough without considering future states of affairs which hold tremendous uncertainty. Constants become variables; little can be taken for granted. The rate of technological progress, an opponent's estimate of your reaction to his latest series of moves based on his reaction to yours, whether or not atomic war will occur, what it will be like, whether we shall have warning, whether the system we are working on will cost anything close to current estimates and whether it will be ready within five years of the due date—on most of these matters, there are no objective probabilities to be calculated.

An effective dealing with uncertainty must be a major goal of systems analysis. Systems analysis is characterized by the aids to calcu-

---

[23] See Glenn H. Snyder, *Deterrence and Defense* (Princeton, 1961).

[24] Wohlstetter in Quade, *op. cit.*, p. 122.

[25] E. S. Quade, *op. cit.*, p. 157. Quade attempts to soften the blow by saying that businessmen and military officers know more about their business than any one else. But the import of the analogy is clear enough.

[26] *Ibid.*, pp. 156–157.

lation it uses, not to conquer, but to circumvent and mitigate some of the pervasive effects of uncertainty. Before a seemingly important factor may be omitted, for example, a sensitivity analysis may be run to determine whether its variation significantly affects the outcome. If there is no good basis for calculating the value of the factor, arbitrary values may be assigned to test for extreme possibilities. Contingency analysis is used to determine how the relative ranking of alternatives holds up under major changes in the environment, say, a new alliance between France and Russia, or alterations in the criteria for judging the alternatives, such as a requirement that a system work well against attacks from space as well as earth. Contingency analysis places a premium on versatility as the analyst seeks a system that will hold up well under various eventualities even though it might be quite as good for any single contingency as an alternative system. Adversary procedures may be used to combat uncertainty. Bending over backwards to provide advantages for low ranking systems and handicaps for high ranking systems is called a fortiori analysis. Changing crucial assumptions in order to make the leading alternatives even, so that one can judge whether the assumptions are overly optimistic or pessimistic, is called break-even analysis.[27] Since all these methods add greatly to the burden of calculation, they must be used with some discretion.

A variety of insurance schemes may also be used to deal with uncertainty. In appraising what an opponent can do, for instance, one can assume the worst, the best, and sheer inertia. In regard to the development of weapons, insurance requires not one flexible weapon but a variety of alternatives pursued with vigor. As development goes on, uncertainty is reduced. Consequently, basic strategic choice involves determining how worthwhile paying for the additional information is by developing rival weapons systems to the next stage. The greater the uncertainty of the world, the greater the desirability of having the widest selection of alternative weapons to choose from to meet unexpected threats and opportunities. Alchian and Kessel are so wedded to the principle of diversified investment that they "strongly recommend this theorem as a basic part of systems analysis."[28]

As a form of calculation, systems analysis represents a merger of quantitative methods and rules of thumb. First, the analyst attempts to solve the problem before he knows a great deal about it. Then he

[27] Herman Kahn and Irwin Mann, *Techniques of Systems Analysis* (Santa Monica, The RAND Corporation, 1957), believe that *"More than any single thing,* the skilled use of a fortiori and break-even analyses separate the professionals from the amateurs."* They think that convincing others that you have a good solution is as important as coming up with one.

[28] Armen A. Alchian and Reuben A. Kessel, *A Proper Role of Systems Analysis* (Santa Monica, RAND Corporation, 1954), p. 9.

continuously alters his initial solution to get closer to what he intuitively feels ought to be wanted. Means and ends are continuously played off against one another. New objectives are defined, new assumptions made, new models constructed, until a creative amalgam appears that hopefully defines a second best solution, one that is better than others even if not optimal in any sense. In the famous study of the location of military bases conducted by Albert Wohlstetter and his associates at the RAND Corporation, widely acknowledged as a classic example of systems analysis, Wohlstetter writes:

The base study . . . proceeded by a method of successive approximations. It compared forces for their efficiency in carrying a payload between the bases and targets without opposition either by enemy interceptors or enemy bombers. Then, it introduced obstacles successively: first, enemy defenses; then enemy bombardment of our bombers and other elements needed to retaliate. In essence, then, the alternative systems were tested for their first-strike capability and then they were compared for their second-strike capacity. And the programmed system performed in a drastically different way, depending on the order in which the opposing side struck. In the course of analyzing counter-measures and counter-counter-measures, the enemy bombardment turned out to be a dominant problem. This was true even for a very much improved overseas operating base system. The refueling base system was very much less sensitive to strike order. It is only the fact that strike order made such a difference among systems contemplated that gave the first-strike, second-strike distinction an interest. And it was not known in advance of the analysis that few of the programmed bombers would have survived to encounter the problem of penetrating enemy defenses which had previously been taken as the main obstacle. The analysis, then, not only was affected by the objectives considered, it affected them.[29]

The advantage of a good systems study is that by running the analysis through in theory on paper certain disadvantages of learning from experience may be avoided.

If the complexity of the problems encountered proved difficult in cost-benefit analysis, the burdens of calculation are ordinarily much greater in systems analysis. Many aspects of a problem simply must be put aside. Only a few variables can be considered simultaneously. "Otherwise," Roland McKean tells us, "the models would become impossibly cumbersome, and . . . the number of calculations to consider would mount in the thousands."[30] Formulas that include everything may appear more satisfactory but those that cannot be reduced "to a single expression are likely to convey no meaning at all. . . ."[31] Summing up their experience, Hitch and McKean assert that:

[29] Albert Wohlstetter in E. S. Quade, *op. cit.*, pp. 125–26.

[30] R. N. McKean, "Criteria," in E. S. Quade, *op. cit.*, p. 83.

[31] E. S. Quade, *op. cit.*, p. 310.

. . . analyses must be piecemeal, since it is impossible for a single analysis to cover all problems of choice simultaneously in a large organization. Thus comparisons of alternative courses of action always pertain to a part of the government's (or corporation's) problem. Other parts of the over-all problem are temporarily put aside, possible decisions about some matters being ignored, specific decisions about others being taken for granted. The resulting analyses are intended to provide assistance in finding optimal, or at least good, solutions to sub-problems: in the jargon of systems and operations research, they are sub-optimizations.[32]

Although admitting that much bad work is carried on and that inordinate love of numbers and machines often get in the way of creative work,[33] practitioners of systems analysis believe in their art. "All of them point out how the use of analysis can provide some of the knowledge needed, how it may sometime serve as a substitute for experience, and, most importantly, how it can work to sharpen intuition."[34] Systems analysis can increase explicitness about the assumptions made and about exclusions from the analysis. The claim is that systems analysis can be perfected; sheer intuition or unaided judgment can never be perfect.

Yet there is also wide agreement that systems analysts "do philosophy,"[35] that they are advocates of particular policy alternatives. What Schelling calls "the pure role of expert advisor" is not available for the analyst who "must usually formulate the questions themselves for his clients."[36] Beyond that, Wohlstetter argues that systems analysts can perform the function of integrating diverse values. New systems can sometimes be found that meet diverse objectives.[37] The politician who gains his objectives by inventing policies that also satisfy others, or the leader of a coalition who searches out areas of maximum agreement, performs a kind of informal system analysis.

All these men, however, work within the existing political structure. While cost-benefit analysis may contain within it implicit changes in existing governmental policies, it poses no direct challenge to the general decision-making machinery of the political system. Program budgeting is a form of systems analysis that attempts to break out of these confines.

[32] Charles J. Hitch and Roland N. McKean, *The Economics of Defense in the Nuclear Age* (Cambridge, Harvard University Press, 1961), p. 161.

[33] See Hitch on "Mechanitis—putting . . . machines to work as a substitute for hard thinking." Charles Hitch, "Economics and Operations Research: A Symposium. II," *Review of Economics and Statistics*, August, 1958, p. 209.

[34] E. S. Quade, *op. cit.*, p. 12.

[35] *Ibid.*, p. 5.

[36] T. C. Schelling, "Economics and Operations Research: A Symposium. V. Comment," *Review of Economics and Statistics*, August, 1958, p. 222.

[37] Albert Wohlstetter in E. S. Quade, *op. cit.*, p. 122.

PROGRAM BUDGETING

It is always important, and perhaps especially so in economics, to avoid being swept off one's feet by the fashions of the moment.[38]

So this new system will identify our national goals with precision . . .[39]

On August 25, 1965, President Johnson announced that he was asking the heads of all Federal agencies to introduce "a very new and revolutionary system" of program budgeting. Staffs of experts set up in each agency would define goals using "modern methods of program analysis." Then the "most effective and the least costly" way to accomplish these goals would be found.[40]

Program budgeting has no standard definition. The general idea is that budgetary decisions should be made by focusing on output categories like governmental goals, objectives, end products or programs instead of inputs like personnel, equipment, and maintenance. As in cost-benefit analysis, to which it owes a great deal, program budgeting lays stress on estimating the total financial cost of accomplishing objectives. What is variously called cost-effectiveness or cost-utility analysis is employed in order to select "alternative approaches to the achievement of a benefit already determined to be worth achieving."[41]

Not everyone would go along with the most far-reaching implications of program budgeting, but the RAND Corporation version, presumably exported from the Defense Department, definitely does include "institutional reorganization to bring relevant administrative functions under the jurisdiction of the authority making the final program decisions." In any event, there would be "information reporting systems and shifts in the power structure to the extent necessary to secure compliance with program decisions by the agencies responsible for their execution."[42] Sometimes it appears that comprehensiveness—simultaneous and complete examination of all programs and all alternatives to programs every year—is being advocated. Actually, comprehensiveness has been dropped (though not without regret) because "it may be too costly in time, effort, uncertainty, and confusion."[43] There exists considerable ambivalence as to whether decisions are im-

---

[38] Prest and Turvey, *op. cit.*, p. 684.

[39] David Novick, Editor, *Program Budgeting* (Cambridge, Harvard University Press, 1965), p. vi.

[40] *Ibid.*, pp. v–vi.

[41] Alan Dean, quoted in D. Novick, *ibid.*, p. 311.

[42] R. N. McKean and N. Anshen in D. Novick, *ibid.*, pp. 286–87. The authors say that this aspect of program budgeting is part of the general view adopted in the book as a whole.

[43] Arthur Smithies in *ibid.*, p. 45.

plicit in the program categories or merely provide information to improve the judgment of governmental officials.

Programs are not made in heaven. There is nothing out there that is just waiting to be found. Programs are not natural to the world; they must be imposed on it by men. No one can give instructions for making up programs. There are as many ways to conceive of programs as there are of organizing activity,[44] as the comments of the following writers eloquently testify:

It is by no means obvious . . . whether a good program structure should be based on components of specific end objectives (e.g., the accomplishment of certain land reclamation targets), on the principle of cost separation (identifying as a program any activity the costs of which can be readily segregated), on the separation of means and ends (Is education a means or an end in a situation such as skill-retraining courses for workers displaced by automation?), or on some artificially designed pattern that draws from all these and other classification criteria.[45]

Just what categories constitute the most useful programs and program elements is far from obvious. . . . If one puts all educational activities into a broad package of educational programs, he cannot simultaneously include school lunch programs or physical education activities in a Health Program, or include defense educational activities (such as the military academies) in the Defense Program. . . . In short, precisely how to achieve a rational and useful structure for a program budget is not yet evident.[46]

In much current discussion it seems to be taken for granted that transportation is a natural program category. But that conclusion is by no means obvious.[47]

A first question one might ask is whether, given their nature, health activities merit a separate, independent status in a program budget. The question arises because these activities often are constituents of, or inputs into, other activities whose purpose or goal orientation is the dominating one. Outlays by the Department of Defense for hospital care, for example, though they assist in maintaining the health of one segment of the population, are undertaken on behalf of national defense, and the latter is their justification.[48]

[44] A look at the classic work by Luther Gulick and Lyndall Urwick, *Papers on the Science of Administration* (New York, Columbia University Press, 1937), reveals considerable similarity between their suggested bases of organization and ways of conceptualizing programs.

[45] M. Anshen in D. Novick, *op. cit.*, pp. 19–20.

[46] G. A. Steiner in *ibid.*, p. 356.

[47] A. Smithies in *ibid.*, p. 41.

[48] Marvin Frankel in *ibid.*, pp. 219–220. I have forborne citing the author who promises exciting discussion of the objectives of American education and ends up with fascinating program categories like primary, secondary, and tertiary education.

The difficulties with the program concept are illustrated in the space program. A first glance suggests that space projects are ideally suited for program budgeting because they appear as physical systems designed to accomplish different missions. Actually, there is a remarkable degree of interdependence between different missions and objectives—pride, scientific research, space exploration, military uses. etc.—so that it is impossible to apportion costs on a proper basis. Consider the problem of a rocket developed for one mission and useful for others. To apportion costs to each new mission is purely arbitrary. To allocate the cost to the first mission and regard the rocket as a free good for all subsequent missions is ludicrous. The only remotely reasonable alternative—making a separate program out of the rocket itself—does violence to the concept of programs as end products. The difficulty is compounded because the facilities that have multiple uses like boosters and tracking networks tend to be very expensive compared to the items that are specific to a particular mission.[49] Simple concepts of programs evaporate upon inspection.

Political realities lie behind the failure to devise principles for defining programs. As Melvin Anshen puts it, "The central issue is, of course, nothing less than the definition of the ultimate objectives of the Federal government as they are realized through operational decisions." The arrangement of the programs inevitably affects the specific actions taken to implement them. "Set in this framework," Anshen continues, "the designation of a schedule of programs may be described as building a bridge between a matter of political philosophy (what is government for?) and . . . assigning scarce resources among alternative governmental objectives."[50]

Because program budgeting is a form of systems analysis (and uses a form of cost-benefit analysis), the conditions that hinder or facilitate its use have largely been covered in the previous sections. The simpler the problem, the fewer the interdependencies, the greater the ability to measure the consequences of alternatives on a common scale, the more costs and benefits that are valued in the market place, the better the chances of making effective use of programs. Let us take transportation to illustrate some of the conditions in a specific case.

Investments in transportation are highly interdependent with one another (planes versus cars versus trains versus barges, etc.) and with decisions regarding the regional location of industry and the movements of population. In view of the powerful effects of transportation investment on regional employment, income, and competition with other modes of transport, it becomes necessary to take these factors

---

[49] See the excellent chapter by M. A. Margolis and S. M. Barro, *ibid.*, pp. 120–145.

[50] *Ibid.*, p. 18.

into account. The partial equilibrium model of efficiency in the narrow sense becomes inappropriate and a general equilibrium model of the economy must be used. The combination of aggregative models at the economy-wide level and inter-region and inter-industry models that this approach requires is staggering. It is precisely the limited and partial character of cost-effectiveness analyses, taking so much for granted and eliminating many variables, that make them easy to work with for empirical purposes. Furthermore, designing a large-scale transportation system involves so close a mixture of political and economic considerations that it is not possible to disentangle them. The Interstate Highway Program, for example, involved complex bargaining among Federal, State, and local governments and reconciliation of many conflicting interests. The development of certain "backward" regions, facilitating the movement of defense supplies, redistribution of income, creating countervailing power against certain monopolies, not to mention the political needs of public officials, were all involved. While cost-utility exercises might help with small segments of the problem, J. R. Meyer concludes that, "Given the complexity of the political and economic decisions involved, and the emphasis on designing a geographically consistent system, it probably would be difficult to improve on the congressional process as a means of developing such a program in an orderly and systematic way."[51]

On one condition for effective use—reorganization of the Federal government to centralize authority for wide-ranging programs—proponents of program budgeting are markedly ambivalent. The problem is that responsibility for programs is now scattered throughout the whole Federal establishment and decentralized to State and local authorities as well. In the field of health, for example, expenditures are distributed among at least twelve agencies and six departments outside of Health, Education, and Welfare. A far greater number of organizations are concerned with American activities abroad, with natural resources and with education. The multiple jurisdictions and overlapping responsibilities do violence to the concept of comprehensive and consistent programs. It "causes one to doubt," Marvin Frankel writes, "whether there can exist in the administrative echelons the kind of overall perspective that would seem indispensable if Federal health resources are to be rationally allocated."[52] To G. A. Steiner it is evident that "The present 'chest of drawers' type of organization cannot for long be compatible with program budgeting."[53] W. Z. Hirsch declares that "if we are to have effective program

[51] J. R. Meyer in *ibid.*, p. 170. This paragraph is based on my interpretation of his work.

[52] M. Frankel, *ibid.*, p. 237.

[53] *Ibid.*, p. 348.

budgeting of natural resources activities, we shall have to provide for new institutional arrangements."[54] Yet the inevitable resistance to wholesale reorganization would be so great that, if it were deemed essential, it might well doom the enterprise. Hence, the hope is expressed that translation grids or crossover networks could be used to convert program budget decisions back into the usual budget categories in the usual agencies. That is what is done in Defense, but that Department has the advantage of having most of the activities it is concerned with under the Secretary's jurisdiction. Some program analysts believe that this solution will not do.

Recognizing that a conversion scheme is technically feasible, Anshen is aware that there are "deeply frustrating" issues to be resolved. "The heart of the problem is the fact that the program budget in operation should not be a mere statistical game. Great strategic importance will attach to both the definition of program structure and content and the establishment of specific program objectives (including magnitude, timing, and cost)."[55] The implications of program budgeting, however, go far beyond specific policies.

It will be useful to distinguish between policy politics (which policy will be adopted?), partisan politics (which political party will win office?), and system politics (how will decision structures be set up?). Program budgeting is manifestly concerned with policy politics, and not much with partisan politics, although it could have important consequences for issues that divide the nation's parties. *My contention is that the thrust of program budgeting makes it an integral part of system politics.*

As presently conceived, program budgeting contains an extreme centralizing bias. Power is to be centralized in the Presidency (through the Budget Bureau) at the national level, in superdepartments rather than bureaus within the executive branch, and in the Federal government as a whole instead of State or local governments. Note how W. Z. Hirsch assumes the desirability of national dominance when he writes: "These methods of analysis can guide Federal officials in the responsibility of bringing local education decisions into closer harmony with national objectives."[56] G. A. Steiner observes that comprehensiveness may be affected by unrestricted Federal grants-in-aid to the states because "such a plan would remove a substantial part of Federal expenditures from a program budgeting system of the Federal government."[57] Should there be reluctance on the part of State and local officials to employ the new tools, Anshen states "that the Federal government may employ familiar incentives to

---

[54] *Ibid.*, p. 280.

[55] *Ibid.*, pp. 358–59.

[56] *Ibid.*, p. 206.

[57] *Ibid.*, p. 347.

accelerate this progress."[58] Summing it up, Hirsch says that "It appears doubtful that a natural resources program budget would have much impact without a good deal of centralization."[59]

Within the great Federal organizations designed to encompass the widest ramifications of basic objectives, there would have to be strong executives. Cutting across the sub-units of the organization, as is the case in the Department of Defense, the program budget could only be put together by the top executive. A more useful tool for increasing his power to control decisions vis-à-vis his subordinates would be hard to find.[60]

Would large-scale program budgeting benefit the Chief Executive? President Johnson's support of program budgeting could in part stem from his desire to appear frugal and also be directed at increasing his control of the executive branch by centralizing decisions in the Bureau of the Budget. In the case of foreign affairs, it is not at all clear whether it would be preferable to emphasize country teams, with the budget made by the State Department to encompass activities of the other Federal agencies abroad, or to let Commerce, Agriculture, Defense, and other agencies include their foreign activities in their own budgets. Program budgeting will unleash great struggles of this kind in Washington. An especially intriguing possibility is that the Bureau of the Budget might prefer to let the various agencies compete, with the Bureau coordinating (that is, controlling) these activities through a comprehensive foreign affairs program devised only at the Presidential level.

Yet it is not entirely clear that Presidents would welcome all the implications of program budgeting. It is well and good to talk about long-range planning; it is another thing to tie a President's hands by committing him in advance for five years of expenditures. Looking ahead is fine but not if it means that a President cannot negate the most extensive planning efforts on grounds that seem sufficient to him.[61] He may wish to trade some program budgeting for some political support.

In any event, that all decisions ought to be made by the most central person in the most centralized body capable of grabbing hold of them is difficult to justify on scientific grounds. We see what has happened.

[58] *Ibid.*, p. 365.

[59] *Ibid.*, p. 280.

[60] See my comments to this effect in *The Politics of the Budgetary Process* (Boston, 1964), p. 140. For discussion of some political consequences of program budgeting, see pp. 135–142.

[61] See William H. Brown and Charles E. Gilbert, *Planning Municipal Investment: A Case Study of Philadelphia* (Philadelphia, University of Pennsylvania Press, 1961), for an excellent discussion of the desire of elected officials to remain free to shift their commitments.

First pure efficiency was converted to mixed efficiency. Then limited efficiency became unlimited. Yet the qualifications of efficiency experts for political systems analysis are not evident.[62]

We would be in a much stronger position to predict the consequences of program budgeting if we knew (a) how far toward a genuine program budget the Defense Department has gone and (b) whether the program budget has fulfilled its promise. To the best of my knowledge, not a single study of this important experiment was undertaken (or at least published) before the decision was made to spread it around the land. On the surface, only two of the nine program categories used in the Defense Department appear to be genuine programs in the sense of pointing to end purposes or objectives. Although strategic retaliation and continental defense appear to be distinct programs, it is difficult to separate them conceptually; my guess is that they are, in fact, considered together. The third category —general purpose forces—is presumably designed to deal with (hopefully) limited war anywhere in the world. According to Arthur Smithies, "The threat is not clearly defined and neither are the requirements for meeting it. Clearly this program is of a very different character from the other two and does not lend itself as readily to analysis in terms either of its components or of its specific contribution to defense objectives."[63]

What about the program called airlift and sealift? These activities support the general purpose forces. Research and development is

---

[62] It may be said that I have failed to distinguish sufficiently between planning, programming, and budgeting. Planning is an orientation that looks ahead by extending costs and benefits or units of effectiveness a number of years into the future. Programming is a general procedure of systems analysis employing cost-effectiveness studies. In this view program budgeting is a mere mechanical translation of the results of high level systems studies into convenient storage in the budgetary format. No doubt systems studies could be done without converting the results into the form of a program budget. This approach may have a lot to be said for it and it appears that it is the one that is generally followed in the Department of Defense in its presentations to Congress. But if the systems studies guide decisions as to the allocation of resources, and the studies are maintained according to particular program categories and are further legitimatized by being given status in the budget, it seems most unlikely that programming will be separated from budgeting. One is never sure whether too much or too little is being claimed for program budgeting. If all that program budgeting amounts to is a simple translation of previous systems studies into some convenient form of accounting, it hardly seems that this phenomenon is worth so much fuss. If the program categories in the budget system are meaningful, then they must be much more than a mere translation of previously arrived at decisions. In this case, I think that it is not my task to enlighten the proponents of program budgeting, but it is their task to make themselves clear to others.

[63] A. Smithies in Novick, *op. cit.,* p. 37.

carried on presumably to serve other defense objectives, and the same is true for the reserve forces.

No doubt the elements that make up the programs comprise the real action focus of the budget, but these may look less elegant when spread into thousands of elements than they do in nine neat rows. When one hears that hundreds of program elements are up for decision at one time,[64] he is entitled to some skepticism about how much genuine analysis can go into all of them. Part of the argument for program budgeting was that by thinking ahead and working all year around it would be possible to consider changes as they came up and avoid the usual last minute funk. Both Hitch[65] and Novick[66] (the RAND Corporation expert on defense budgeting) report, however, that this has not worked out. The services hesitate to submit changes piecemeal, and the Secretary wants to see what he is getting into before he acts. The vaunted five year plans are still in force but their efficacy in determining yearly decisions remains to be established.

One good operational test would be to know whether the Department's systems analysts actually use the figures from the five year plans in their work or whether they go to the services for the real stuff. Another test would be whether or not the later years of the five year projections turn out to have any future significance, or whether the battle is really over the next year that is to be scooped out as part of the budget. From a distance, it appears that the services have to work much harder to justify what they are doing. Since McNamara's office must approve changes in defense programs, and he can insist on documentation, he is in a strong position to improve thinking at the lower levels. The intensity of conflict within the Defense Department may not have changed, but it may be that the disputants are or will in the future be likely to shout at a much more sophisticated level. How much this is due to McNamara himself, to his insistence on quantitative estimates, or to the analytic advantages of a program budget cannot be determined now. It is clear that a program budget, of which he alone is master, has helped impose his will on the Defense Department.

It should also be said that there are many notable differences between decision-making in defense and domestic policy that would render suspect the transmission of procedures from one realm to the other. The greater organizational unity of Defense, the immensely

[64] See U.S. House Appropriations Committee Subcommittee on Department of Defense Appropriations for Fiscal 1965, 88th Congress, 2nd Session, IV, p. 133. McNamara asserted that some 652 "subject issues" had been submitted to him for the fiscal 1965 budget.

[65] Charles Hitch, *Decision-Making for Defense* (Berkeley, University of California Press, 1965).

[66] Novick, *op. cit.*, p. 100.

large amounts of money at stake, the extraordinarily greater risks involved, the inability to share more than minimal values with opponents, the vastly different array of interests and perceptions of the proper roles of the participants, are but a few of the factors involved.

The Armed Services and Appropriations Committees in the defense area, for example, are normally most reluctant to substitute their judgment on defense for that of the President and the Secretary of the Department. They do not conceive it to be their role to make day to day defense policy, and they are apparently unwilling to take on the burden of decision. They therefore accept a budget presentation based on cavernous program categories even though these are so arranged that it is impossible to make a decision on the basis of them. If they were to ask for and to receive the discussion of alternative actions contained in the much smaller program elements on which McNamara bases his decisions, they would be in a position to take the Department of Defense away from its Secretary.

There is no reason whatsoever to believe that a similar restraint would be shown by committees that deal with domestic policies. It is at least possible that the peculiar planning, programming, and budgeting system adopted in Defense could not be repeated elsewhere in the Federal establishment.

POLITICAL RATIONALITY

Political rationality is the fundamental kind of reason, because it deals with the preservation and improvement of decision structures, and decision structures are the source of all decisions. Unless a decision structure exists, no reasoning and no decisions are possible. . . . There can be no conflict between political rationality and . . . technical, legal, social, or economic rationality, because the solution of political problems makes possible an attack on any other problem, while a serious political deficiency can prevent or undo all other problem solving. . . . Nonpolitical decisions are reached by considering a problem in its own terms, and by evaluating proposals according to how well they solve the problem. The best available proposal should be accepted regardless of who makes it or who opposes it, and a faulty proposal should be rejected or improved no matter who makes it. Compromise is always irrational; the rational procedure is to determine which proposal is the best, and to accept it. In a political decision, on the other hand, action never is based on the merits of a proposal but always on who makes it and who opposes it. Action should be designed to avoid complete identification with any proposal and any point of view, no matter how good or how popular it might be. The best available proposal should never be accepted just because it is best; it should be deferred, objected to, discussed, until major opposition disappears. Compromise is always a rational procedure, even when the compromise is between a good and a bad proposal.[67]

[67] Paul Diesing, *Reason in Society* (Urbana, 1962), pp. 198, 203–204, 231–32.

We are witnessing the beginning of significant advances in the art and science of economizing. Having given up the norm of comprehensiveness, economizers are able to join quantitative analysis with aids to calculation of the kind described by Lindblom in his strategy of disjointed incrementalism.[68]

Various devices are employed to simplify calculations. Important values are omitted entirely; others are left to different authorities to whose care they have been entrusted. Here, sensitivity analysis represents an advance because it provides an empirical basis to justify neglect of some values. Means and ends are hopelessly intertwined.

The real choice is between rival policies that encapsulate somewhat different mixes of means and ends. Analysis proceeds incrementally by successive limited approximations. It is serial and remedial as successive attacks are made on problems. Rather than waiting upon experience in the real world, the analyst tries various moves in his model and runs them through to see if they work. When all else fails, the analyst may try an integrative solution reconciling a variety of values to some degree, though meeting none of them completely. He is always ready to settle for the second or third best, provided only that it is better than the going policy. Constrained by diverse limiting assumptions, weakened by deficiencies in technique, rarely able to provide unambiguous measures, the systems, cost-benefit, and program analysis is nonetheless getting better at calculating in the realm of efficiency. Alas, he is an imperialist at heart.

In the literature discussed above there appears several times the proposition that "the program budget is a neutral tool. It has no politics."[69] In truth, the program budget is suffused with policy politics, makes up a small part of President Johnson's partisan politics, and tends towards system politics. How could men account for so foolish a statement? It must be that they who make it identify program budgeting with something good and beautiful, and politics with another thing bad and ugly. McKean and Anshen speak of politics in terms of "pressure and expedient adjustments," "haphazard acts . . . unresponsive to a planned analysis of the needs of efficient decision design." From the political structure they expect only "resistance and opposition, corresponding to the familiar human disposition to protect established seats of power and procedures made honorable by the mere facts of existence and custom."[70] In other places we hear of "vested interests," "wasteful duplication," "special interest groups," and the "Parkinson syndrome."[71]

[68] Braybrooke and Lindblom, *op. cit.* See also Lindblom, *The Intelligence of Democracy* (New York, 1965).

[69] M. Anshen in D. Novick, *op. cit.*, p. 370.

[70] *Ibid.*, p. 289.

[71] *Ibid.*, p. 359.

Not so long ago less sophisticated advocates of reform ignored the political realm. Now they denigrate it. And, since there must be a structure for decision, it is smuggled in as a mere adjunct of achieving efficiency. Who is to blame if the economic tail wags the political dog? It seems unfair to blame the evangelical economizer for spreading the gospel of efficiency. If economic efficiency turns out to be the one true religion, maybe it is because its prophets could so easily conquer.

It is hard to find men who take up the cause of political rationality, who plead the case for political man, and who are primarily concerned with the laws that enable the political machinery to keep working. One is driven to a philosopher like Paul Diesing to find the case for the political:

> . . . the political problem is always basic and prior to the others. . . . This means that any suggested course of action must be evaluated first by its effects on the political structure. A course of action which corrects economic or social deficiencies but increases political difficulties must be rejected, while an action which contributes to political improvement is desirable even if it is not entirely sound from an economic or social standpoint.[72]

There is hardly a political scientist who would claim half as much. The desire to invent decision structures to facilitate the achievement of economic efficiency does not suggest a full appreciation of their proper role by students of politics.

A major task of the political system is to specify goals or objectives. It is impermissible to treat goals as if they were known in advance. "Goals" may well be the product of interaction among key participants rather than some "deus ex machina" or (to use Bentley's term) some "spook" which posits values in advance of our knowledge of them. Certainly, the operational objectives of the Corps of Engineers in the Water Resources field could hardly be described in terms of developing rivers and harbors.

Once the political process becomes a focus of attention, it is evident that the principal participants may not be clear about their goals. What we call goals or objectives may, in large part, be operationally determined by the policies we can agree upon. The mixtures of values found in complex policies may have to be taken in packages, so that policies may determine goals as least as much as general objectives determine policies. In a political situation, then, the need for support assumes central importance. Not simply the economic, but the *political* costs and benefits turn out to be crucial.

A first attempt to specify what is meant by political costs may bring closer an understanding of the range of requirements for political

[72] Paul Diesing, *op. cit.*, p. 228.

rationality.[73] Exchange costs are incurred by a political leader when he needs the support of other people to get a policy adopted. He has to pay for this assistance by using up resources in the form of favors (patronage, logrolling) or coercive moves (threats or acts to veto or remove from office). By supporting a policy and influencing others to do the same, a politician antagonizes some people and may suffer their retaliation. If these hostility costs mount, they may turn into reelection costs—actions that decrease his chances (or those of his friends) of being elected or reelected to office. Election costs, in turn, may become policy costs through inability to command the necessary formal powers to accomplish the desired policy objectives.

In the manner of Neustadt, we may also talk about reputation costs, i.e., not only loss of popularity with segments of the electorate, but also loss of esteem and effectiveness with other participants in the political system and loss or ability to secure policies other than the one immediately under consideration. Those who continually urge a President to go all out—that is, use all his resources on a wide range of issues—rarely stop to consider that the price of success in one area of policy may be defeat in another. If he loses popularity with the electorate, as President Truman did, Congress may destroy almost the whole of his domestic program. If he cracks down on the steel industry, as President Kennedy did, he may find himself constrained to lean over backwards in the future to avoid unremitting hostility from the business community.

A major consequence of incurring exchange and hostility costs may be undesirable power-redistribution effects. The process of getting a policy adopted or implemented may increase the power of various individuals, organizations and social groups, which later will be used against the political leader. The power of some participants may be weakened so that the political leader is unable to enjoy their protection.

The legitimacy of the political system may be threatened by costs that involve the weakening of customary political restraints. Politicians who try to suppress opposition, or who practice election frauds, may find similar tactics being used against them. The choice of a highly controversial policy may raise the costs of civic discord. Although the people involved may not hate the political leader, the fact that they hate each other may lead to consequences contrary to his desires.

The literature of economics usually treats organizations and institutions as if they were costless entities. The standard procedure is to consider rival alternatives (in consideration of price policy or other criteria), calculate the differences in cost and achievement among

---

[73] I am indebted to John Harsanyi for suggestions about political rationality.

them, and show that one is more or less efficient than another. This typical way of thinking is sometimes misspecified. If the costs of pursuing a policy are strictly economic and can be calculated directly in the market place, then the procedure should work well. But if the costs include getting one or another organization to change its policies or procedures, then these costs must also be taken into account.[74] Perhaps there are legal, psychological, or other impediments that make it either impossible or difficult for the required changes to be made. Or the changes may require great effort and result in incurring a variety of other costs. In considering a range of alternatives, one is measuring not only efficiency but also the cost of change.

Studies based on efficiency criteria are much needed and increasingly useful. My quarrel is not with them as such, at all. I have been concerned that a single value, however important, could triumph over other values without explicit consideration being given these others. I would feel much better if political rationality were being pursued with the same vigor and capability as is economic efficiency. In that case I would have fewer qualms about extending efficiency studies into the decision-making apparatus.

My purpose has not been to accuse economizers of doing what comes naturally. Rather, I have sought to emphasize that economic rationality, however laudable in its own sphere, ought not to swallow up political rationality—but will do so, if political rationality continues to lack trained and adept defenders.

[74] In the field of defense policy, political factors are taken into account to the extent that the studies concentrate on the design of feasible alternatives. In the choice of overseas basing, for example, the question of feasibility in relation to treaties and friendly or unfriendly relationships with other countries is considered. Thus it seems permissible to take into account political considerations originating outside of the country, where differences of opinions and preferences among nations are to some extent accepted as legitimate, but apparently not differences internal to the American policy.

SYSTEMS ANALYSIS AND THE POLITICAL PROCESS

JAMES R. SCHLESINGER

My purpose in this paper is to evaluate the role for systems analysis—particularly as it functions in a highly politicized environment. I shall not devote any attention to discussing whether cost effectiveness procedures are hypothetically desirable. Far too much attention—in Congress and elsewhere—has been wasted in this strange dialectical tilting ground. Viewed abstractly, systems analysis implies rigorous thinking, hopefully quantitative, regarding the gains and the resource-expenditures involved in a particular course of action—to insure that scarce resources are employed productively rather than wastefully. It is almost tautological therefore to state that systems analysis effectively employed will be beneficial. The real questions arise when we descend from a high-level of abstraction and begin to grapple with the practical issues. Attention must be given to such questions as (1) the quality of information bases and analyses, (2) methodology, (3) bias, (4) the impact of politicized environments on analytical efforts and analytical results.

These issues cannot be treated wholly in isolation. The quality of information, for example, is very much influenced (and biased) by the structure of and alliances within the bureaucracy. The methodology chosen for analytical efforts will in itself introduce a specific form of bias. These in turn, reinforced by the specific interests and functions of

From *Systems Analysis and the Political Process* (Santa Monica: The Rand Corporation, June 1967), monograph, P-3464. James Schlesinger is currently Assistant Director of the U.S. Bureau of the Budget. Reprinted with permission of the author and the Rand Corporation.

separate sections of the bureaucracy, will increase tensions within the Government and make more costly the introduction of changes which might objectively be regarded as desirable. Nonetheless, the effort to sort out different classes of issues must be made. One may categorize issues (1) and (2) as "mechanical" and issues (3) and (4) as "organizational." Without implying a judgment regarding the relative importance of these problems, it is plain that a paper directed to political scientists should concentrate on the latter class of problems. After a few words on the way in which the data base and methodology may influence the quality of analysis, the balance of the paper will be devoted to the implications of these broader organizational issues.

Where gross wastage and irrationality have flourished it is relatively easy (in principle) to indicate very improved patterns of resource allocation even in the face of rather skimpy data. In all other cases the quality of the underlying data will determine the quality of analysis. The fact must be recognized that the data presently available to the Government for analytical work are not in good shape. One of the reasons for the success of systems analysis in the DoD [Department of Defense] under McNamara is that considerable prior effort had been invested in the development and study of the data relevant to defense problems. For most of its other functions the Government faces an uphill fight simply in developing useful data. In part, this problem will yield to steady effort especially as more trained personnel become available. However, it would be utopian to expect agencies automatically to provide data useful for analytical purposes. Knowledge is a form of power, and most institutions exhibit an understandable reluctance to dissipate this power in the absence of compensating advantages. While newer or favored agencies, which anticipate expanded budgets, are likely to prove cooperative, the old-line agencies, especially those that have established a degree of independence, are likely to prove obdurate. In many cases data of appropriate quality can only be obtained through the wholehearted cooperation of the relevant agencies. Since the indicated tactic for many agencies will be to hide some information and to release much of the balance in warped form, many decisions will continue to be based on deficient information with only limited confidence being placed in the results.

The problems that established methodology can create ought not be ignored, even though a sense of proportion suggests that in relation to the enormous potential payoff of systems analysis the errors attributable to methodological bias should be relatively small. While at its best systems analysis insists only on "rigorous thinking," the background of systems analysis in lower-order operations research problems has resulted in a lingering preference for formal models, preferably mathematical. In numerous cases this leads to the neglect of important variables which are not readily subject to manipulation to the existing methods. The normal association of model-building and simplification cannot be avoided in analytical work in the social sciences, but there is cause for concern if such analytical work becomes the sole basis for decision-making. The stress on quantifiable elements is particularly risky in cost-benefit work where objectives are hard to define or subject to change. In most cases the cost elements can be reduced to money terms. By contrast, objectives may be numerous, mutually incommensurable, and reducible to money terms only on the basis of rather arbitrary and subjective judgments by the analyst.[1] The result is that what started as a cost-benefit analysis becomes primarily a crude cost comparison—with inadequate attention either to a number of the potential benefits or to the adaptability of the preferred alternative to a number of unforeseen contingencies. Countervailing tendencies toward prodigality in pursuit of misconceived or ill-defined objectives may bulk larger overall, yet there is no assurance that such tendencies will serve as direct offsets to the biasing of specific analyses toward the choice of the low-cost alternative. When and if systems-analytical work becomes routinized, the risks implicit in methodological bias will rise.

As distinct from methodological bias, the more general forms of bias reflect the pressures of a large and variegated organizational structure. Among the causes of bias are: asymmetry in the sources of information, disproportionate attention by the analyst to preferred information sources, prior intellectual commitment on the part of the analyst, selectivity in organizational recruitment, and other bureaucratic pressures. From these sources a great deal of bias, reinforced by slipshod and mechanical work, inevitably slips in, even on those occasions that it is not deliberately introduced. It scarcely needs saying that in so complex an organization as the United States Government, viewed from its highest levels, that deliberate introduction of misinformation and distortion is no insignificant problem in itself, as will be seen below. The point being made here is that a very large proportion of total bias springs from honest conviction rather than the attempt to deceive, and it is particularly difficult to compensate for bias in this form. Contrary to a widespread hope the solution does not lie in the training and upgrading of personnel—in getting more honest (or more intelligent and capable) personnel. The most damaging forms of bias spring from an honest, if misguided, conviction of the correctness of one's own views. Where biases clash they may be viewed with less apprehension under the classification of the "competition of ideas." But all too frequently biases are mutually reinforcing.

[1] It is infeasible to go into the criterion problem at any length. Suffice it to say that for most higher-order problems adequate measures of merit have yet to be devised. Even if some improvement may be hoped for, the irreducibly subjective element in such measures will remain substantial.

And, in any event, the introduction of bias (inevitable in all save the lowest-order decisions) contaminates the detached and quantitative analysis which a widespread myth holds to be attainable.

The final question bearing on the effectiveness of systems analysis for governmental decision-making is the impact of politicized environments on analytical efforts and analytical results. The deliberate introduction of distortion and fuzziness to improve the competitive position of one's own agency or division is an unavoidable and dominant feature of the bureaucratic landscape. At lower levels the tendency to pick and choose those data which support one's position result in analyses which may be uncritically accepted at higher levels, if the conclusions are palatable. Only if the conclusions are unpalatable, will searching questions be raised regarding the underlying data. Not infrequently, the very agencies whose premises are most questionable, are the very ones which are most adept in handling the new quantitative tools, and in developing a superficially convincing presentation that may beguile those charged with responsibility for review.

The techniques of deception are legion; the effectiveness of intelligence operations and the available sanctions frequently low. In the variegated structure of the Government (with innumerable agencies and sub-agencies), deliberate distortion is reinforced by honest conviction, bias, recruitment, limited information, and the structure of power. It becomes impossible to separate one such element from another. In a perpetual rutting season, these mutually-reinforcing tendencies coagulate in their separate sectors of the lattice structure of the Government. How much systems analysis can do to counteract the pernicious results of such coagulative tendencies remains an open question. Certainly it can accomplish something—hopefully a great deal. Nonetheless, the resistance to the application of systematic and rigorous analysis in a highly politicized environment are sufficient to make even the stoutest heart grow faint. Our purpose is to examine how analytical techniques will fare in this political environment. Let us consider four aspects of the problem: (1) the general limitations, (2) the relevancy of experience in the Department of Defense, (3) bureaucratic problems in a wider compass, and (4) what systems analysis can accomplish.

GENERAL LIMITATIONS

With perhaps a tinge of self-satisfaction on the part of its practitioners, systems analysis has been advertised as the application of logical thinking to broad policy issues. The implication is that logic comes in only one guise. Yet, whatever the doubts of those who seek to rationalize politics, the political process is dominated by a species of logic of its own, one that diverges from the brand germane to systems analysis. The domain of politics is a far broader system than that to which systems analysis is typically applied. Systems analysis applies to substantive issues susceptible to definition, where linkages exist among costs, technologies, and closely-related payoffs. The criterion is some substantive (and presumably measurable) utility which is more-or-less directly relevant to the enhancing of national security or citizen well-being. The pride of systems analysis is its ability to take a long run view and to disregard prior commitments, if they are too costly or non-productive.

By contrast, in politics one is concerned with more than the substantive costs and benefits involved in a specific decision area. One is engaged in mobilizing support by words and by actions over a wide range of ill-defined issues. The ultimate criterion will remain the psychological and voting responses of the general electorate and of important pressure groups. Positive responses in this realm are only irregularly correlated with those actions preferred on the basis of cost-benefit criteria. The focus of political action tends to be short run. The wariness with which the approaching election is watched is tempered only by the precept that the half life of the public's memory is approximately three months.

Put quite briefly, political decision operates under the normal constraint to avoid serious risk of the loss of power. The tool of politics (which frequently becomes its objective) is to extract resources from the general taxpayer with minimum offense and to distribute the proceeds among innumerable claimants in such a way as to maximize support at the polls. Politics, so far as mobilizing support is concerned, represents the art of calculated cheating—or more precisely how to cheat without being *really* caught. Slogans and catch phrases, even when unbacked by the commitment of resources, remain effective instruments of political gain. One needs a steady flow of attention-grabbing cues, and it is of lesser moment whether the indicated castles in Spain ever materialize. The contrast to the systems-analytic approach with its emphasis on careful calculation of resources required to implement real alternatives could not be greater. In political decision, the *appearance* of effort, however inadequate, may be overwhelmingly more remunerative than the costly (and thereby unpleasant) implementation of complete programs.

Consider two of the guiding principles of systems analysis: (1) the avoidance of foot-in-the-door techniques leading to an unintended commitment to large expenditures, and (2) the orientation of analysis and allocation decisions toward output rather than input categories. These go to the heart of systems analysis with respect to the quest for the proper relating of resources provided and goals adopted. Output-orientation is designed to measure the extent to which adopted goals are actually achieved. Avoidance of foot-in-the-door is designed to prevent the preliminary wastage of resources on purposes for which one is unwilling to pay full costs. These are laudable principles, but they conform poorly to the realities of political decision.

Politics, it was hinted above, requires the systematic exploitation of foot-in-the-door techniques. One wishes to attract current support from various voting groups by indications or symbolic representations that the government will satisfy their aspirations. One wishes to attract the support of many groups, but there are limits to the size of the budget. Consequently, resources are applied thinly over a wide array of programs. The symbolism of concern is enough and the last thing that is desired is the toting up of the full costs of a program with the implication that one should not go ahead unless willing to incur the costs involved.

Similarly, in the real world of political decision it is immensely difficult to concentrate on outputs rather than inputs. A very large proportion of political pressure is concerned with the sale or preservation of specific types of socio-economic inputs. The preservation or expansion of vested interests implies that political decision will be much concerned by and may be overwhelmed by inputs rather than ouptuts. No doubt, the behavior of politicians reflects a total disregard of Kant's categorical imperative, but that viewed realistically is the name of the game. Classical liberals may stress the desirability of advancing one's component of the general interests rather than one's special interests, but it requires no great amount of shrewdness on the part of politicians to see that such behavior will not lead to political success. The systems analyst may search for new and more efficient means for achieving objectives, but these new means are by definition likely to have little political support both within and without government, depending on the affected groups. Both within and without the government (depending on the locus of affected interests) the opposition to new methods will be powerful. Consequently political leaders who are interested in maintaining a consensus (as all political leaders must be) must continue to pay close attention to input-oriented interest groups.

As a result, there is an inevitable note of paradox when systems-analytic techniques are endorsed at the highest political level. For such an endorsement implies, in principle, the partial renunciation of the most effective tools of the politician. That systems-analytic techniques are being diffused throughout the Federal bureaucracy in response to a directive of President Johnson is both understandable and ironical. It is understandable in that the pressures for sensible use of resources will be most keenly felt during an administration with high aspirations and expanding programs (much more so than, for instance, in the Eisenhower administration). Yet, it is also ironical in that no recent administration has been more alert to the direct political implications of domestic programs. Lyndon Johnson prides himself on the widespread recognition of his superb political instincts —and on his understanding of what makes the electorate click. Repeatedly he has extracted political gain through the announcement (during the low-cost initial stages) of new programs—before the costs have been thought through or the bills presented for payment. Though this be the political replica of what the analyst decries as foot-in-the-door techniques, few political leaders will be restrained by such an observation. Politics is geared to the hopes of the voters rather than to the calculation of the cost accountant. In politics one is almost driven to overstate the benefits and understate the costs of controversial programs.

The keynote of the Great Society has been the launching of new programs associated with substantial increases in government expenditures. Goals have been announced (like the elimination of poverty) before the means of achieving them have been developed. Neither alternative policies nor the costs have been studied until *after a decision has been reached.* No one would suggest that such programs as "demonstration cities"[2] or rent subsidies have been carefully analyzed with respect to benefits in cost, especially in relation to the alternative employment of the same resources. My point here is neither to ascribe praise or blame to what is effective politics, nor is it to raise questions regarding the merits of the programs themselves. Rather it is to suggest the inherent difficulties of reconciling such procedures with the precepts of systems analysis.

These problems are not new ones. For generations men have sought methods for introducing more "rationality" into the government allocations. Systems analysis is a powerful technique, but like all techniques, it will be germane only when there is a willingness to employ it systematically in dealing with issues of public policy. In fact, systems analysis is only the latest in a series of attempts to achieve more rational allocation. Moreover, prior attempts bear at least a family

[2] "Doing more for the cities" has become the latest arena for political competition. The new programs are to be superimposed on the old without too much study. Indicative of the pre-existing casualness in the attitude toward costing (one of the two legs of cost-benefit analysis) are two recent items bearing on the Federal Government's urban programs. First, in testifying on New York City's budgetary problems, Mayor Lindsay was unable to indicate "what is the total Federal figure?" (Senator Kennedy's words)—in assistance to the City. No one was able to establish whether Federal contributions were closer to the half billion dollar mark or the billion dollar mark. Second, Senator Abraham Ribicoff, whose subcommittee is investigating the problem, stated in an interview: "No one really knows how much we are spending on the program to help cities. . . . What are these programs doing? What should they be doing? Have the cities the men to spend this money properly? What have they duplicated, what have they wasted?"

resemblance to what we now propose to do with systems analysis. For example, Public Law 801, passed in 1956, required the presentation of five-year cost estimates when new programs were adopted. The five-year cost estimates have a familiar ring, but the law is a dead letter. It has been ignored, not because it is undesirable, but because it expresses a pious hope but disregards the underlying realities of political life. Once again it suggests the barriers of imposing upon political decision a method for efficiently using resources to provide direct, substantive benefits.

There is an old yarn which concerns a farmer who was approached by an enthusiastic extension agent pushing a new technique which allegedly would raise the farmer's output by 10 percent. The farmer is supposed to have replied: "I'm only farming half as well as I know how to, right now." It was just too much bother to take advantage of opportunities for improvement. There is a moral in the story for the improvement of the operation of the Government. In many, perhaps most, lines of activity, we already know—even without systems analysis—how to improve efficiency and shave costs by eliminating obsolescent activities. In principle, we could easily do far better. The problem is not absence of knowledge; it is rather that appropriate actions are constrained by political factors reflecting the anticipated reactions of various interest groups. In such lines of activity, if analysis is to be useful, it will not be by contributing to knowledge, but rather by serving as a political instrument through which the relevant political constraints can be relaxed. This is both a more modest and a more ambitious objective for systems analysis than is generally stated, but it is suggestive of the true role that analysis can play once we recognize the serious limitations imposed upon it by the political process.

THE RELEVANCY OF DoD EXPERIENCE

The application of cost-effectiveness techniques in the Department of Defense since 1961 is regarded as a model for reform. While unspoken, there exists an underlying premise that "what's good for the DoD, is good for the rest of the government bureaucracy." While this is, of course, true with regard to the *role* of analytical probing, it is not necessarily the case with regard to the *implementation* of analytical results. It is necessary, therefore, to explore certain differences between the Department of Defense and other elements of the bureaucracy. Moreover, we should examine the actual workings of the new procedures in the DoD, for a somewhat idealized picture has been disseminated which diverges in part from the reality. In so doing we shall be stressing the structural and political aspects of decision-making rather than the substantive issues that have been a controversy since 1961. In a sense, this represents an injustice to Secretary McNamara and his aides, for omitting reference to the substantive issues ignores the truly remarkable way in which the new team took hold with respect to the main strategic and postural issues in 1961.

Controversies regarding budgetary allocations in defense are fought out *within* a single Department. Outsiders, even the Congress itself, have only a nominal influence on allocation. Since the Defense Reorganization Act of 1958, the Secretary of Defense has had sufficient authority to impose his will on the Services. Moreover, the DoD does not supply final goods and services highly valued by influential portions of the electorate, nor is its use of specific inputs such that affected interest groups are normally in a position to block specific allocative decisions. In the United States the military has a relatively weak political position. In the absence of influential public support the traditional tactic of cultivating Congress is inadequate. When the Executive Branch stands firm behind its budgetary decisions (whether based on sound analysis or not), the military has no real alternative to accepting the decision.[3] The means of direct resistance, available to other components of the bureaucracy, are largely denied to the military.

Consequently the Department of Defense, relative to other components of the bureaucracy, has provided an abnormally easy place to apply program budgeting and systems analysis. Only in the case of the closing of the obsolete or redundant bases were vested interests sufficiently involved requiring major political courage to override. With the support of the President the Department of Defense can follow *internally-generated* guidelines, rational or otherwise, with only ineffectual resistance from below or outside. Moreover, the bulk of Defense's allocative decisions are internal to the Department. The linkages to allocative decisions by other Departments or Agencies are relatively weak, by contrast to the major civilian programs.

For those civilian programs in which improved-performance-through-analysis is hoped for, the situation is far less favorable. A number of the newer Departments represent a gathering-in of pre-existing entities with the tradition of independence and outside sources of support serving to sustain that independence. The Secretary is in a weak position to impose decisions; he is rather like a weak

---

[3] While this judgment conflicts sharply with the interpretation represented by General Eisenhower's "military-industrial complex" or C. Wright Mills' "power elite"—to say nothing of the standard Leninist view, I believe that the evidence will bear out that only in periods of national hysteria does the "complex" have much influence on broad defense allocations. One need inquire only into what has happened to the Strategic Air Command under McNamara, and compare the results with the many long-lived and obsolete civilian programs.

feudal overlord attempting to control some ill-governed baronies. The equivalent of the Defense Reorganization Act of 1958 does not exist to establish the authority of the Secretary. This condition applies, moreover, to some of the older Departments in which nominally subordinate units are in reality independent baronies.

The services provided by the various bureaus and agencies regularly create clienteles within the electorate, whose interests it is politically risky for the President to override in preparing his Budget. These interests are strongly represented in Congress, and even a bold President could not afford to take on too many of them within a brief span of time.

The weakness of the Departments, relative to the DoD, implies that allocative decisions cannot be based upon *internally-generated* guidelines. Consequently guidelines must be imposed from above, which is both difficult and politically risky for the President and his principal aides. More important, the appropriate analytical and decision-making domain is much broader than the individual bureaus and agencies in question. There are important linkages and spillovers in costs, in technologies, and particularly in payoffs across agency lines. The improvements to be obtained by intra-organizational changes are small relative to those obtainable by inter-organizational adjustment. This is particularly dramatic, for example, in the natural resources area. Here the Bureau of Reclamation, the Corps of Engineers, the National Park Service, the Forestry Service, the Bureau of Land Management, and the Bureau of Mines are only the more prominent among the *Federal* Agencies involved (whose activities must be reconciled with such State entities as the Texas Railway Commission). Each has a position to maintain and a "suboptimizing" mission to perform, and as we shall see later, the concept of that mission is frequently based upon obsolescent views and obsolescent professional functions. Each, moreover, is involved in a symbiotic relationship with a clientele, which it partially supports and from which it gains significant political backing. The "systems" to which "analysis" should be applied are far broader than the ones which are the concern of the existing entities. Yet, the existing organizational structure makes it virtually impossible to implement the recommendations which would come from good analyses. Thus, the underlying question remains: how strong is the will and ability to achieve a modernization of the structure of the Federal Government?[4]

To this must be added one final point. Both intensive and extensive research had been done on the problems of defense before 1961. This

---

[4] The recent refusal of the Congress to sanction the transfer of the Maritime Administration from the Department of Commerce to the new Department of Transportation is symptomatic of the broader problem of achieving a more coherent structure for Federal Government activities.

body of research was available to Secretary McNamara when he began to introduce his reforms in 1961, and the reforms underlay many of the decisions regarding allocations. For most of the civilian programs, very little policy-oriented research bearing on allocative decisions has been done. In some areas the problems have not even been formulated. Consequently, there is no capital of pre-existing research to be milked. It may be years before adequate analyses have been performed. While in no way does this suggest that analytical effort should not be pushed, it does suggest that our expectations should not be pitched too high with respect to immediate benefits.

Let us turn briefly to consider the other relevant aspect of DoD experience: the actual workings of the evaluative procedures as opposed to the idealized model. In understanding the results we must bear in mind that analytical work is performed and decisions are reached, not by disinterested machines, but by individuals with specific views, commitments, and ambitions. The normal bureaucratic tendencies may be weakened, but will not disappear. We might anticipate the following.

Where centralized evaluative procedures are applied, certain proposals, towards which the reviewers are predisposed, will be subject to less rigorous scrutiny than will other proposals.

An administrator will have powerful incentives to preserve his own options by vigorously suppressing foot-in-the-door attempts by *his* subordinates, he may have a strong desire to commit his superiors or his successors to those policies that he personally favors. Moreover, there may be a weak impulse to preserve options favored by subordinates, but which he opposes.

Finally, while the impulse to justify the commitments or disguise the errors in judgment of subordinates may be weak, the impulse to justify policies and programs to which one's own name has become attached may be correspondingly strong. Consequently, the hope that prior commitments can be disregarded appears utopian. Over time current decision-making may increasingly be influenced by prior decisions.

Manifestation of such tendencies have not disappeared in the DoD since 1961. The Department's leaders have been capable men—and their preferences quite defensible. Yet, one must examine how such bureaucratic tendencies might influence the results, not only if the DoD's decisions were in the hands of men of lesser caliber, but also when the tendencies are exhibited in the more politicized environment affecting the civilian programs. For example, under the first heading above, contract definition procedures require the judgment that the relevant technology is in hand before signing. It is rumored that DDR&E [Office of Director of Defense Research and Engineering] takes a far more tolerant view of "technology in hand" when it wants a contract than when it does not. While I cannot confirm this assertion from direct observation, I would not find it surprising.[5]

On the second point, it is plainly desirable to suppress the attempts of subordinates to commit a Department or the Government to certain courses of action, even when this does not preclude such attempts at higher levels. The point we must keep in mind is that outside the DoD there may be a closer identification of senior officials with the proposals made by subordinate units in their Departments. There may be less ability to control and suppress attempts to gain Departmental support. In that case the willingness of senior administrators to push for commitments at higher levels would not imply a willingness to suppress such pressures from below. Consequently, the Departments could become transmission belts to move the pressure for commitments from lower units to higher political levels.

Enough has been said to suggest that there is some discrepancy between the theory and the practice of systems analysis. While the theory is unexceptionable, the practice is subject to the temptations and distractions that characterize the real world. Actual experience in the DoD ought not be treated as synonymous with the idealized theoretical statement of the procedures. Perfection and elegance exist but rarely in the real world. When the natural impediments to implementation, which were encountered in DoD experience, are extended to the more raucous and politicized environment of the civilian programs, we should not be too surprised if the DoD experience proves to be a rather inexact model for what will actually take place.

THE ENCOUNTER WITH THE BUREAUCRACY

In predicting how systems analysis will fare as it encounters the passive resistance of the bureaucracy, one might start with E. L. Katzenbach's observation in his classic study of the Horse Cavalry that "history . . . is studded with institutions which have managed to dodge the challenge of the obvious."[6] The reference is to military history, but observers as diverse as Thomas Jefferson and C. Northcote Parkinson suggest that the dictum may also be relevant to the civilian bureaucracy. For the military, as Katzenbach indicates, the

[5] Such an attitude of easy tolerance could be disastrous in the civilian programs. As we shall see below, certain civilian agencies take quite readily to the language of systems analysis and are able to construct superficially plausible, but basically misleading analyses. Where strong political pressures are involved, there may be no inclination to scrutinize and challenge superficially plausible analyses, and consequently costly and ineffective programs may win easy acceptance.

[6] E. L. Katzenbach, Jr., "The Horse Cavalry in the Twentieth Century: A Study in Policy Response," *Public Policy*, 1958, Graduate School of Public Administration, Harvard University, p. 121.

difficulty of serious inter-war testing of the effectiveness of forces partially accounts for the longevity of obsolescent institutions. But Katzenbach wrote prior to the impact of systems analysis, and it is arguable that the new techniques have eased the problem of testing and have made it more difficult for obsolescent institutions to withstand the challenge of the obvious. In civilian activities, however, the problem is less one of devising suitable instruments for testing than of overcoming inertia and the political strength of supporting constituencies. It is rare that the obsolescence of civilian functions becomes *obvious*. The dramatic evidence of an opponent's military capability is absent. The civilian agencies make contributions to the well-being of portions of the electorate, and it is difficult to make a persuasive case that the functions or technologies in question have been superseded. Perhaps only dramatic, interest-arousing events are sufficient to persuade the public that the productive period of an institution's life is near its end.

The barriers to the effective utilization of analysis are formidable. The older agencies, anxious to preserve their traditional orientations and functions, will be reluctant to view problems in terms of "broader systems." Given the narrow perspective of most agencies, the spillovers are already large and growing. Yet, if the spillover problem is seriously attacked, it would certainly imply radical change in the well-established ways of doing business and could imply a shrinkage of budgets. By contrast, the DoD has energetically dealt with the issues of spillovers between the Services. Spillovers from the DoD to the outside are perhaps another matter, but these are relatively small —in comparison to those existing at the relevant decision-making level in the civilian agencies.

Collectively the programs of the Government are like an iceberg with only a small portion appearing above the surface. Most of the existing arrangements continue from year to year, in a brief period only relatively minor perturbations are feasible, whereas to implement analytical conclusions may require radical modernization. Thus, the difficulties are substantial. The older agencies will resist either the imparting of information or the development of analyses which would cut into their treasure troves. Unhappily, the new agencies, from which better things might be hoped, are put under unremitting pressure to produce glamorous new programs—before the necessary analysis has been performed.

These are the "obvious" obstacles, but there are others more subtle and less obvious.

First, there is the ease with which all parties may fall into describing as "end use" or as outputs what are essentially inputs. The temptation is strong to continue to describe as an output what it has always been the agency's purpose to produce. The organization of the Government for providing "outputs" has normally been on an "input" basis.[7] The Forestry Service produces forests; the Bureau of Reclamation builds dams; the Corps of Engineers creates canals and flood control projects; the Atomic Energy Commission is charged with the responsibility aggressively to push the development of nuclear power. What is needed is a broader view of power developments or water resources developments or land use—with the evaluation of the relative benefits that component programs could provide on an integrated basis. But the existing organizations are in no position, either structurally or temperamentally, to provide such an evaluation. Even where an agency is organizationally charged with a broader responsibility, confusion may remain regarding just what the "output" is. The Forestry Service is charged not only to manage the forests efficiently for production purposes, but to provide recreation for the public. However, the Forestry Service is dominated or strongly influenced by professional foresters, sometimes known as "timber beasts." Foresters certainly love trees and productive forests as such, and may view the town-dwellers who invade their forests as a nuisance to be tolerated. Consequently, the suggestion is hardly surprising that the Forest Service has overinvested in timber production and underinvested in recreation. Moreover, the Forest Service is interested in *timber* rather than in *lumber*. Yet, from the national standpoint, it is arguable that small sums invested in research and development on sawmill operations would have a much higher payoff than much larger sums invested in expanded tree production.

This leads into the second difficulty, which may be the most baffling and intractable of all. This is the orientation of research personnel in the agencies to prevailing notions of professional standards and scientific integrity. This orientation tends to overshadow a concern for the broader policy objectives of the agency. Reduced payoffs in this case reflect the highest rather than the lowest motives, but the impact on government efficiency may be the same. Researchers who respond mainly to the interests of their professional peers in universities and elsewhere may keep the research shop so pure that it is of little use to the agency in developing improved techniques or policies. This is the opposite extreme from use of research as an unimaginative and low-level tool for management, but it can occur within the same organization. A portion of the Forestry Service's research personnel are primarily concerned with maintenance of professional status among foresters located in large measure outside the Service. Perhaps a more interesting example is the Geological Survey, which played so large a role in stimulating hydrological research in this country. In any attempt to achieve a coordinated water research program in the

---

[7] The establishment of single-function agencies is both a reflection of and a promoter of what may be called "resource ideologies"—in which "water," "nuclear energy," "timber," and the like become valued for their own sake and become the measure of value.

Government, the Geological Survey would be a key element. However, Survey personnel have been reluctant to be included in any such plan for fear that the Survey would become embroiled in policy issues and lose its identification with pure science. One is not without sympathy for such an attitude. Yet, effective policy research—at an intermediate level high science and prosaic managerial research—must be carried out somewhere in the Government, if the new analytical techniques are to be exploited. The reorientation and broadening of professional attitudes is an essential ingredient for the more effective performance of many governmental functions. Yet, it is a problem that is easier to indicate than to solve. At best, many years will be required before the professional bodies are appropriately reoriented.

Third, there exist certain fundamental issues of choice, which even complete modernization of the governmental structure cannot resolve. Analysis cannot bridge the gap between irreconcilable objectives. At its best, analysis can shed some light on the costs of accepting one objective at the expense of others. But there is a danger that analysis may help to disguise fundamental choice problems as efficiency problems. Analytical techniques have been most successful in obtaining efficient mixes through the compromising of several objectives. But some objectives are not susceptible to compromise, and such objectives could easily be ignored in the simple-minded quest for efficient solutions. Consider one important form of land use, that of wilderness preservation. The now dominant approach to land use analysis is that of multiple use with utilities balanced at the margin. But, by definition, a wilderness cannot be "improved" for other purposes. The preservationist impulse is one of exclusionary use of unique ecological or geological settings. One must face the fundamental choice issue *before* one seeks efficiency, or the issue of choice will be prejudged. The difficulty in the extended discussions of improved managerial or analytical tools is that it distracts attention from these more fundamental questions which deserve study in depth. By establishing efficiency as a goal one is deflected from examining those positions in which the question is: how much "efficiency" should we sacrifice in order to preserve a particular style of life or physical environment?

These are examples of the less obvious obstacles in the path of improved-government-service-at-lowered-unit-cost through analysis. But enumeration of these problems should not be taken to imply that we should be deterred from pushing ahead with the development and the exploitation of analytical techniques. These problems will yield to persevering effort. In the long run, they may prove to be less of a barrier than the more obvious one embodied in the formidable powers of resistance represented by the existing organizational structure and division of labor within the government.

Without modernization of the bureaucratic structure, a large portion of the potential gains of the broad application of systems analysis will be foregone. The existing structure, organized in large measure around inputs and supported by clienteles with sizable political influence, may become adept at presenting drastically-suboptimized (input-oriented) or misleading analyses, which it is more convenient to accept than reject. To accept the spirit of systems analysis is exceedingly hard, but to learn the language is rather easy. There is a danger that the same old programs will be presented in new costumes. In this regard our little experience is not altogether encouraging. A number of the agencies which were early users of cost-benefit techniques have demonstrated a proficiency in presenting questionable cost-benefit analyses for questionable programs. Quantitative documentation is presented in full, but with a willing audience it appears subject to easy manipulation.

One glaring example is in water resources, for there Congress early required responsible agencies to justify proposals in terms of cost-benefit calculations. But Congress displays a willingness to be persuaded, even when the calculations are only *pro forma*. In developing the case for the Marble Canyon dam, the Bureau of Reclamation calculated costs on the assumption that the load factor would be 80 percent. More recently, in response to certain criticism, the Bureau has indicated that the dam would be used for firming power—and the estimated load factor has slipped to 50 percent. No one has insisted that the Bureau go back to recalculate its estimates of costs on the basis of the adjusted figure. When there is a willingness to be persuaded, fundamental changes in the data may be treated as minor perturbations.

Another example, happily more straightforward, is the case presented by the Atomic Energy Commission to keep in operation the three gaseous diffusion plants at Oak Ridge, Paducah, and Portsmouth —which are no longer required for military production. The Commission's argument is that there will be a strain on production facilities around 1980, and there should be "pre-production"[8] of slightly enriched uranium to provide for power reactors some 15 years in the future. Given any reasonable rate of discount, 5 percent for purposes of discussion, the Commission's argument says, in effect, that it will be unable 15 years hence to perform separative work at less than double the present cost. Since work is going forward on improving gaseous diffusion and other technologies; since it may be more efficient (given the pattern of demand) to scrap the present plants and build new ones at a later date; and since a main cost item in the gaseous diffusion process is the cost of electric power (which the

---

[8] The term "stockpiling" has acquired some unfortunate connotations and is going out of favor.

Commission repeatedly has insisted will be reduced), it would seem that one might reasonably forecast a fall in the cost of separative work rather than an increase. Nonetheless, it would not be wise to assume that the Commission will be unsuccessful in pressing its case or that the diffusion plants will, in fact, be closed down when the existing power contracts have been terminated.

These cases may indicate the shape of things to come in the future. It should come as no great surprise that Government agencies, like other entrenched interests, will fight vigorously to preserve their activities.

WHAT CAN SYSTEMS ANALYSIS ACCOMPLISH?

The number of apprehensions that have been expressed might make it appear that I am indifferent, or even opposed, to the attempt to introduce systems analysis throughout the Government. On the contrary, I am hopeful and even, within moderation, enthusiastic. This is a case of two and a half cheers for systems analysis. But before we begin to cheer we should be fully aware of what systems analysis cannot accomplish as well as what it can.

In the first place, systems analysis cannot achieve wonders: it cannot transmute the dross of politics into the fine gold of Platonic decision-making, which exists in the world of ideas rather than the world of reality. Political decisions in a democratic society can hardly be more "rational" than the public, the ultimate sovereign is willing to tolerate. All of the old elements remain: the myths and ideologies, the pressure groups, the need for accommodation and compromise, the decision made under duress. Systems analysis may modify, but it cannot extirpate these elements. Analysis is not a substitute for any form of decision-making, but for political decision-making it will be an even less effective guide than in narrower decision contexts.

As long as the public displays an insatiable appetite for "constructive new ideas" (whether or not they have been systematically designed) democratic politics will inevitably revolve around the foot-in-the-door techniques that the analysts criticize. As long as interested clienteles will support inefficient or counter-productive government activities, obsolescent functions will be preserved. Democratic politics will remain unchanged: a combination of pie in the sky and a bird in the hand. Tokenism, catch-phrases, and cultivation of various interests will remain the guideposts.

What then can systems analysis accomplish? The question is perhaps most relevant for the long run, since we must recognize the problem of transition. The qualities that make for good analysis—detachment, breadth, interdisciplinary sympathies—do not appear like manna from heaven. It will take time to train an adequate supply of personnel and to produce good analysis. One cannot put new wine into old bottles. Even though the language of cost-effectiveness analysis is adopted by the agencies, one cannot expect a miraculous change of attitudes. At best, it will be years before analysis begins to have a significant influence in many agencies.

Nonetheless, even in the shorter run analysis will serve an educative function. In ways that may go unrecognized, analysis will begin to reshape the way that agencies view their own problems. While the desire to preserve empires will not disappear, the concept of the agency's functions will undergo change. Perhaps this is the major accomplishment of analysis: it sharpens and educates the judgments and intuitions of those making decisions. Even when analytical drapings are employed consciously or unconsciously as a camouflage for prejudged issues, the intuitions will have become sharper.

In the early stages, this educative function may be reinforced by the shock effect. The need to respond to probing questions will shake up many a stale mill pond. An advantage of all new techniques of managerial decision-making is that it forces management to think through its problem anew. In an environment so readily dominated by routine, this cannot help but have a favorable impact.

The other major function of analysis is to smoke out the ideologies and the hidden interests. By introducing numbers, systems analysis serves to move arguments from the level of ideology or syllogism to the level of quantitative calculation. Of course, numbers alone are not necessarily persuasive. The ideologies and the established interests may not be rooted out, but the whole character of the discussion is changed. There will be a far greater awareness of how much it costs to support programs revolving about particular interests or resources. The public may be willing to pay the price—at least temporarily—but such a program is put on the defensive. Ideology alone will no longer suffice. In the longer run less resources are likely to be committed to the program and less will be wasted than if the cost-effectiveness calculations had not been done.

Finally, we must remember that there is a certain amount of gross wastage in the Government, which serves nobody's purpose. These situations reflect not differences of opinion, nor interests, nor ideologies, but simply the failure to perceive dominant solutions. It is in this realm that McNamara achieved his great savings within the Pentagon. With the elimination of these obvious sources of waste, analyses have had to become more subtle and recondite, but they are not necessarily as productive. Sources of gross waste may have been more common and certainly easier to get at in the Services than in the civilian programs. But within the civilian programs there remains a margin which can be squeezed out—even without the modernization of the Government's administrative structure.

THE IMPACT OF ANALYSIS ON BARGAINING IN GOVERNMENT

WILLIAM M. CAPRON

Does the current addition to Washington's alphabetic vocabulary—PPBS—signify that a real and important change is occurring in the Federal government's decision-making process? Or do the techniques, devices, and ground rules summed up in the terms for which those initials stand—Planning-Programming-Budgeting Systems—merely represent a systematic eruption which will leave unaffected the real elements—and the actual results of—the "bargaining," or decision-making process, in government? . . .

IS ANALYSIS "ANTI-POLITICAL"?

I would like to get one rather basic point out of the way at the outset: to my mind (and as far as I know, in the minds of others who helped to initiate PPB) there is no question that this system is very much a part of the political process. Indeed, if it is not—or at least does not become a political instrument—then it will be for naught. Professor Aaron Wildavsky . . . suggests that some of us at least do indeed view systems analysis as "superior" to the "ordinary" political process and antithetical to that process. I dissent from this view. Any suggestion that we are somehow degrading politics and political judgments, that we are substituting "rationality" for the "irrationality" of the political

Paper delivered before the American Political Science Association Annual Meeting, New York City, September 1966. William M. Capron, formerly with the Brookings Institution, is currently Associate Dean of the John F. Kennedy School of Government, Harvard University. Reprinted with permission of the author and the American Political Science Association.

process lies only, as far as I can tell, in the minds of those who have made this charge. I will grant that I recognize that in the dialogue of the last 18 months and, indeed, going back over the last 10–15 years, there have been some advocates of a greater use of systematic analysis of one form or another who have perhaps given the impression that they were promoting an approach to public policy issues which was in some way antithetical to politics and to "political" decision-making. Perhaps some analysts have felt that this was what they were up to. But it seems to me a complete misunderstanding of the basic decision-making structure of our system of government and the role of the Executive, the Congress, interest groups, and the public at large to view the greater reliance on more formal analysis of policy issues and alternatives as in some sense basically (and necessarily?) changing the underlying process, relationships, and roles which are embedded in our system and have been throughout our history.

While accepting PPB as a part of the political process in this country, it seems to me perfectly consistent for me to go on to suggest that in my view, to the extent that this system is in fact accepted and becomes a fully working part of the budgetary and program decision-making process, it must certainly have a significant impact on that process. It may be perfectly true, as has been suggested, that a broad range of decisions will not be affected no matter how skillful and splendid the analysis provided by the Executive Branch: the pork barrel will still offer a rich and tempting diet of pork (though this "pork" is usually poured concrete) and we may still have Cross-Florida barge canals and Arkansas River projects—and even perhaps dams on the Colorado—even if we substantially improve the quality and sophistication of the "cost-benefit analysis" applied to evaluating such proposals.

THREE IMPACTS OF ANALYSIS

Accepting this point, I would still assert three claims for the potential of the wider use of systematic analysis in government:

—the *dialogue* between the parties involved (the bureaus, the departments, the Executive Office of the President, the Congress, the private interest groups and "constituencies") will be conducted differently and will certainly be "impacted" by PPB

—*some* decisions will be different from what they otherwise would be without this approach

—and *some* of these decisions will be *better* than they would have been absent the use of more formalized analysis.

Of these three claims, the second is certainly more difficult to substantiate than the first, and the third incomparably more difficult to substantiate than the first or second. Indeed, until the art and science of political science and economics (and philosophy?) have advanced beyond their present stage of very rudimentary development, the last statement can only, in the final analysis, be defended as an individual value judgment and cannot in any meaningful sense be "substantiated."

I have used and will continue to use the term "budget process" and "budget decision" as a short-hand to encompass not only the dollars and cents decisions but also the *program* decisions and *policy* decisions which are affected by and reflected through the budgetary process. This is a usage which seems to me increasingly appropriate in Washington at least since 1961, since the Bureau of the Budget has become the focal point, as far as the Presidency is concerned, for the organization of the President's legislative program, a key part of which is the Budget itself. (As I recall my days (and nights) as Assistant Director of the Bureau of the budget, a very large fraction of my time was involved in dealing with policy and program issues which had only a peripheral connection and relation to expenditures in a quantitative sense.)

I am more than willing to adopt the basic framework and language to which Professor Lindblom first introduced me in order to consider the role of analysis and its impact in government decision-making. The Lindblom language is reflected, of course, in the title of this paper: "bargaining." And having for a while played a role in what can usefully be considered a bargaining process, I find this comfortable and relevant as a framework for considering the role of analysis. In this framework, I suppose the key question can be put as follows: is the bargaining *process* and/or the result of the "bargain" significantly affected if one or more of the "players" in the bargaining process employs systematic, explicit analyses of one variety or another? As I have already indicated, my tentative answer is "yes" to this question and, indeed, "yes" to both the *process* and *result* aspects of the question. Does this mean that judgment, intuition and "hunch" are downgraded or eliminated in the decision-making or bargaining process? To ask the question I think is to answer it, and this for two reasons. In the first place, I would be a poor advocate for the greater and greater use of analysis, and a poor supporter of efforts to expand the areas in which we develop a facility in using various analytic tools and an increase in the sophistication and breadth and reach of analysis, if I were to argue that analysis allows us to bring a kind of "neutral rationality" to government decisions so that we can turn to the computer to grind out the answers to policy issues untouched by human hands—or minds. I would be a poor advocate to try and argue this point because it is trivially easy to demonstrate it is a point with feet of clay—indeed, it is made of clay up to its armpits!

THE HIERARCHY OF DECISIONS AND OF ANALYTIC FORMS: COST-EFFECTIVENESS, COST-BENEFIT, SYSTEMS ANALYSIS

It is perhaps appropriate to say a word about terms like "systems analysis" and "cost-effectiveness" and "cost-benefit analysis." There is I think growing consensus on the use of these terms, though still a good deal of fuzziness in individual cases as to how a particular kind of analysis should be properly denominated. One convenient way of looking at the various art forms which go under the generic heading of "analysis" in this context is to recognize that we have a hierarchy of decisions which we can view either from the "top" or from the "bottom." Starting from the top, we have the very basic and broadest policy issues and policy choices. Should our marginal tax dollar be devoted to education or to transportation or to health or to an increase in the defense budget? Should a broad new Federal program be instituted not only to land a man on the moon but to attempt to start a whole civilization there—or perhaps on Mars? Questions at this pinnacle of the decision hierarchy may be (and, I would argue, should be) profoundly affected by the results of analyses at lower levels in this decision hierarchy but are not themselves the subject of useful formal and systematic analysis—at least at this stage. There are two reasons for this. First, the awesome complexity of comparing such alternatives, each with so many sweeping implications and ramifications for our society, is well beyond our capacity, given the status of the analytic art and the sciences this art employs, and I suspect this will be the case for a long, long time to come. Second, and more fundamental, these choices between basic and broad alternative public purposes and their rank order and weight depend so fundamentally on basic and illusive value judgments which (absent an explicit social welfare function) must be the personal judgment of each of us. As we move down the decision hierarchy, analysis becomes more manageable and also more directly influential and significant in the choices that are made. For example, once we accept, at least provisionally, the notion that the Federal government should give support to elementary and secondary education, the analyst can then—still at a rather high level of suboptimization—lay out alternatives for those who must make these decisions.[1] However, it is for this kind of choice that the

---

[1] The phrase "those who make these decisions" and are potential customers of the analyst's output include, in the case of education (in ascending order), the Commissioner of Education, the Secretary of Health, Education, and Welfare, the President (rather, "the Presidency" which includes his key advisers, especially the Director of the Bureau of the Budget), and the relevant subcommittees and committees of the Congress, and finally the House and Senate. There are four relevant subcommittees and committees, the authorizing commit-

impact of analysis on bargaining becomes rather easy to identify, namely, the way the alternatives are put and the explicit measures which are developed may be very much affected by the analysis—and the analyst (e.g., the choice between alternative techniques and levels of support to achieve "improvement in elementary and secondary education").

Analysis can only be said to "make decisions" at the very lowest level of suboptimization. Once an appropriation has been passed by the Congress and where a program's purposes are reasonably clear-cut and quantifiable, the choice of particular techniques to implement these programs may be made completely (or at least heavily controlled) by the results of one form of "analysis" or another. A clear-cut (though some may argue trivial) example is the job of air traffic control by the FAA. While human judgment still plays a significant role in the day-to-day, hour-to-hour, and minute-to-minute decisions of the air traffic controller, he relies more and more on automatic decision-making generated by various types of computerized and electronic gear and "analysis." And systems in the works may largely eliminate the human decision altogether. However, once one goes above this level—and in some programs one never gets down to this level— judgment plays a role and, as one moves up the hierarchy, judgment plays a more and more important role. At the middle and higher reaches, indeed, the judgment of the analyst is crucial, because at this level of "systems analysis" (or cost-benefit, or cost effectiveness), objectives are only given to the analyst in the vaguest form and, since typically more than one objective is involved, the analyst is required to make many judgments as to the way in which the multiple objectives —typically competing objectives (at least at the margin)—are to be melded and molded into the analysis. It has been suggested that some of the most significant efforts in systems analysis have actually been more important in the discovery and specification of *objectives* than they have been in elucidating alternative *means* of reaching objectives.

REASONS FOR INTRODUCING PPBS

In assessing the potential effect of government-wide use of systematic analysis, it is instructive to examine the motives of those who have played key roles in pushing the Establishment in this direction. I know from my own experience that one of the principal factors which

---

tees and the appropriating committees. To make the list complete, I should include a wide variety of interest groups such as the NEA, perhaps state school superintendents, major school superintendents, PTA groups, and so forth and so on at great length.

motivated people in the Budget Bureau to insist on a greater use of analysis has been the fact that, typically, both program and budget recommendations coming to the President from the Departments and agencies have not contained any alternatives and have denied the President the option of making meaningful choices. The options have been screened out before the President has had an opportunity to choose among them. This great failure is frustrating to the Budget Bureau and to the President. Moreover, not only is the typical budget request as it comes forward to the Budget Bureau lacking in alternatives, but there is not even available to the Budget Director and the President he advises the kind of information which allows one to judge the effect on a given program of either a decrease or an increase in the funding level finally recommended to the Congress. The result of this is that the judgment of Budget Bureau staff is often superimposed on the judgment of those presumably much more knowledgable about the program. And the Budget Bureau inevitably acts, at least sometimes, in a very arbitrary fashion—arbitrary because those required, say, to cut X-hundred million dollars from a given program area have nothing before them to indicate the impact of that cut, or the impact of the manner in which they allocate that cut among various program elements. Equally significant to some of us has been the conviction that the application of systematic analysis to programs all across the board will not only encourage the examination of alternative ways of meeting program objectives, but will actually lead to the invention of new techniques for achieving public purposes. This, indeed, is the hallmark of a really good systems analysis, namely, that quite new ways of looking at problems have led in turn to the development of quite new *and better* ways of meeting problems.

IS PPB REVOLUTIONARY?

Having mentioned some of the reasons lying behind the move to PPB, I would emphasize that I, at least, do not regard PPB and, more particularly, the emphasis on systematic analysis in the Federal establishment as really revolutionary. The whole system seems to me to be a quite natural *evolution* and the emphasis on analysis, while intense and ubiquitous, is, after all, neither wholly new nor revolutionary. Some sectors of Federal activity have for many, many years been subjected to systematic and regular procedures of analysis. In fact, one of the difficulties in getting enthusiastic support for this new emphasis on analysis is the deservedly bad repute in which some types of analysis have come to be held. The outstanding candidate for this role, in my view, is water resource cost-benefit analysis where, typically, the quality of analysis has been mediocre and the "guidance" to policy has been at best imperfect and irrelevant, at worst plain wrong. The fact that bad analysis can be done and the fact, moreover, that the water resource field is replete with examples of the manner in which the analyst can twist his assumptions to get the politically desired result is a powerful argument indeed for those skeptical of this whole effort. My response to this skepticism is the obvious one, namely, that because an approach and set of techniques have been abused in the past does not mean inevitably that they must be.

What can be done about "cheating" by the analysts who are directed to "make the case" for the projects and program the agency (and its constituency) have already decided they want? This will happen—witness the questionable assumptions (often hidden) in water-resource cost-benefit analysis. How can the abuse of analysis be handled? For one thing, elements in the organizational structure at echelons above the level at which the analysis is performed as well as "competing" agencies at the same echelon (especially, it is hoped, the Cabinet officer in whose department the program being analyzed is located) should insist that the analyst:

make *assumptions explicit*

carry out analysis with *alternative assumptions*

conduct *sensitivity analyses*

Occasionally (perhaps on a sampling basis), the analyses will have to be redone independently to make sure the results are not biased by key hidden assumptions, quirks in the methodology, etc.

THE ROLE OF THE BUREAU OF THE BUDGET

The role of the Bureau of the Budget deserves a special word in this context. It is, of course, just another player in the bargaining process of Federal budget decision-making, but the Bureau, at least at its best, performs as the President's agent, which means that it takes a Presidential view of the decisions that come before it. Now, there is no question that the Presidential view is a very political view. But it is a political view which has by its nature a breadth which is lacking in almost any other player in the bargaining process: the bureau and department, the Congress (and particularly the Congressional Committee) and all the private interest groups. The very fact that the President must balance conflicting interests for his own political purposes in a sense places a requirement for a more systematic and analytic approach than is typical when one speaks as an advocate of a particular agency or interest group point of view. The fact that many values and the interests of many elements in the community must be taken into account in coming to final Presidential decisions lends added value to the use of an articulated systematic approach. As the President's major staff arm on program and budget matters, the Bureau sometimes likes to think of itself as, and to play the role of, "the taxpayers' counsel" at the government bargaining table. In particular, it is at the Budget Bureau level that the competition among major program areas comes to a head. At least one force for resisting the seemingly insatiable appetite for funds on the part of the advocates of many program areas is a simple fact which the Bureau and the President are required to recognize: if Program A gets more funds, other programs will get less. This is a fact of budgetary life, at least in the short run.

DOES PPB REQUIRE CENTRALIZATION?

This leads me to comment briefly on the organizational implications of PPB and to discuss more specifically the suggestion which has been strongly urged by Wildavsky (and less publicly by many in Washington) that PPB requires a significant increase in the *centralization* of the whole decision-making process. Briefly, this seems to me to be a complete misreading of PPB. Potentially, at least, PPB will permit, if properly implemented, a rationalization of the centralization-decentralization relationships from the President to the Cabinet officer and major agency head to the bureau and division level and down to the suborganization units which go to make up the Federal hierarchy. As one moves up the hierarchy, if the inputs called for in the PPB system are adequately developed, it would be possible for the decision-maker at any level to make the choices among the elements for which he has responsibility, but to a large extent to devolve on the decision-makers below him responsible for each one of these elements the choices *within* each of these elements. In the present system, unhappily, the cabinet officer is almost compelled (if he wishes to really manage his department and to discharge the responsibility which is nominally his) to "second guess" those way down the line in his agency. Likewise, as I suggested above, the Bureau of the Budget, because of the paucity of relevant information available to it under the pre-PPB system for Presidential budget decision-making, is frequently compelled to involve itself in detailed decisions which it is inherently less capable of comprehending and properly deciding than those more directly involved in the implementation and execution of the program. It seems to me, for example, an excessive centralization when the Budget Director makes decisions with regard to the details of the staffing of regional offices of a given Federal agency; and yet if he has no information before him which really indicates what that agency and what its individual offices are up to and yet is constrained to keep some rein on expenditure levels, he is almost compelled to make rather arbitrary (and, I am sure in some instances, capricious and unfortunate) decisions. In short, the present system seems to me to lead to a pernicious and promiscuous kind of centralization all the way up the line, and it is this perverse centralization in the present system which hopefully at least PPB will go some way to correcting. PPBS, when developed, can be a powerful force for a rationalization of the Federal decision structure and for *decentralization.*

PPB AND REORGANIZATION

Wildavsky and others who have commented in the same vein are certainly right, it seems to me, in suggesting that the development of a sensible program structure does contain within it significant reorganization implications for the Federal establishment—even though not necessarily reorganization leading to greater centralization. Just to cite one example: if there had not already been a strong move to establish a Department of Transportation, I suspect that two or three years with PPBS would have provided the President and his chief advisors with a strong, if not compelling, reason for moving to establish such a department. No matter what the program structure, however, there will continue to be, as there is in any budgeting system, the need for the central authority—the Presidency—to pay particular attention to what in today's jargon are identified as the significant "interfaces" among various major program categories. There is no question that the program budget, insofar as possible, should be structured so that the program categories, subcategories, and program elements make sense from a *program* standpoint. And for obvious reasons, a program budgeting system can operate much more effectively to the extent that the *organizational* structure corresponds more or less to the program structure. Since our present organizational structure reflects a whole series of "accidents of history," I agree with the suggestion that, over time at least, reorganizations will be, if not compelled, at least strongly encouraged by the development of a sensible program structure. But, I repeat, I see no reason to expect greater centralization to result.

Some of the inadequacies in the initial attempts to develop program budgets in the last several months have unquestionably resulted from the fact that present *organizational* structure in some areas has little relation to a sensible view of *program* structure. Since PPB must be viewed primarily as a tool and technique for improving Presidential budget decision-making and not primarily as a tool for guiding budget implementation (e.g., the actual expenditure of funds once appropriated by the Congress), it is very important, in my opinion, that the rationalization of the program budget be guided primarily by the development of sensible and viable program categories and components of those categories and that the demands of the organizational structure as it presently exists play a distinctly secondary role. I would add that in practice I recognize that compromises must be made to accommodate the existing organizational structure, at least until the necessary reorganizational moves have been made. One must recognize that even if we go to a structure which is more highly centralized than at present, there will always be difficult choices to be made as to where to place particular program sub-categories and program elements since in at least some significant instances a case can be made that a given program belongs in two or more places in the overall structure. Finally, it would be foolish to ignore the fact that we are not starting from scratch, that important ties, loyalties and the strongly held views of groups represented at the bargaining table are going to leave us—no matter how hard we push in the direction that I'm suggesting—with some (to say the least) rather peculiar alignments of program and organization. This, though, is yet another instance which supports my basic thesis, namely, that the PPBS effort is bound to have an effect on the bargaining process and on its outcome, even though it will not in every instance control that outcome. Relationships which are now suppressed or ignored will be put on the bargaining table and may force people to recognize interrelationships (or, if you like, "interfaces") which up until now have conveniently been forgotten.

THE ROOT VS. THE BRANCH: LINDBLOM'S VIEW AND ANALYSIS

Another of Professor Lindblom's contributions to the discussion of government decision-making can be read to reject the notion that systems analysis can be of much use, except perhaps in very special cases. In "The Science of 'Muddling Through,'" he contrasts two approaches to public policy decision-making. One he identifies as the "rational-comprehensive" or root method; the other as the "successive limited comparisons" or branch approach. While recognizing and accepting many of the difficulties with the former (rational comprehensive) approach and further recognizing that more often than not the "successive limited comparisons" approach is what we observe in practice, it does not seem to me that an emphasis on articulate systematic analysis is inconsistent with Lindblom's preference for the successive limited comparisons approach, which he considers to be the more realistic and reasonable of the two methods. He points, for example, to the difficulty in starting out with a clearly articulated statement of the objectives before one begins empirical analysis. As I have indicated above, one of the hallmarks of good systems analysis as it has come to be practiced is that simultaneously with a definition and testing of alternative means is the refinement and specification of objectives. Furthermore, the *comprehensiveness* of any given systems analysis will depend on the ingenuity of the analyst, the kind of data available to him, and the amount of resources that are at his command in undertaking the analysis. I would urge even if Lindblom's preferred approach—successive limited comparison—is selected as appropriate to the case in hand, that it should be undertaken *systematically* with assumptions clearly specified. This is particularly necessary since in this approach, as he points out, many of the interrelationships with other parts of the system are ignored. It is important that those who will use the results of the "analysis" have called to their attention the limited nature of the analysis so that the limited, partial and incomplete nature of the argument will be understood. I am not so concerned with "comprehensiveness" or the lack thereof, but rather with the use of a very casual and inarticulate "analysis" in place of a specific, "spelled-out" analysis. The "consumer" of the results should be in a position to judge whether or not the particular analysis is in fact useful to him—whether he wants to be guided, in whole or in part, by the results of that "analysis."

Another idea associated with Lindblom's name and closely related to the above is his emphasis on "incrementalism" in public policy decision-making. Again, I would insist that this is *not* necessarily inconsistent with the philosophy underlying PPB. Most analyses will, indeed, be at the middle range of the decision hierarchy and will focus on relatively marginal changes in existing programs. However, there are occasions when it is appropriate to attempt a more ambitious analysis, an analysis which moves toward the end of the spectrum identified by Lindblom as the "rational-comprehensive" method. The use of a more sweeping, broader analysis (in the terms employed by some, "systems analysis" instead of "cost-benefit" or "cost-effectiveness" analysis) will be appropriate in at least two situations: first, where whole new program areas are being considered, that is, where the President, for example, is contemplating the initiation of Federal activity in an area in which the Federal government has not before performed. Very often in this situation there will be a number of options open to the President. It may very well be, and indeed in general I would urge that it is ordinarily the desirable strategy, that the first actual program moves be small and that experimentation characterize the initial efforts in a new area, since I fully share with Professor Lindblom and others skepticism at our ability through analysis to develop a very sure-footed understanding of the effect of government activity in an area where it has not been tried. This is so particularly because relationships are difficult to determine *a priori* in many instances and that in this situation we are largely working by analogy of one sort or another and have little or no directly applicable empirical evidence upon which to draw. However, it is in these instances of really new undertakings where a system-analytic approach, in the hands of a skilled analyst, often can lead us to be very inventive in developing new approaches and new techniques. The second area where a fairly broad sweep in a systems analysis is appropriate—where incrementalism won't do, at least as far as the analysis goes—arises where we have become seriously dissatisfied with the effectiveness of an existing program and where we wish to undertake major redirection and revision of a given Federal activity.

THE VALUE OF OBSCURITY ON OBJECTIVES

I must refer to one other theme which is frequently emphasized by the skeptics,[2] namely, the value in many areas of government activity in *not* being explicit about objectives. Representatives of this view have pointed out that at least in some instances agreement on specific programs is possible, even though the interests of various affected groups in the program may be not only quite different but, in terms of their overall value schemes, antithetical. From this one *might* draw the inference that an attempt at articulating an analysis which identifies objectives will actually make agreement on programs and on budgets *more* difficult than reliance on implicit reasoning and bargaining to arrive at the program's contours and level. It is, moreover, pointed out that the implicit "analysis" in a bargaining system with various interests and values "taken care of" by the representation of these interests and values by one or more players at the bargaining table is a good and workable system. I would agree that, by and large, the system has been pretty good and pretty workable and I further agree that one can undoubtedly identify specific cases (especially where feelings run high) which might be put back rather than forward by an attempt to subject the program to an explicit analysis— or at least to make that analysis public. (But the Executive Branch can develop its position based on analysis without injecting analysis into public debate.) However, I am not persuaded by this view as a regular and basic guide. For one thing the fact that there are different interests and different values concerned with particular programs does not mean that systematic analysis will necessarily make agreement on specific program decisions and specific budget decisions impossible. It is possible, for example, to reflect explicitly the degree and extent to which different objectives or values will be realized under different alternative approaches and different levels in a given program area. Thus, the interested parties will be able to identify the extent to which *their* own particular interests—their own particular weighing of the outcomes—will be achieved. Furthermore, as I indicated at the outset, PPBS does *not* mean a basic nor drastic alteration in the bargaining

[2] I had intended to identify this group as the "Yale School" but knowledgeable friends in political science warned me that this would be unfair to some at or from New Haven and also, perhaps, unclear.

system relationships. Nor does it signify the non-representation of all the present players in the game.

In brief, while I find much that is useful and insightful in the "skeptics" view of the governmental process, I think I can do so and still maintain a faith in the value and efficacy in an increased reliance on systematic analysis as an aid in making public policy choices.

PPB AND CONGRESS

Turning to another topic, it is frequently asked what will be the effect of PPBS on the relations between the Executive Branch and the Congress and on the authorizing and appropriating process within the Congress? I do not have the background or expertise to discuss this question with any kind of completeness—and I can certainly not speak from the Congressional point of view. However, there are several points that should be understood. In the first place, let me reiterate a point made above: PPBS was designed and is being pushed as a technique or set of techniques which will improve the *Presidential* budget decision process. The President, having made his decisions, can forward his recommendations to the Congress in a variety of forms. It is worth emphasizing that in any case the *implementation* of the President's budget once the Congress has authorized and appropriated funds requires expression of these budgetary decisions in the familiar "object class," input-oriented, and organizational-unit oriented terms of the traditional budget. There is no special difficulty or extra burden placed on the Executive Branch in translating the results of the program budget and the decisions reflected therein to the Congress in the familiar terms which they seem, at least up until now, to prefer. Thus, I see no particular technical difficulty in acceding to the apparent will of Congress that the familiar budget structure be maintained with regard to their deliberations.

There is, however, one central and sensitive point involved in the implications of PPB for Congressional-Executive relations: a key element in the new system is its emphasis on *multi-year* programming and budgeting. The standard pattern is that each program be developed in terms of a five-year program plan and that this be translated into a five-year financial plan. It has been suggested that this is in a sense impossible for a President to live with since he does not wish "to give up his options" (to use a phrase President Johnson has made familiar)—that he does not wish to tie his hands earlier than he must with regard to the future. The President need only make recommendations to the Congress with regard to the *next* year's appropriation levels, plus recommendations with regard to the new programs (or amendments to old programs) on which he is *now* (in the current session) requesting action by the Congress. Even though the President decides not to submit formally the five-year program and financial plans to the Congress, there is little question, given the facts of life in Washington, that the existence of these plans will not only be well known but that they will, one way or another—above or below the table—come into the hands of the Congress. I recognize that there is a certain amount of risk for the President in this situation. Only by the repeated and steadfast reiteration of the fact that the plans for each program beyond the next budget year—the year for which he must make specific recommendations—are only tentative and do *not* represent any kind of Presidential determination or commitment, can he avoid creating the impression that he is committed for the future. And even if the President does this, he will occasionally and inevitably be embarrassed—but Presidents have been embarrassed by "commitments" for the future in the past, and have managed to survive this embarrassment. One way of minimizing the danger of an apparent premature commitment to funding levels and program development is to have program and financial plans (beyond the current and next budget year) presented in terms of two or more alternative funding and activity levels. It is worth noting that Secretary McNamara for the last several years has discussed the defense five-year program plan and force structure with the relevant committees of the Congress and has not been embarrassed especially that these plans have been revised from year to year. While the Secretary's relations with Senator McClellan, Congressman Rivers and other key figures on the Hill have not always been completely placid, it is not at all clear that his difficulties have been due to PPB!

My own forecast, for whatever it is worth, with regard to Congressional attitudes toward PPBS is that over the next several years in at least some areas, the Congressional committees (both substantive and appropriation) will come to discuss administration recommendations in terms of the dialogue of PPBS. In other words, I think that it will not only affect the bargaining *within* the Executive Branch (e.g., among the agencies and between the President and the agencies), but that it will also directly enter the bargaining dialogue between the Administration and the relevant focal points in the Congress—and the private constituencies. Indeed, already there are moves afoot on the Hill to develop staffing available to, and responsible to, the Congress to review systems analyses, program budgets and the like. Just as the Budget Bureau (at least on a sampling basis) must carefully review the various analyses performed within the agencies, so I think—even though it will make some of my former colleagues and associates very uncomfortable—it is desirable that on a sampling basis the Congress have available to it the necessary expertise to review in depth and very carefully the kinds of analyses being performed in the Executive Branch. Indeed, I see nothing inappropriate with the Congress itself initiating analyses of various programs, examining various alternative ways of accomplishing program purposes, and evaluating the effectiveness of existing undertakings.

DOES PPB MATTER: THE McNAMARA CASE STUDY

It would be too much to ask that I end this discussion without calling your attention to the best demonstration of many of the points that I have suggested above and, most importantly, the fact that an increasing reliance on systems analysis throughout the Federal establishment will indeed have a significant effect on the bargaining process and on the results of that process. This "evidence for the prosecution" —or rather, for the defense, since this is the American Political Science Association—is, of course, provided by the McNamara years in the Pentagon. While Wildavsky and others have questioned to what extent the use of a PPBS system has *really* had much effect and have pointed out that no one within the Establishment has yet laid out the case that this, in fact, has occurred, I find it hard to understand how even the most casual observer, dependent only on the *New York Times* as his information source, can question that at least the dialogue has been profoundly affected, if not the result. In the nature of the case, of course, it is impossible to establish in any irrefutable fashion that the results of the decision-making process have been affected by changes in that process since we are never able to develop an acceptable and rigorous test of the question—no specific decision is ever reached under the "pre" and "post" McNamara systems. The very fact that the Services have developed the capacity for performing very sophisticated systems analyses (perhaps in self-defense against the whiz-kid onslaught from on high) is certainly evidence of the impact which analysis has had on the bargaining process.

Has systems analysis within the defense decision area not only affected the dialogue in which the bargaining has been conducted between the Secretary and the Services (and particularly between the Secretary and the Joint Chiefs) but also affected the actual decisions which have been made? There is at least some evidence available to the outsider which strongly suggests that certain crucial decisions made . . . by Mr. McNamara and approved by the President have indeed been directly and even dominantly affected by the analysis. The most important of these analyses have been performed under the direction of Alain Enthoven. . . . It is my impression, for example, that the airlift-sealift decisions which have been made in the last year or two have been strongly influenced by systems analysis results. The decision to develop and acquire the C-5—a large logistics carrier—and the characteristics of that carrier were strongly influenced by analytic results produced in the last few years. The composition of the airlift-sealift forces—the "mix" of systems—has likewise been much influenced, if not dictated, by the analyses which have been performed both in the Office of the Secretary and by the Air Force and the Navy. And the still-disputed TFX decision was, from all indications, not unaffected by systems analysis.

Furthermore, I would offer in evidence the brief but incisive description of the development and implementation of PPB in the Defense Department in the period beginning in 1961 provided by Charles Hitch. . . . It is clear that Mr. Hitch is anything but an unbiased witness. It is furthermore clear that this book does not pretend to be the kind of systematic "systems analysis" of the impact of systems analysis which apparently is called for by skeptics like Wildavsky. Yet, a reading of this work, making all the allowances for the undoubted prejudice with which Hitch understandably addresses this subject, offers a rather impressive dossier with regard to the radical changes in the dialogue, and perhaps in the quality and nature of the defense decisions taken in the period since 1961.

A final note on the McNamara revolution: While this phenomenon has been tied closely to the Secretary as an individual and has been in large measure a personal triumph, I am convinced that the Mc-Namara-Hitch system will have a major impact on Defense decision-making for years to come. No successor could undo all McNamara has wrought—even if he wished to—and even if his successor is a person of the same rare quality.

WILL IT WORK ACROSS THE POTOMAC?

Will the same impact emerge—if we are willing to accept at least some impact from systems analysis on the defense scene in the last few years—over the coming five years on the domestic side as a result of President Johnson's dramatic memorandum of last August 25 announcing his determination to develop and apply PPB on a government-wide basis? It is too soon to tell and one would be foolish to make any kind of a flat forecast. We can perhaps, however, make some conjectural predictions. It is not too bold to suggest that we can be sure that the performance across programs will be very uneven. Indeed, within the defense decision-making arena itself, the impact of the systems analytic approach and the development of a program budget system has been uneven. Some problems and some program. areas are more amenable to this approach, given the present state of our understanding and knowledge, than are others. And the same is obviously true on the domestic side of Federal activity. Furthermore, the aggressive and effective application of this new approach certainly depends on a number of factors. To cite just a few:

The viewpoint of the key players in the game. It is certainly clear, no matter how strong and insistent the exhortation from the President and the Budget Director, that without the whole-hearted understanding and support of the Cabinet and independent agency heads the effect of PPB will be marginal. Certainly the major, or at least, a major reason for the effectiveness of PPB in the Defense context has been that the Secretary has grasped this (as Wildavsky himself has noted) as the major management tool by which he has "conquered" the Services and made himself the master of the Defense Department in a way far exceeding the degree to which any previous Secretary of Defense has ever exerted his authority and run his own show.

The effectiveness of the bureaucracy in alliance with its constituent groups and their representatives in Congress in resisting the effective implementation of PPB. There is little doubt on the part of those who have been in Washington in the last few months that there are certain loci of strong and effective resistance to changing the whole budgetary and program decision process. The success of this resistance will be very much dependent on the *de facto* control which the Presidency has over the activities in question and over the key personnel in the bureaucracy responsible for those activities. One can be sure that there will be certain program areas where resistance will continue to be more or less effective in blunting the attempt to make anything more than a pro-forma modification in the actual decision-making process and where only the most superficial and irrelevant attempts at analysis will be undertaken. I would suggest that this is not a peculiar characteristic of PPBS or systems analysis. Any attempt to modify significantly the rules of the bargaining game will be strongly resisted by at least some elements of a bureaucracy as large and varied and, in some cases, as well entrenched as the Federal bureaucracy. As a first approximation, one can say that those who find the present arrangements comfortable and effective from their own self-interest and special interest view-point will resist changes of any kind, since change introduces uncertainty. The results of change for the individual bureaucrat, the individual agency, the individual Congressman and committee, and the individual special interest group may turn out to be good. They may also turn out to be bad. If things are reasonably satisfactory and comfortable now, the question facing these people and institutions is: "Why go along with attempts to rock the boat?" As an aside, I might add that one strong reason for supporting PPB lies precisely here: Quite apart from the intrinsic potential value of this new system should it be effectively implemented—or, put differently, even if it is not effectively implemented—there is real value in a periodic shake-up of the key centers in the Federal nervous system. And certainly if it has accomplished nothing else,

PPB has already done this. It has forced people to rethink their own roles, the agency's roles; it is raising questions and providing a context in the bargaining framework in which questions can be raised which have largely been ignored in the past. All of this I submit is healthy and good as long, of course, as the boat-rocking is not too severe as to do more than ship a little water—we don't, after all, want to swamp the ship of State, just keep it responsive to changes in the currents, tides, and winds of government activity.

An assessment of the impact of analysis on bargaining in government must at this juncture be cautious and conjectural. I have tried to refrain from "overselling" or expressing wild optimism that the increased emphasis on analysis—and PPB *in toto*—will transform the quality of Federal decision and vastly improve public policy. On the other hand, I have indicated that I cannot share the view of those political scientists and old-hand Washington bureaucrats who think that PPBS is yet another passing fancy which will have no noticeable impact on anything—and will shortly fade away. Some representatives of this skeptical group seem to feel, in the absence of a violent revision in our basic governmental structure and process, that a modification as modest as PPB can have no impact. They appear to view the whole Federal decision process as involving "who is in what job and where is the real power" and "what will Mr. A do for Mr. B so that Mr. B will support A's pet project" and "what's in it for me, Jack?" This is not only a possible but sometimes useful way of looking at government. But viewed as the totality of the governmental process it is, I submit, badly misleading and incomplete. Even the most venal parochial party to governmental bargaining can be forced to take account of cogent systematic analysis—as long as some others at the bargaining table insist on making it part of the dialogue. My bet is that PPB (and its emphasis on analysis in particular) will have a far greater impact than the skeptics are ready to admit.

COMMENTARY

The purpose of this chapter is to probe to the value center of systematic analysis, and a logical starting point is Wildavsky's composite image of the program analyst as a political imperialist with an extreme centralizing bias toward total efficiency. Stripped of its histrionics, the Wildavsky article does provide an excellent device for developing a value profile of the rationalists along three dimensions.

First, the rationalist is obviously not a political animal in the bargaining-incremental tradition. The anti-politics image of the rationalist projected by Wildavsky may even be accurate to the extent that "politics"—i.e., the incremental allocation of limited resources on the basis of bargained agreements among professional political actors—is considered neither as efficient nor as effective as program budgeting in meeting the needs and wants of the body politic. But to be anti-politics is not necessarily the same as being anti-political, and if the comments of Hitch, McKean, Enthoven, Capron, and Schlesinger can be taken as a guide, PPB and systems analysis are not divorced from the normal political process. The statement by Melvin Anshen, accurately quoted by Wildavsky, is foolish and offensive to anyone who understands the intricacies of organizational behavior. There are no neutral tools in administration, public or private, and if PPB knows no politics, it will learn in short order if it is to survive. The truth of the matter is that most responsible proponents of PPB who have been directly and officially involved in the executive decision-making process agree that PPB is not a neutral, apolitical instrument.

Capron, a former Assistant Budget Director, states at the outset of his paper that PPB is very much a part of the political process.

Schlesinger, an Assistant Budget Director under President Nixon, could hardly make his sense of political realism shine through any brighter. McKean, Hitch, Enthoven—all former Defense Department officials under McNamara—recognize without qualification that the ultimate decision-making responsibility must be assigned to the top-level political executives. In short, no one would disagree with Wildavsky that political questions demand political answers. Proponents of PPB would simply add that the search for these answers might be advanced and improved through systematic and rigorous analysis. However, analytical answers or solutions must be translated into a political context, and this, quite properly, is a function of the political official, not the systems analyst.

Second, the political imperialism of the rationalists is discernible when their extreme centralizing bias is examined, but even here the impression which emerges is somewhat less dramatic than that which Wildavsky attempts to convey. For instance, it is difficult to find any advocate of program budgeting who has made a concerted effort to hide the fact that PPB is designed to alter the traditionally fragmented and decentralized decision structure of the executive branch. PPB requires centralized coordination to be effective, and this, in turn, demands a greater degree of centralized authority. Capron notes that the effectiveness of PPB will depend upon the extent to which the President has *de facto* control over the programs and over the key bureaucratic officials who are responsible for the implementation of these programs. Since the goal of PPB is the integration of program outputs and policy objectives, and since it is not likely that such integration will bloom forth spontaneously, control and coordination must be centralized.

Furthermore, it should be noted that centralization cannot be referred to as intrinsically good or bad. It is a management device that can be applied in a variety of ways. The manner in which it is applied may be good or bad—i.e., effective or ineffective, functional or dysfunctional—but the device itself cannot have a value ascribed to it. Therefore, to claim that the rationalists reveal an extreme centralizing bias is simply to say that given the type of decision-making structure these individuals seek to employ, centralized coordination and authority is more effective in attaining their goals than a decentralized pattern. Given the nature of program budgeting this is not a bias—it is an empirical fact. Thus, to attribute to the rationalists a value motive (with an unfavorable connotation, no less) is unwarranted.

Power and authority are clearly centralized in the PPB context, but it is Capron who advances the seemingly ironical notion that if PPB is correctly and effectively carried out, the initial centralized structure will ultimately yield a highly productive (and, by implication, a more equitable) decentralized decision-making structure. Or, as Paul Appleby said many years ago, "you have to centralize before you can decentralize." Indeed, one of the features of the bargaining-incremental system which Capron hopes PPB can correct is the almost absolute centralization of arbitrary and capricious authority in the Bureau of the Budget.

The third thrust of Wildavsky's critique is that PPB represents the culmination of the move toward "total efficiency." "Note what has happened," Wildavsky warns. "First pure efficiency was converted to mixed efficiency. Then limited efficiency became unlimited." Unlimited or total efficiency, as defined by Wildavsky, is evidenced when the structure of the political system is altered to accommodate the alterations applied to the available resources and stated objectives. In other words, Wildavsky's concept of total or unlimited efficiency implies that nothing is taken for granted including the existing structure of the political system. Schlesinger's comments in this regard certainly confirm Wildavsky's fears for reasons which the latter would most probably reject: "Without modernization of the bureaucratic structure, a large portion of the potential gains of . . . systems analysis will be foregone. The existing structure, organized in large measure around inputs and supported by clienteles with sizable political influence, may become adept at presenting drastically suboptimized (input-oriented) or misleading analyses which are more convenient to accept than reject."

If one accepts the notion—as, seemingly, one must—that structure influences, if not dictates, process, then the prevailing bargaining-incremental decision-making process is, to a great extent, a product of our decentralized and fragmented administrative structure. The rational-comprehensive decision-making process, on the other hand, requires a more centralized and integrated administrative structure if it is to be implemented effectively. To this extent, therefore, it is true that the rationalists seek to alter the structure of the existing political system. But rather than imputing to the rationalists a clandestine motivation to subvert the democratic process ("It is hard to find men . . . who are primarily concerned with the laws that enable the political machinery to keep working."), it would seem more accurate to emphasize that they are primarily concerned with changing the decision-making structure. Admittedly, as Wildavsky points out, the decision-making structure lies at the core of system politics, but unless there is something intrinsically good and beautiful about the bargaining-incremental decision-making process, and something intrinsically bad and ugly about the rational-comprehensive approach, there seems to be no compellingly apparent reason why the former should enjoy a sacrosanct position in our administrative process.

Of course, all incrementalists have good reason to be disturbed by the prospect of a rational-comprehensive decision structure. On a philosophical level, PPB is a source of uneasiness for political pluralists. The application of systematic and quantitative methods for conflict resolution and resource allocation has never been recognized as an absolutely valid operating principle either in pluralist political thought or in our pluralist political system. Majority rule is not an immutable concept. The emphasis placed on rigorous, systematic, and quantitative analysis thus revives a latent fear among the pluralists, who feel much more at ease in a decision-making atmosphere which places a premium on qualitative, subjective, and intuitive judgments. PPB's quantification of hard and soft data through systems and cost-benefit analyses is just as unacceptable as the quantification of political opinions through the majoritarian principle. On a more temporal level, PPB is viewed with equal distrust. For the principal actor in the pluralist system—the political bargainer—the success of PPB will certainly end the need for his services, at least as those services have been defined within the incremental process. On the attitudinal level, PPB is seen as a major departure from the bargaining-incremental orientation, and in this respect, it probably represents the single, most important value bias of the rationalists.

The political attitude and value orientation of the incrementalist is primarily subnational in the sense that his effectiveness is maximized if political values remain diversified, political groups retain their autonomy, political conflict is narrowly contained, and popular political activity is limited. The movement of PPB, by contrast, is up, not down. That is to say, the political attitudes and values fostered by this approach are essentially national, and even transnational. Programmatic goals are established by top-level government officials on a long-range basis of national and international priorities. The centralized mobilization of government resources to meet these goals follows as a given.

The rhetoric of our democratic creed emphatically abounds with references to the ultimate sovereignty and sanctity of the Public Interest or the General Welfare. But, as Dahl correctly points out, in actual practice public policy decisions are formed by putting together a coalition of a majority of minorities through the bargaining-incremental process. The overriding bias of the rationalists is that such terms as the Public Interest and the General Welfare can be made operationally valid—that is, as a result of a systems analytical approach these terms can be objectively identified, and the effectiveness of the means designed to achieve these ends can be quantitatively measured. Their position is that national priorities can be established through the application of PPB methods. This, of course, assumes that the major domestic problems confronting the government today *should* be recognized as national problems requiring coordinated, long-range national solutions. This is the fundamental value premise of the rationalists, and it clashes directly with the subnational orientation and value premise of the incrementalists.

This is not to suggest, of course, that systems analysis "stops at the water's edge." In the grand design of a systems approach to politics, every system is but a subsystem in a higher scheme of relationships. While, for our purposes here, it is sufficient to note that the rationalist proponents of PPB reflect a very definite national—as opposed to a subnational—orientation, it is important to bear in mind that for the true rationalist, trans- and supranational systematic analyses are but a logical extension of PPB.

A really good systems analysis, Capron tells us, provides "new ways of looking at problems" which, hopefully, will lead to "the development of quite new and better ways of meeting problems." Despite the delicate and circumspect manner in which Capron advances his thesis ("PPB will insure that relationships which are now suppressed or ignored will be put on the bargaining table. . . . Even the most venal parochial party to governmental bargaining can be forced to take account of cogent systematic analysis—as long as some others at the bargaining table insist on making it a part of the dialogue."), rationalists and incrementalists alike will recognize the direction in which his propositions are bound to lead. As a consequence, the retrenchment of the incrementalists is an inevitable development. And, if the diagnosis of the current status of PPB and systems analysis by Schlesinger is correct (". . . the resistances to the application of systematic and rigorous analysis in a highly politicized environment are sufficient to make even the stoutest heart grow faint." and "Democratic politics will remain unchanged: a combination of pie in the sky and a bird in the hand. Tokenism, catch phrases, and cultivation of various interests will remain the guide posts."), then his prognosis for the future of systems analysis in the federal government ("I am hopeful and even, within moderation, enthusiastic.") has to be based on unmitigated faith alone.

The one area mentioned by Schlesinger (but frequently overlooked by others) where systems analysis could have a major impact is in the determination of existing or approaching obsolescence. For PPB to be fully effective a continuous reassessment of all existing programs must be instituted to insure that each program maintains a favorable cost-benefit ratio and that its outputs are directly related to its objectives. Properly applied, systems analysis serves as an early warning device of impending program obsolescence. As a consequence, program analysts are given enough lead time to prepare sets of alternative proposals for change. But even here Schlesinger recognizes that the barriers to the effective application of analysis in determining existing or approaching obsolescence are formidable. "In [non-military] functions . . . obsolescence rarely becomes obvious. [Domestic] agencies make contributions to the well-being of portions of the electorate, and it is difficult to make a persuasive case that the functions or technologies in question have been superseded."

Obsolescence is the bane of any administrative system. If not recognized or if recognized and not acted upon, it can drain administrative vitality to the point of enfeeblement. The disturbing fact is, however, that obsolescence is a common-sense phenomenon that is frequently lost in its own simplicity. Schlesinger is correct—even without systems analysis we are capable of identifying obsolescent activities if only intuitively. As he points out the basic problem is not the lack of knowledge but rather "that appropriate actions are constrained by political factors reflecting the anticipated reactions of various groups." Consequently, as Schlesinger views the future of systems analysis in the federal government, at least as a technique to be applied in the assessment of on-going operations, he concludes, "if analysis is to be useful, it will not be by contributing to knowledge, but rather by serving as a *political instrument* through which the relevant political constraints can be relaxed" (italics added).

The Madisonian constraints of prudential pragmatism built into our pluralistic political structure are tenacious, but, if Capron's prediction proves correct, PPB may alter the incremental dialogue, and possibly the existing political constraints may be eliminated, or, more precisely, "relaxed." A classic little study of the Bureau of Labor Statistics is a case in point.* Prior to World War II labor union officials probably placed cost-of-living index reports in the same category as weather reports—both were to be read cursorily. However, during the war period, when for most major unionized industries wage increases were tied to the cost-of-living index, union officials had a major incentive to examine the index in more detail. Using their own economic analysts they challenged the standard index. They forced executive and legislative officials to take into account the union's form of cogent systematic analysis. They made explicit for public discussion relationships which had been suppressed or ignored. They used analysis to alter the existing political dialogue, and, as a consequence, their form of analysis became a most effective political instrument which was used to "relax"—i.e., change—the political constraints imposed on the wage scales of their members.

Used in this fashion, analysis of any kind can prove to be an effective device for breaking away from the inertia of the status quo, but, as Schlesinger concludes, "It will be years before analysis begins to have a significant influence in many agencies." For the rationalist this is hardly a comforting prospectus; for the incrementalist, time is

* Kathryn Smul Arnow, "The Attack on the Cost of Living Index," in *Public Administration and Policy Development,* Harold Stein (ed.), pp. 775–853.

on his side. For both, however, a third force may be developing which could dramatically reject both approaches in favor of a hybrid version of the two. There is virtually no evidence to suggest, for instance, that the political, social, economic, and moral turbulence erupting throughout the entire world shows any signs of diminishing in the foreseeable future. Within our own nation, the volume of the demands for drastic and radical change grows almost daily and is exceeded only by the inability of the multitude of governmental units in this country to cope with these demands. To a great extent the turbulent elements of our society reject both the incremental and rationalist decision-making approaches to the allocation of resources. This has led some to search for a "new public administration" which would substitute a true sense of decentralized social equity and social justice as defined by Jefferson for Madison's concept of political equity carried forth by incrementalists, or Hamilton's vision of centralized executive efficiency pursued by the rationalists. A pure version of any of these three models has not nor is likely to emerge. Interestingly, however, the hybrid model which appears to show limited signs of responding most effectively to the social turbulence, especially on the part of local governments throughout the nation, is a combination of the Jeffersonian and Hamiltonian administrative philosophies. The selections and the commentary in the final chapter are designed to explore this proposition, and, in the process, to return to the point from which we began.

ADMINISTRATION IN A TURBULENT ENVIRONMENT 9

SYSTEMS POLITICS AND SYSTEMS BUDGETING

ALLEN SCHICK

Change in budgeting means change in politics. Any doubts on this score ought to have been dispelled by Aaron Wildavsky's *The Politics of the Budgetary Process*. This implies that the arrival of planning-programming-budgeting, however brief its current run, heralds or reflects transformations in American political life. The politico-budgetary world is much different from what it was in 1965 when PPB was launched, and it probably will not be the same again. While PPB cannot claim parentage for many of the changes, neither can it be divorced from the ferments now sweeping the domestic political scene. Uniting the emergent changes in politics and budgeting is one of the popular metaphors of our times.[1] The central metaphor of the old politics and budgeting was *process;* the key metaphor of the new politics and budgeting is *systems.*[2]

With the process-systems dichotomy as the pivot, I will try to: (1) identify the distinctive and contrasting elements of old and new; (2) analyze the persistence of process politics and the challenge of systems politics; (3) assess the preparedness of politics and budgeting

---

[1] See Martin Landau, "On the Use of Metaphor in Political Analysis," 28 *Social Research,* 1961.

[2] Of course, there are other ways to view the changes currently unfolding. I use the systems concept because it unites study and practice and politics and budgeting.

From *Public Administration Review,* Vol. 29 (March–April 1969), pp. 139–150. Allen Schick is Professor of Political Science, Tufts University. Reprinted with permission of the author and the American Society of Public Administration.

for the systems view; and (4) develop a taxonomy of political process deficiencies.

PROCESS AND SYSTEM

The salient feature of process politics is the activity by which bargains are struck and allocations negotiated—the so-called rules of the game and the strategies of the contestants. There is a presumption that if the process is working properly, the outcome will be favorable. Hence, there is no need for an explicit examination of outcomes; one can evaluate the process itself to determine its performance and desirability. The *sine qua non* of systems politics is the outcome, not the activity, but what results from it. Take away this component and you do not have a system.[3] In systems politics allocations are formally related to preferred outcomes or objectives. Its assumption is exactly contrary to that which undergirds the process approach: unless outcomes are evaluated specifically, the results will be suboptimal or undesirable.

In systems budgeting the distinctive element is the analysis of alternative opportunities, while in process budgeting it is the bargaining apparatus for determining public actions. (To avert a possible misunderstanding, let me note that process and system are portrayed in pure form. In the hybrid world, analysis and bargaining coexist.[4]) Contrary to some interpretations, neither approach requires or rejects a zero-based determination of government programs. Systems politics does not force an all-or-nothing choice. The alternatives are always at the margins, and the margins, like the increments in process politics, can be large or small—a one percent increase in the appropriation for a bureau or a billion dollars for a new Medicaid program.[5] The critical difference is that the increments are negotiated in bargains that neglect the outcomes, while the systems margins are determined via an analysis of outcomes. Nor does systems politics require

[3] It should be noted that systems politics and systems analysis are of much more modest proportions than "general systems theory" defined by Kenneth Boulding as the quest "for a body of systematic theoretical constructs which will discuss the general relationships of the empirical world." See Walter Buckley (ed.), *Modern Systems Research for the Behavioral Scientist* (Chicago: Aldine Publishing Company, 1968).

[4] See William M. Capron, "The Impact of Analysis on Bargaining in Government," presented to the 1966 Annual Meeting of the American Political Science Association.

[5] A hint of the closing of the gap between incrementalism and systems analysis is implicit in the latest version of Wildavsky's views, "Toward a Radical Incrementalism: A Proposal to Aid Congress in Reform of the Budgetary Process," in Alfred deGrazia (ed.), *Congress: The First Branch of Government* (Garden City, N.Y.: Doubleday Anchor Books, 1967).

that every program be compared to all others; programs can be divided into parts for the purpose of analysis and choice. This is the familiar methodology of suboptimization. But unlike the fragmented and piecemeal tactics of process politics in which the part stands alone, in a systems view the part always is viewed in some relation to the whole. Systems politics does not require that everything be decided all at once or once and for all. Systems analysis is both serial and remedial, with iterative feeding back from means to ends.

In process politics the contestants tend to view the options from the perspectives of their established positions (existing legislation, last year's budget, the "base," etc.). Theirs is a retrospective bias. Budgeting is treated as the process of financing existing commitments and of creating some new commitments (the increments). Systems politics tends to have a prospective bias; budgeting is regarded as the allocation of money to attain some future value (the outcome or objective). This year's budget, in systems terms, is an installment in buying that future.

Because of its future orientation, systems budgeting is likely to induce somewhat larger annual budget shifts than might derive under process rules. But this does not mean a zigzag course of events, each successive budget disowning the previous allocations. All political life, whether process or systems, must achieve stability and continuity. Process politics accomplishes these through a chain of incremental adjustments; systems politics by embracing a large number of years and values within its analytic frame.

In process politics the strategy is that of mobilizing interests, and in process budgeting of mobilizing funds. In systems politics and budgeting it is the allocation and rationing of values and resources among competing powers and claimants. Process politics (and budgeting), therefore, tends to favor the partisans such as agencies, bureaus, and interest groups, while systems politics (and budgeting) tends to favor the central allocators, especially the chief executive and the budget agency. Systems politics also can be used to bolster certain officials who have mixed mobilizing-rationing roles. A few department heads such as Robert McNamara have used systems budgeting in this fashion. But this is likely to occur only when top officials have mobilizing values that diverge from those of their subordinates.

Systems politics takes a relatively holistic view of objectives compared to the partial view associated with process politics. As many pluralists have asserted, the group process produces public objectives as derivatives or aggregates of the special, limited interests of the groups. Systems politics encompasses a broader range of public purposes, including some which cannot be extracted from or negotiated via the usual group interactions. But it would be erroneous to attribute to systems politics a global concern with objectives. That would tax the political system with an overload of calculation and conflict management. All politics has to work with limits on cognition and with the realities of multiple and conflicting objectives. To cope with these constraints, systems politics relies on the indispensable division of analytic and political labors furnished by group bargaining. Systems politics, in short, does not eschew group objectives, but it certainly is not confined to them.

The important facts of process budgeting have been portrayed in Aaron Wildavsky's *The Politics of the Budgetary Process*. Process budgeting is "incremental, fragmented, non-programmatic, and sequential."[6] There is a tendency to accept last year's budget as the base for next year's and to use an array of non-analytic tactics to reduce the complexities and conflicts of budget making and to strengthen the opportunities of agencies to obtain funds. These tactics have stabilized into the rules and roles of bargaining that govern the incremental budget process. Although Wildavsky has underestimated the program content of traditional budgeting, he correctly observes that there is little explicit consideration of objectives and policies and almost no search for alternatives. The line-item method is one technical manifestation of process budgeting.

Systems budgeting is represented by the planning-programming-budgeting systems now being established in many government jurisdictions. While there are many versions of PPB and PPB is not the only appropriate expression of systems in budgeting, all PPB systems direct allocative choice to future outcomes, to the costs of achieving public objectives, and to alternative means of pursuit. The technology of PPB—the program memoranda, program and financial plans, and other federal documentation or the variant methods used in other jurisdictions—are of considerable relevance in the conversion of the systems idea into practice, but it is the concept of systems budgeting that overrides and ultimately must determine the techniques.

THE DOMINANCE OF PROCESS

The process school dominated American politics from the early 1950's through the mid-1960's. From David Truman's *The Governmental Process* (1951) through Wildavsky's justly praised budget study (1964) there prevailed the confidence that pluralist politics—particularly transactions among interest groups—produces favorable outcomes. For the most part, the politics of the period was practiced as described by the pluralists and incrementalists. The emphasis was on

[6] Aaron Wildavsky, *The Politics of the Budgetary Process* (Boston: Little, Brown and Company, 1964), p. 136.

consensus and stability, on limiting the scope and intensity of conflict by allocating to each group its quota of public satisfactions. Change was gradual and piecemeal, with departures from the status quo limited by established rules and by the actions of the "partisan mutual adjusters" who orchestrated the group process.[7] Despite their slavish lip service to Lasswell's formulation of politics as "who gets what, when, how," the pluralists gave scant attention to the outcomes of group interactions. One can search the vast pluralist literature and locate only scatterings of concern with "who gets what" from the power distribution in a community or from the established government policies. The pluralists were deterred from looking into such questions by their own focus on process.

Wildavsky's study is an excellent illustration of the pluralist methodology. After two lengthy chapters on "Calculations" and "Strategies" devoted to the partisan process of budget making, and with hardly a word about outcomes,[8] Wildavsky opens the next chapter with a strong rebuke to budget reformers:

There is little or no realization among the reformers, however, that any effective change in budgetary relationships must necessarily alter the outcomes of the budgetary process. . . . proposed reforms inevitably contain important implications for the political system; that is, for the "who gets what" of governmental decisions.[9]

Yet nowhere in *The Politics* does the author evaluate "who gets what" from traditional budgeting. Instead, there is a *deux ex machina* faith in the goodness of the pluralist process:

The process we have developed for dealing with interpersonal comparisons in government is not economic but political. Conflicts are resolved (under agreed upon rules) by translating different preferences through the political system into units called votes or into types of authority like a veto power.[10]

Why have the pluralists neglected to study the outcomes of their process? What inspired their awesome respect for the ability of that process to deliver the right results time and again? There are a num-

[7] The best statement of pluralist process for purposes of this paper is Charles E. Lindblom, *The Intelligence of Democracy* (Glencoe, N.Y.: The Free Press, 1965).

[8] While his work contains numerous illustrations and anecdotes, Wildavsky does not deal explicitly with which interests win or lose as a consequence of the budget process, or with the outcomes of the process, for example, with the question of whether people are well or poorly housed.

[9] Aaron Wildavsky, *The Politics of the Budgetary Process, op. cit.*, p. 127.

[10] *Ibid.*, p. 130.

ber of explanations which manifest the potency and attractiveness of the pluralist view.

American political science is habituated to confidence in the formal relations among power holders. Just as the Constitution makers believed that government would be good (non-tyrannical) if power were divided among the several branches, the pluralists have argued that government is good (responsible) because power is shared by many groups. A social checks and balances system has replaced the legal checks and balances as the "democratizing" process of government. The pluralists also have been swayed by the market model of economic competition. In the same way that the unseen hand of the market effectively and fairly regulates supply and demand, the interactions of competing groups yields the desired supply of political good, and at the right price. Moreover, the proper functioning of both private and public markets hinges on the partisanship of the contestants. Social welfare is maximized by the self-interest of buyers and sellers, not by an attempt to calculate the general welfare. If either economic man or political man abandoned his partisan role, the expected result would be a misallocation of resources.

The pluralists were impressed by their "discovery" of interest groups. In the pluralist mind, not only do groups supplement the electoral process by providing additional channels of influence and information, they also compensate for some of the limitations of electoral politics, notably its inability to transmit unambiguous policy preferences (mandates) from voters to public officials or to accommodate differentials in the intensity of preferences. By virtue of the overlapping pattern of group identifications, interest groups also were esteemed as effective brakes on socioeconomic conflict. Accordingly, the pluralists came to regard the group process as the cornerstone of modern democratic government, possessing a representative capability superior to the voting process.

According to this pluralist interpretation, government is sometimes a representative of special interests (for example, a bureau advocating the interests of its clientele), and sometimes an arbiter of interests (for example, the budget bureau allocating the shares among the various agencies). But its role is not that of promoting some overarching public interest. Its job is to keep the process going, not to maximize some consistent set of policy objectives. Bureaucracies were considered faithful reflectors of group preferences; consequently, their growth to enormous power was not deemed a threat to norms of representation.

Once they were sold on the efficacy of interest groups, the pluralists stopped worrying about the ends of government. They were persuaded by a tautological, but nonetheless alluring, proof that the outcomes of the group process are satisfactory. If the bargain were not the right one, it would not have been made. Since it was made, it must be the right one. Unlike many economists who have become cognizant that market imperfections and limitations, such as external costs and benefits or imperfect competition, can produce unfavorable outcomes, most pluralists stayed solidly convinced group competition has no major defects.

The process approach offered a convenient escape from difficult value questions. A decisional system that focuses on the outcomes and objectives of public policy cannot avoid controversy over the ends of government, the definition of the public interest, and the allocation of core values such as power, wealth, and status. But the pluralists bypassed their matters by concentrating on the structure and rules for choice, not on the choices themselves. They purported to describe the political world as it is, neglecting the important normative implications of their model. The pluralists scrupulously avoided interpersonal comparisons and the equally troublesome question of whose values shall prevail. Instead, they took the actual distribution of values (and money) as Pareto optimal, that is, as the best that could be achieved without disadvantaging at least one group.

These political scientists, along with many others, assumed that politics is a giant positive sum game in which almost everyone comes out ahead. This perspective was inspired by the affluent mood of the period and by the "out of sight, out of mind" predicament of the poor. It had a powerful analog in the Keynesian model of economic growth and stabilization; if everyone benefits from economic development, it is hard to ask the question "development for what?" For verification of their interpretation, the pluralists resorted to a "fail-safe" tautology. If there were any losers, surely they would have joined into groups to protect their interests. If a disadvantaged group had a great deal at stake, it would have been able to veto the proposed bargain or to demand compensation for its losses. The affluence, everyone wins presumptions removed any compulsion for an evaluation of policy outcomes; satisficing solutions would do. (Pareto solutions are, by definition, satisficing conditions, *modus vivendi* worked out to the satisfaction of those groups whose interests are involved.) Satisficing became a way of political life and a justification for the status quo, not merely a means of cutting down the cost of choice.[11] "Second best" became the preferred solution because the best would have required some agonizing reappraisal of policy and purpose, along

[11] When he introduced the concept, Simon's argument was "that men satisfice because they have not the wits to maximize. . . . If you have the wits to maximize, it is silly to satisfice." Herbert A. Simon, "The Decision-Making Schema: A Reply," *Public Administration Review*. Winter, 1958.

with a renegotiation of delicate group relationships. More than a decade ago Robert C. Wood explained why America was doing little to reconstruct her cities despite the warnings of reformers:

Despite our predictions, disaster has not struck: urban government has continued to function, not well perhaps, but at least well enough to forestall catastrophe. Traffic continues to circulate; streets and sewers are built; water is provided; schools keep their doors open; and law and order generally prevail.[12]

It is only at the point of crisis that satisficing no longer is good enough and governments are compelled to reexamine what they are doing and where they are heading. But the crises that surround our public institutions today were remote, or at least underground, a few years ago.

Affluence enables winning groups to compensate their competitors. For this reason, log-rolling among interests was viewed as an efficient mechanism for negotiating side-payments. The quality of the "pork," in terms of some public interest criterion, was not taken into account —only the success of the groups in obtaining agreement. The fact that the groups consented to the exchange was taken as sufficient evidence of its utility. It is easy to understand that under conditions of scarcity the quality of the exchange would more likely be subjected to scrutiny. But these were not perceived as times of scarcity.

The pluralists emphasized the remedial features of incrementalism. A decision made today is provisional; it can be modified tomorrow. If this year's budget is deficient, corrections can be made next year. One need not search for the optimal outcome, nor need one attempt to take all factors into account before deciding. Some pluralists argued that better results can be achieved through a series of partial adjustments than through a systematic canvass of alternatives. The serial and remedial aspects of incremental politics were regarded as especially helpful in reducing the complexities and controversies involved in the negotiation of a $185 billion national budget.

The pluralists were impressed by the ability of the budgetary process to limit political and bureaucratic conflict. The annual competition over billions of dollars has the potential of generating explosive and divisive conflicts. The fact that this competition usually is waged peacefully and leaves few scars attests to the effectiveness of the traditional process. The pluralists tend to view anything that might broaden the scope of intensity of conflict as undesirable, and they believe that an explicit and systematic evaluation of public objectives,

---

[12] Robert C. Wood, "Metropolitan Government, 1975: An Extrapolation of Trends," 52 *American Political Science Review*, March 1958, p. 112.

accompanied by emphasis on alternatives, trade-offs, and the outcomes of competitive resource allocations, will increase the level of conflict.

Finally, the pluralists looked at the American political scene and liked what they saw—abundance, growth, consensus, stability, satisfaction with the American way. (It should be remembered that the pluralist age followed a great depression and a great war.) Given these "success indicators," the pluralists readily assumed that the shares were being divided equitably and to the satisfaction of the citizenry. They saw no need to quicken the pace of change or to effect radical redistribution in political values. And, of course, they saw no need to question the entrenched politico-budgetary process or to reexamine the outcomes of that process.

In many ways, the political life of the times was a faithful image of the pluralist view. Political practice was geared to consensus, an avoidance of the big ideological issues. The economy was buoyant, the mood optimistic. Writing of "The Politics of Consensus in an Age of Affluence," Robert Lane identified this mood as a key to understanding the political behavior of the common man:

Since everyone is "doing better" year by year, though with different rates of improvement, the stakes are not so much in terms of gain or loss, but in terms of size of gain—giving government more clearly the image of a rewarding rather than a punishing instrument.[13]

It was not a time for thinking about purposes or worrying about priorities. Perspectives did not extend much beyond this year and the next. There was great confidence in the capability of the political process to produce the right results. Muddling through was canonized as the American virtue. It was a time of governmental immobilism, capable neither of disowning the New Deal legacy nor of forging new directions in economic and social life. If there was an industrial-military-political cartel, it was outside the range of pluralist inquiry, above the middling levels of politics. If there were nonvoters, or apathetic voters, or uninformed voters, that all was good, for it cooled the level of political excitement and demonstrated the basic satisfactions with the process. If there were losers in American politics, there was no need for concern, for they, too, could look to a better tomorrow when they would share in the political bargains.

The politicians practiced what the pluralists described.

[13] Robert E. Lane, "The Politics of Consensus in an Age of Affluence," 59 *American Political Science Review*, December 1965, p. 893. For a fuller picture on the optimism of the common man in the 1950's, see Robert E. Lane, *Political Ideology: Why the American Common Man Believes What He Does* (Glencoe, N.Y.: The Free Press, 1962).

THE SYSTEMS CHALLENGE

It is well known that the main impetus for PPB came from the new decisional technologies associated with economic and systems analysis, not from public administration or political science. Accordingly, it was possible for the governmentwide introduction of PPB to occur at the time that the pluralists' bargaining model had reached its academic apogee, approximately one year after the publication of major works by Lindblom and Wildavsky. Yet a full appreciation of the sources and implications of systems politics and budgeting must take into account a wider range of influences and ferments. To move from process to systems requires at least the following: (1) dissatisfaction with the outcomes resulting from the established process and (2) confidence that better outcomes can be obtained via the systems approach.

The entry of economists into positions of political influence was important on both counts. Economists, unlike their political science brethren, were not committed to the established process. As they applied their specialized norms and perspectives to the political world, many economists became convinced that the process was inefficient and inequitable.[14] Moreover, economists already possessed sophisticated methodologies for examining outcomes: the positivist input-output models and the normative welfare economics concepts.

However, few political scientists qualified for the systems approach during the 1950's and 1960's. Rather than showing concern about political outcomes, they were preoccupied with celebrating an *ancien régime* that exhibited few signs of the traumas developing within.[15] There were some stirrings by men of prominence, but their work was premature or too late. David Easton did his first work on systems politics, but only in recent years have his input-output categories been filled with useful data.[16] On the normative side, Lasswell's call for a policy science to "enable the most efficient use of the manpower, facilities, and resources of the American people," [17] evoked a feeble

14 More than anything else, this skeptical view of public spending prodded economists to be the leading sponsors of PPB.

15 See Leo Strauss, "An Epilogue," in Herbert J. Storing (ed.), *Essays on the Scientific Study of Politics* (New York: Holt, Rinehart and Winston, 1962), p. 327. This caustic yet penetrating critique of the pluralist method was "buried" by the establishment.

16 David Easton, *The Political System* (New York: Alfred A. Knopf Inc., 1953). See, also, his *A Systems Analysis of Political Life* (New York: John Wiley & Sons, 1965).

17 Harold D. Lasswell, "The Policy Orientation," in Daniel Lerner and Harold D. Lasswell (eds.), *The Policy Sciences* (Stanford: Stanford University Press, 1951), p. 3. The call for policy or systems analysis often is coupled with a comment on resource scarcity and the need for optimization.

response from his colleagues. (After all, if someone is convinced of the efficacy of the ongoing process, what incentive does he have to examine its outcomes?) A major methodological development has been the comparative study of state politics. Some scholars have taken advantage of the opportunities for multijurisdictional comparisons to correlate policy outcomes with certain economic and political characteristics.[18] Several of these studies call into question the pluralist assumption and desirable outcomes. Where these first methodological steps will lead is difficult to anticipate. Yet if it is true that researchers tend to follow their methodologies, the development of new systems techniques will have an impact on future conceptions of political reality. We might expect novel efforts to evaluate the performance of political systems and the quality of public policies. This is the forecast issued by Gabriel Almond in his 1968 Benedict Lectures at Boston University.[19] It is likely that when political scientists begin to probe policy outcomes, many will cast off the pretense of neutrality and take explicitly normative positions in evaluating the outcomes.[20]

More influential than the methods will be the level of dissatisfaction with political life. As more scholars become sensitive to politics in which there are losers and to a political world beset by scarcities, there will be a growing unwillingness to accept the process and its outcomes as givens. In this connection Michael Harrington's *The Other America* warrants notice because of the actions it provoked. For so many, the book was a revelation, bringing into sight and mind what long had been obscured by the pluralists' decision-making models. Its message was forthright: not everyone is protected and represented by the group mechanism. Not everyone benefits from the way politics works in the United States. There are unfavorable outcomes, and some of them are the results of the very processes and policies that have been established over the past 35 years. Once the spotlight was turned on outcomes, the weaknesses of the old processes became more conspicuous. Hence the search for new processes: community action, "maximum feasible participation," income guarantees, neighborhood cooperations, taking to the streets.

[18] Thomas R. Dye, *Politics, Economics, and the Public: Policy Outcomes in the American States* (Chicago: Rand McNally, 1966); and Ira Sharkansky, *Spending in the American States* (Chicago: Rand McNally, 1968).

[19] Gabriel Almond, *Perspectives on Political Development,* Benedict Lectures on Political Philosophy, March 18–20, 1968, Boston University.

[20] In explaining why behavioral political scientists have emphasized process over content, Austin Ranney observes that many scholars "think that focusing on content is likely to lead to evaluations of present policies and exhortations for new ones," "The Study of Policy Content: A Framework for Choice," in *Items* (Washington, D.C.: Social Science Research Council, September 1968).

The systems mood became political reality when the President decided to "go public" with PPB. Viewed from the White House, what might have been some of the attractive features of PPB? During the initial part of his presidency, Lyndon Johnson displayed two characteristics that might have induced dissatisfaction with the pluralist processes: (1) a desire for involvement and initiative in program development and (2) an insistence on scrutinizing existing programs. Both characteristics required some modification in the rules of incremental choice; the first because it meant presidential rather than bureau leadership in program development; the second because it meant presidential rejection of the "preferred position" of last year's budget.

The traditional budget processes are unsuited for an active presidential role. In the usual bureaucratic pattern, budgetary power is located at the lower echelons, with successively higher levels having declining power and less involvement. By the time the budget reaches the President, most of the decisions have been made for him in the form of existing programs and incremental bureau claims. Barring unusual exertion, the President's impact is marginal, cutting some requests and adding some items of his own. PPB may have been perceived as a means of establishing the presidency earlier and more effectively in the making of budgetary and program policy. (No claim is made here that the President saw PPB as a vitalizer of his budgetary power or in a systems context. But the very arrival of PPB is strong evidence of high-level dissatisfaction with the status quo processes.)

Dissatisfaction is not enough to sway political leaders to underwrite an innovation. They also must have confidence that the new way is workable and desirable. This optimism was fueled by the Great Society mood. There was confidence in the ability of government to eradicate hard-core social and human problems, and in its ability to specify and reach long-ranch objectives. A few years earlier President Kennedy had predicted a moon landing in this decade; why not set concrete targets for a wide range of social endeavors? PPB was perceived as an effective apparatus for identifying legitimate national objectives and for measuring progress toward their attainment. PPB's objectives would be operational and reachable, politically appealing yet based on socioeconomic analysis, not just the expedients of politicians or the dreams of futurists. PPB's objectives would be presidential, marking the accomplishments of his administration.

The legislative explosion of the first Johnson years may have supplied another incentive. A President who was intensely concerned with building a program and legislative record was impelled to become an administrative innovator. This pattern parallels the course of New Deal politics. Following his unsurpassed legislative accomplishments, President Roosevelt appointed his Committee on Administrative Management and embarked on a battle for reorganization that was to culminate in the establishment of the Executive Office of the President and the growth of the budget function to its contemporary status. In both the New Deal and the Great Society, basic changes in program goals aggravated and exposed the organizational deficiencies rooted in the bureau-congressional committee-interest group axis that dominates the pluralists processes. There is reason to believe that the President viewed PPB as an opening prong in a major overhaul of federal organization, an expectation that was aborted by the Vietnam situation.

While economists and analysts have been credited and debited for PPB's debut, many hands and influences have been involved. One can even go back to the waning years of the Eisenhower Administration, to the commissions on national goals and purpose. These quests reflected disenchantment with the drift of the period, the lack of purpose or progression. As one expression of this temper, PPB has attracted both conservative and liberal sponsorship. The conservative version is based on the conviction that public outputs are not worth the private cost and that multiyear projections would disclose the ominous growth in government spending implicit in current policies. The motives of the liberals are more complex. They are confident that public objectives are worth the cost, but they also feel that existing programs are not producing optimal outcomes.[21]

POLITICAL PROCESS DEFICIENCIES

If systems politics is in step with the times, it is because the political process has been found wanting. The imperfections have produced unsatisfactory outcomes. But it would be senseless to discard the process because it is deficient: we can compensate for its weaknesses. This is what economists have done with the market.

The pluralist process is based on competition among interest groups. Its archtype is the economic model of competition among buyers and sellers. But the economists have come to reject a total reliance on the market's capability to allocate all resources efficiently or equitably. They have identified several classes of market limitations, the most important of which pertain to public goods and external costs and benefits. They also have identified certain characteristics of imperfect markets, in which competition is restricted, supply and demand are controlled or manipulated, and prices are admin-

[21] Thus Governor Reagan has emphasized multi-year projections in his application of PPB in California government. A liberal's concept of PPB is suggested in Michael Harrington's *Toward a New Democratic Left* (New York: Macmillan, 1968).

istered. The pluralists still are in their *laissez faire* period. They attribute few faults to their political market. But the economic market supplies useful analogs for the appraisal of the political process. It is reasonable to expect that a political process which is modeled on market competition will exhibit many of the deficiencies of the economic market itself. Yet for many of the market defects and limitations, economists have looked to government for corrective action. Accordingly, the political process might reinforce rather than combat market inadequacies. As a first step toward conceiving a political process that is free of market-like defects, I propose to develop a taxonomy of political process deficiencies.

PUBLIC GOODS

Goods that are available to all consumers, whether or not they pay for them, cannot be supplied efficiently by the private economy. For such public goods, nonmarket institutions, usually but not exclusively governmental, are used for determining how much should be provided.

In transferring the case of public goods from the private sector to the polity, economists assume that collective values will prevail. But the political process, as conceived by the pluralists, operates via competition. Is the process of political competition superior to, or different from, the process of market competition in deciding public goods issues? If government were to provide public goods on the basis of some public interest determinant—in terms of systems criteria—it might be superior to the market, for there would be a means of evaluating the social costs and benefits to the whole polity of an investment in national defense, space exploration, or other public goods. But when private group influences prevail, the result is that public goods are produced and distributed on the basis of private calculations. Perversely, something which economists regard as a public good, our pluralists regard as a private good. Take the case of defense. An economist would argue that we all receive, more or less, the same benefits. The pluralists would have to argue, however, that we do not benefit equally, for the defense establishment and military contractors get more out of defense spending than the rest of us do. Thus, while each of us is equally defended, we do not equally benefit from the production of defense.

Whether the supply of public goods will be distorted by the polity depends on the shape of group politics. When an influential group gains disproportionately from a public good, society may produce too much of it. Since we all gain some benefit from defense, we do not have the usual checks and balances that operate in the case of private goods. A swollen or misallocated defense budget may result. When the public good is promoted by a weak group, too little of the good might be produced. Perhaps this is what has hobbled the national movement for pure air. (Some pluralists now speak of two polities, one with the ordinary interplay of group interests, the other where the group process is subordinate.[22] The latter sector consists mainly of the national security and foreign policy areas which consume a huge portion of our public wealth and deal with the survival of this nation and the world.)

EXTERNALITIES

A second class of allocative decisions which cannot be entrusted completely to the competitive market pertains to external costs and benefits. A classic case of an external cost is the discharge of pollutants into the air; the polluter does not pay for the social cost he engenders. An external benefit results when the beneficiary does not have to pay for another's largess. Some economists regard education as such a benefit because society benefits but does not pay for the investments I make in my own education. While the market can supply goods that carry external costs or benefits, it is not capable of producing them in the optimal quality or quantity. It would tend to overproduce goods that have external costs, and to underproduce those that provide external benefits.

Because of this market disability, the public sector gets the call. In the case of an external cost such as air pollution, the job of government would be to make the polluter pay (through taxation, regulation, fines, or some other mode) so that his cost equals the social cost. For an external benefit such as education, government would require all members of the community to pay some share of the cost. But in a competitive polity, the group process might stimulate rather than inhibit the production of goods with external costs. After all, one of the aims of an interest group is to get others to pay for your benefits or to avoid paying your share of the costs. As a result, government can and does play Robin Hood in reverse, taking from the poor and giving to the rich. Urban renewal is a case in point. Government's fiscal and legal powers were used by developers to impose all sorts of costs on residents and shopkeepers in the renewal area. Sometimes powerful interests can engineer public policy to obtain rewards for imposing costs on the community. Thus we hear proposals to award tax credits to air polluters in order to motivate them to cease their harmful activity. Where there are external benefits, powerful beneficiaries may refuse to tax themselves for their gain.

Why doesn't the unseen hand of group competition keep everyone honest, making the polluter pay for the costs he imposes and society

[22] Ex., Aaron Wildavsky, "The Two Presidencies," *Trans-Action*, December 1966, pp. 7–14.

for the benefits it receives? The obvious answer is that not all interests are equally powerful. Pollutors probably have better lobbies than city residents who breathe the air. And they use their political power to ratify, not to countermand, the edict of the market.

INCOME DISTRIBUTION

Left to its own wills, the market will produce a distribution of income in which some have very much and some have very little. In a capitalist polity, we tend not to regard the possession of wealth as an evil, but we have become concerned about those who are poor. Hence the array of welfare programs that have grown over the past 35 years. Certainly these programs have resulted in a net redistribution of income in favor of low-income groups. But the results are not one-sided, as indicated by the regressive social security tax structure, the welfare problems, and some of the housing programs.

But the basic income distribution established by the market has not been greatly affected by public micropolicy. (Macropolicy, the stimulation of economic growth, definitely has had considerable impact on the numbers of people living below the poverty line.) The poor subsist under welfare; they also subsisted under the poor laws. Often the poor are denied the bootstraps that might enable them to rise above the poverty level. We rarely redistribute wealth by giving the poor money; instead we give them benefits in kind. These are woefully inefficient from an economic point of view (as the conservatives tell us) and woefully inadequate from a social viewpoint (as the liberals have discovered). Somehow, however, they are efficient and desirable from a political standpoint. There are several explanations for this anomaly (see the paragraphs below on imperfect competition and ideology). The main reason is that the poor lack not only money but political power as well. They cannot compete fully in political life because they lack money, status, self-confidence, political skill, and group and bureaucratic representation. Perhaps there can be no effective redistribution of income unless there is a concomitant redistribution of political power. But the established group structure is committed to the prevailing distribution of power because it is advantaged by that distribution, just as those who are economically potent tend to approve the market distribution of incomes. In order to achieve a meaningful redistribution of political resources, it might be necessary to challenge the group norms that undergird the political process, that is, to contest the legitimacy of the process itself.

IMPERFECT COMPETITION

A market with few buyers and sellers will not produce the right outcomes; neither will a polity which is itself oligopolistic. The political process possesses the same tendencies toward concentration that drive competition from the market. In both instances there are advantages in bigness and in the ability to control resources. We have the Big Three in automobile production and the Big Two in political parties. While they are not interchangeable players, the robber baron and the boss had much in common, and so do the contemporary elites in business and government.[23] Powerful men have not been known to favor competition when competition does not favor them. In pluralist politics there is a special kind of market imperfection. Four-fifths of the population, according to most reckonings, is fairly affluent. When we speak of 30 or 40 million poor people, we tend to forget the political implications of the 160 or 170 million who are not poor. It is of great ideological import that the rise of pluralist politics coincided with the emergence of an advantaged majority and disadvantaged minority. At the very time the pluralists were celebrating minorities rule,[24] we had become a homogeneous majority of affluents. Under the guise of consensus, we had a new kind of tyranny of the majority. Not a deliberate or invidious tyranny, but one of political incapability to deal with the interests of the minority. John K. Galbraith spelled out the economic and social implications in *The Affluent Society*.[25] As Mills argued, what passed for political competition were petty family quarrels, but the big issues went unchallenged.

How then have things begun to change in the cities and the ghettos? I would not leave altruism out of the answer, nor the efforts of activists and analysts who have warred against the established process and its stark outcomes. But the number one factor is that the poor and the blacks are becoming majorities in our inner cities, those strategic centers of communications and commerce that remain vital to suburban interests.

Not only did the affluence of the period create a new set of majority interests, it also turned would-be competitors into allies. As Galbraith has pointed out, countervailing power (which he carefully differentiates from pluralist competition) does not function well "when there is inflation or inflationary pressure on markets."[26] Unions can conspire with management to gain higher wages and to pass the cost on to consumers. In the political arena, interests can logroll and pass the cost on to taxpayers. Only under conditions of scarcity is competition

23 It is not necessary, however, to accept Mills' view of interlocking military-industrial-political directorates to acknowledge the affinities in their behavior.

24 The "minorities rule" phrase along with its theoretical elaboration is in Robert A. Dahl, *A Preface to Democratic Theory* (Chicago: University of Chicago Press, 1956).

25 Much of Galbraith's thesis was misunderstood, and especially his comments on poverty (Boston: Houghton Mifflin, 1958).

26 John Kenneth Galbraith, *American Capitalism* (Boston: Houghton Mifflin Company, Sentry Edition, 1962), p. 128 ff.

an efficient allocator of resources. This is one important reason why systems politics converges with the politics of scarcity.

IDEOLOGY

According to the principles of competition, both economic man and political man know their own interests and fight for them against the competing interests of others. But one of the things a political process can do is to make people not know their own interests. In the market it is somewhat difficult to misdirect people; there is the profit motive and the relatively unambiguous price mechanism. In politics it's a lot easier; you use ideology to do the job. Any successful mode of political inquiry becomes a set of biases, encumbering its practitioners from viewing the world from some alternative perspective. Pluralism, more and more of us are willing to concede, became a statement of the way politics ought to be, not merely a descriptive summing up of the way it is. As political reality began to move from group pluralism to group conflict, many political scientists were debarred by their concepts from recognizing the changes that were occurring. Only the cumulative hammerings of urban, racial, fiscal, diplomatic, and military crises have uprooted growing numbers from their pluralists anchorage.

To study the workings of political interests, the pluralists refined the art and science of public opinion polling, asking citizens about every conceivable issue and reporting the results with statistical fidelity. They also studied power to communities to determine who participates in the making of decisions and which interests get their way. Both techniques assume that there are no ideological impediments to interest formation and expression. Two very different scholars, C. Wright Mills and Joseph Schumpeter, argued to the contrary. The Marxist thread in Mills leads to this statement:

What men are interested in is not always what is to their interest; the troubles they are aware of are not always the ones that beset them . . . it is not only that men can be unconscious of their situations; they are often falsely conscious of them.[27]

Schumpeter took the view that the conditions of modern politics inevitably dull man's capacity to form a political will:

Thus the typical citizen drops to a lower level of mental performance as soon as he enters the political field. He argues and analyzes in a way which he would readily recognize as infantile within the sphere of his real interests. . . . the will of the people is the product and not the motive power of the political process.[28]

[27] C. Wright Mills, *White Collar* (New York: Galaxy Books, 1956), p. xix.

[28] Joseph A. Schumpeter, *Capitalism, Socialism and Democracy,* Third Edition (New York: Harper Torchbooks, 1962) pp. 262–263.

Schumpeter anticipates and rejects the pluralist response that groups act as surrogates for individual interests, converting the ignorance of the voter into a powerful political asset, and possessing a collective intelligence that compensates for the citizen's lack of knowledge. But rather than serving as representatives of individual interests, groups "are able to fashion and, within very wide limits, even to create the will of the people. What we are confronted with in the analysis of political processes is largely not a genuine but a manufactured will."[29]

The community power studies often were exhaustive in their coverage, but they covered very little. Banfield was able to find only six controversies of citywide importance in the Chicago of 1957 and 1958, and none of them dealt with the guts of living in a mass urban environment. Apparently the political process already had dried up the wells of conflict, relegating the important things to what Bachrach and Baratz aptly termed "nondecisions." It is the "mobilization of biases," E. E. Schattschneider wrote in his last antipluralist work, that determines the scope of political conflict.[30]

Ideology is one critical reason why people do not always know their own interests, why there are so few controversies. The political process socializes its citizens to accept certain norms and rules as legitimate, not to be challenged or questioned. The myopics who have climbed the political socialization bandwagon (the successor to community power studies) look at the small things like who is Democratic and who is Republican, as if Tweedledee and Tweedledum made much difference, and all the time they neglect the big questions of the citizens' linkage to the polity.

"My chief objection," Christian Bay has said, "is not to a pluralist society but to a pluralist political theory." This theory "does not jibe with what political scientists *know* about the power of elites or the techniques of mass manipulation."[31] Under the cover of pluralism elites flourished, but they were given new, deceptive titles; the active minority, opinion leaders, decision makers. Rarely were they identified in terms of the power they wielded or in terms of the gaps between mass and elite, powerful and powerless, manipulator and manipulated. All were given statistical equality and anonymity in the opinion polls.

The pluralists thought that their age was "The End of Ideology." Looking backward, we can see it as the triumph of an ideology—the

---

[29] *Ibid.*, p. 263.

[30] E. E. Schattschneider, *The Semisovereign People* (New York: Holt, Rinehart, & Winston, 1960).

[31] Christian Bay, "Needs, Wants, and Political Legitimacy," *Canadian Journal of Political Science*, September, 1968, p. 252.

ideology of pluralism. For pluralism became more a norm than a fact, the glorification of the bargain and the status quo, the sanctification of consensus and stability. Elite interests benefited from these norms; minority interests were constrained by them.

IMMOBILITY OF RESOURCES

Unlike water, economic resources such as labor and capital do not always flow to the right place. There can be barriers to their mobility. Unemployed miners remain in Appalachia and subsistence farmers on their farms. Bankers put their money downtown, not in Harlem where the interest rates are higher. One responsibility of government is to stimulate mobility via subsidies, loans, and regulatory devices.

There also can be immobility of political resources, by which I mean the failure of the political process to behave in response to numbers. For in a democratic polity, numbers (weighted for intensity of interest) is the key resource. Over the long run, this political resource tends to attract power. If Negroes move into a city and come to outnumber the whites, they ultimately will take over the elective offices, much as the Irish displaced the Yankees. But there are at least two kinds of impediments to the free flow of numbers—structural and ideological. All sorts of structural roadblocks stand in the way of interests which have the votes and want the power. Legislative apportionment, the committee system, parliamentary rules, seniority, federalism, the balkanization of metropolitan regions, bureaucratic patterns, election laws—whatever justification they may have, these structures have the potential of depriving interests of their just political fruits. Sometimes the structures are contrived for this purpose (gerrymandering, for instance); sometimes they evolve over many years of inaction (urban sprawl); sometimes they are abolished (as in the case of legislative malapportionment).

The second factor is a product of the incremental character of political choice. What economics writes off as sunk cost, politics rewards as a vested interest. The incremental ideology has the effect of immobilizing numbers because it protects status quo interests. Each incremental move forecloses additional opportunities, with the consequence that the iron grip of the past is tightened with each successive decision. Of the $180 billions in the budget, only a tiny fragment is actionable. A President who would war on poverty today has fewer options than Franklin Roosevelt had in his time. By the time the pluralist process reached its zenith, the political world was almost immobilized by the accumulation of previous commitments. (In his study of state expenditures, Ira Sharkansky shows that previous expenditures are an excellent predictor of current spending. For selected years between 1913 and 1965 he has computed the deviation between actual and incrementally predicted spending. For the years prior to 1957, an average of 22 states had a deviation of at least 15 percent. But for the years between 1957 and 1965, only seven states had a 15 percent deviation of actual from predicted spending.)[32] Lindblom was right. You can move far with incrementalism, but only in the direction in which you started.[33]

It is not surprising that Pareto norms became popular to some sophisticated pluralists. The economists' justification of the status quo had more appeal than their own "veto group" concept. By 1965 politics was a massive Pareto optimum. In politics the optimum almost always is what is; at least one person (or group) would be displeased by any proposed change. Every moment of the Vietnam war has been Pareto optimal; regardless of the political or military conditions, every moment was justifiable in terms of any alternative.[34]

REPRESENTATION

There is one kind of imperfection in the political process that has no market analogy. While the market is impelled by hidden levers, the polity is dependent on a representative mechanism, whether electoral, bureaucratic, or group. There is no other way to convert numbers and preferences democratically into policy. Many have written on the inadequacies of representation; the structural impediments mentioned above; the ignorance of the electorate and its limited "yes-no" vocabulary; the under- or over-representation of group interests; the tendency of group leaders to represent themselves rather than their members; the conspiratorial relationship between bureaucracies and their clienteles. The research of Nelson Polsby has added one more to this formidable inventory: the "institutionalization" of the House of Representatives (and, I suspect, of many other legislative bodies.)[35]

It would take papers the length of this one to map all the blockages between citizens and their representatives. The sociopsychological studies of mass and elite call into question many critical aspects of voting and interest group theory. In sum, regarding all the modern institutions of representation, one can apply the characterization of Erich Fromm concerning the voting process:

[32] Ira Sharkansky, *op. cit.*, Table III-8.

[33] See Charles E. Lindblom, *A Strategy of Decision* (Glencoe, N.Y.: The Free Press, 1963).

[34] In this light, it is understandable why public opinion polls fluctuated with Administration policy in Vietnam before the Tet crisis. Tet revealed some of the true outcomes of the war.

[35] See Nelson Polsby, "The Institutionalization of the U.S. House of Representatives," *American Political Science Review*, March 1968.

Between the act of voting and the most momentous high-level political decisions is a connection which is mysterious. One cannot say that there is none at all, nor can one say that the final decision is an outcome of the voter's will.[36]

THE STATUS OF SYSTEMS BUDGETING

Just as the process strategies described by Wildavsky suited the politics of its times, so the systems vistas of PPB are in tune with the politics of its times. PPB is part of a larger movement of revision in political study and adjustment in political practice. But just as upheavals in political life have produced disorder and confusion, the new wave in budgeting has generated a good deal of costly disruption and obfuscation.

PPB has had a rough time these past few years. Confusion is widespread; results are meager. The publicity has outdistanced the performance by a wide margin. In the name of analysis, bureaus have produced reams of unsupported, irrelevant justification and description. As Schumpeter said of Marxism: it is preaching in the garb of analysis. Plans have been formulated without serious attention to objectives, resource constraints, and alternative opportunities. PPB's first years have been an exercise in technique. There have been the bulletins and the staffings, the program memoranda, and the program and financial plans. Those who have been apprehensive over possible threats to cherished political values can find no support for their fears in what has happened during these years. Those who had hoped that PPB would not succumb to the tyranny of technique can find much disappointment in what has happened. PPB's products have become its end-products. For so many practitioners, PPB is not some majestic scrutiny of objectives and opportunities, but going through the motions of doing a program structure, writing a program memorandum, of filling in the columns of a program and financial plan.

It is tempting to attribute PPB's difficulties to the manner in which it was introduced, for the implementation strategy has been faulty. But the decisive factor has been the prematurity of PPB.

The conceptual side of PPB presents something of a paradox. The important ideas are few in number and easy to understand. But they happen to run counter to the way American budgeting has been practiced for more than half a century. The concepts which took root in economics and planning will have to undergo considerable mutation before they can be successfully transplanted on political soil. PPB

[36] Erich Fromm, *The Sane Society* (New York: Holt, Rinehart & Winston, Inc., 1955), p. 191.

is an idea whose time has not quite come. It was introduced governmentwide before the requisite concepts, organizational capability, political conditions, informational resources, and techniques were adequately developed.[37] A decade ago, PPB was beyond reach; a decade or two hence, it, or some updated version, might be one of the conventions of budgeting. For the present, PPB must make do in a world it did not create and has not yet mastered.

It is hard to foretell PPB's exact course of development. Certainly there will be many PPB's arising out of the diverse roots and images of systems politics and budgeting, and also out of the diverse perceptions of budget participants and the diverse capabilities of governments. In a technical and methodological sense, there will be continual upgrading in the sophistication of systems budgeting. But there will be no revolutionary overthrow of process in politics. There is an understandable tendency in politics to rely on stable, consensual processes. The pluralists were right about many of their claims for the existing process, the way it reduces conflict and complexity. One can make much the same case for any established process which governs the relationships among competing interests. A permanent systems politics might mean permanent crisis, constant struggle over public ends and means.

I have indicated that the systems ferment is grounded in the conviction that the existing process produces unfavorable outcomes. If systems people had confidence in the process, it would make little sense to go through the costly and possibly divisive reappraisals involved in a system analysis of objectives and alternatives. How, then, can we reconcile the tendency toward process equilibrium with the challenges to the established process? I think the answer is that systems politics will induce a revision in the process. The systems approach enables us to ascertain why the process yields imperfect outcomes. But like the market, we need not throw out the political process because it is deficient; we can compensate for its weaknesses. The task of systems politics is to correct for the defects by making adjustments in the process and by creating new institutions of power and choice. Optimally, the political process should have some gyroscopic capability to assess its outcomes rather than accept them on blind faith as the pluralists have. Budgeting will have a leading role in this readjustment because it is the closest thing politics has to a system for choice. The hybrid process that will emerge will be more responsive and efficient by virtue of the feedback from outcome to process.

[37] These prematurities have been examined in Allen Schick, "PPB's First Years: Premature and Maturing," Washington, D.C.: U.S. Bureau of the Budget, September 1968, mimeo.

ADMINISTRA-TIVE DECENTRAL-IZATION AND POLITICAL POWER

HERBERT KAUFMAN

BUREAUCRACIES AT BAY

How strange it would sound today if a leading social reformer dedicated a book to "Bill Bureaucrat!" Yet when Paul Appleby, a prominent New Deal official, did so in 1945, it was perfectly in keeping with the liberal temper of his time.[1] The burgeoning bureaucracies were seen by many as the executors of the peaceful, lawful, and necessary social revolution then taking place, and were viewed as bringing a high level of professional competence and dedication to their tasks. They were the shaft, if not the spearhead, of social reform.

A generation later, bureaucracies find themselves under fire from many of the same elements of the population who were once their champions. The bureaucracies administering welfare, public schools, public housing, highways, police, urban renewal, employment security, city planning, not to mention the perennial target, foreign policy, have been assailed from many quarters, including, in some cases, the very clienteles they serve. Indeed, even Chief Executives have voiced anxiety about the administrative machinery they allegedly command: President Truman, preparing to depart from the White House, ex-

[1] Paul H. Appleby, *Big Democracy* (New York: Knopf, 1945). Actually, the dedication was "To John Citizen and Bill Bureaucrat."

Paper delivered before the American Political Science Association Annual Meeting, Washington, D.C., September 1968. Herbert Kaufman is Professor of Political Science, Yale University. Reprinted with permission of the author and the American Political Science Association.

pressed sympathy for the frustrations he knew his successor would experience when he discovered his orders would often produce no administrative response.[2] President Eisenhower left office warning of the dangers of the military-industrial complex to a democratic polity.[3] President Kennedy urged his aides to record the history of the Bay of Pigs episode to ensure that the versions being written in the agencies involved would not be the only accounts of the event.[4] President Johnson entrusted direction of the poverty program to an administrator known to believe that the old-line administrative agencies did not have the drive or the imagination to prosecute the war against poverty effectively.[5]

What happened in one generation to produce these changes of position? They cannot be ascribed to a reversal of direction of the part of the bureaucracies, comparable to the shift of the Supreme Court that would turn its liberal critics of the 'thirties into its most ardent defenders and its conservative supporters of the 'thirties into its most vehement censurers; the bureaucracies underwent no such dramatic policy transformation, but merely continued to do what they always had done.

Therein, of course, lies the answer. They have not changed drastically, but the times have. Much of the present impatience and discontent clearly stem from this lag.

The tensions were predictable—and predicted. More than a decade ago, it was said:

To many students of public administration trained in the 'twenties, 'thirties, and 'forties, the new atmosphere will be a strange and perhaps a bewildering one, fraught with hostilities. To students trained in the 'sixties, the literature of the earlier period, with its "principles," may seem quaint and even naive. Political scientists of the remoter future, looking back, may well conclude that it is not easy to bridge the gap between a generation seeking to encourage the growth of a professional bureaucracy and a generation in turmoil over how to control it.[6]

The basis of this prediction was the identification of a pattern in the rhythms of change in the design of our governmental machinery.

[2] Richard E. Neustadt, *Presidential Power* (New York: Science Editions, 1964).

[3] See Section IV of his farewell address to the Nation, *The New York Times,* 18 January 1961.

[4] Arthur M. Schlesinger, Jr., *A Thousand Days* (Boston: Houghton Mifflin, 1965), p. xi.

[5] John C. Donovan, *The Politics of Poverty* (New York: Pegasus, 1967), pp. 30–31; Advisory Commission on Intergovernmental Relations, *Intergovernmental Relations in the Poverty Program* (Washington: 1966), pp. 21, 25.

[6] Herbert Kaufman, "Emerging Conflicts in the Doctrines of Public Administration," *The American Political Science Review,* Vol. 50, No. 4 (December 1956), p. 1073.

From this pattern, we can forecast the next stage in our governmental institutional development and in the doctrines of public administration.

A CYCLE OF VALUES

The prediction that the last third of the twentieth century would be a period of tensions about governmental organization was deduced from a hypothesized cycle in the values strongly influencing governmental design (among other things) at any given time. These values —representativeness, politically neutral competence, and executive leadership—it was suggested, are all exhibited in our governmental institutions all the time, but they succeed each other in relative emphasis, so that each plays a larger part than the others in different periods.

That is not to say the values are pursued abstractly, as ends in themselves, or that there is universal agreement on which should be emphasized at any given time. On the contrary, different segments of the population feel differentially disadvantaged by the governmental machinery in operation at any given moment, and agitate for structural changes to improve their position—i.e., to increase their influence—in the system. Discontent on the part of various groups is thus the dynamic force that motivates the quest for new forms. Some groups feel resentful because they consider themselves inadequately represented; some feel frustrated because, though they are influential in forming policy, then policy decisions seem to be dissipated by the political biases or the technical incompetence of the public bureaucracies; some feel thwarted by lack of leadership to weld the numerous parts of government into a coherent, unified team that can get things done. At different points in time, enough people (not necessarily a numerical majority) will be persuaded by one or another of these discontents to support remedial action—increased representativeness, better and politically neutral bureaucracies, or stronger chief executives as the case may be. But emphasis on one remedy over a prolonged period merely accumulates the other discontents until new remedies gain enough support to be put into effect, and no totally stable solution has yet been devised. So the constant shift in emphasis goes on.

Thus, it was argued in the paper quoted above, our earliest political institutions at all levels were shaped by reaction against executive dominance in the colonial era. Extreme reliance was placed instead on representative mechanisms, which made the post-Revolutionary years an interval of great power for legislatures and elective officials and of comparative weakness for executives in most jurisdictions. By the middle of the nineteenth century, however, legislative supremacy, the long ballot, and the spoils system resulted in widespread disillusionment with our political institutions, which in turn gave impetus to efforts to take administration out of politics by lodging it in independent boards and commissions and by introducing the merit system to break the hold of parties on the bureaucracies. But the fragmentation of government reduced both efficiency and representativeness, and the search for unification led to the popularly elected chief executives; the twentieth century was marked by a rapid growth in their powers.

Although each successive reform was not conceived as an attack on representativeness, the pursuit of the other values does in fact seem to have contributed to a growing sense of alienation on the part of many people, to a feeling that they as individuals cannot effectively register their own preferences on the decisions emerging from the organs of government.[7] In short, they feel inadequately represented, if not totally excluded. To be sure, it is not *merely* the structure of government that engenders a sensation of helplessness; the burgeoning of large-scale organizations in every area of life may be an even more important factor.[8] But institutional arrangements unquestionably intensify what would probably have been a problem under any circumstances. Already, efforts to redress the balance among the values are evident, and the quest for a political solution is adding to the strains on old institutions and perhaps giving rise to some new ones.

CURRENT DISSATISFACTION

America is not wanting in arrangements for representation. More than half a million public offices are still elective.[9] Legislatures and

[7] Murray Levin, The Alienated Voter (New York: Holt, Rinehart, and Winston, 1960), Chap. 4.

[8] See for example, Robert Presthus, The Organizational Society (New York: Knopf, 1962), pp. 39–49; Bertram M. Gross, The Managing of Organizations (Glencoe: Free Press, 1964), Vol. 1, Chap. 4; Roderick Seidenberg, Post-Historic Man (Boston: Beacon Press, 1957); W. Lloyd Warner, Darab B. Unwalla, and John H. Trimm (eds.), The Emergent American Society: Volume 1, Large-scale Organizations (New Haven: Yale University Press, 1967).

[9] U.S. Bureau of the Census, 1957 Census of Governments, Vol. 1, No. 4, Elective Offices of State and Local Governments (Washington: Government Printing Office, 1958), p. 4. These figures were not updated in the 1962 Census of Governments, and the totals in the 1967 Census were not available at the time of this writing, although details were; see U.S. Bureau of the Census, Census of Governments 1967: Elective Offices of State and Local Governments, Preliminary Report (Washington: Bureau of the Census, 1967). A tentative review of the details suggests the 1967 figures will be of approximately the same magnitude as the 1957 totals.

individual legislators retain immense powers, and do not hesitate to wield them liberally. Parties are still strong and attentive to the claims of many constituencies. Interest groups are numerous and press their demands through myriad channels. The mass media serve as watchdogs of governmental operations. Administrative agencies incorporate manifold procedures for representation into their decision-making processes, including quasi-judicial and quasi-legislative hearings, representative or bipartisan administrative boards, and advisory bodies.[10] Opportunities for participation in political decisions are plentiful. Why, then, is there dissatisfaction with these arrangements?

Fundamentally, because substantial (though minority) segments of the population apparently believe the political, economic, and social systems have not delivered to them fair—even minimally fair —shares of the systems' benefits and rewards, and because they think they cannot win their appropriate shares in those benefits and rewards through the political institutions of the country as these are now constituted. These people are not mollified by assurances that the characteristics of the system thwarting them also thwart selfish and extremist interests; it appears to them that only the powerful get attention, and that the already powerful are helped by the system to deny influence to all who now lack it. Thus, the system itself, and not just evil men who abuse it, is discredited.

At least three characteristics of the system contribute heavily to this impression on the part of the deprived: First, existing representative organs are capable of giving only quite general mandates to administrative agencies, yet it is in the day-to-day decisions and actions of officials and employees in the lower levels that individual citizens perceive the policies. There are often gross discrepancies between the promise of the programs (as construed by the populace to be served) and performance—sometimes because the expectations of the populace are unrealistically optimistic, sometimes because programs are impeded by difficulties that could not be foreseen, and sometimes because bureaucracies are too bound by habit or timidity to alter their customary behavior in any but the most modest ways. Whatever the specific reasons for the discrepancies, the result is disillusionment with the machinery through which the general mandate is given and a search for methods of influencing the more particular, small-scale actions of officialdom.[11]

[10] Avery Leiserson, *Administrative Regulation: A Study in Representation of Group Interests* (Chicago: The University of Chicago Press, 1942).

[11] See, for instance, the criticism of professional bureaucracy and the demand for "public participation" in resource management decisions by Yale Law School Professor Charles A. Reich in his *Bureaucracy and the Forests* (Santa Barbara: Center for the Study of Democratic Institutions, 1962).

Second, the pluralistic nature of the political system provides abundant opportunities for vetoes by opponents of change. Each proposed innovation must run a gamut of obstacles, and ends as a product of bargains and compromises. In general, political structure and procedure tend to favor the status quo, and to place a heavy burden on the advocates of major change. So change usually comes slowly, by small advances, in bits and pieces. Those who regard particular problems as requiring urgent, immediate action are prone to condemn a system that behaves so "sluggishly." For them, at that moment in time, the virtues of the system seem far outweighed by its defects.

Third, the scale of organization in our society has grown so large that only through large-scale organization does it seem possible to have a significant impact. This impression alone is enough to make individual people feel helplessly overwhelmed by huge, impersonal machines indifferent to their uniqueness and their humanity. In addition, however, some interests—notably, those of Negroes and of youth—have recently begun to develop the organizational skills to mobilize their political resources only to find that it takes time to build channels of access to political structures. Rather than wait for admission to these structures—where, incidentally, they are likely to encounter larger, more experienced, well-entrenched organizations opposed to them—these groups, while continuing to strive for recognition in the older institutions, have adopted a strategy of deriding those institutions and seeking to build new ones in which they can have greater, perhaps dominant, influence.

Thus, the plenitude of traditional modes of representation no longer suffices; the existing methods do not adequately accommodate many of the demands upon them. Just as the adaption of governmental design during the past century has gravitated toward furnishing expertise and leadership, so it is now under pressure from several quarters to accord a greater role to representativeness.

INCREASING REPRESENTATIVENESS THROUGH ADMINISTRATIVE CHANGE

The quest for representativeness in this generation centers primarily on administrative agencies. Since administrative agencies have grown dramatically in size, function, and authority in the middle third of this century, this is hardly surprising. Chief executives, legislatures, and courts make more decisions of sweeping effect, but the agencies make a far greater number of decisions affecting individual citizens in intimate ways. In them lies the source of much present unrest; in them, therefore, the remedies are sought.

One type of proposal for making administrative agencies more representative is traditional in character; situating spokesmen for the interests affected in strategic positions within the organizations. Often, this means nothing more than filling vacancies on existing boards and commissions with appointees enjoying the confidence of, or perhaps even chosen by, those interests.[12] In the case of the controversial police review boards, it involves injecting into administrative structures new bodies, dominated by ethnic minority groups or their friends to survey and constrain bureaucratic behavior. Architecturally, such plans do not require drastic modifications of existing organizations, and their objectives could probably be met by changes in personnel at high organizational levels. So they are not sharp departures from prevailing institutions and practices, but they do reflect the mounting uneasiness about lack of some kinds of representativeness in administration.

More unorthodox, but swiftly gaining acceptance, is the concept of a centralized governmental complaint bureau, clothed with legal powers of investigation, to look into citizen complaints against administrative agencies and to correct inequities and abuses—the office of "ombudsman."[13] Once, it was chiefly through his representative in the appropriate legislative body, or through the local unit of his political party, that a citizen of modest status and means petitioned for a remedy of a grievance. But professionalization of administration and the insulation of bureaucrats from party politics has reduced the ability of the parties to be of real help, and the constituencies of legislators have grown so large that they rarely intervene in more than a *pro forma* fashion on behalf of most individual constituents. Today, some observers contend that only a specialized, full-time official, wise in the ways of bureaucracy, having a vested interest in correcting its errors, and supported by adequate staff and authority, can perform this function effectively; apparently, it takes a bureaucrat to control a bureaucrat. Advocates of this proposed new agency defend it on the grounds that it would constitute a channel of representation for people who now have no satisfactory alternative.

The most sweeping expression of the unrest about lack of representativeness is the growing demand for extreme administrative de-

[12] For example, *The New York Times* reported on 29 November 1967 that "A [New York City] citizen group demanded yesterday that a Negro and a Puerto Rican be named to the city's nine-man Community Mental Health Board." And a high-ranking city antipoverty administrator (suspended for failing to file tax returns) went on a hunger strike to dramatize his demand that Puerto Ricans be named to the Board of Education, the State Board of Regents, the citywide Model Cities Advisory Committee, the Civil Service Commission, and the City Housing Authority; *The New York Times,* 29 June 1968.

[13] Walter Gellhorn, *When Americans Complain* (Cambridge: Harvard University Press, 1966) and *Ombudsmen and Others* (Cambridge: Harvard University Press, 1966); Stanley Anderson (ed.), *Ombudsmen for American Government* (Englewood Cliffs: Prentice-Hall, 1968).

centralization, frequently coupled with insistence on local clientele domination of the decentralized organization. Dramatic manifestations of this movement occurred in the anti-poverty program and in education.

In the anti-poverty program, the original legislation included a provision that community action be "developed, conducted, and administered with maximum feasible participation of residents of the areas and members of the groups served." Initially by interpretation of the Office of Economic Opportunity, and later by statute, the provision was construed to mean that community action boards should try to allot some of their chairs to the poor, so that the poor would have a voice in the highest policy councils of the community programs. Whatever the original intent of the drafters of the phrase (about which there is some disagreement) it has come to mean the program is to be run in substantial degree *by* the poor, not merely *for* the poor.[14]

In public education, the new trend is exemplified by recent events in New York City. In the spring of 1967, the mayor asked the state legislature for additional financial assistance for education on the grounds that the city embraced five countries and deserved to be treated as having five educational systems rather than one. Legislative leaders advised him the system would have to be truly decentralized if that were to be his argument. In the summer and fall, three separate reports proposed steps to this end: One was an academic study. One was a study by an Advisory Committee on Decentralization (headed by McGeorge Bundy of the Ford Foundation) appointed by the mayor. One was a study by the State Board of Regents, which called for even more sweeping changes than the other two.[15]

The City Board of Education, the United Federation of Teachers, and the Council of Supervisory Associations, were unanimously critical of all three studies.[16] The Board twice made concessions to

14 *The New York Times,* 29 October 1967; Advisory Commission on Intergovernmental Relations, *op. cit.,* pp. 48–55. But there was opposition; see John C. Donovan, *op. cit.,* pp. 54–61. Nevertheless, many communities have complied with OEO requirements by providing for neighborhood election of at least some of the board members of local anti-poverty agencies; see, for example, *The New York Times,* 6 May, 1968, and William L. White, *The Power of the Poor: Resident Participation in New Haven's Community Action Program* (Unpublished Scholar of the House thesis, Yale College, 1967).

15 For the history of these phases of the New York City school decentralization battle, see *The New York Times,* 13 August, 12 November, and 20 November 1967.

16 For the reactions of these groups to the decentralization proposals, see *The New York Times,* 26 October, 10 November, and 4 December 1967; 25 April, 28 April, and 29 April, 1968.

the demands for decentralization by enlarging the authority of its local advisory boards, but these did not satisfy the advocates of change.[17] In the spring of 1968, the mayor sent to the state legislature an adaptation of the Bundy plan—more extensive than the Board of Education and the officials and teachers of the city system favored, less drastic than the recommendations of the Regents.[18]

In the face of opposition from those who thought his plan went too far (the United Federation of Teachers spent $200,000 to defeat strong decentralization measures[19]) and those who thought it was too mild, his bill fared poorly. The mayor therefore swung to the side of the Regents' measure, which had the Governor's support, in hopes of keeping the measure alive. But the legislators grew uneasy as the opponents exerted increasing pressure. In the closing hours of the session, therefore, a much weaker compromise bill was passed and signed by the Governor.[20] Though a disappointment to those who wanted prompt, extensive action, it was nevertheless a step in the direction of decentralization, and clearly not the last one. The thrust toward decentralization and neighborhood control of the schools could be slowed but not stopped.

The outcry has not been limited to the war on poverty and to education. It was taken up in public housing when the Secretary of Housing and Urban Development unveiled a program to modernize low-rent projects that included an augmented role for tenants in their operation.[21] At a meeting of the American Institute of Planners, a dissenting group, calling itself Planners for Equal Opportunity, demanded a larger place for the poor in city planning, and exhorted its members to engage in "advocate planning," which is to say expert counsel for neighborhood associations unhappy with official plans for renewal in their areas.[22] New York City recently began experimenting with a process of "affiliating" its public hospitals with voluntary hospitals that would be responsible for their administration, a plan that would presumably include lay boards representing the community served by each institution,[23] and its Police Department is

---

[17] *The New York Times,* 20 October 1967, 8 March and 30 March 1968.

[18] *The New York Times,* 30 March 1968.

[19] *The New York Times,* 13 June 1968.

[20] *The New York Times,* 28 April, 15 May, 17 May, 21 May, 26 May 1968.

[21] *The New York Times,* 18 November 1967. John W. Gardner, former Secretary of Health, Education, and Welfare, and currently chairman of the Urban Coalition, went even further and urged a larger role for Negroes in helping solve the urban crisis generally, *The New York Times,* 6 May 1968.

[22] *The Washington Post,* 3 October 1967.

[23] Martin Cherkasky, "The City Should Get Out of the Hospital Business," *The New York Times Magazine,* 8 October 1967, pp. 53ff.

cooperating with experimental community security patrols of locally recruited young people.[24] Similarly, a neighborhood council in Washington "asked for more citizen control over police, either in the form of local police aides or resurrection of the auxiliary police force used here in World War II."[25] The American Assembly, assessing the role of law in a changing society, called for development of "rapid procedures at the neighborhood level . . . to adjudicate disputes over simple transactions."[26] In response to the Poor People's Campaign in Washington, "Five agencies—Health, Education and Welfare, Agriculture, Labor, Housing and Urban Development and the Office of Economic Opportunity—said they would review their plans to involve poor people themselves in local decisions affecting welfare, food, employment, housing and other anti-poverty programs."[27]

The movement is not confined to public agencies; it reaches into colleges and universities, where students, often by direct action, have been asserting a claim to participation in the policies of these institutions—one activist reportedly going so far as to predict that American universities will soon resemble Latin American institutions, in which students hire and fire professors and determine the curriculum.[28] A sociologist recently suggested establishment of closed-circuit television stations in which the neighborhood listeners might control programming.[29] In the Roman Catholic Archdiocese of New York, a committee of priests presented a petition to the archbishop-designate requesting, among other things, a voice in the selection of auxiliary bishops and other high officials, and establishment of a Pastoral Council of priests, nuns, and laymen to be consulted in advance on projected programs and budgets, a request to which he partially acceded on taking office;[30] later, priests formed a national organization, the National Federation of Priests Councils, to seek a stronger voice in Church affairs.[31] In Washington, classes at a high school were suspended in the face of a boycott by students demanding "a real say on what goes on inside the school."[32]

[24] *The New York Times,* 19 March 1968.

[25] *The Washington Post,* 2 April 1968.

[26] *Report of the American Assembly on Law and the Changing Society* (Center for Continuing Education, University of Chicago, 14–17 March 1968).

[27] *The New York Times,* 30 June 1968.

[28] *The Wall Street Journal,* 14 February 1968. See also, *The New York Times,* 6 May 1968.

[29] Seymour J. Mandelbaum, "Spatial and Temporal Perspectives in the U.S. City," mimeo., University of Pennsylvania, 1968.

[30] *The New York Times,* 14 March and 17 May 1968.

[31] *The New York Times,* 21 May 1968.

[32] *The Washington Post,* 9 December 1967.

But it is in the government sphere that the tendency has been winning widest endorsement. Indeed, some of our general forms of government, as well as specific agencies, have come under attack. The President of the American Political Science Association, for example, in his 1967 presidential address,[33] raised questions about the compatibility of large units of government—national, state and urban —with the principles of democracy. Searching for a unit large enough to avoid triviality yet "small enough so that citizens can participate extensively," he suggested 50,000 to 200,000 as the optimum size range for democratic city governments. Moreover, he concluded that even in polities of this size, "participation is reduced for most people to nothing more than voting in elections," and he therefore commended experimentation to decentralize power and authority still further in order to discover viable "smaller units within which citizens can from time to time formulate and express their desires, consult with officials, and in some cases participate even more fully in decisions." Similarly, the Advisory Commission on Intergovernmental Relations in Washington, at almost the same time, was recommending[34] that "Neighborhood initiative and self-respect be fostered by authorizing counties and large cities to establish, and at their discretion to abolish, neighborhood subunits endowed with limited powers of taxation and local self-government." At Ithaca, New York, the Office of Regional Resources and Development concluded that larger metropolitan centers should be decentralized because they have reached a point at which "it is almost impossible to deal with human problems on a human scale," and called for investigation of strategies for more effective use of cities with 50,000 to 500,000 residents—proposals that won the editorial plaudits of *The Washington Post*.[35] A meeting of Americans for Democratic Action was warned by Daniel P. Moynihan, an outspoken liberal, that "Liberals must divest themselves of the notion that the nation, especially the cities of the nation, can be run from agencies in Washington."[36] Senator Robert F. Kennedy, campaigning for the Democratic presidential nomination in Los Angeles, promised audiences a revolution in the distribution of political power that would, among other things, reduce the authority of the federal bureaucracy in Washington; "I want," he said, "the control over your destinies to be decided by the

[33] Robert A. Dahl, "The City in the Future of Democracy," *The American Political Science Review*, Vol. 61, No. 4 (December, 1967), pp. 967, 969.

[34] Advisory Commission on Intergovernmental Relations, *Ninth Annual Report* (Washington: 1968), p. 21.

[35] 10 October 1967.

[36] *The New York Times*, 24 September 1967. But he criticized school decentralization a short time later; *The New York Times*, 5 June 1968.

people in Watts, not by those of us who are in Washington."[37] Richard M. Nixon similarly urged the federal government to relinquish some of its powers to state and local governments, voluntary associations and individuals, saying, "One reason people are shouting so loudly today is that it's far from where they are to where the power is," and that power should be brought closer to them rather than exercised from remote centers.[38] In important respects, the Heller-Pechman plan, devised by two advisors to the President, rests partly on the premise that federal surpluses should be shared with states and cities in time of peace because they can be more effectively spent by the smaller units of government than by Washington directly.[39]

In short, "decentralization" of administration is in the air everywhere.[40] While it is sometimes defended on grounds of efficiency, it is more frequently justified in terms of effective popular participation in government. Reformers of earlier generations succeeded in raising the level of expertise and professionalism in the bureaucracies, and, to a lesser extent, in improving the capacity of chief executives to control the administrative arms of government. Now, people are once again turning their attention to representativeness, which was more or less taken for granted in earlier reforms and which therefore lost ground relatively, and are trying to elevate it to a more prominent place in the governmental scheme of things.

[37] *The Washington Post,* 26 March 1968. See also the arguments of a former Foreign Service Officer for "dismantling the present overgrown bureaucratic apparatus" in Washington; Gordon Tullock, *The Politics of Bureaucracy* (Washington: Public Affairs Press, 1965), Chap. 25.

That liberals have thus adopted a position taken by conservatives in New Deal days is an irony to which attention has been drawn by James Q. Wilson, "The Bureaucracy Problem," *The Public Interest,* Vol. 2, No. 6 (Winter, 1967), pp. 3–4. Note the similarities between the new liberal language and the position of former Governor George C. Wallace of Alabama: "I would," he said, "bring all those briefcase-toting bureaucrats in the Department of Health, Education and Welfare to Washington and throw their briefcases in the Potomac River . . . ," *The New York Times,* 9 February 1968. His attack on bureaucrats is, of course, based on their zeal in defense of civil rights; the liberals' indictment is constructed on a diametrically opposite appraisal. The impulse toward decentralization thus comes from both the political right and the political left for entirely different reasons—but with combined force.

[38] *The New York Times,* 28 June 1968.

[39] "Revenue sharing expresses the traditional faith most of us have in pluralism and decentralization . . . All of us have a direct stake in the financial health of state-local governments for the simple reason that they perform the bulk of essential civilian services in the country." Walter W. Heller and Joseph A. Pechman, *Questions and Answers in Revenue Sharing* (Washington: The Brookings Institution, 1967), pp. 12–13.

[40] Like all slogans, it means different things to different people, however. It is a much more complex and ambiguous concept than it seems; see p. 417, below, and Note 47.

THE CONTINUING SEARCH FOR LEADERSHIP

Public bureaucracies are under fire not only from critics outside the machinery of government, but also from inside. Chief executives who once championed measures to insulate the bureaucracies from partisan politics as steps toward enlarging their own control over administrative agencies discovered that these measures did not make the agencies more responsive to executive direction; rather, it increased their independence. This independence, in turn, makes it difficult for the executives to secure enthusiastic adoption of new approaches to social problems; money pumped into new programs administered by established agencies tends to be used more for intensification of traditional ways of operating than for inventive departures from familiar patterns. Furthermore, it results in massive problems of coordination of effort, and even in dissipation of energies in interbureau rivalries. Consequently, just as segments of the public are upset by the alleged unresponsiveness of administration to their demands, so chief executives have been increasingly concerned about the unresponsiveness of agencies to their leadership.[41]

We may therefore look forward to new waves of administrative reorganization proposals. One principal thrust of the movement will, as in the past, be toward rationalizing, enlarging, and strengthening the executive-office staffs of the heads of governmental units at all levels, and toward building up the staffs of the administrators who report directly to the heads. More and more, chief executives will reach out for new devices to coordinate policy decisions, to work up fresh programs to deal with emergent problems, and to maintain the momentum of innovations adopted.[42] Executive offices will be redesigned; the U.S. Bureau of the Budget, for example, has only recently undergone a major reorganization.[43] New vigor will be applied to the exploration of "super-departments," with the Department of Defense as a prototype; Mayor Lindsay, for instance, has expended much political capital on introducing this concept into the govern-

[41] See, for example, Schlesinger, *op. cit.*, pp. 679–86.

The problem is not exclusively American. Premier Fidel Castro of Cuba opened a "battle against bureaucracy," but complained after a couple of years that the anti-bureaucratic campaign itself had become mired in bureaucracy; *The New York Times,* 21 February 1967, 24 May 1967.

[42] The Executive Office of the President was created in 1939, when the federal budget was under $9 billion. It has grown since, but not nearly as much as the budget, now fifteen times larger and many hundreds of times more complex. Some reordering seems almost inevitable.

[43] U.S. Bureau of the Budget, "Work of the Steering Group on Evaluation of the Bureau of the Budget: A Staff Study," July, 1967. The reorganization took effect shortly afterwards.

ment of New York City.[44] Programming-Planning-Budgeting Systems, in many variants, will continue to spread.[45] There will be a new burst of literature calling attention to the relative powerlessness of our highest public executives.[46]

Another stream of recommendations will urge strengthening executive leadership through what its advocates will call "decentralization," but which, in fact, is better characterized as organization by area as opposed to the present almost exclusive organization by functional departments and bureaus.[47] The justification for it will be couched in terms of efficiency—the need to speed decisions in the field without referral to headquarters and without loss of coordination among field personnel in different bureaus. The consequences will extend further, however, because areal officers in the field would give top executives lines of communication and control alternative to existing functional channels, thus actually strengthening central authority. At the federal level, this will mean renewed attempts to

[44] *The New York Times,* 11 December 1966, 16 February 1967, 23 April 1968. By the middle of the summer, 1968, four of the ten proposed super-departments still had not been approved by the City Council and signed into law.

[45] The origins of PPBS are many and varied; see Allen Schick, "The Road to PPB," *Public Administration Review,* Vol. 26, No. 4 (December, 1966), pp. 243–58. But it was the system's utility to the Secretary of Defense from 1961 on in gaining control of his own department that gave widespread currency to the idea and induced the President to make it governmentwide in 1965; see U.S. Senate, 90th Congress, 1st Session (1967), Committee on Government Operations, Subcommittee on National Security and International Operations, *Program-Planning-Budgeting: Official Documents,* pp. 1–6, and *Program-Planning-Budgeting: Hearings, Part 1* (23 August 1967). This new impetus will doubtless lead to adaptive imitation in other governments.

[46] Schlesinger, *op. cit.,* pp. 679–80, reports, "he [President Kennedy] had to get the government moving. He came to the White House at a time when the ability of the President to do this had suffered steady constriction. The clichés about the 'most powerful office on earth' had concealed the extent to which the mid-century Presidents had much less freedom of action than, say, Jackson or Lincoln or even Franklin Roosevelt. No doubt the mid-century Presidents could blow up the world, but at the same time they were increasingly hemmed in by the growing power of the bureaucracy and of Congress. The President understood this." Similarly, President Johnson's assistant for domestic programs, Joseph A. Califano, Jr., recently complained publicly of the limitations of presidential power, observing that the powers of the office have not kept pace with its growing responsibilities; *The Washington Post,* 6 May 1968. See also, Sayre and Kaufman, *op. cit.,* pp. 669–79.

[47] James W. Fesler, *Area and Administration* (University, Alabama: University of Alabama Press, 1949), especially pp. 8–18, and "Approaches to the Understanding of Decentralization," *The Journal of Politics,* Vol. 27, No. 3 (August 1965), pp. 557–61. See also the essay by John D. Millett, "Field Organization and Staff Supervision," in *New Horizons in Public Administration: A Symposium* (University, Alabama: University of Alabama Press, 1945), pp. 96–118.

set up much stronger regional representatives of the heads of cabinet departments than any we have had in the past. It will also mean intensified efforts to establish regional presidential representatives in the field.[48] Similarly, we may anticipate governors and their department heads will follow the same strategies with respect to regions within the states. At the local level, Mayor Lindsay has already sought—with very limited success—to win approval for "little City Halls" throughout New York, and may ultimately find himself engaged in new bureaucratic struggles as the administrators of his new super-departments try to introduce regional coordinators to supervise the field operations of the bureaus under their command. Distinctively American versions of the European prefect may yet make an appearance.

In short, dissatisfaction with public bureaucracies will furnish ammunition for the defenders of executive leadership as well as for the proponents of increased representation of the consumers of public services. The bureaucracies will be pressed from both above and below.

CONFLICT AND COALITION

SOURCES OF CONFLICT

It has long been recognized that much public policy is shaped largely by clusters of bureaus, their organized clienteles, and legislative committees and legislators specializing in each public function[49]— health, education, welfare, etc. The arguments for strengthening chief executives and their department heads vis-à-vis the clusters are based chiefly on the need to offset the resulting fragmentation of government by introducing sufficient central direction to unify the policies and administration of these separate centers of power. The arguments for new modes of participation by the public in these centers rest on the conviction that hitherto excluded and unorganized interests have little to say about decisions that affect them profoundly. But it is most unlikely that the pressures of either kind will be welcomed by those already in key positions in each decision center.

They will resist not simply out of abstract jealousy of their own power or stubborn unwillingness to share their influence with each other, though these motives will doubtless not be absent. They will

[48] James W. Fesler, *Area and Administration*, pp. 88–89. Fesler's writing on this subject anticipated long in advance the problems that were to engender a more general awareness when programs of the New Frontier and the Great Society overwhelmed the administrative machinery.

[49] See J. Leiper Freeman, *The Political Process: Executive Bureau-Legislative Committee Relations* (New York: Random House, 1955), and the works therein cited in Chapter One.

oppose because, in addition, the proposed reforms threaten those values which present arrangements protect. Bureau chiefs and the organized bureaucracies perceive intervention by political executives as the intrusion of partisan politics into fields from which doctrine has for many years held that politics should be excluded; they see jeopardy for the competence nurtured so carefully and painfully against political distortion or extinction. Similarly, opening the system to lay members of local communities looks like a negation of the expertise built up by the specialists. Legislators regard strong regional officials responsive to chief executives and their cabinets as executive attempts to invade legislative districts and usurp the representative function of legislative bodies. In like fashion, local control of administrative programs could conceivably weaken the representative basis of legislative institutions, a development that men of goodwill may fear for quite public-spirited reasons.

So the champions of executive leadership and the evangelists of expanded representativeness have many obstacles to overcome before they have their respective ways. For example, Congress has been cautious about presidential recommendations of added funds and personnel for the heads of Cabinet departments, and has always looked with suspicion on so relatively innocuous an innovation as field offices for the Bureau of the Budget.[50] The Office of Economic Opportunity in the Executive Office of the President always operated chiefly through established bureaus and engaged in independent administration only in limited ways; gradually, through delegation, it has been relinquishing its control over programs to the bureaus, and the future of even those programs it manages directly is uncertain.[51] Moreover, its community-action program aroused resentment among both Congressmen and local executives, to whom the action agencies appeared as springboards for political rivals; consequently, legislation in 1967 authorized greater control of the agencies by local governments.[52] In New York City, the mayor's "little City Halls," which he presented as a device for bringing the people and their government

[50] Bureau of the Budget field offices were set up in mid-1943, but were eliminated in the early years of the Eisenhower administration. Recent efforts to revive them, even on a limited basis, ran into stiff opposition; see U.S. Senate, 90th Congress, 1st Session, Subcommittee of the Committee on Appropriations, *Hearings on H.R. 7501: Treasury, Post Office, and Executive Office Appropriations for Fiscal Year 1968* (Washington: Government Printing Office, 1967), pp. 973–990. Note especially the comments of Senator Monroney at p. 981: "The reason the committee cut your request for additional personnel last year was because it did not wish to have field offices established . . . My impression was that we were afraid they would grow into a 50-State bureaucracy with State and regional offices."

[51] See John C. Donovan, *op. cit.,* p. 51.

[52] *The New York Times,* 7 February 1968.

closer together, were soundly defeated by a City Council (dominated by the opposite party) denouncing the plan as a strategy for establishing political clubhouses throughout the city at public expense.[53] And, as noted earlier, when the "Bundy plan" for school decentralization appeared, the largest teachers' union and the Board of Education, which not long before had been at each other's throats in labor disputes, each took a similar firm stand against it.[54] In Board-sponsored experiments with community control of schools in Harlem and in Brooklyn, the community leaders and the head of the same teachers' union engaged in acrimonious battles with each other.[55] The reformers are not having an easy time of it.

A COALITION OF EXECUTIVES

To advance their cause, troubled chief executives at all levels, all suffering similar frustrations, could conceivably make common cause with one another. Thus, the President may well find it strategically advantageous to build closer ties with governors and big-city mayors than was ever the case before; Congress would find it more uncomfortable to resist presidential demands for creation of strong field representatives with jurisdiction over bureau field personnel if state and local officials in their own home areas support the demands than if the President alone advances them. And these state and local officials may be receptive to such an association because the fragmentation of the system is as vexing to them as it is to the President himself.

Gubernatorial and big-city mayoral vexations spring from three sources. First, procedures in many intergovernmental programs are

[53] The mayor proposed 35 local mayor's offices soon after his inauguration; *The New York Times*, 27 January 1966. Encountering opposition in the Board of Estimate, he tried to set up five by executive order; *ibid.*, 29 January 1966. But the City Council refused to support him (*ibid.*, 2 February 1966, 17 February 1966, 16 April 1966, 16 January 1967), and the Comptroller refused to approve payment of their bills (*ibid.*, 24 December 1966). The mayor tried again in May, 1967, but was again rebuffed by the Council and the Board of Estimate (*ibid.*, 9 May 1967, 10 May 1967, 12 May 1967, 24 May 1967). Eventually, four local offices were opened, but they were much weaker than was originally anticipated (*ibid.*, 26 January, 9 June 1967, 31 July 1967). For the time being, at least, the plan seems emasculated.

[54] Note 16, above.

[55] In both instances, the union and the parents clashed over the appointment and removal of teachers and principals, with the parents insisting on control of these decisions and the union refusing to acknowledge their authority. On the Harlem dispute see *The Washington Post*, 2 October 1967, and *The New York Times*, 5 November 1967. On the Brooklyn controversy, see *The New York Times*, 11 May, 12 May, 15 May, 17 May, and 23 May 1968.

irritatingly slow; it often takes months—sometimes more than a year, in fact—to get decisions on projects and financing from federal agencies, partly because so much business is referred to Washington for approval.[56] To be sure, state and municipal executives have no wish to speed negative decisions on their requests, but hanging decisions are even worse; they can neither plan programs nor try to get the decisions reversed. They can only wait while dangerous pressures build up in their jurisdictions, and whole networks of interrelated programs are slowed or brought to a halt.

Second, procedures are often labyrinthine and uncoordinated,[57] so that it takes specialists to keep track of terminal dates, filing of applications for renewal of grants, compliance with accounting requirements, meshing of separate grants in individual projects, and explanations of variations in allowances (such as differences in relocation allowances for businesses and individual tenants moved for highway construction on the one hand and urban renewal on the other) that bewilder and annoy the public. These intricacies almost paralyze action at the grassroots, and divert needed manpower from substantive program operations to administrative routine.

Third, federal grants for very specific purposes encourage a tendency toward what the 1955 Commission on Intergovernmental Relations referred to as "a more or less independent government of their own" on the part of functional specialists at all levels of government who are only nominally under the control of their respective chief executives.[58] In point of fact, the chief executives are apparently reduced in many instances to virtually ceremonial ratification of the intergovernmental arrangements worked out by such specialists, and to the most superficial oversight of the administration of the arrangements.

So governors and big-city mayors have reason to applaud the introduction of federal regional officers with authority to rationalize the actions of federal field personnel in the bureaus. For reasons of their own, they may well find the "prefectoral" pattern of organization, which, as we have seen, will suggest itself ever more insistently to the President, coincides with their own preferences.

This congruence of presidential, gubernatorial, and mayoral interests is not entirely speculative; indications of it have already appeared. Late in 1966, for example, President Johnson sent to a number

---

[56] Stephen K. Bailey, "Co-ordinating the Great Society," *The Reporter*, Vol. 34, No. 6 (24 March 1966), p. 39.

[57] *Ibid.*

[58] *The Final Report* of the Commission on Intergovernmental Relations (Washington: Government Printing Office, 1955), p. 44. See also Colman B. Ransome Jr., *The Office of the Governor of the United States* (University, Alabama: The University of Alabama Press, 1956), p. 249.

of his top officials a memorandum[59] directing that federal assistance programs "be worked out and planned in a cooperative spirit with those chief officials of State, county and local governments who are answerable to the citizens. To the fullest practical extent, I want you to take steps to afford representatives of the Chief Executives of State and local governments the opportunity to advise and consult in the development and execution of programs which directly affect the conduct of State and local affairs." A few months later, to implement the President's memorandum, the Bureau of the Budget issued a circular[60] spelling out procedures for consultation, and identifying as one of its central policies the requirement that "The central coordinating role of heads of State and local governments, including their role of initiating and developing State and local programs, will be supported and strengthened." Meanwhile, former Florida governor Farris Bryant, director of the Office of Emergency Planning in the Executive Office of the President, was leading teams of federal officials to forty state capitals for discussions with Governors and other state administrators;[61] Vice President Humphrey was conducting a program of visits and discussions with mayors, county officers, and other local executives;[62] and the President was formulating and announcing a plan to assign each member of his cabinet responsibility for liaison with four or five states, "with instructions to maintain personal contact between the Governors and the White House."[63] And in early 1968, the Advisory Commission on Intergovernmental Relations recommended that "1. Coordination of Federal grant programs being administered by a variety of Federal departments and agencies be strengthened through the Executive Office of the President; 2. The authority to review and approve plans developed as a condition of Federal formula-type grants to State and local governments be decentralized to Federal regional offices and the wide

---

[59] "The President's Memorandum to Heads of Certain Federal Agencies. November 11, 1966. Subject: Advice and Consultation with State and local officials."

[60] Bureau of the Budget Circular No. A–85, 28 June 1967.

[61] Advisory Commission on Intergovernmental Relations, *Ninth Annual Report* (Washington: 1968), p. 12.

[62] *Ibid.*, pp. 12–13.

[63] The plan grew out of "Mr. Johnson's continuing determination to build domestic as well as foreign bridges by working to sort out the tangled Federal-state relations that have been increasingly complicated by the administration of the Great Society Programs." *The New York Times*, 8 June 1967. See also Terry Sanford, *Storm Over the States* (New York: McGraw-Hill, 1967), pp. 164–66; here, a former governor calls on the White House to help state and local governments and quotes James Reston's comment that "He [the President] is reaching out to the governors and mayors of America for a new political, social, and economic partnership."

variations in boundaries of Federal administrative regions be reduced."[64] An alliance of public chief executives is already taking
shape.

THE CONFLUENCE OF REPRESENTATIVENESS
AND LEADERSHIP

At the same time, groups clamoring for local control of administrative
programs, confronted with the suspicion and resentment of bureaucracies and their legislative and interest-group allies, will probably
discover that they get their most sympathetic hearings from chief
executives, especially from big-city mayors. For such groups can
provide the executives with the counterweights to the bureaucracies:
they constitute an alternative channel of information about administrative performance, reducing executive dependence on the bureaucracies on the one hand and on the mass media (with their bias
toward the sensational) on the other. The groups are a constituency
that can be mobilized to help exert leverage on bureaucracies resistant
to executive leadership. They furnish a direct conduit to localities
from the executive mansions. They can serve as the nuclei of discrete,
executive-oriented campaign organizations. Chief executives probably could not create the groups if they set out deliberately to do so,
but it would be surprising if they did not eventually perceive the
advantages of collaborating with them now that a variety of complaints has brought the groups spontaneously into being.

It will be an uneasy, mutually wary relationship. To neighborhood
and community associations, the paradox of turning to remote chief
executives in a quest for local control will be disturbing. To chief
executives, the risks of opening a Pandora's box and releasing incon-
trollable disintegrative forces will give pause. Yet each can gain so
much from an alliance with the other that it is hard to avoid the
feeling the attractions will overcome the anxieties. I do not mean to
imply the alliance will be formal or structured. I mean only to suggest each side will turn to the other as appropriate occasions arise,
and that the occasions will arise with increasing frequency in the
years ahead.

Thus, the new voices of representatives and the more familiar
voices of executive leadership will be joined in a common challenge
to those who speak for neutral competence and for older institutions
of representation. The marriage of convenience between executives
and bureaucracies that broke the dominant hold of the parties over
public employment, a union visibly headed for the rocks twelve years

[64] Advisory Commission on Intergovernmental Relations, *Ninth Annual Report*
(Washington: 1968), p. 22.

ago,[65] will dissolve entirely. The new coalition will fly the standards, "democracy," "participation," "coordination," "dynamism," and will level charges of "unresponsiveness," "red tape," and "administrative chaos." The old forces will invoke the symbols of expertise and experience, and hurl accusations of political interference in professional decisions and of dilettantism. The game will thus go on much as it has in the past, but the renewed emphasis on representativeness will bring in some new players and lead some old ones to switch strategies.

THE SUBSEQUENT PHASE OF THE CYCLE

Because of the pluralism of the American political system and the American society, change is damped, and tends to come gradually. The realignment of the partisans of the three values shaping governmental design will therefore produce no sudden and dramatic shifts.

Nevertheless, the building pressures appear to be gaining sufficient strength to effect some modifications. Some decentralization will take place; concessions will be made to the demands for greater local influence on public programs. And there will be some headway toward establishing territorial officers with at least limited authority over field personnel of the functional bureaus.

It will not take long for the price of these changes to make itself felt. Decentralization will soon be followed by disparities in practice among the numerous small units, brought on by differences in human and financial resources, that will engender demands for central intervention to restore equality and balance and concerted action; the factors underlying the movement toward metropolitan units of government and toward conditional federal grants-in-aid will, in other words, reassert themselves. Decentralization will stand in the way of other goals, such as school integration (as did "states' rights" doctrines in other times). It will give rise to competition among the units that will be disastrous for many of them, which will find it more difficult to attract talent and money than others that start from a more advantageous position. In some units, strong factions may well succeed in reviving a new spoils system, thus lowering the quality of some vital services. Decentralization of public administration will not necessarily be accompanied by decentralization of the other institutions with which public units deal, such as unions of public employees, so that the local units may find themselves at a serious disadvantage in negotiations and unable to resist the pressures of special interests. Economies of scale, which are admittedly overstated very frequently, nevertheless do exist, and the multiplication of overhead costs in local units will divert some resources from sub-

[65] Kaufman, *op. cit.*, pp. 1069–73.

stantive programs to administrative housekeeping. Initially, all these costs will be regarded by those concerned with representativeness as well worth paying, but the accumulation of such grievances over time will inspire a clamor for unification and consolidation.[66]

Similarly, area officials reporting directly to chief executives will soon develop autonomous bases of political power in the regions to which they are assigned. Rapid rotation from area to area will help to reduce their independence, but the rate of rotation will decline because each new assignment will necessitate a period of familiarization with the new territory during which actions and decisions are held in abeyance, and because local interests, having established comparatively stable relationships with their regional officers, will protest and resist frequent transfers. As the regional officers get more and more involved in regional complexes, they will become more and more ambassadors from the regions to the chief executives instead of the executives' men in the regions.[67] Regional differences and competition will become sources of irritation and controversy. Moreover, regional posts may become convenient and effective springboards to elective office. At first, these dangers will seem remote and therefore less important than the immediate gains, but time is likely to reverse the balance.

So the wave of reform after the one now in progress will rally under a banner of earlier days: Take administration out of politics and politics out of administration. Disappointed partisans of the current movement on behalf of representativeness, having won some of their points, will acquiesce in the efforts of a new generation of idealists to elevate the quality, the consistency, the impartiality, the morale, and the devotion to duty of bureaucrats by strengthening and broadening central control and supervision. Chief executives anxious to regain command of the administrative field forces in each of their regions will rediscover the virtues of strong central direction of those forces by functional administrative agencies whose chiefs identify with the executives,[68] and whose standards can be applied

---

[66] Some anxieties about the costs of decentralization have already been voiced in Irving Kristol, "Decentralization for What?" *The Public Interest,* Number 11, Spring 1968, p. 17, and echoed by Daniel P. Moynihan as he assailed school decentralization as likely to lead to segregated bureaucracies; *The New York Times,* 5 June 1968. Note also the dissents by Governors Rhodes and Rockefeller from a hearty endorsement of neighborhood subunits with limited powers of taxation and local self-government; Advisory Commission on Intergovernmental Relations, *op. cit.,* p. 21.

[67] Herbert Kaufman, *The Forest Ranger* (Baltimore: The John Hopkins Press, 1960), pp. 75–80.

[68] A hint of what lies ahead is suggested by the experience with regional development commissions. Encouraged by the federal government, their establishment

evenhandedly everywhere. From above and below, to escape the distortions of purpose inflicted by the vigorous factional politics of localities and regions (as they once sought to free themselves from the toils of selfseeking factions in state and Congressional District politics), the apostles of good government will turn back to insulating the bureaucracies against such political heat. The neutrality and independence of the civil service will again be extolled. Until, in the more remote future, the problems of stressing this value accumulate, and the devotees of representativeness and of executive leadership once again grow anxious. Thus does the cycle run.

It should not be inferred that the process is fruitless because the succession of values is repetitive. Wheels turning on their own axles do advance. Each time the balance among the values is redressed, only to require redress again, some new accommodation among the myriad interests in the society is reached. Modification of structure or procedure alters the political system and its distribution of rewards and benefits enough to satisfy at least some of the demands of those who feel aggrieved. Representativeness *will* be improved. Executive leadership *will* be exerted. The very real benefits of bureaucratic organization *will* be safeguarded. The alternation of values helps prevent the loss of any of them, keeping the whole system flexible and adaptive as conditions change.

Because of this process, the years immediately ahead are, as predicted, turning out to be years of turmoil over control of bureaucracies. Precisely what shape the subsequent resurgence of natural competence will take in the years beyond, it is impossible to prophesy now. But if the hypothesized cycle of values is at all valid, then strange as it may seem to this generation of reformers, innovators of tomorrow will defend many of the very institutions (as transformed in the course of current controversies) under attack today. And many a forgotten tome and obscure article on public administration, long gathering dust on unpatronized shelves and in unopened files, will be resurrected and praised for its prescience, only to subside again into temporary limbo when another turn of the wheel ends its brief moment of revised relevance.

---

was hailed as a step toward decentralization. But their plans began to conflict and compete with each other, and with the work of other federal and state agencies; moreover, powerful political blocs began to aggregate around them. The President had to direct the Secretary of Commerce to coordinate them, giving him strong powers of review over their proposals and the aid of a council of assistant secretaries from ten federal agencies, a measure greeted as a partial recentralization. *The Washington Post,* 30 December 1967. This dilemma was explicitly foreseen by James W. Fesler, *Area and Administration,* especially at pp. 100–02.

POLITICAL ENDS AND ADMINISTRA- TIVE MEANS

DAVID M. LEVITAN

ONE

More than half a century has elapsed since Woodrow Wilson published his essay on "The Study of Administration."[1] This marked the first effort, in America, at a systematic delineation of the scope and meaning of the field of administration. The essay was soon followed by Goodnow's Politics and Administration,[*] in which the subject matter of administration was again emphasized. Great progress has since been made in the clarification and systematization of the discipline brought to light by these earlier works. In fact, the outstanding development during the twentieth century in the field of public administration has been the evolution of a separate discipline concerned with the execution of public policy, as distinguished from the function of policy determination. The study of administration has become a study of techniques, a study of the "means" as distinguished from the "ends"—a concept aptly summarized in White's statement that "administration is a process."

This identification of administration with techniques, most elab-

[1] Political Science Quarterly 197–222 (1887).

[*] Goodnow, Politics and Administration (The Macmillan Company: New York, 1900).

From Public Administration Review, Vol. 3 (Winter, 1943), pp. 353–359. David Levitan is Adjunct Professor of Political Science, Long Island University. Reprinted with permission of the author and the American Society of Public Administration.

orately developed by Willoughby, has been called the "institutional" approach, perhaps because of its resemblance to the approach of institutional economics. Whatever the origin of the term, the attention focused on administrative techniques, processes, and procedures has contributed much to the improvement of administration in the modern state.

But, valuable as the institutional approach has been for the development of administration, it has also led to the appearance of some dangerous tendencies in modern administrative theory. It is easy to advance from the concept of "administration is a process" to the view that its principles can be scientifically stated, that it can be developed as a separate science, and that, once discovered, administrative principles have universal applicability.

In regarding administration as a separate discipline no one, of course, claims that administration exists in a vacuum; it is generally recognized as a tool for putting into effect policy decisions—for carrying out the purposes of the state. But it is in the tendency to regard it as a tool which, once perfected, can be used for the effectuation of *any* policy decisions, for carrying out *any* purposes, that the danger lies.

Two specific instances may be cited of trends resulting from this view which have highly dangerous potentialities. The first is its effect on administrative personnel, present and future. If sound administrative principles and techniques are equally applicable in any situation, it follows logically that a good administrator need know only these principles and techniques in order to fulfill his functions adequately. And, in fact, the emphasis on administration as concerned only with techniques fosters among some present administrative employees the development of a bureaucratic point of view and a total unconcern with the broader implications of administrative action or, in the case of those with broader training, a deep feeling of resentment as to the lack of importance of their work. Almost every day in Washington one encounters some friend of college or school days who bemoans his plight with red tape, his total frustration as a result of his preoccupation with "administrivia." Most of these people have simply failed to see the fundamental nature of their work and its relation to the broader aspects of government and public policy, because it has so often been emphasized to them that their job is to deal with techniques and that broad questions of policy and theory are outside the scope of administration. They no longer search for the more fundamental. They see only a "paper-shuffling" job.

The same emphasis portends some serious shortcomings as to the training of future administrative officials. The tendency is clear. The growth of schools of public administration with their type of program is indicative of the trend with respect to the scope of the training of the administrative official of the future. The emphasis is on courses dealing with "Introduction to Administration." "Principles of Personnel Administration," "Techniques of Classification," "Principles of Budgeting," "Principles of Overhead Management," and the like. This type of training, unless founded on a broad theoretical and historical background, will greatly influence the type of students who turn to the study of administration and as a result will greatly influence the type of administration. The administration of the modern service state places a premium upon administrative officials with imagination and insight; yet students with a flair for the broad and endowed with a faculty for assimilating the general will view askance the study of administration. There is a very real concern among many administrators regarding the supply of younger administrators—men with broad vision and understanding. Mr. Paul Appleby, Undersecretary of the Department of Agriculture, emphasized this problem in a paper read before the Washington Chapter of the American Society for Public Administration in the fall of 1942, stressing the importance for higher administrative work of broad training, imagination, and capacity for abstract thinking.

The second unfortunate tendency which has its genesis in the view of administration as a tool which can be used for the effectuation of any policy is the (again logical) extension of this idea to include the belief that administrative machinery can be transplanted from one system of government to another; if it works well in the one, it will work well in the other. Wilson has stated this belief succinctly:

> If I see a murderous fellow sharpening a knife cleverly, I can borrow his way of sharpening the knife without borrowing his probable intention to commit murder with it; and so, if I see a monarchist dyed in the wool managing a public bureau well, I can learn his business methods without changing one of my republican spots.[2]

The dangerous fallacy implicit in this view needs to be clearly understood in order to avoid transplanting into this country from other governments administrative techniques intrinsically incompatible with the underlying philosophy of democratic government.

It should be pointed out that the men who were responsible for the development of the institutional approach themselves realized the importance of the relation between the administration and the broad underlying philosophy of a government. The emphasis on administration as concerned with techniques and means rather than with ends has been so great that sight is often lost of an equally definite aspect of their philosophy of administration. Wilson, after stating the value of a comparative study of techniques of administration, showed that

[2] *Ibid.*, p. 220.

he fully realized the dangers inherent in transmitting systems of administration without regard to the local philosophy:

> By keeping this distinction in view—that is, by studying administration as a means of putting our own politics into convenient practice, as a means of making what is democratically politic towards all administratively possible towards each—we are on perfectly safe ground, and can learn without error what foreign systems have to teach us.[3]

Even more pointed is his admonition that "the principles on which to base a science of administration for America must be principles which have democratic policy very much at heart."

Similarly, Goodnow recognized the close relation between administration and the underlying philosophy of the government. He stated clearly that the nature of the state is as much influenced by the administrative system as by the underlying philosophical principles, that "a system of government" refers to both its principles and its administrative system. "The administrative system has, however, as great influence in giving its tone to the general governmental system as has the form of government set forth in the constitution."[4] And he refers with approval to the view of the German jurist and administrator, Gneist, that "English parliamentary government could not be understood apart from the administrative system."

Other students of the administrative process have also emphasized the closeness of the relationship between administration and political and social philosophy. For example, White, writing in the *Encyclopaedia of the Social Sciences*, says:

> The general character of administration has always been governed by the physical basis of state organization, by the prevailing level of social and cultural organization, by the development of technology, by theories of the function of the state and by more immediate governmental and political traditions and ideals.

There is, therefore, nothing new in the recognition of an organic relationship between the basic principles of a system of government and its administration. In view of the dangerous tendencies already noticed, however, it would seem to be necessary to reemphasize and to clarify this concept. That a need for such reemphasis and clarification exists is made further evident by such statements as that of Schuyler C. Wallace in his *Federal Departmentalization** (pp. 231–33):

[3] *Loc. cit.*

[4] *Politics and Administration*, p. 5.

* Schuyler Wallace, *Federal Departmentalization* (Columbia University Press: New York, 1941).

There exists a tendency on the part of many of those who deal with administration to concentrate upon some particular aspect of the general field and to ignore or neglect its relations to the process of government as a whole. . . . Those who deal with administration generally do not look upon the study of that subject as requiring the study of government as a whole —much less as necessitating a broad consideration of the economic, social, and psychological characteristics of the society in which they are operating.

At this time, when many are turning their attention to the solution of the problems related to the establishment of a postwar world order, a genuine understanding of the significance of the administrative and procedural is especially important.

TWO

Administrative procedural machinery is much more than a *tool* for the implementation of a political ideology. Administrative procedural machinery is an integral *part* of each political ideology—it is a part of a system of government.

Any system of government is composed of the sum total of its political and philosophical principles and the administrative procedural machinery established for their effectuation. The democratic system of government includes not only such principles as that government is based on the consent of the governed, that the individual is the basis of all legitimate governmental authority, and that the dignity of the individual must be preserved, but also the fundamental administrative procedural machinery to implement these principles. It follows that a system of government cannot be considered as a democratic system, even though its theoretical foundation be the principles included by political theorists in their statement of the democratic dogma, if it is not accompanied by administrative machinery for the realization of the principles.

A striking example is found in the Middle Ages. Recent studies, such as McIlwain's brilliant volume, *Growth of Political Thought in the West** have done much to clarify our thinking about the political philosophy of the Middle Ages. It had been customary to speak of that era as a period of supreme absolutism. Even now one sometimes hears the statement that Hitlerism or fascism marks a return to the philosophy of the Middle Ages. Nothing could be further from the truth. The truth is that the notion of unlimited government—government not subject to a higher law—is foreign to the Middle Ages. The modern doctrine of sovereignty was first enunciated by the apologists for papal authority and church supremacy at the beginning of the

* Charles H. McIlwain, *Growth of Political Thought in the West* (The Macmillan Company: New York, 1932).

fourteenth century. Much of the democratic philosophy was part of the tradition of the Middle Ages, finding expression in the writings of both students and rulers. Yet no one would include the system of government of the Middle Ages in a list of democratic governments, even if the concept include states espousing democratic principles but formally headed by a monarch, as is the case with Great Britain today.

The distinguishing feature between modern democratic governments of the past apparently based on democratic principles is the establishment of procedures, of administrative machinery for the effectuation of the basic democratic tenets. The real contribution of modern democracy is not in the development of new principles, or what the lawyer calls "substantive" law, but rather in the development of "procedural" law—the implementation of broad philosophical principles with concrete administrative machinery. The "due process of law" concept, in its true historical sense, is at the very foundation of democratic government.

The fact that in the mind of the average man Hitlerism, barbarism, unfettered government are associated with the idea of the Middle Ages is itself illustrative of this point. Since it is clearly established that no adequate procedural guarantees for checking the authority of the ruler were in existence during the Middle Ages, the system of government has become identified in the popular mind with absolutism; and rightly so. It is a gross error for a student of theory to identify fascism with the philosophy of the Middle Ages, but it is natural for the common man to identify one with the other, for with regard to the things that concern him—his actual rights and liberties— Hitlerism and the governments of the Middle Ages have much in common.

The importance of the administrative and procedural was eloquently summarized by Quincy Wright at the time of the Munich settlement:

> The fundamental legal criticism of the settlement rests on the fact that the statesmen responsible for it placed the substance of the settlement ahead of the procedure by which it was achieved. They thus duplicated the error of the statesmen at Versailles twenty years earlier. . . .
>
> Constitutional government consists in a determination of the citizens of the state that adherence to the procedures set forth in the constitution shall be treated as more important than any specific grievance, demand, or reform. Until the people of the world are similarly determined to place procedures ahead of substance, we may expect the world to alternate between dictates of Versailles and dictates of Munich, with little respite from wars and rumors of wars.[5]

[5] "The Munich Settlement and International Law," 33 *American Journal of International Law* 31–32 (1939).

Students of American foreign affairs will need little prodding to realize the role of procedural machinery. The fate of the Versailles Treaty is still too fresh in our minds.

What is true with regard to basic procedures in relation to the basic structure and constitutional framework of the state is equally true with regard to procedures and administrative machinery for the effectuation of the day-by-day decisions and legislation. Social legislation, whether dealing with minimum wages, maximum hours, social security, or labor relations, can have little significance to the citizen; it begets meaning only when supported by detailed "administrivia." A liberal government has value only when based on liberal legislation supported by administrative machinery.

The nature of the administrative procedural machinery is thus seen to be as important as, if not more important than the nature of the philosophical principles of government. Democratic government means democracy in administration, as well as in the original legislation. It is of supreme importance that the administrative machinery established for the execution of legislation be permeated with democratic spirit and ideology, with respect for the dignity of man.

Few would gainsay the truth of Wilson's warning: "Liberty cannot live apart from constitutional principle; and no administration, however perfect and liberal its methods, can give men more than a poor counterfeit of liberty if it rest upon illiberal principles of government." But it is apparently not so generally recognized that the converse is likewise true—that no principles of government, however perfect and liberal, can give men more than a poor counterfeit of liberty if they are not implemented by democratic administrative machinery. Administrative authoritarianism, officiousness, and arbitrariness are much more serious threats to the rights and liberties of the individual than arbitrary legislation. The German historian, Niebuhr, summarized this view in his statement that "liberty depends incomparably more upon administration than upon constitutions." Unwise legislation may be mitigated somewhat by considerate and humane administration, but the citizen has no "cushion" against arbitrary officialdom, often hidden behind the cloak of "administrative necessity." The real protection of the citizen lies in the development of a high degree of democratic consciousness among the administrative hierarchy.

Continued emphasis on the universal applicability of administrative principles tends to obfuscate this organic relationship between the political and social theory of the government as a whole and the political and social theory underlying its administration. There is little real basis for a comparative study of the administrative machinery in Nazi Germany and in democratic America. The fact that German administrative machinery is geared to effectuate a philosophy which recognizes no rights of the individual, which denies the very dignity of the human personality—either of the citizen or of the public servant—while the American system is based on the very opposite philosophy makes the German experience of little value, so far as the United States is concerned, not only as to methods and machinery for dealing with the citizen, but even as to internal management. Administrative procedures cannot be transplanted from one system of government to another, but must have their roots in the political and social philosophy underlying their own system of government.

All this is not to deny the existence of any general applicable principles of administration, but to affirm that such principles must be interpreted and applied in a manner consistent with the basic philosophy of the state, and that as so interpreted and applied they exhibit fundamental differences from the same principles applied elsewhere. For example, the concept of "unity of command" has assumed different meanings in Germany and in America. It is one thing to say that in the administration of any program someone must be empowered to make final decisions, after a genuine exchange of ideas up and down the hierarchy. It is a totally different thing to say that in the administration of any program there must be one man to give orders and issue commands. The *Fuehrerschaft* principle denies that all men have the capacity to make some contribution; consequently it is useless to establish channels for the exchange of ideas up and down the hierarchy. In the American system a public servant is not only an employee but also a citizen and, above all, a human being, who retains his basic rights and is therefore entitled to dignity and respect.

The natural human tendency to emulate what others have done is so great, especially if it has appeared successful, that unless the limited aspect of "transplantable administration" is constantly emphasized and the importance of the frame of reference reiterated, much that is contrary to the fundamental spirit of the forum will be transplanted. The danger is especially great where some are interested in changing the spirit of the forum, and the advocated measures carry the blessings of the god of "efficiency." Only maximum vigilance by the administrative hierarchy, based upon a clear understanding and acceptance of the philosophy of the state, will effectively check such efforts.

THREE

Up to this point, stress has been laid on the prime importance of procedural machinery in effectuating the ends of government and on the necessity for gearing administrative machinery to the basic philosophy of the state. It is also important to realize that, while the existence of such machinery is basic, the machinery itself may be modified from time to time; in fact, must be modified if it is to continue to implement the fundamental principles of the government under changing social and economic conditions.

One of the discouraging symptoms of the myopic condition prevailing among some students of administration is manifested in their failure to see the relation between administrative techniques and social and political environment. On more than one occasion I have heard such students decry the Jacksonian system of administration—the spoils system—without the slightest indication of any realization on their part that the spoils system was based on a very genuine theory of democracy. The technique may be a bad one by our standards; but it was in tune with the social and political philosophy of its day.

Those desiring the *status quo ante* or a return to "normalcy" inevitably rely on old established procedural safeguards, though under the new conditions they are only legal fictions, no longer serving the purposes which they were intended to serve. Students of American constitutional and administrative law will readily recall the "sham" of the due process doctrine. This doctrine, long a bulwark of individual freedom, became under changed conditions an instrument for the miscarriage of justice.

The administrator, whether in a court of law or executive department, must at all times ask himself: "Is the established administrative machinery effectuating the policy—the end which the law sought to accomplish?" Ends broadly and adequately conceived will remain valid for long periods of time, if there are no fundamental changes in the basic philosophy of the government. Such is not the case, however, with regard to the detailed machinery of government. Whereas the ends of a just government have changed little from the days of Plato and Aristotle to our own, the machinery and the specific legal enactments necessary for the realization of these ends have completely changed and will continue to change with the modifications of the physical, technological, social, and economic world about us.

Administrative machinery, then, as an important—perhaps the most important—part of a system of government, must be constantly reexamined in terms of the ends it is intended to serve—in terms of the results which are to be accomplished. Further, the maintenance in this manner of procedural machinery which is in accord with the basic philosophy of the state is, in the long run, more important for the achievement of those ends than is the enactment of substantive law.

This last generalization should, of course, be understood as referring to such broad and intangible ends as liberty of the individual or a just world order. When we are dealing with specific and clearly defined ends, we must not permit ourselves to get so involved in the administrative machinery as to lose sight of the ends; policy decisions will necessarily come before administrative considerations in realizing the ends in view. But even then the importance of the administrative machinery should always be kept in mind; and, in connection with the broader, long-term ends, it should be recognized as paramount.

FOUR

An outstanding government administrator once remarked that "administration must have a soul." That, in a way, magnificently summarizes the thesis I have been developing. It needs to be added, however, that administration should contribute to the fuller development of the soul of the state. I have tried to point out that the administrative machinery and the political and philosophical principles together determine the system of government; that a democratic state must be not only based on democratic principles but also democratically administered, the democratic philosophy permeating its administrative machinery and being manifested in its relations both with the citizen outside the government and with the citizen inside the government, the public servant; that administrative procedures are even more important in effectuating the basic principles of government than is substantive law; and that these procedures must therefore be constantly reexamined in terms of the ends they serve and changed when the changing social and economic milieu requires different means to attain these ends.

The institutional approach has contributed greatly to the development of administrative theory and practice, but if we so misinterpret it as to regard administration as concerned with "means" and nothing more, we shall be dealing a serious blow not only to administration itself, but to the democratic principles which we are striving to put into effect. The administrators of tomorrow must be men with a clear understanding and acceptance of the philosophy of the state and with the broad vision and imaginative power to gear the administrative machinery to that philosophy.

COMMENTARY

Elton Mayo believes that one consequence of the hypothesis that people are a rabble of unrelated individuals is authoritarian control. Where
the nature of people in groups is misunderstood, it is easy to deal with
them as though they weren't people. They can be treated instead as
layers of matter supporting what one writer has called "an apex of super-
intelligences." Assume that they are disorderly unless confined, and it is
logical to confine them. The unnaturalness of such impositions is abundantly testified to by the struggles they invariably provoke to throw off the
restraints. . . .

It is not an over-calculation . . . to suggest that new approaches to
bureaucracy, both public and private, need to be considered. . . . Society at
this moment in history is neurotic and disintegrated. Before we return to
the arboreal life, we should try once to see if we can be as smart about
people as we have about engines, if indeed it isn't too late.

The fact that Earl Latham ended his 1943 article, "Hierarchy and
Hieratics" (p. 157 above) with these comments would be of little
consequence for the purpose of this inquiry were it not for the fact
that it seems to provide a contemporary and relevant introduction
to a summary discussion of public administration in a turbulent
environment. Compare, for example, the Latham comments to those
made more recently by the former Secretary of the Department of
Health, Education, and Welfare, John Gardner. Gardner focuses on
the urban problem in America and, in the style of Dawes and Lindblom, is drawn—possibly inevitably—to the lure of the metaphor of
the ships and the sea.

I have looked at all the various problems of the city—the snarled traffic, the polluted air and water, crime, overcrowded schools, inadequate health services, breakdowns in public order, and so on and on. And I have listened attentively to the special explanations as to why each of these problems has arisen. But out of all these crises a conclusion begins to emerge that is more alarming than any one of them: Our greatest cities have lost command of themselves and their future. They lie helpless as the multiple waves of crisis roll over them, like half-sunken battleships battered by heavy seas.*

At the present time, a crisis of increasing proportions seems to be developing within the body politic due to the failure of substantial segments of the population to recognize 1) the validity of the norm of reciprocity between generations, 2) the validity of the values which govern the basic rules of democratic procedure, and 3) the efficacy of the formal public organization as an equitable and responsive problem-solving mechanism. Given the increasingly widespread degree of disillusionment with the representative and responsive character of the governmental administrative process, it seems appropriate to agree with Latham that new approaches to bureaucracy, both public and private, need to be considered. Not only our cities, but virtually all of our governmental administrative structures—national, state, and local—seem to have lost command of themselves and their future. In short, the Madisonian or pluralist model of administrative bargaining and incrementalism is being seriously questioned by some, and totally rejected by others as an acceptable policy-making, resource-allocating, and problem-solving device.

The incremental pattern is certainly not new to the American political scene, nor has it functioned flawlessly over the years. On various occasions selected "publics" in the body politic have incurred losses which were not offset by subsequent gains. Conflict has, on occasion, expanded, both in scope and intensity, and the bargaining arena, normally occupied solely by professionals, has been cluttered with amateur advocates. But if the incremental pattern has not been always successful in its policy of conflict containment, to date its practitioners (the professionals) have been "lucky" in having most of these confrontations scheduled on their own "home court," so to speak. That is, until recently they have been successful in ensuring that aggrieved parties seek redress for their grievances through the normal and acceptable channels of the democratic process. However, to an increasing extent, various minority groups have reached the conclusion that by observing the traditional rules of the bargaining-in-

---

* *Science and Technology and the Cities,* A Compilation of Papers prepared for the Tenth Meeting of the Panel on Science and Technology. Committee on Science and Astronautics, U.S. House of Representatives, Committee Print (1969), p. 3.

cremental process they are being hopelessly buried in a "no-win" situation.

Justifications for the deviant, "anti-social" behavior of the urban poor, the blacks, and the young people of the nation have been provided by a wide range of contemporary scholars, journalists, activists, and propagandists. Social protest, of course, represents a recurring theme of the American heritage. Indeed, when justifications for past protest movements can be applied with almost total relevance to the turbulence of the present, an attempt to assign "new" significance to the current situation may impress some as frivolous. The following excerpt written in 1914 by Herbert Croly, a dynamic intellectual force of the early Progressive movement, provides an excellent example of how the past may be easily adapted to the present.

The insistence by American conservatives . . . on a morality of restraint, is a most trustworthy indication of the want of democracy in our traditional legalism. When the conservatives declare that the traditional American political system depends upon the character of the American people, what they mean by character is self-control, moderation, and circumspection. . . . Legalism was an enormous improvement on the official tyranny of a class or an individual. It introduced into political and social organization the rule of live-and-let-live and some of the spirit of that rule. But in practice the rule of live-and-let-live has never successfully expressed its underlying spirit of fair play. Its usefulness has been impaired by an unfair division of labor. Upon the rich have been conferred the opportunity and the obligation of living; upon the poor, the opportunity and the obligation of let-living. The moral code of moderation and self-repression is intended for [the benefit of the poor].*

As has been implied in Chapter Six the morality of restraint referred to by Croly is, indeed, an integral aspect of the current bargaining-incremental framework. Self-control, moderation, and circumspection are the cardinal virtues of prudential politics. The morality of restraint is the foundation of the value structures of the professional political actors—the operatives in the incremental complex. They are expected to adhere to a discipline which, as seen by many contemporary social critics, stems more from Stoicism than from the Judeo-Christian ethic. Nor is the discipline of moral restraint limited only to the professionals; as Lindblom observed, any group which feels strongly enough about any issue has the opportunity to express its feelings, and if sufficiently influential and effective can have its feelings enacted into law. The assumption for Lindblom was, of course, that such group expressions would be—indeed, must be—

* Herbert Croly, *Progressive Democracy* (New York: The Macmillan Company, 1914), pp. 418–19.

made within the given limits of the rules of the game. In the bargaining-incremental context, restraint and stability are reciprocal factors which are most likely to produce the ultimate of all goals—stable consensus. The discussion of ends can be disruptive of the incremental equation; discussion of means is much more productive. Therefore, the virtues of self-control, moderation, and, most especially, circumspection, become highly valued. Ends become incidental to the means. In fact, ends must become indistinguishable from means, and political efforts should be dedicated to the mastery of procedural details and the complexities of strategy and counter-strategy, bargaining and counter-bargaining. Emotional detachment is essential; disciplined behavior itself becomes a valued end. Robert Michaels using an allegory offers essentially the same prescription for democracy as that advanced by contemporary incrementalists.

The peasant, in the fable, when on his death bed, tells his sons that a treasure is buried in the field. After the old man's death the sons dig everywhere in order to discover the treasure. They do not find it. But their indefatigable labor improves the soil and secures for them a comparative well-being. The treasure in the fable may well symbolize democracy. Democracy is a treasure which no one will ever discover by deliberate search. But in continuing our search, in laboring indefatigably to discover the undiscoverable, we shall perform a work which will have fertile results in the democratic sense.*

Keep digging for the treasure in the field, the incrementalists would say, and in the process one may very well become an expert in excavation techniques, forgetting the initial lure of the treasure. However, as viewed by an increasing segment of the body politic, the concept of moral restraint has created a socially irrelevant politics and a morally bankrupt administrative process. Croly's comments on this stoical discipline again seem completely relevant to the current dilemma.

In a democracy the people may and will necessarily be asked to submit to discipline, but not to discipline for its own sake. The mass of people will need to have the discipline made interesting to them. They will rightly demand the same motive for submitting to discipline that their conquerors have had. A man can reasonably be asked to impose self-restraint upon himself, whenever self-restraint is necessary as a part of a positive and desirable individual or social activity; but he cannot fairly be asked to accept a life of which self-restraint is the preponderant character. That, in substance, is what the social conservators are asking the democracy to accept. The democracy is not listening to them and is quite right in its inattention. . . . sacrifices were demanded and offered in obedience to the

* *Political Parties: A Sociological Study of the Oligarchical Tendencies of Modern Democracy* (New York: Collier Books, 1962), p. 368.

general ideas that they were assuring the creation of a consummate community. . . . Such ideas are losing their authority. The consummate community is not a fact to which the good citizen must bow down, or a prophecy which can exercise constraint on events. . . . If it is to exist . . . it must be partly realized in the aspirations and opportunities of living men and women. It must have an immediate and a positive moral value for the democracy of today. It must bring with it a new and frank assertion of humanism.*

The need for a "frank assertion of humanism" has, to a very real extent, become the clarion call for those who advocate the development of a socially relevant public administration. As Kaufman notes, ". . . The scale of organization in our society has grown so large that only through large-scale organization does it seem possible to have a significant impact. This impression alone is enough to make [individuals] feel helplessly overwhelmed by huge, impersonal machines indifferent to their uniqueness and their humanity." The scientific and technological revolution of this generation has resulted in increased complexity, increased ambiguity, and increased turbulence. Consequently a growing segment of the body politic seems convinced that bureaucratic officials either do not understand, or worse do not care, about the simple nature of people, or, as Latham wrote nearly twenty-five years ago, "where the nature of people in groups is misunderstood, it is easy to deal with them as though they weren't people." For many individuals democracy at the present time simply represents a hypocritical delusion, and the administrative structures of the executive branches of our governments are increasingly viewed as repressive forces which stifle the expansion of human dignity and the improvement of human nature.

The live-and-let-live philosophy cited by Croly has been manifested by incrementalists in the form of simply accepting human nature as it is. The willingness to "satisfice," particularly in areas involving human welfare and social equality, is a most obvious example. Liberal democracy in America gains its heritage from Jefferson. The cornerstone of that heritage rests on the basic goodness of man and on an immovable faith in the ultimate perfectibility of human nature. It is an avowedly optimistic appraisal which openly rejects the "good enough" or satisfactory solutions to the problems of social equality. But for too many years the ideals of Jefferson have provided soft background music for the prudential pragmatism of James Madison. Until recently the fundamental flaw in our Jeffersonian heritage has been its futuristic character. Human perfectibility implies a future to be achieved, as well as the corollary assumption (based on faith alone) that such a future is capable of being

* Croly, *Progressive Democracy*, pp. 414–415.

achieved. If, however, one starts with the assumption that in matters involving the social and political interactions of individuals the future cannot be defined, much less achieved, then public policy and administrative decisions which are "good enough" to meet immediate needs (as those needs are defined and constrained by past performance) are all that one can realistically expect. To posit a future goal assumes that one is *capable* of proceeding rationally and comprehensively toward that goal. But as we have seen in Chapter Six, modern incrementalists explicitly reject that assumption. As Lindblom remarked, "One should never ever [sic] be as 'comprehensive as possible' whatever that means," and elsewhere, " 'It is better to answer as many questions as possible in advance' is not an acceptable axiom for decision-making."* In the search for social equality specifically, the incrementalists quite explicitly prefer to "satisfice." Again, in the words of Lindblom,

Most of us in the Western tradition would, if faced with a practical choice, probably sanction any degree of inequality necessary to maintain a government based on consent rather than a high degree of repression. We might doubt that a highly inequalitarian government could command consent, but if it could we would prefer it to a repressive egalitarianism.†

In the midst of the current turbulent crisis, the never-ending search for social equality has reasserted itself once again but with one important difference—long-range planning of public policy decisions cán no longer be considered as futile expeditions into fantasy. Although as previously noted, systematic analysis is not without its limitations and pitfalls, it does offer an alternative to the incremental allocation of resources—an alternative which, most significantly, clearly distinguishes ends from means and presents ends as definable goals to be achieved. This is in direct contrast to the situation in 1915 when Croly moved in the direction of a "systems analytical" solution to the social inequities that were generated by the political system of his day. For Croly, an administrative structure had to be developed with a capacity to act with "a clear, conscious, resolute, and inclusive purpose." It had to be "organized for the acquisition of knowledge" in order to plan "as far ahead as conditions permit or dictate." Croly prophetically defined the primary purpose of his proposed administrative system in terms which are totally relevant today:

The difficulty is not the lack of facts, but the ability to accumulate, to compare, and to digest them. The planning department of a progressive democratic state . . . will always be planning, and it will, in a sense, al-

* Charles Lindblom, *The Strategy of Decision*, pp. 47, 126.

† Charles Lindblom and David Braybrooke, *The Intelligence of Democracy*, p. 260.

ways be fighting chiefly to convert its enemies, but it will be planning not for the sake of fighting, but for the sake of learning and building.*

However, despite the social ethic heavily imprinted on the Progressive movement, Croly's administrative vision remained a fanciful dream. Again the theories of Jefferson were matched with those of Madison by Croly's contemporaries in the management science school of thought who focused almost exclusively on internal organizational control, discipline, loyalty, and efficiency.

The promise of America, for Croly, depended on a linkage between the ethical-moral philosophy of Jefferson and the nationalistic philosophy of Hamilton, with both being substantially modified in the ultimate hybrid model.

Americans have always been both patriotic and democratic. . . . but in neither case have they brought the two ideas or aspirations into mutually helpful relations. As democrats they have often regarded nationalism with distrust. . . . As nationalists they have frequently regarded essential aspects of democracy with a wholly unnecessary and embarrassing suspicion. They have been after a fashion Hamiltonian, and Jeffersonian after more of a fashion; but they have never recovered from the initial disagreement between Hamilton and Jefferson. If there is any truth in the idea of a constructive relation between democracy and nationality this disagreement must be healed. . . . The alliance between the two principles will not leave either of them intact; but it will necessarily do more harm to the Jeffersonian group of political ideas than it will to the Hamiltonian. The latter's nationalism can be adapted to democracy without an essential injury to itself, but the former's democracy cannot be nationalized without being transformed. . . . It must cease to be a democracy of indiscriminate individualism, and become one of selected individuals who are obliged constantly to justify their selection; and its members . . . must become a democracy devoted to the welfare of the whole people by means of a conscious labor of individual and social improvement; and that is precisely the sort of democracy which demands for its realization the aid of the Hamiltonian nationalistic organization and principle.†

An excellent, and much more contemporary discussion of this same theme is offered by Rossiter who views Hamilton as a mixed-economy pragmatist and a community-minded individualist.‡ Rossiter notes that Croly's preference for Hamilton was viewed by other intellectuals of the Progressive movement as "interesting but bizarre," and

---

* Croly, *Progressive Democracy*, pp. 370–371.

† Croly, *The Promise of American Life* (New York: The Macmillan Company, 1909), pp. 213–214.

‡ Clinton Rossiter, *Alexander Hamilton and the Constitution* (New York: Harcourt, Brace & World, Inc., 1964), p. 178.

for himself, he comments that "one has to be an eccentric soul to share the American commitment to democracy and still like Hamilton better than Jefferson."*

The essential point is, however, not whether one "likes" Jefferson more, or "dislikes" Hamilton less, but, rather, can the two philosophies of administration be combined in some fashion to provide a socially relevant, morally committed, and operationally efficient administrative model as an alternative to the prevailing Madisonian tradition of the bargaining-incremental model? If the social and political turbulence of this generation does, as considered likely by many observers, increase both in scope and intensity with the coming of future generations, can some means be devised which will facilitate the channeling of these social energies in positive, constructive directions? Can we learn not only to live in a state of perpetual turbulence, but can we learn to confront it, exploit it, direct it to beneficial ends? One conclusion appears certain: these turbulent forces cannot be confronted by public administration with responses which are anchored deep in an essentially nonresponsive political system. The moral restraint which has served the pluralist, the bargainer, the incrementalist seems totally inappropriate to a future of unpredictable and complex change. The dynamic, imaginative, innovative dimension of Hamilton must somehow be combined with the moral, ethical, almost spiritual quality of Jefferson. Choosing alternately between the two would simply generate impassioned excesses from both extremes. A "new and frank assertion of humanism" must be infused with a systems approach to administration. Some of the more progressive corporate and industrial organizations already have directly confronted this problem as it affects their social and economic positions, and their responses have been highly imaginative and truly creative. However, the spill-over effects of these experiments into the public administrative spheres have been minimal thus far. In politics, as in aerodynamics, lag-time is directly related to wind resistance. Engineers can modify their designs to minimize resistance, but social and political scientists have, as yet, to demonstrate comparable ingenuity. The product they are working with, of course, is much more complex, but the demand for solutions is much more desperate. People must become a central object of concern for public administration. The major dialogue between administrative agencies and selected segments of the body politic is once again composed of ethical-moral discussions of human dignity and self-determination.

There comes a time in the history of every nation when its independence of spirit vanishes unless it emancipates itself in some measure from its traditional illusions; and that time is fast approaching for the American

---

* Rossiter, *Alexander Hamilton and the Constitution*, pp. 234, 235.

people. They must either seize the chance for a better future, or else become a nation which is satisfied in spirit merely to repeat indefinitely the
monotonous measures of its own past.*

Herbert Croly offered this observation in 1909, but for many of his
contemporaries, undoubtedly, the implied crisis existed only in the
eyes of Croly. His warnings were overwhelmed by our most basic
traditional illusion—America the Invincible. Given this most cherished illusion, how seriously need the social and political critics of
today be taken? Huntington, in his article on page 231, provides us
with one answer:

The prophecies of economic calamity by the old critics proved erroneous
and their demands for reform superfluous. The American people moved out
of the depression without resorting to constitution reform, disciplined
parties, or cabinet government, and even in the face of a gradual decline
of presidential leadership from its high point of 1933–1935. This was due
more to fortuitous circumstance, which moderated and redirected the
challenge, than to the demonstrated ability of the governmental system
to meet the challenge. The economic challenge disappeared in World War
II and was replaced by the strategic challenge. The likelihood of fortuitous
circumstances moderating or eliminating the latter appears reasonably
remote.

The prudential pragmatists of our political system place great reliance on the element of fortuitous circumstance. However, given the
strategic challenge aimed at the United States from abroad, plus the
strategic challenge to the government generated from within the
domestic sphere, one feels that the sands of time are clearly running
out. A "new public administration" must be devised to respond effectively to the many new and different participatory patterns and demands emerging from an increasingly turbulent environment. The
literature on the general subject, "The Year 2000," is already of considerable size; literature on the specific subject, "Public Administration in the Year 2000," is virtually nonexistent. The Jackson subcommittee memorandum reflects the confidence that "if PPBS develops
into a contest between experts and politicians, it will not be hard to
pick the winners. They will be the politicians in the Congress and
the White House." The accuracy of the statement, unfortunately,
cannot be questioned. For so many of our professional political actors
and academicians, the future is restricted to the present which, to a
great extent, is defined by the past. To accept the challenge of the
future in a confident, forthright spirit requires a high degree of
optimism and faith in the basic goodness of man. For Jefferson, the
alternative was totally unacceptable.

* Croly, *The Promise of American Life*, p. 279.

The Gothic idea that we were to look backwards instead of forwards for the improvement of the human mind, and to recur to the annals of our ancestors for what is most perfect in government . . . is worthy of those bigots in . . . government by whom it has been recommended, and whose purposes it would answer.

If we are to dream, the flatteries of hope are as cheap, and pleasanter than the gloom of despair.*

This choice between hope and despair need not be left to resolution by fortuitous circumstances. A wide gulf separates the individual member of the body politic from the solemn heights of the public policy pinnacles of the federal government. The type of administrative approaches which are applied to present and future social and political problems will determine whether this gap is bridged in an effective, socially relevant manner or whether an additional barrier is to be imposed between the governed and the governors. The former provides an element of hope; the latter, the gloom of despair. In either instance the administrative process and most especially the individual administrator hold the key to the future of democracy in a turbulent age.

* Quoted in Adrienne Koch, *The Philosophy of Thomas Jefferson* (Chicago: Quadrangle Books, 1964), p. 117. © 1943, Columbia University Press, New York.